1st Workshop on Language Technologies for Historical and Ancient Languages (LT4HALA 2020)

Marseille, France
11-16 May 2020

Editors:

Rachel Sprugnoli
Marco Passarotti

ISBN: 978-1-7138-1269-2

LREC 2020 Workshop
Language Resources and Evaluation Conference
11–16 May 2020

**1st Workshop on Language Technologies for
Historical and Ancient Languages,
(LT4HALA 2020)**

PROCEEDINGS

Editors: Rachele Sprugnoli and Marco Passarotti

$$\textbf{Proceedings of the LREC 2020}$$
$$\textbf{1}^{\textbf{st}} \textbf{ Workshop on Language Technologies for}$$
$$\textbf{Historical and Ancient Languages}$$
$$\textbf{(LT4HALA 2020)}$$

Edited by: Rachele Sprugnoli and Marco Passarotti

For more information:
European Language Resources Association (ELRA)
9 rue des Cordelières
75013, Paris
France
http://www.elra.info
Email: lrec@elda.org

Preface

These proceedings include the papers accepted for presentation at the 1st Workshop on Language Technologies for Historical and Ancient Languages (LT4HALA: `https://circse.github.io/LT4HALA`). The workshop was supposed to be held on May 12th 2020 in Marseille, France, co-located with the 12th Edition of the Language Resources and Evaluation Conference (LREC 2020). Unfortunately, the gravity of the Covid-19 pandemic prevented the conference from taking place. However, since the spread of the pandemic started to rise at world-level when the reviewing process and the notifications of acceptance/rejection of the proposals were just concluded, the organizers decided to publish the proceedings of both LREC 2020 and the co-located workshops as planned in May 2020, to valorize the work done by authors and reviewers, as well as to provide an overview of the state of the art in the field.

The objective of the LT4HALA workshop is to bring together scholars who are developing and/or are using Language Technologies (LTs) for historically attested languages, so to foster cross-fertilization between the Computational Linguistics community and the areas in the Humanities dealing with historical linguistic data, e.g. historians, philologists, linguists, archaeologists and literary scholars.
Despite the current availability of large collections of digitized texts written in historical languages, such interdisciplinary collaboration is still hampered by the limited availability of annotated linguistic resources for most of the historical languages. Creating such resources is a challenge and an obligation for LTs, both to support historical linguistic research with the most updated technologies and to preserve those precious linguistic data that survived from past times.
Historical and ancient languages present several characteristics, which set them apart from modern languages, with a significant impact on LTs. Typically, historical and ancient languages lack large linguistic resources, such as annotated corpora, and data can be sparse and very inconsistent; texts present considerable orthographic variation, they can be transmitted by different witnesses and in different critical editions, they can be incomplete and scattered across a wide temporal and geographical span. This makes the selection of representative texts, and thus the development of benchmarks, very hard. Moreover, texts in machine-readable format are often the result of manuscript digitization processes during which OCR systems can cause errors degrading the quality of the documents. Another peculiarity is that most of the texts written in historical and ancient languages are literary, philosophical or documentary, therefore of a very different genre from that on which LTs are usually trained, i.e. news. This is strictly connected to the fact that the final users of LTs for historical and ancient languages are mostly humanists who expect a high accuracy of results that allows a precise analysis of linguistic data.

Such a wide and diverse range of disciplines and scholars involved in the development and use of LTs for historical and ancient languages is mirrored by the large set of topics covered by the papers published in these proceedings, including methods for automatic dating ancient texts and performing semantic analysis, processes for developing linguistic resources and performing various natural language processing (NLP) tasks, like lemmatization and semantic role labelling, and applications of machine translation and distributional semantics, speech analysis and diachronic phonology, automatic inflectional morphology and computational philology.

As large as the number of topics discussed in the papers is that of the either ancient/dead languages or the historical varieties of modern/living ones concerned. In total, the languages tackled in the proceedings are 21 (note that some papers deal with more than one language), namely: Latin (5 papers), French (3), English (2), Hebrew (2), Italian (2), Spanish (2), Ancient Greek (1), Aramaic (1), Armenian (1), Georgian (1), German (1), Norwegian (1), Old Chinese (1), Portuguese (1), Romanian (1), Serbian (1), Slovene (1), Syriac (1), Vedic Sanskrit (1) and the unknown writing system of the so-called Voynich manuscript (1).

In the call for papers, we invited to submit proposals of different types, such as experimental papers, reproduction papers, resource papers, position papers and survey papers. We asked both for long and short papers describing original and unpublished work. We defined as suitable long papers (up to 8 pages, plus references) those that describe substantial completed research and/or report on the development of new methodologies. Short papers (up to 4 pages, plus references) were instead more appropriate for reporting on works in progress or for describing a singular tool or project.

We encouraged the authors of papers reporting experimental results to make their results reproducible and the entire process of analysis replicable, by distributing the data and the tools they used. Like for LREC, the submission process was not anonymous. Each paper was reviewed but three independent reviewers from a program committee made of 25 scholars (12 women and 13 men) from 15 countries.

In total, we received 23 submissions from 47 authors of 13 countries: China (7 authors), France (6), Ireland (5), The Netherlands (5), Poland (5), United Stated (5), Malta (4), Belgium (3), Israel (2), Spain (2), Estonia (1), Italy (1) and Switzerland (1). After the reviewing process, we accepted 15 submissions (8 long and 7 short papers), leading to an acceptance rate of 65.22% .

Beside these 15 contributions, the program of LT4HALA would have featured also a keynote speech by Amba Kulkarni (Department of Sanskrit Studies, University of Hyderabad, India) about the challenges raised by the development of computational tools for Sanskrit. We had invited Professor Kulkarni to give a talk on this topic, because Sanskrit holds a prominent position among historical and ancient languages, being one of the oldest documented members of the Indo-European family of languages.

LT4HALA was supposed to be also the venue of the first edition of EvaLatin, the first campaign devoted to the evaluation of NLP tools for Latin (`https://circse.github.io/LT4HALA/EvaLatin`). Just because of the limited amount of data preserved for historical and ancient languages, an important role is played by evaluation practices, to understand the level of accuracy of the NLP tools used to build and analyze resources. By organizing EvaLatin, we decided to focus on Latin, considering its prominence among the ancient and historical languages, as demonstrated also by the high number of papers dealing with Latin in these proceedings. The first edition of EvaLatin focussed on two shared tasks (i.e. Lemmatization and PoS tagging), each featuring three sub-tasks (i.e. Classical, Cross-Genre, Cross-Time). These sub-tasks were designed to measure the impact of genre and diachrony on NLP tools performances, a relevant aspect to keep in mind when dealing with the diachronic and diatopic diversity of Latin texts, which are spread across a time span of two millennia all over Europe. Participants were provided with shared data in the CoNLL-U format and all the necessary evaluation scripts. They were required to submit a technical report for each task (with all the related sub-tasks) they took part in. The maximum length of the reports was 4 pages (plus references).

In total, 5 technical reports of EvaLatin, corresponding to as many participants, are included in these proceedings. All reports received a light review by the two of us, to check the correctness of the format, the exactness of the results and ranking reported, as well as the overall exposition. The proceedings also feature a short paper detailing some specific aspects of EvaLatin, like the composition, source, tag set and annotation criteria of the shared data.

Although we are very sorry that the LT4HALA workshop and EvaLatin could not be held, as an exciting opportunity to meet in person the authors who contributed to these proceedings, we hope that this will give us a further argument to organize a second edition of both initiatives. Indeed, as demonstrated by the good number of papers submitted to LT4HALA and participants of EvaLatin, the research field concerned is wide, diverse and lively: we will do our best to provide the scholars working in such field with a venue where they can present their work and confront with colleagues who share their research interests.

Rachele Sprugnoli
Marco Passarotti

Organizers:

Rachele Sprugnoli, Università Cattolica del Sacro Cuore (Italy)
Marco Passarotti, Università Cattolica del Sacro Cuore (Italy)

Program Committee:

Marcel Bollmann, University of Copenhagen (Denmark)
Gerlof Bouma, University of Gothenburg (Sweden)
Patrick Burns, University of Texas at Austin (USA)
Flavio Massimiliano Cecchini, Università Cattolica del Sacro Cuore (Italy)
Oksana Dereza, Insight Centre for Data Analytics (Ireland)
Stefanie Dipper, Ruhr-Universität Bochum (Germany)
Hanne Eckoff, Oxford University (UK)
Maud Ehrmann, EPFL (Switzerland)
Hannes A. Fellner, Universität Wien (Austria)
Heidi Jauhiainen, University of Helsinki (Finland)
Julia Krasselt, Zurich University of Applied Sciences (Switzerland)
John Lee, City University of Hong Kong (Hong Kong)
Chao-Lin Liu, National Chengchi University (Taiwan)
Barbara McGillivray, University of Cambridge (UK)
Beáta Megyesi, Uppsala University (Sweden)
So Miyagawa, University of Göttingen (Germany)
Joakim Nivre, Uppsala University (Sweden)
Andrea Peverelli, Università Cattolica del Sacro Cuore (Italy)
Eva Pettersson, Uppsala University (Sweden)
Michael Piotrowski, University of Lausanne (Switzerland)
Sophie Prévost, Laboratoire Lattice (France)
Halim Sayoud, USTHB University (Algeria)
Olga Scrivner, Indiana University (USA)
Amir Zeldes, Georgetown University (USA)
Daniel Zeman, Charles University (Czech Republic)

Invited Speaker:

Amba Kulkarni, University of Hyderabad (India)

Table of Contents

Proceedings of 1st Workshop on Language Technologies for Historical and Ancient Languages, pages 1–9
Language Resources and Evaluation Conference (LREC 2020), Marseille, 11–16 May 2020

Dating and Stratifying a Historical Corpus with a Bayesian Mixture Model

Oliver Hellwig
Department of Comparative Linguistics
University of Zurich
hellwig7@gmx.de

Abstract

This paper introduces and evaluates a Bayesian mixture model that is designed for dating texts based on the distributions of linguistic features. The model is applied to the corpus of Vedic Sanskrit the historical structure of which is still unclear in many details. The evaluation concentrates on the interaction between time, genre and linguistic features, detecting those whose distributions are clearly coupled with the historical time. The evaluation also highlights the problems that arise when quantitative results need to be reconciled with philological insights.

Keywords: Textual chronology, Bayesian mixture model, Vedic Sanskrit

1. Introduction

While the historical development of the classical Chinese and European (Latin, Greek) literature is well understood, the chronology of ancient corpora from the Near and Middle East (Sumerian, Egypt, Hebrew) as well as from South Asia is often heavily disputed. The situation is especially complicated for the Vedic corpus (VC) of ancient India. Vedic is the oldest form of Sanskrit, an Indo-Aryan language that is the predecessor of many modern Indian languages (Masica, 1991, 50–53). The VC presumably has been composed between 1300 and 400 BCE, and consists of metrical and prose texts that describe and discuss rituals and their religious significance (Gonda, 1975; Gonda, 1977). Being a large sample of an old Indo-European language, the VC often serves as a calibration point in diachronic linguistic studies. Moreover, it provides the foundations for the major religious and philosophical systems of India. Therefore, it is important to have a clear idea of its temporal axis.

Studying the diachronic linguistic development of Vedic is challenging, because external historical and archaeological evidence is unclear, missing or has not been explored so far (Rau, 1983; Witzel, 1995), and the texts do not provide datable cross-references. The situation is further complicated by the lack of reliable authorial information and of old manuscripts or even autographs (Falk, 1993, 284ff.), as well as by the fact that many, or even all, ancient Indian texts, in their current form, have been compiled from different sources or may have originated from oral literature. Moreover, even the Rigveda (ṚV), the oldest Vedic text, shows traits of an artificial language that was no longer in active use (Renou, 1957, 10). While it is easy to distinguish Old from Middle English just by reading a few lines of text, diachronic linguistic changes in post-Rigvedic Sanskrit are difficult to detect with philological methods. As a consequence, dates proposed for individual texts in the secondary literature can differ by several hundreds of years or are often not given at all.

In spite of these difficulties, 150 years of Vedic studies have produced a coarse chronology of the VC. This paper introduces a Bayesian mixture model called ToB ("time or background") that refines and clarifies this chronology. While most Bayesian mixture models with a temporal component focus on deriving linguistic trends from known temporal information (see Sec. 2.), the model proposed in this paper takes the opposite approach and derives temporal information from linguistic features. For this sake, it integrates the current state of knowledge in the text-historical domain as a subjective Dirichlet prior distribution, and models refined dates of composition with a hidden temporal variable. Non-temporal factors that may influence the linguistic form of texts are modeled with a background branch (Chemudugunta et al., 2007), and the decision between time or background is based on the subtypes of linguistic features.

This design choice is due to the philological and text-historical orientation of the model: An important aspect of its evaluation consists in finding linguistic features that can serve as diachronic markers in Vedic. Most research has concentrated on the ṚV as the oldest Vedic document and on rare linguistic features that disappear soon after the Rigvedic language (e.g., the subjunctives of all tenses). These studies are therefore of limited use for dating later Vedic texts. This paper uses a broader range of features including lexical as well as non-lexical ones, which are generally assumed to be less dependent from the topic of texts (Stamatatos, 2009; Mikros and Argiri, 2007). By inspecting the conditional distributions of the trained model, I will show that simple linguistic features such as, for instance, the frequencies of certain POS n-grams are good predictors of time, as they reflect changing syntactic preferences in late Vedic texts. The underlying syntactic developments were discussed in linguistic studies (see Sec. 2.) as well as in recent publications using quantitative frameworks (Hellwig, 2019).

Regarding the role of background distributions, the interaction between linguistic surface and non-temporal factors such as the genre (Hock, 2000; Jamison, 1991) or the place of origin of a text (Witzel, 1989) is well known, but has not been assessed in a quantitative framework in Vedic studies so far. The design of the model discussed in the paper provides a principled approach for distinguishing between time-related features and those that are generated by non-temporal factors. The latter can serve for extending future versions of the proposed model with further non-temporal hidden variables. Section 5.1. will show that the genre of

Vedic texts is a prime candidate for such an extension.

The rest of the paper is structured as follows. After a brief overview of related research in Sec. 2., Sec. 3. sketches the model and Sec. 4. describes the data used in this paper. The main part of this paper (Sec. 5.) deals with the evaluation of the results. The problem formulation itself – refining a disputed chronology of texts – implies that there is no accepted gold standard for the extrinsic evaluation of the model. Since the composition of the ṚV, the oldest and most famous Vedic text, has been studied extensively in previous research, Sec. 5.4. uses this text as a test case for a detailed philological evaluation of the model results. Section 6. summarizes this paper and discusses future extensions of the proposed model. – Data and script are available at `https://github.com/OliverHellwig/sanskrit/tree/master/papers/2020lt4hala`.

2. Previous Research

Vedic studies have examined the temporal structure of the VC for more than 150 years, starting with a chronology that is tightly coupled with the content of texts and implicitly still used in many publications (Levitt, 2003). Since external historical evidence is not available, linguistic features, the meter and the content were used as chronological markers for studying the temporal structure of the ṚV (Avery, 1872; Lanman, 1872; Arnold, 1905). Large parts of the post-Rigvedic corpus were only sporadically considered in diachronic studies. Most scholars concentrated on limited sets of words (Wüst, 1928; Poucha, 1942) or morpho-syntactic features they assumed to indicate the old or young date of a text. These features include variations in the frequencies of case terminations (Lanman, 1872; Arnold, 1897a) or verbal moods (Arnold, 1897b; Hoffmann, 1967; Kümmel, 2000). Witzel (1989) extended the set of diachronically relevant features and studied the relationship between geographical clues found in the texts and their linguistic form. More recently, a limited number of publications applied statistical (Fosse, 1997), information theoretic (Anand and Jana, 2013), and discriminative machine learning methods (Hellwig, 2019). As the temporal granularity of quantitative results is often much coarser than expected by philologists, reconciling these results with traditional scholarship remains an open problem.

Many NLP papers that deal with diachronic data do not focus on the temporal information as such, which is assumed to be known. Instead, they use it to detect, for example, semantic changes in diachronic corpora (Kim et al., 2014; Hamilton et al., 2016; Frermann and Lapata, 2016) or the historical distribution of ideas (Hall et al., 2008). Several authors have integrated temporal information into mixture models either by imposing constraints on the mixture parameters (Blei and Lafferty, 2006) or directly sampling time stamps of documents from a continuous distribution (Wang and McCallum, 2006). As it is often difficult to decide if linguistic variation inside a text is due to time or to different authors, models for authorship attribution as proposed by Rosen-Zvi et al. (2004), Seroussi et al. (2012) or, with a Dirichlet process, Gill and Swartz (2011) are equally relevant for this paper.

3. Model

Linguistic variation in historical corpora spanning a long time range can be due to diachronic changes in the language as well as other factors such as different textual styles, genres or geographic variation. The model proposed in this paper accounts for these causes of linguistic variation by combining two admixture sub-models (see Fig. 1). The first of these sub-models, which is responsible for sampling the latent time variable $\mathbf{t}$, obtains a subjective time prior τ. The second sub-model is initialized with an uninformative prior α and represents background distributions, which are meant to capture non-temporal trends in the data (Chemudugunta et al., 2007).

When a token x_{dku} of feature subtype k (e.g. case=accusative) is sampled in document d, its feature type decides if it is drawn from the time related distribution $\theta_{t_{dku}}$ or from a background distribution $\psi_{s_{dku}}$. This approach differs from the one proposed by Chemudugunta et al. (2007), where the sampling path is chosen on the basis of document distributions. Since this paper focusses on the diachronic distribution of features, this design decision is considered a relevant part of the model.

The latent discrete time variable $\mathbf{t}$, which denotes the true (but unknown) dates of composition of individual text sections, is split into 30 time bins. The size of these bins corresponds to slices of approximately 35 years, a value often assumed to span one generation of authors. Results of previous text-historical research (see Sec. 4.) are integrated using a section-wise subjective Dirichlet prior τ_d of the latent time variables $\mathbf{t}$, which represents text-historical knowledge about the approximate dates of composition of each text section. For constructing this prior, text-historical information, as listed in Sec. 4., is first encoded as a range of section-wise lower and upper dates l_d, u_d. Value i of the prior τ_d (representing the prior of time bin i for text section d) is then modeled using the cumulative density function (cdf) of a Normal distribution with $\mu_d = \frac{1}{2}(l_d + u_d)$ and $\sigma_d^2 = (u_d - mu_d)/z_d$. The z-value z_d is chosen such that l_d and u_d represent the lower and upper limits of the 70% confidence interval of the corresponding Normal distribution. The prior can now be calculated as the difference of the cdfs of two adjacent time bins:

$$\tau_{di} = \mathrm{cdf}\big(\mathcal{N}(i|\mu_d, \sigma_d^2)\big) - \mathrm{cdf}\big(\mathcal{N}(i-1|\mu_d, \sigma_d^2)\big) \quad (1)$$

Using standard Dirichlet integration and the notation given in Fig. 2, the posterior predictive for a collapsed Gibbs sampler can be obtained from the joint distribution of all variables by integrating out the variational parameters $\Omega = \{\omega, \phi, \mu, \theta, \psi\}$ (see Fig. 1 for details):

$$p(t_n, s_n, g_n | \mathbf{t}^{-n}, \mathbf{s}^{-n}, \mathbf{g}^{-n}, \tau, \alpha, \beta, \gamma, \delta)$$
$$= p(\mathbf{t}, \mathbf{s}, \mathbf{g} | \tau, \alpha, \beta, \gamma, \delta)$$
$$= \int_\Omega p(\mathbf{t}, \mathbf{s}, \mathbf{g}, \Omega | \tau, \alpha, \beta, \gamma, \delta) d\Omega$$
$$\propto (B_{km}^{-n} + \beta_m) \times$$

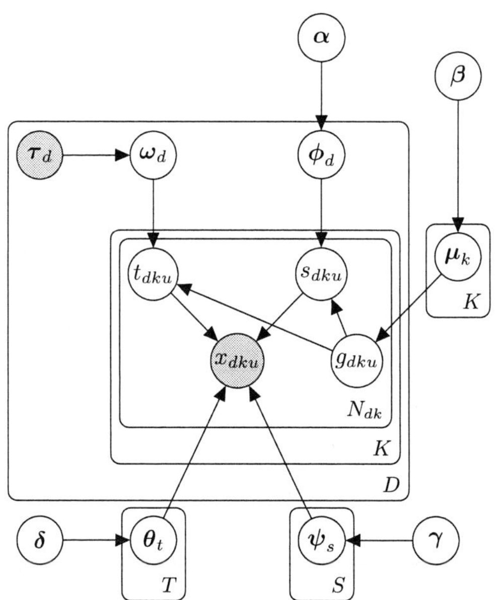

Figure 1: Plate notation of the model proposed in this paper (Eq. 2); see Fig. 2 for the notation.

- D Number of documents
- K Number of feature types (N_{dk}: of feature type k in document d)
- T Number of time bins
- S Number of background distributions
- θ, ψ Time-feature and background-feature proportions
- ω, ϕ Document-time and document-background proportions
- $\alpha, \beta, \gamma, \delta, \tau$ Dirichlet priors
- $n := dku$ (document d, feature type k, occurrence u)
- Counters for the Gibbs Sampler:
  A_{ds} # genre s assigned to document d
  B_{km} # feature k generated by the time ($m = 0$) or the topic ($m = 1$) distributions.
  C_{sk} # feature k generated by genre s
  D_{tk} # feature k generated by time t
  E_{dt} # time t assigned to document d

Figure 2: Notation used in Fig. 1 and Eq. 2

$$\begin{cases} \frac{E_{dt}^{-n} + \tau_{dt}}{\sum_u^T E_{du} + \tau_{du}} \cdot \frac{D_{tk}^{-n} + \delta_k}{\sum_u^K D_{tu}^{-n} + \delta_u} & \text{if } g_n = 0 \\ \frac{A_{ds}^{-n} + \alpha_s}{\sum_u^S A_{du}^{-n} + \alpha_u} \cdot \frac{C_{sk}^{-n} + \gamma_k}{\sum_u^K C_{su}^{-n} + \gamma_u} & \text{else} \end{cases} \quad (2)$$

Since mixture models are often sensitive to the choice of hyperparameters (Wallach et al., 2009; Asuncion et al., 2009), $\alpha, \beta, \gamma, \delta$ are updated after each iteration of the sampler using the estimates described by Minka (2003).

4. Data and features

4.1. Linguistic features

The data are extracted from the Digital Corpus of Sanskrit (DCS, Hellwig (2010 2020)), which contains more than 200 Sandhi-split texts in Vedic and Classical Sanskrit along with manually validated morphological and lexical information for each word.[1] The Vedic subcorpus of the DCS, as used in this paper, contains 35 texts with a total of 540,000 words. In contrast to previous philological work (see Sec. 2.), this paper uses a wide range of linguistic features (see Hellwig (2019, 4-7)), including, among others, the counts of the 1,000 most frequent words in the Vedic subcorpus of the DCS, cases, POS tags, verbal classes, tenses and moods. As post-Rigvedic Sanskrit was not in active daily use, previous research has claimed that most linguistic changes took place in its vocabulary. Apart from the actual vocabulary, this paper therefore pays special attention to etymology[2] and derivational morphology, two word-atomic feature types that reflect changes on the lexical level. It has been claimed that post-Rigvedic Sanskrit incorporates an increasing amount of non-Indo-Aryan words due to its contact with substrate languages (Witzel, 1999), so that higher ratios of words with a non-Indo-Aryan etymology may indicate a later date of texts (Hellwig, 2010).

Derivational rules were used to derive new words (preferably nouns) from verbal stems and other nouns. Such processes can be as simple as using the verbal root as a noun or adjective (*diś-* 'to show' → *diś-* 'indication, direction'), but may also involve complex phonological transformations applied to already derived or compounded nouns (*sukara-* 'easy-to do' → *saukārya-* 'the state of being easy to do'). While Hellwig (2019) used only a limited amount of derivational information, this paper inspects the distribution of 84 rules based on the treatment in Wackernagel and Debrunner (1954). Lexicalizing compounds was another popular method for deriving new words; e.g. *saroruhāsana* = *saras-ruha-āsana* = 'lake-growing-seat' = 'having a lotus as his seat' = 'name of the god Brahman'. Previous research has not used the number of elements in such compounds systematically for studying the chronology of Sanskrit (a few brief notes in Wackernagel (1905, 6-9, 24-26)). Currently, etymological or derivational information is available for 61,5% of all Vedic word types. Derivational morphology and lexical compounding are mutually exclusive and are therefore subsumed under a single feature type "derivation".

Apart from these word-atomic features, two multi-word features are also considered. Recent research has provided evidence for an increasing degree of configurationality in Indo-Aryan, i.e. to use word order for marking grammatical functions (Reinöhl, 2016). As a syntactic treebank is only available for a small subset of Vedic texts (Hellwig et al., 2020), the most frequent 500 bi- and trigrams of POS tags are used as a coarse approximation of syntactic chunks (Hellwig, 2019). The second multi-word feature encodes the lengths of non-lexicalized compounds. While compounds in the ṚV and the AV have at most three members (Wackernagel, 1905, 25-26), their length is not limited in Classical Sanskrit (Lowe, 2015, 80-83), so that, as a working hypothesis, increasing counts of long compounds may be indicative of late Vedic texts.

Each text is split into sections of 200 words. Since each word contributes multiple atomic features (e.g. POS, derivational information) and forms part of POS bi- and tri-

---

[1]Conllu files are available from https://github.com/OliverHellwig/sanskrit/tree/master/dcs/data/conllu.

[2]This term is used here in its restricted meaning as "étymologie-origine"; see Mayrhofer (1992, IX-XIV).

grams, each text section contains 440 data points on average.

4.2. Temporal priors

The model described in Sec. 3. requires temporal priors τ (see Eq. 1) that encode chronological proposals made in previous literature. Based on Renou (1957, 1-16), Witzel (1989), and Kümmel (2000, 5-6), this paper uses a fivefold temporal split of the VC:

Rigvedic (RV) 1300-1000 BCE; ṚV 1-9

Mantra language (MA) 1100-900 BCE; ṚV 10, Atharvaveda Saṃhitās, Ṛgveda-Khilāni, metrical parts of the Yajurveda Saṃhitās

Old prose (PO) 900-700 BCE; Aitareya Brāhmaṇa 1-5, Śatapatha Brāhmaṇa 6-9, 10.1-5; prose parts of the Yajurveda Saṃhitās

Late prose (PL) 700-400 BCE; major Brāhmaṇas not contained in PO, old Upaniṣads

Sūtra level (SU) 600-300 BCE; late Upaniṣads and Brāhmaṇas (e.g., the Gopatha Brāhmaṇa), the ritual handbooks called Sūtras

5. Evaluation

Section 5.1. studies the information that is encoded in the background distributions of ToB. Section 5.2. compares ToB with a baseline LDA model, using perplexity for the intrinsic and temporal predictions for the extrinsic evaluation. Here, the extrinsic evaluation is being complicated by the fact that the only diachronic information at our disposal is already encoded in the subjective priors τ. Section 5.3. takes a closer look at features that are generated by the time path of ToB, and discusses their philological relevance. The concluding Sec. 5.4. examines the temporal predictions for the ṚV.

5.1. The role of the background distributions

The background distributions are expected to capture the proportion of linguistic variation that cannot be explained by diachronic changes. In order to determine the optimal number of these background distributions, perplexity and accuracy are measured on the held out sets of cross-validations for varying numbers of background distributions.[3] As discussed in Hellwig (2019), randomly assigning text sections to the train and test sets underestimates the error rates on the test set of a discriminative model, because the linguistic evidence from the train sections is often strong enough to cause overfitting. Therefore the same splitting scheme as proposed in Hellwig (2019) ("textwise CV") is used in this paper. Here, each text is in turn used as the test set, and the model is trained with the remaining

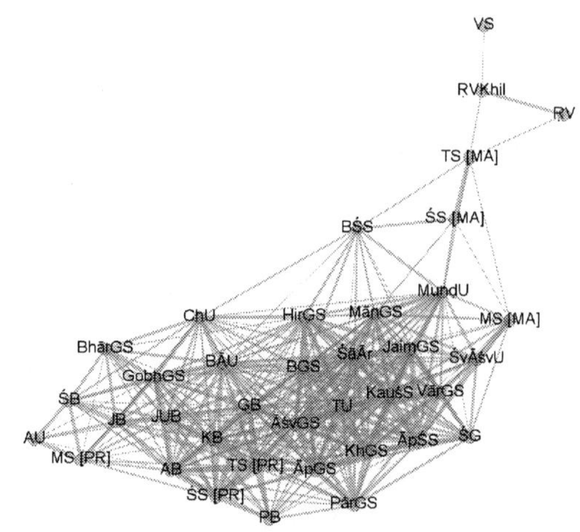

Figure 3: Undirected graph resulting from textwise similarities of background distributions; edge sizes are proportional to the textwise similarities. The graph induces a distinction between old metrical texts (top, green; ṚV, Ṛgveda-Khilāni, ŚS), prose texts (bottom left, blue; names ending on B = Brāhmaṇas) and ritual handbooks (bottom right, red; names ending on S[ūtra]). The Upaniṣads (names ending on U and Up) mediate between prose and Sūtras.

$T - 1$ texts. When varying the number S of background distributions between 1 and 30, the setting $S = 3$ results in the lowest perplexity and highest accuracy. This setting is used for all following experiments.

In order to understand which type of linguistic variation is encoded in the background, the counts of background assignments per text are accumulated and normalized, resulting in T distributions $\mathbf{b}_t$. The Euclidean distance between $\mathbf{b}_i$ and $\mathbf{b}_j$ is chosen for calculating the distance between a pair of texts (i, j). Using these Euclidean distances as edge weights results in the undirected graph that is shown in Fig. 3. The structure of the graph indicates a threefold split of the VC into early metrical texts (ṚV, Ṛgveda-Khilāni, ŚS), the works composed in prose and the ritual handbooks composed in the elliptic Sūtra style, which differs significantly from the style of other prose texts (Gonda, 1977, 629-647). Major Upaniṣads (esp. the Chāndogya Up. [ChU] and the Bṛhadāraṇyaka Up. [BĀU]) occupy an intermediate position between prose texts and Sūtras, although they were originally part of Brāhmaṇa texts. The structure of the graph therefore suggests that the background distributions primarily encode stylistic and genre-specific linguistic variation, as the differences in content between the three main groups go along with obvious differences in style.

5.2. Model comparison

While the evaluation of the background distributions (Sec. 5.1.) suggests that the text genre is a relevant factor when studying linguistic variation in Vedic, it cannot be taken for granted that ToB, the model proposed in this paper, is best suited for detecting time-dependent linguistic varia-

---

[3]Accuracy is a short-hand term for the probability that the model prediction has been generated by the normal distribution that is derived from the coarse Vedic chronology given in Sec. 4.2.; see the discussion of τ on p. 2. When the training is completed, section-wise date predictions for the left out text are obtained using "folding in".

tion. ToB is therefore compared with a modified version of LDA (Blei et al., 2003) in which the flat prior of standard LDA is replaced with the subjective temporal prior τ of ToB.

For the intrinsic comparison, I perform textwise CVs (see Sec. 5.1.), using an uninformative temporal prior for each tested text, and compare the perplexities of the two models on the test texts using a pairwise Wilcoxon rank sum test. Under the alternative hypothesis that ToB has a lower perplexity than the baseline LDA, the test yields a highly significant p-value of $3.62e^{-8}$. The lower perplexity (i.e. higher likelihood) of ToB can be due to overfitting, as it has more parameters than LDA. Therefore the Bayesian Information Criterion (BIC; Schwarz (1978)), which penalizes higher numbers of parameters and thus favors plain LDA, is calculated for all tests. In around 70% of all cases, LDA has a higher BIC than ToB and is thus more appropriate than ToB according to this metric. Repeating the Wilcoxon test with the BIC values, however, yields a p-value of 0.016, which is not significant at the 1% level. When plotting the BIC values of LDA against those of ToB (not shown in this paper), it can be observed that for lower BICs ToB performs better than LDA. The respective texts are, in general, the earlier ones (ṚV, ŚS), and they contain samples of the Brāhmaṇa style, which may be more prone to textual interpolation than the Sūtra texts for which LDA has a lower BIC than ToB. A follow-up study should evaluate if this apparent correlation between time, genre and the BIC is systematic.

For performing an extrinsic comparison, it is evaluated how well the temporal range of each text (see Sec. 4. and Fn. 3) is predicted, again using uninformative temporal priors for each tested text. It is important to emphasize once more that these temporal ranges do not constitute a proper gold standard, because multiple historical strata can, in principle, occur in any text of the VC. A model that works correctly can therefore generate temporal predictions for individual sections of a text that massively deviate from the temporal priors. Keeping these restrictions in mind, the priors are again assumed to constitute Normal distributions (see Sec. 3.) and the z-standardized value of each prediction given the respective Normal distribution is calculated. In this scenario, values closer to 0 correspond to a better model fit. A Wilcoxon test that compares the z-values of both models (alternative hypothesis: ToB generates lower z-values than plain LDA) yields a p-value of less than $2.2e^{-16}$ and thus a highly significant result.

5.3. Time-correlated features

A central motivation for developing ToB is to extend the set of linguistic features that show systematic diachronic variation and can thus be used for dating and stratifying the VC (see Sec. 2.). The switch between temporal and background distributions in ToB (variable g in Fig. 1) can be used to find feature types that are predominantly generated by the time path of the model. When the feature types examined in this paper are ordered by the proportions with which they are generated by the time path of ToB, the top position is occupied by compounds (only generated by time), followed by infinite verbal forms (89,5%), lexical in-

formation (83,6%), tenses and modes (82,7%) and POS trigrams (76,5%). All remaining feature types are also preferably generated by the time path except for etymological information (39,2%).

The increasing use of compounds for expressing syntactic constructions including coordination, nominal subordination, and exocentric relations has often been described in secondary literature (Lowe, 2015). Since compounds with more than two components only appear in larger numbers at the end of the Vedic period (esp. in the Sūtra texts), this result is mainly relevant for dating texts composed in (early) Classical Sanskrit.

The important role of the lexicon and of finite verbal forms is not surprising, as these feature types have been used regularly in previous attempts to date early Vedic texts (e.g., Arnold (1905), Poucha (1942)). More interesting insights are provided by the POS n-grams. When plotting the POS type-token ratios (TTR) against the time slots predicted by the model (see Fig. 4), it can be observed that the TTRs of all POS n-grams are maximal for the ṚV and later on decrease with the predicted dates. This suggests that the syntactic variability of post-Rigvedic Sanskrit decreases as well, perhaps caused by processes of grammaticalization and configurationality which are in effect in Middle- and New Indo-Aryan languages (Heine and Reh (1984, 67), Reinöhl (2016)). It is also instructive to inspect the POS trigrams that are preferably associated with the two temporal extremes of the VC. In the earliest layer we find, for example, the sequence preverb – noun (in various cases) – finite verb (CADP-NC.*-V), which represents tmesis (i.e. separation of preverb and verb) in many passages such as the Soma hymn ṚV 9.86.31a (matching pattern underlined): *prá rebhá ety áti vā́ram avyáyam* "The husky-voiced one [= the Soma] goes forth across the sheep's fleece" (Jamison and Brereton, 2014, 1324); or, more frequently, with a noun in the accusative in central position (ṚV 10.67.12ab, about Indra's deeds): *índro mahnā́ maható arṇavásya ví mūrdhā́nam abhinad arbudásya* "Indra with his greatness split apart the head of the great flood, of Arbuda" (Jamison and Brereton, 2014, 1490). Eventual misassignments as at ṚV 9.73.2b (*ūrmā́v ádhi venā́ avīvipan* 'the longing ones have made him (Soma) tremble on the wave'), where *ádhi-* 'on, in' is used as a postposition, but not as a preverb, could be avoided when a treebank of the complete VC is available. At the other end of the historical spectrum, late Vedic texts have a preference for absolute constructions of compound verbs in clause final position (trigram NC.acc-CADP-CGDA), as at JUB 4.9.9: *prāṇebhyo 'dhi mṛtyupā́śān unmucya-athainaṃ* ... *sarvamṛtyoḥ spṛṇāti* 'having released the fetters of death from his breaths, he releases him from all (kinds of) death'.

Temporal predictions for derivational features reflect many diachronic trends described in previous literature. When the derivational features are ordered by the mean date assigned to them, the first (= earliest) position is occupied by the suffix *-tāti*, which is used to derive abstract nouns from other nouns as in *sarvá-tāti-* 'complete-ness' (< *sárva-* 'complete, all') and known to be restricted to the oldest parts of the VC (Wackernagel and Debrunner, 1954,

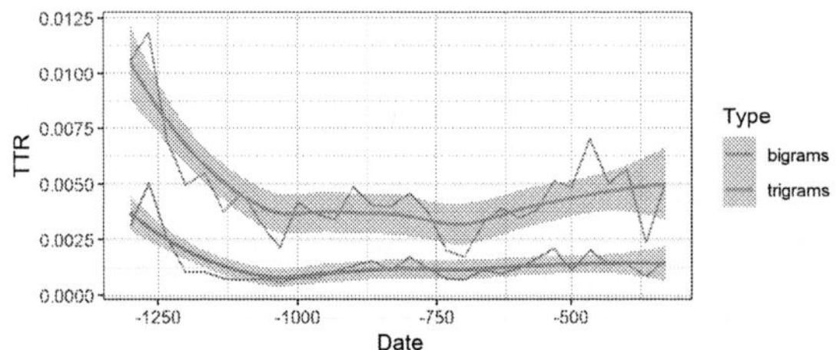

Figure 4: Type-token ratios of POS n-grams (y-axis) dependent from the predicted dates (x-axis). The curves demonstrate the decreasing syntactic variability of post-Rigvedic Sanskrit.

§464). Suffixes assigned to the latest time slots contain, among others, the comparative suffix *-tara* (e.g., *kṣipratara-* 'faster'), which replaces the older comparative suffix *-īyas* (e.g., *kṣépīyas-* 'faster', see Wackernagel and Debrunner (1954, §450)), or the suffix *-ika* with vṛddhi of the first syllable, which is often used to derive adjectives from (compounded) nouns (e.g., *aíkāh-ika-* 'lasting one day' < *eka-aha-* 'one day' with vṛddhi e → ai; see Wackernagel and Debrunner (1954, §194 b β) for a historical sketch). As often, results for the earliest Vedic strata are well known, while features associated with intermediate and late time ranges have the potential to promote philological research. As mentioned on p. 3, lexicalized compounds are subsumed under the feature type derivation. Conforming to the general trend observed for compound formation (see above), the model assigns an earlier average date to words with two compound members (e.g., *vanas-pati-* 'lord of the wood, tree') than to those with three (e.g., *a-prajás-tā-* 'childlessness'). It should, however, be noted that 63% of the three-element compounds are inflected forms of the word *sv-iṣṭa-kṛt-* 'offering a good sacrifice', the name of a special sacrifice to the god Agni (Mylius, 1995, 140), which is almost exclusively discussed in the late Sūtra texts. Even this brief overview shows the importance of derivational information for inducing the temporal structure of the VC. Wüst (1928), who studied a related set of features for the ṚV, did not meet enthusiastic support in Vedic studies – it may be worthwhile to reconsider his approach with new quantitative methods.

5.4.   Detail study: Temporal stratification of the Rigveda

The ṚV, the oldest work of Vedic Sanskrit, is a collection of ten books of religious poetry composed by multiple authors (Witzel, 1997, 261-264). Among all Vedic texts, the ṚV has been studied most intensively and can thus serve as a test case for the temporal predictions made by ToB. On the basis of linguistic criteria, citations, and the textual content, it is generally assumed that ṚV 10 is the youngest book of the whole collection (Renou, 1957, 4). The so-called Family Books (ṚV 2-7) are usually considered to be old or even to constitute the core of the ṚV (Witzel, 1997, 262-264). ṚV 9 is also often accepted as old, while the status of ṚV 1 and especially ṚV 8 is disputed (Hopkins (1896), Gonda (1975, 8-14), Jamison and Brereton (2014, 9-13)). Overall, the split (1-9) (10) has emerged as the most widely accepted

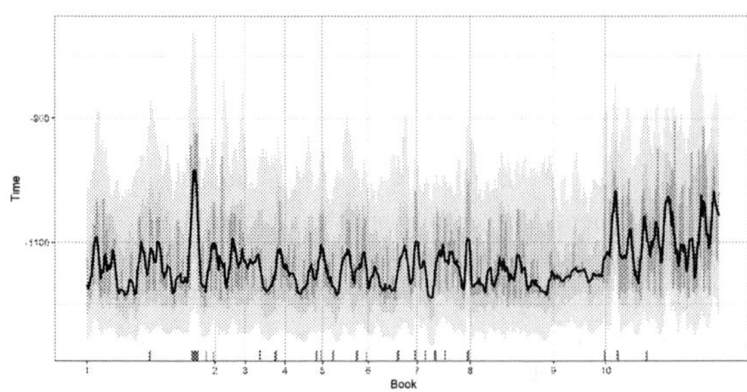

Figure 5: Predicted dates for the ṚV. The polygons show the smoothed 50% and 90% quantiles, the black line is the smoothed median, and the grey line is the unsmoothed median.

stratification of the ṚV.

Figure 5 shows the median and two quantiles of the dates predicted by ToB.[4] The overall trend observed in Fig. 5 confirms the most frequently postulated stratification of the ṚV: While book 10 is late, there are no clear temporal separations between the remaining nine books. For deriving a temporal ranking of the ten Rigvedic books, one-sided Wilcoxon rank sum tests between pairs of books (i, j) are performed. If the test for (i, j) is significant at the 10% level, an ordering constraint $i < j$ is recorded. When a minimum location shift of one time step is assumed, the resulting constraints induce the "canonical" ordering $(1 - 9) < (10)$. Leaving the location shift unspecified[5] induces the ordering $(4, 8) < (1 - 3, 5 - 7, 9) < (10)$, which deviates from the most widely accepted split (1-9) (10) by labeling RV 4 and 8 as the earliest books, as already postulated for book 8 by Lanman (1872, 580) and Arnold (1897a, 319) (strongly contested by Hopkins (1896)) and for book 4 by Wüst (1928).

Further binomial tests are performed for all features that are preferably assigned to the earliest time slots, assessing if they are significantly more frequent in RV 4 and 8 than in the rest of the text (RV 10 can be omitted as obviously younger). These tests produce a list of 92 features, most of which have been considered as archaic in previous research: (1) perfect subjunctive and injunctive (see Arnold (1905, 31)); (2) the suffixes *-tave*, *-vane*, *-aye* and *-ase*, all of which form dative verbal nouns (Wackernagel and Debrunner, 1954, s.v.); (3) the derivational suffixes *-tvana* (abstracts) and *-vat* (in *pra-vat-* 'elevation'; see Wackernagel and Debrunner (1954, §530,703)); (4) five POS n-grams containing, among others, the sequence noun-infinitive (as in old constructions like *jyók ca súryaṃ dṛśé* 'in order to see the sun for a long time'); (5) and a list of 79 words.

In 1888, the scholar H. Oldenberg claimed that the hymns in each book of the ṚV are arranged according to the numbers of their stanzas, and that hymns violating this rule represent the youngest layer of Rigvedic poetry ("appendices"; Oldenberg (1888, 191-197, 265)). As Oldenberg's work is still among the most frequently cited studies on the textual

---

[4]Continuous quantiles are calculated by interpolating the discrete counts.

[5]Note that significant p-values can result from the mere sample sizes in this setting.

history of the R̥V, it may be useful to compare his results with the output of ToB. The 31 hymns identified as appendices in Oldenberg (1888, 197-202, 222-223) are marked by the rug plot at the bottom of Fig. 5, and obviously coincide with some of the peaks in the predicted times.[6] A Wilcoxon rank sum test that compares the times predicted for Oldenberg's appendices with those of the rest of R̥V 1-7, 9 produces a highly significant p-value of less than $2e1^{-16}$, which suggests that Oldenberg's ideas are supported by the output of ToB. A closer inspection, however, shows that this strong effect is mainly caused by a few of Oldenberg's appendices marked as especially young by the model. These hymns comprise, among others, R̥V 1.162-164 (including the famous "riddle hymn" 1.164, which may be related to the pravargya ritual; see Houben (2000)); the "frog hymn" 7.103, which shows traits of later religious ideas (Lubin, 2001); the Atharvanic hymn R̥V 7.104 (Lommel, 1965, 203ff.); the Soma hymn 9.113, which foreshadows a concept of heaven occurring in much later texts (Jamison and Brereton, 2014, 1304) and notably mentions a group of Gandharvas instead of a single Gandharva only, an idea often considered as late (Oberlies, 2005, 106); 10.19, a hymn composed in easy language that addresses cows who have gone astray, but is found, somehow unfittingly, at the end of a series of funeral hymns (Jamison and Brereton, 2014, 1401); and 10.60, which pays much attention to the Atharvanic topic of healing. The remaining appendices, esp. those contained in the Family Books R̥V 2-7, are not marked as particularly late by the model, but some of them even as quite old as, for example, the "praise of giving" (*dānastuti-*) in R̥V 5.27, whose status as an appendix has been challenged by Jamison and Brereton (2014, 688) on metrical grounds.

6. Summary

This paper has introduced a Bayesian mixture model with a temporal component that is used for chronological research in Vedic literature. Although the VC is used as the text corpus in this paper, the proposed method is not specifically designed for Vedic Sanskrit, but can be applied to any corpus with a disputed historical structure as long as linguistic annotations for this corpus are available. As Sections 3. and 5. have shown, the actual challenge is rather the evaluation of such a model than its design. While the underlying probabilistic processes are well understood, the interpretation of the model output requires a close interaction between quantitative methods and text-historical scholarship, especially since the data with which the model are evaluated do not constitute a proper gold standard (see Sec. 5.1. and 5.2.). The brief evaluation of the R̥V in Sec. 5.4. functions as a test case that indicates some possible approaches. Although a closer inspection of the results for the R̥V will unveil more insights into its structure, more interesting candidates for in-depth studies are certainly found among the post-Rigvedic texts as, for example, the two recensions of

---

[6]Only full hymns marked as appendices are considered in this paper, i.e. R̥V 1.104, 162-164, 179, 191; 2.42-43; 3.28-29, 52-53; 4.48, 58; 5.27-28, 61, 87; 6.47, 74-75; 7.17, 33, 55, 103-104; 9.112-114; 10.19, 60.

the Atharvaveda (see Whitney and Lanman (1905, cxxvii-xclii) and Witzel (1997, 275-284)) or early prose treatises such as the Maitrāyaṇī-Saṃhitā (see Amano (2009, 1-6) on the state of research).

On the mathematical side, the model proposed in this paper is a prototype that can be extended in various aspects. Its most serious drawback is the inflexible structure of the admixture models, which will be replaced by a Hierarchical Dirichlet Process (HDP, Teh et al. (2005)) in a follow-up study. In addition, the fixed size of the text windows (see Sec. 4.1.) prevents textual strata from being directly induced from the data (instead of constructing them in a post-processing step). Combining HDPs with a Markov Random Field, as proposed by Orbanz and Buhmann (2008) for image segmentation, appears to provide a viable solution for this challenge.

7. Bibliographical References

Amano, K. (2009). *Maitrāyaṇī Saṃhitā I–II. Übersetzung der Prosapartien mit Kommentar zur Lexik und Syntax der älteren vedischen Prosa*. Hempen, Bremen.

Anand, D. A. and Jana, S. (2013). Chronology of Sanskrit texts: An information-theoretic corroboration. In *National Conference on Communications (NCC)*, pages 1–5. IEEE.

Arnold, E. V. (1897a). Literary epochs in the Rigveda. *Zeitschrift für vergleichende Sprachforschung auf dem Gebiete der Indogermanischen Sprachen*, 34(3):297–344.

Arnold, E. V. (1897b). Sketch of the historical grammar of the Rig and Atharva Vedas. *Journal of the American Oriental Society*, 18:203–353.

Arnold, E. V. (1905). *Vedic Metre in its Historical Development*. University Press, Cambridge.

Asuncion, A., Welling, M., Smyth, P., and Teh, Y. W. (2009). On smoothing and inference for topic models. In *Proceedings of the Twenty-fifth Conference on Uncertainty in Artificial Intelligence*, pages 27–34. AUAI Press.

Avery, J. (1872). Contributions to the history of verb-inflection in Sanskrit. *Journal of the American Oriental Society*, 10:219–324.

Blei, D. M. and Lafferty, J. D. (2006). Dynamic topic models. In *Proceedings of the 23rd International Conference on Machine Learning*, pages 113–120.

Blei, D. M., Ng, A. Y., and Jordan, M. I. (2003). Latent Dirichlet Allocation. *Journal of Machine Learning Research*, 3:993–1022.

Chemudugunta, C., Smyth, P., and Steyvers, M. (2007). Modeling general and specific aspects of documents with a probabilistic topic model. In *Advances in Neural Information Processing Systems*, pages 241–248.

Falk, H. (1993). *Schrift im alten Indien: Ein Forschungsbericht mit Anmerkungen*. Gunter Narr Verlag, Tübingen.

Fosse, L. M. (1997). *The Crux of Chronology in Sanskrit Literature*. Scandinavian University Press, Oslo.

Frermann, L. and Lapata, M. (2016). A Bayesian model of diachronic meaning change. *Transactions of the Association for Computational Linguistics*, 4:31–45.

Gill, P. S. and Swartz, T. B. (2011). Stylometric analyses using Dirichlet process mixture models. *Journal of Statistical Planning and Inference*, 141(11):3665–3674.

Gonda, J. (1975). *Vedic Literature (Saṃhitās and Brāhmaṇas)*, volume 1 of *A History of Indian Literature*. Otto Harrassowitz, Wiesbaden.

Gonda, J. (1977). *The Ritual Sūtras*, volume 1, Fasc. 2 of *A History of Indian Literature*. Otto Harrassowitz, Wiesbaden.

Hall, D., Jurafsky, D., and Manning, C. D. (2008). Studying the history of ideas using topic models. In *Proceedings of the EMNLP*, pages 363–371.

Hamilton, W. L., Leskovec, J., and Jurafsky, D. (2016). Cultural shift or linguistic drift? comparing two computational measures of semantic change. In *Proceedings of the Conference on Empirical Methods in Natural Language Processing. Conference on Empirical Methods in Natural Language Processing*, volume 2016, page 2116. NIH Public Access.

Heine, B. and Reh, M. (1984). *Grammaticalization and Reanalysis in African Languages*. Helmut Buske Verlag, Hamburg.

Hellwig, O., Scarlata, S., Ackermann, E., and Widmer, P. (2020). The treebank of Vedic Sanskrit. In *Proceedings of the LREC*.

Hellwig, O. (2010). Etymological trends in the Sanskrit vocabulary. *Literary and Linguistic Computing*, 25(1):105–118.

Hellwig, O. (2010–2020). DCS - The Digital Corpus of Sanskrit. http://www.sanskrit-linguistics.org/dcs/index.php.

Hellwig, O. (2019). Dating Sanskrit texts using linguistic features and neural networks. *Indogermanische Forschungen*, 124:1–47.

Hock, H. H. (2000). Genre, discourse, and syntax in early Indo-European, with emphasis on Sanskrit. In Susan C. Herring, et al., editors, *Textual Parameters in Older Languages*, pages 163–196. John Benjamins, Amsterdam/Philadelphia.

Hoffmann, K. (1967). *Der Injunktiv im Veda*. Winter, Heidelberg.

Hopkins, E. W. (1896). Prāgāthikāni, I. *Journal of the American Oriental Society*, 17:23–92.

Houben, J. E. M. (2000). The ritual pragmatics of a Vedic hymn: The "Riddle Hymn" and the pravargya ritual. *Journal of the American Oriental Society*, 120(4):499–536.

Jamison, S. W. and Brereton, J. P. t. (2014). *The Rigveda: the Earliest Religious Poetry of India*. Oxford University Press, New York.

Jamison, S. W. (1991). Syntax of direct speech in Vedic. pages 40–56. E.J. Brill, New York, Kopenhagen, Köln.

Kim, Y., Chiu, Y.-I., Hanaki, K., Hegde, D., and Petrov, S. (2014). Temporal analysis of language through neural language models. In *Proceedings of the ACL 2014 Workshop on Language Technologies and Computational Social Science*, pages 61–65.

Kümmel, M. J. (2000). *Das Perfekt im Indoiranischen. Eine Untersuchung der Form und Funktion einer ererbten Kategorie des Verbums und ihrer Entwicklung in den altindoiranischen Sprachen*. Reichert, Wiesbaden.

Lanman, C. R. (1872). A statistical account of noun-inflection in the Veda. *Journal of the American Oriental Society*, 10:325–601.

Levitt, S. H. (2003). The dating of the Indian tradition. *Anthropos*, 98(2):341–359.

Lommel, H. (1965). Vasiṣṭha und Viśvāmitra. *Oriens*, 18/19:200–227.

Lowe, J. J. (2015). The syntax of Sanskrit compounds. *Language*, 91(3):71–115.

Lubin, T. (2001). Vratá divine and human in the early Veda. *Journal of the American Oriental Society*, 121(4):565–579.

Masica, C. P. (1991). *The Indo-Aryan Languages*. Cambridge University Press, Cambridge.

Mayrhofer, M. (1992). *Etymologisches Wörterbuch des Altindoarischen. I. Band*. Carl Winter, Heidelberg.

Mikros, G. and Argiri, E. (2007). Investigating topic influence in authorship attribution. In *Proceedings of the International Workshop on Plagiarism Analysis, Authorship Identification, and Near-Duplicate Detection*, pages 29–35.

Minka, T. P. (2003). Estimating a Dirichlet distribution. Technical report.

Mylius, K. (1995). *Wörterbuch des altindischen Rituals*. Institut für Indologie, Wichtrach.

Oberlies, T. (2005). Der Gandharva und die drei Tage während 'Quarantäne'. *Indo-Iranian Journal*, 48(1):97–109.

Oldenberg, H. (1888). *Die Hymnen des Ṛigveda. Band I: Metrische und textgeschichtliche Prolegomena*. Wilhelm Hertz, Berlin.

Orbanz, P. and Buhmann, J. M. (2008). Nonparametric Bayesian image segmentation. *International Journal of Computer Vision*, 77(1-3):25–45.

Poucha, P. (1942). Schichtung des Ṛigveda. *Archív Orientální*, 13:103–141, 225–269.

Rau, W. (1983). *Zur vedischen Altertumskunde*. Steiner, Wiesbaden.

Reinöhl, U. (2016). *Grammaticalization and the Rise of Configurationality in Indo-Aryan*. Oxford University Press, Oxford, UK.

Renou, L. (1957). *Altindische Grammatik, Introduction Générale*. Vandenhoeck & Ruprecht, Göttingen.

Rosen-Zvi, M., Griffiths, T., Steyvers, M., and Smyth, P. (2004). The author-topic model for authors and documents. In *Proceedings of the 20th Conference on Uncertainty in Artificial Intelligence*, pages 487–494.

Schwarz, G. (1978). Estimating the dimension of a model. *The Annals of Statistics*, 6(2):461–464.

Seroussi, Y., Bohnert, F., and Zukerman, I. (2012). Authorship attribution with author-aware topic models. In *Proceedings of the ACL: Short Papers-Volume 2*, pages 264–269. Association for Computational Linguistics.

Stamatatos, E. (2009). A survey of modern authorship attribution methods. *Journal of the American Society for Information Science and Technology*, 60(3):538–556.

Teh, Y. W., Jordan, M. I., Beal, M. J., and Blei, D. M. (2005). Sharing clusters among related groups: Hierarchical Dirichlet processes. In *Advances in Neural Information Processing Systems*, pages 1385–1392.

Wackernagel, J. and Debrunner, A. (1954). *Altindische Grammatik. II, 2: Die Nominalsuffixes*. Vandenhoeck & Ruprecht, Göttingen.

Wackernagel, J. (1905). *Altindische Grammatik. Band II, 1: Einleitung zur Wortlehre. Nominalkomposition*. Vandenhoeck & Ruprecht, Göttingen.

Wallach, H. M., Mimno, D. M., and McCallum, A. (2009). Rethinking LDA: Why priors matter. In *Advances in Neural Information Processing Systems*, pages 1973–1981.

Wang, X. and McCallum, A. (2006). Topics over time: A non-Markov continuous-time model of topical trends. In *Proceedings of the 12th ACM SIGKDD International conference on Knowledge Discovery and Data Mining*, pages 424–433.

Whitney, W. D. and Lanman, C. R. (1905). *Atharva-Veda Samhita*. Harvard University, Cambridge.

Witzel, M. (1989). Tracing the Vedic dialects. In Colette Caillat, editor, *Dialectes dans les littératures indoaryennes*, pages 97–264. Collége de France, Institut de Civilisation Indienne, Paris.

Witzel, M. (1995). Early Indian history: Linguistic and textual parametres. In George Erdosy, editor, *The Indo-Aryans of Ancient South Asia. Language, Material Culture and Ethnicity*, volume 1, pages 85–125. Walter de Gruyter, Berlin, New York.

Witzel, M. (1997). The development of the Vedic canon and its schools: The social and political milieu (Materials on Vedic Sakhas, 8). In Michael Witzel, editor, *Inside the Texts, Beyond the Texts. New Approaches to the Study of the Vedas*, pages 258–348. Cambridge.

Witzel, M. (1999). Substrate languages in Old Indo-Aryan (Ṛgvedic, Middle and Late Vedic). *Electronic Journal of Vedic Studies*, 5(1):1–67.

Wüst, W. (1928). *Stilgeschichte und Chronologie des Ṛgveda*. Deutsche Morgenländische Gesellschaft, Leipzig.

Proceedings of 1st Workshop on Language Technologies for Historical and Ancient Languages, pages 10–16
Language Resources and Evaluation Conference (LREC 2020), Marseille, 11–16 May 2020

Automatic Construction of Aramaic-Hebrew Translation Lexicon

Chaya Liebeskind, Shmuel Liebeskind
Computer Science Department, Jerusalem College of Technology, Lev Academic Center, Israel
liebchaya@gmail.com, israellieb@gmail.com

Abstract

Aramaic is an ancient Semitic language with a 3,000 year history. However, since the number of Aramaic speakers in the world has declined, Aramaic is in danger of extinction. In this paper, we suggest a methodology for automatic construction of Aramaic-Hebrew translation Lexicon. First, we generate an initial translation lexicon by a state-of-the-art word alignment translation model. Then, we filter the initial lexicon using string similarity measures of three types: similarity between terms in the target language, similarity between a source and a target term, and similarity between terms in the source language. In our experiments, we use a parallel corpora of Biblical Aramaic-Hebrew sentence pairs and evaluate various string similarity measures for each type of similarity. We illustrate the empirical benefit of our methodology and its effect on precision and F1. In particular, we demonstrate that our filtering method significantly exceeds a filtering approach based on the probability scores given by a state-of-the-art word alignment translation model.

Keywords: translation, lexicon, Aramaic, Hebrew, word alignment, string similarity

1. Introduction

A translation lexicon is a set of word pairs, where each pair contains one word from the source language and its translation equivalent (has the same meaning as, or can be used in a similar context to) from the target. Translation lexicons are an essential element of any statistical machine translation (MT) scheme. Previous work on MT has shown that, given sufficient parallel training data, highly accurate word translations can be learned automatically (Koehn et al., 2003; Chiang, 2007).

According to UNESCO, some 6,000-7,000 languages are spoken worldwide today. Approximately 97% are spoken by only 4% of the world population, while just 3% of the world speaks 96% of all the remaining languages. Most of those languages, mainly spoken by indigenous people, will alarmingly disappear. Thus, the worldwide preservation, revitalization and promotion of indigenous languages is urgent.

Aramaic is a member of the Afro-Asian language family's Semitic branch. Aramaic is an ancient language (closely related to both Hebrew and Arabic) with a 3,000 year history. Experts believe that Aramaic was main language from 539 BC to 70 AD in the Middle East and probably spoken by Jesus. However, as the number of speakers worldwide is declining, Aramaic is threatened by extinction.

Aramaic is the language of the Biblical books of Daniel and Ezra, and is the primary language of the Talmud (a key Jewish text) and the Zohar (a foundational work in the literature of Jewish mystical thought known as Kabbalah). To enable future scholars to understand and learn from these ancient texts in Aramaic, lexical resources, such as a dictionary, must be developed.

In this study, we present an algorithmic scheme for automatic construction of Hebrew-Aramaic translation lexicon. In particular, we propose and investigate a filtering process over an initial translation lexicon, generated by a state-of-the-art word alignment translation model. Our filtering method computes three types of string similarities, similarity between terms in the target language, similarity between a source and a target term, and similarity between terms in the source language. We examine five string similarity measures for the three types of similarity.

We demonstrate the empirical advantage of our scheme over a parallel Aramaic-Hebrew Biblical corpora and evaluate its impact on accuracy and F1. We show that our filtering method significantly outperforms a filtering approach based on the probability scores provided by the word alignment translation model. The remainder of this paper is organized as follows: we start with a description of word-based translation models that we utilize in our scheme and a brief summary on Aramaic natural language processing (NLP) (Section 2.). Then, we describe our Aramaic-Hebrew parallel corpora in Section 3.. Our main contribution of the algorithmic scheme is detailed in Section 4., followed by an evaluation in Section 5. and conclusions in Section 6..

2. Background

This section describes word-based translation models that we used in our experiments (Section 2.1.), followed by a brief introduction to the applications of NLP on our extinct language, Medium Aramaic, or "post-classical" Aramaic (Section 2.2.). We note that we also applied state-of-the-art neural MT algorithms. However, they did not perform well on our corpus, probably due to the limited amount of data.

2.1. Word-based Translation Models

Word alignment corresponds to word-based translation models (Brown et al., 1993), where the units of correspondence between sentences are individual words. Formally, we say that the objective of the word alignment task is to discover the word-to-word correspondences in a sentence pair $(F_1^J = f_1...f_J, E_1^I = e_1...e_I)$ in which the source and target sentences contain I and J words, respectively.

An alignment A of the two correspondences is defined as (Och and Ney, 2003):

$$A \subseteq \{(j, i) : j = 1, ..., J; i = 0, ..., I\} \quad (1)$$

in case that i = 0 in some (j, i) ∈ A, it represents that the source word j aligns to an "empty" target word e_0.

In statistical word alignment models, the probability of a source sentence given target sentence is written as:

$$P(f_1^J|e_1^i) = \sum_{a_1^J} P(f_1^J, a_1^J|e_1^i) \qquad (2)$$

in which a_1^J denotes the alignment on the sentence pair. Several different parametric forms of $P(f_1^J, a_1^J|e_1^i) = p_\theta(f_1^J, a_1^J|e_1^i)$ have been proposed, and the parameters θ can be estimated using Maximum Likelihood Estimation (MLE) on a training corpus (Och and Ney, 2003).

$$\hat{\theta} = \underset{\theta}{\mathrm{argmax}} \prod_{s=1}^{S} \sum_{a} p_\theta(f_s, a|e_s) \qquad (3)$$

The best alignment of the sentence pair, is called Viterbi alignment.

$$\hat{a}_1^j = \underset{a_1^J}{\mathrm{argmax}} \, p_\theta(f_1^J, a_1^J|e_1^i) \qquad (4)$$

The IBM Models (Brown et al., 1993) are a sequence of word alignment models with increasing complexity, starting with lexical translation probabilities, adding models for reordering and word duplication. The IBM Models, along with the Hidden Markov Model (HMM) (Vogel et al., 1996), serve as the starting point for most current state-of-the-art statistical machine translation systems.

One of the serious drawbacks of the IBM models is that they create a one-to-many mapping. Their alignment function may return the same value for different input, but cannot return multiple values for one input (many-to-one). To resolve this and allow many-to-many mappings, various methods for performing a symmetrization of the IBM directed statistical alignment models are applied. Most of the symmetrization methods apply a heuristic postprocessing step that combines the alignments in both translation directions (source to target, target to source). If we intersect the two alignments, we get a high-precision alignment of high-confidence alignment points. If we take the union of the two alignments, we get a high-recall alignment with additional alignment points. In SMT (Och et al., 1999), a higher recall is more important (Och and Ney, 2000), so an alignment union would probably be chosen.

Och and Ney (Och and Ney, 2003) investigated the space between intersection and union with expansion heuristics that start with the intersection and add additional alignment points. They trained an alignment model in both translation directions and obtained two alignments a_1^J and b_1^I for each pair of sentences in the training corpus. Let $A_1 = \{(a_j, j)|a_j > 0\}$ and $A_2 = \{(i, b_i)|b_i > 0\}$ denote the sets of alignments in the two Viterbi alignments. They combined A_1 and A_2 into one alignment matrix A using the following steps:

1. Determine the intersection $A = A_1 \cap A_2$.

2. Extend the alignment A iteratively by adding alignments *(i, j)* occurring only in the alignment A_1 or in the alignment A_2:

   (a) if neither f_j nor e_i has an alignment in A, **or**

   (b) if both of the following conditions hold:

      i. The alignment *(i, j)* has a horizontal neighbor *(i - 1, j), (i + 1, j)* or a vertical neighbor *(i, j - 1), (i, j + 1)* that is already in A.

      ii. The set $A \cup \{(i,j)\}$ does not contain alignments with both horizontal and vertical neighbors.

In our experiments, we adopted this type of symmetrization methods, which are also known as *grow-diag-x* heuristics. Given this alignment method, it is quite straight-forward to estimate a maximum likelihood translation lexicon.

2.2. Aramaic NLP

Not much research has been done on Aramaic NLP. Some studies have used a corpus of ancient texts in mixed Hebrew and Aramaic language, the Responsa project. These studies discussed different tasks like abbreviation disambiguation (HaCohen-Kerner et al., 2010; HaCohen-Kerner et al., 2013), citations identification (HaCohen-Kerner et al., 2011; Koppel and Schweitzer, 2014), temporal data mining (Mughaz et al., 2017; Moghaz et al., 2019), and diachronic thesaurus construction (Zohar et al., 2013; Liebeskind et al., 2016; Liebeskind et al., 2019). Some of these studies have provided insights into the Aramaic language. However, since the main language of the Responsa project is Hebrew, these studies did not directly focus on Aramaic NLP.

Snyder and Barzilay (2008) presented a non-parametric model that jointly induces a segmentation and morpheme alignment from a multilingual corpus of short parallel phrases from the Hebrew Bible and translations (Targum Onkelos was used for the Aramaic (see Section 3.)). The model uses Dirichlet process prior for each language and for the cross-lingual links. Snyder and Barzilay (2008) applied their model to four languages: Arabic, Hebrew, Aramaic, and English. They showed that the joint model decreased error by up to 24% with respect to monolingual models. When used in languages of the same family, the model achieved better performance. However, since Snyder and Barzilay (2008) did not have gold standard segmentation for the English and Aramaic part of the data, they restrict their evaluation to Hebrew and Arabic.

An exception is the recent work of Porat et al. (2018) on identification of parallel passages in the Babylonian Talmud corpus. In contrast to the Responsa project, the Talmud main language is Aramaic. The method by Porat et al. (2018) allows for changes between the parallel passages on word level and on phrase level. On word level, they focused on the core of the words. First, the input corpus was used to compute the frequency of the Hebrew letters. Then, they identified for each word the two most rare letters and represented the word by these two letters (keep the order of two letters in the word). Since prefixes letters and matres lectionis are the most common letters in the language, The method by Porat et al. (2018) effectively eliminated most of them. They assumed that since they aimed to find sequences of matching two-letter codes, the number of false positives will be reduced later. On phrase level, they compared both n-grams of length 4 and non-contiguous n-grams (termed skip-grams). They extracted all 4-word combinations for every 5-word sequence in the text, which could omit any of the last four words. Finally, to validate a given match, they clustered matching skip-grams by generating a two-dimensional graph. Each skip-grams match was plotted on one axis according to the base skip-gram starting word position, and on the other axis according to the corresponding skip-gram starting word position. Cases where several skip-grams match a cluster on the graph on a more or less diagonal line were considered valid. As the method by Porat et al. (2018) constructs its list of potential matches in a pre-processing step generated via a single pass, it is capable of processing text of any size in $O(N)$ time.

3. Parallel Corpus

Translation lexicon construction requires parallel data for learning. In a sentence-level parallel corpus, for every sentence in the source language there is a translated sentence in the target language. We used two Aramaic-Hebrew corpora:

1. **Targum Onkelos**, the Jewish Aramaic Targum, is an authentic translated text of the Pentateuch (Five Books of Moses), which is believed to have been written in the early 2nd century CE. Its authorship is traditionally attributed to Onkelos, a well-known convert to Judaism in the Tannaic era (c. $35-120$ CE). The Talmud story (Megillah 3a) tells that Targum Onkelos's content was first transferred to Moses at Mount Sinai by God, but later forgotten and recorded by Onkelos. Onkelos' Aramaic translation is a literal word-by-word translation, with very little additional material in the form of non-legalistic exegetical texts (usually where the original Hebrew is an idiom, a homonym, or a metapho). However, in cases where biblical passages are difficult, Onkelos aims at minimizing obscurities and ambiguities.

2. **Targum Jonathan**, the official eastern Aramaic translation to the Nevi'im (Prophets), the second main division of the Hebrew Bible. Its authorship is traditionally attributed to Jonathan ben Uzziel, a pupil of Hillel the Elder. The Talmud (Megillah 3a) states that "from the mouths of Haggai, Zechariah, and Malachi," suggesting Targum Jonathan was based on traditions derived from the last prophets. Its overall style is like Targum Onkelos, originated in the land of Israel and was accepted in Babylonia in the third century. Targum Jonathan was brought to the Diaspora by the Babylonian Academies.

4. Methodology

Translation lexicons usually contain thousands of entries, termed here *source terms*. Each entry holds a list of *target translated terms*, which has the same meaning as, or may be used in a similar context to the source term.

In this paper we assume that a sentence-level parallel corpus is given as input, and run an IBM method to extract a list of candidate target translated terms (termed *candidate translated terms*). Then, we focus on the process of filtering the candidate list and extracting a list of target translated terms for each source term.

Our methodology was performed on a Aramaic-Hebrew parallel corpus, but can be generically applied in other settings.

4.1. Algorithmic Scheme

We used the following algorithmic scheme for translation lexicon construction. Our input is a sentence-level parallel corpus. First, we extract an initial translation lexicon using an IBM word alignment algorithm. Next, to filter incorrect translations, for each term in the initial lexicon we retrieve all its translations and cluster them using some measure of string similarity. For example, the translation cluster of the Aramaic word גברין (men) is {אנשי, אנשים, איש} We consider clusters of more than one translation as valid and further examine clusters of length 1. We compare the similarity between the term and its single translation. A high similarity score indicates the correctness of the translation. For example, the Aramaic word אכלתון (eat) and its translation {אכלתם}. Finally, to check the validity of the remaining clusters (e.g. מדכר (ram)) and avoid losing cases like synonyms, we extract similar terms to the term that we are testing (דכרין) using some measure of string similarity and cluster the translations of all these terms ({אילם, האילים, איל, אילים, אילם}). If the cluster of the tested translation (איל) is contained in one of the extracted clusters, the translation is considered valid. The output is a filtered translation lexicon consisting of the translations which were judged valid by the algorithm.

The algorithm's pseudo code is described in Algorithm 1. String similarity measures are used (in four steps of the algorithm) to calculate three types of similarities; (1) similarity between terms in the target language (lines 4 and 13), (2) similarity between a source and a target term (line 7), and (3) similarity between terms in the source language (line 10).

4.2. String Similarity

Aramaic is a *resource-poor* language that lacks essential resources, such as part-of-speech taggers, necessary for computational linguistics. Thus, to calculate the similarity between two Aramaic words. we can not lemmatize them and compare their lemmas, but we need to apply a string similarity measure. Since Liebeskind et al. (2012) reported that available tools for Hebrew processing perform poorly on a diachronic corpus and our parallel corpora is of a similar genre, we also investigate string similarity measures for Hebrew. For word comparison in different languages (Aramaic and Hebrew), a string similarity measure is also required.

Table 1 lists the prior art string similarity measures considered in our work. Given two similar words with a different orthography, our goal is to find a measure which maximizes their similarity score or minimizes their distance score.

Although, in our corpora, the alphabet of both languages is the Hebrew alphabet. the letter distribution differ between the Aramaic and Hebrew. Figure 1 shows both the letters' frequency in each of the languages. ן and א are common

Algorithm 1: Methodology implementation

---

input : A sentence-level parallel corpus
output: A translation lexicon

```
 1  IntialLexicon ← IBM (parallel corpus) ;
 2  foreach term t in IntialLexicon do
 3      CandidateTransList ←
          GetCandTransList (t);
 4      SimilarCandidateClusters ←
          GetSimCandCls (CandidateTransList) ;
        foreach cluster c in
        SimilarCandidateClusters do
 5          if length(c)>1) then
 6              add c to FilteredTransList
                break;
 7          if IsTermCandSim (t,c) then
 8              add c to FilteredTransList
 9          else
10              SimilarTermList ←
                GetSimilarTermList (t);
11              foreach term t2 in SimilarTermList do
12                  CandidateTransList + =
                      GetCandTransList (t2)
13              SimilarCandidateClusters ←
                GetSimCandCls (CandidateTransList)
                foreach cluster simc in
                SimilarCandidateClusters do
14                  if length(simc) > 1 & c ⊆ simc
                    then
15                      add c to FilteredTransList
16      add < t,FilteredTransList > to
        FilteredLexicon
```

Aramaic suffixes and ד is a common Aramaic prefix. Thus, they are more frequent in Aramaic than in Hebrew. On the contrary, ם is a common Hebrew suffix and ה and ש are common Hebrew prefixes, so they are more frequent in Hebrew.

5. Evaluation

5.1. String Similarity Evaluation

In our experiments, we investigated three types of similarities (see Section 4.1.), namely, Hebrew-Hebrew (HE-HE), Aramaic-Aramaic (AR-AR), and Aramaic-Hebrew (AR-HB). To evaluate the performance of the various string similarity measures presented in Section 4.2., we manually annotated word pairs of the three types. For each type, we annotated word pairs that were tested by the algorithm in the corresponding step. To avoid focusing on trivial cases that can easily be determined by all the measures, we only annotated pairs with at least two common letters, excluding matres lectionis.

Table 2 compares the performance of five string similarity measures for the three types of similarity by four commonly used measures: precision (P), recall (R), F1, and accuracy (Acc). For each configuration, we report the optimal threshold results. The word-level (Porat et al., 2018) measure was

examined with the most two, three, and four rare letters, obtaining the best results with two lettered items for all the configurations.

In the sample of the annotated HE-HE pairs, there are 269 pairs, 187 positive (judged similar) and 82 negative (judged dissimilar). In the sample of the annotated AR-AR pairs, there are 559 pairs, 32 positive and 527 negative. In the sample of the annotated AR-HE pairs, there are 429 pairs, 131 positive and 298 negative. The gap between the number of positive and negative pairs of the corresponding configurations in the AR-AR sample explains the gap between the F1, which do not consider true negatives, and the accuracy, which does consider them.

The best results were obtained by the Jaro similarity measure, using different thresholds, for all the three types of pairs. The similarity thresholds were 0.67, 0.82, and 0.78 for HE-HE, AR-AR, and AR-HE, respectively.

To complete our investigation, we used the Hebrew part-of-speech tagger (Adler and Elhadad, 2006) to lemmatize the HE-HE pairs and compare their lemmas. We obtained recall, precision, F1, and accuracy of 0.4, 0.48, 0.44, and 0.29, respectively.

Next, we evaluated the performance of our algorithmic scheme. In all the reported results, for each similarity type, we used the best similarity measure with its optimal similarity threshold.

5.2. Algorithmic Scheme Evaluation

5.2.1. Evaluation Setting

The results reported in this paper were obtained from a sample of 108 randomly selected source terms from a list of 29,335 terms, generated by the state-of-the-art IBM model 4 using Giza++ (Och and Ney, 2003) open source toolkit[1]. Only source terms with more than one appearance in the corpora were selected. We manually annotated 287 source-target word pairs with an average of 2.66 word pairs per source term. Each source-target word pair was judged as either correct or incorrect translation.

We assessed our algorithmic scheme by evaluating its ability to filter the state-of-the-art IBM model 4 translation lexicon and increase its accuracy. Additionally, we compared our filtering process with a baseline filtering approach of deleting translations with low probability score. We used the probability (i.e. maximum likelihood) score that was assigned by the IBM model.

We used four evaluation measures: precision (P), relative-recall (RR), F1, and Accuracy (Acc). The scores were micro-averaged. Since we do not have any pre-defined translation lexicon, we evaluated the relative-recall. Our relative-recall considered the number of correctly translated source-target pairs from the output of state-of-the-art IBM model as the full set of translated pairs.

Table 3 presents the results of the baseline filtering approach which deletes translations with low probability score. We examined different probability thresholds. The best results were obtained with a threshold value of 0.1, which means almost no filtration. Once the filtering is more

---

[1] http://www.statmt.org/moses/giza/GIZA++.html

#	String Similarity Measure	Description
1	Levenshtein distance (Levenshtein, 1966)	Counts the minimum number of operations (removal, insertion, or substitution of a character) required to transform one string into another.
2	Hamming distance (Hamming, 1950)	Finds the total number of places one string is different from the other.
3	Jaccard similarity coefficient (Jaccard, 1901)	Counts the number of common characters and divides it by the total number of unique characters.
4	Jaro similarity (Jaro, 1989)	Highly scores strings with the same characters, but at a certain distance from each other, as long as the order of the matches is similar.
5	Word-level match (Porat et al., 2018)	Represents the words by their n most rare letters (keeps the order of the letters in the word) and requires an exact match.

Table 1: Prior art string similarity measures considered in our work

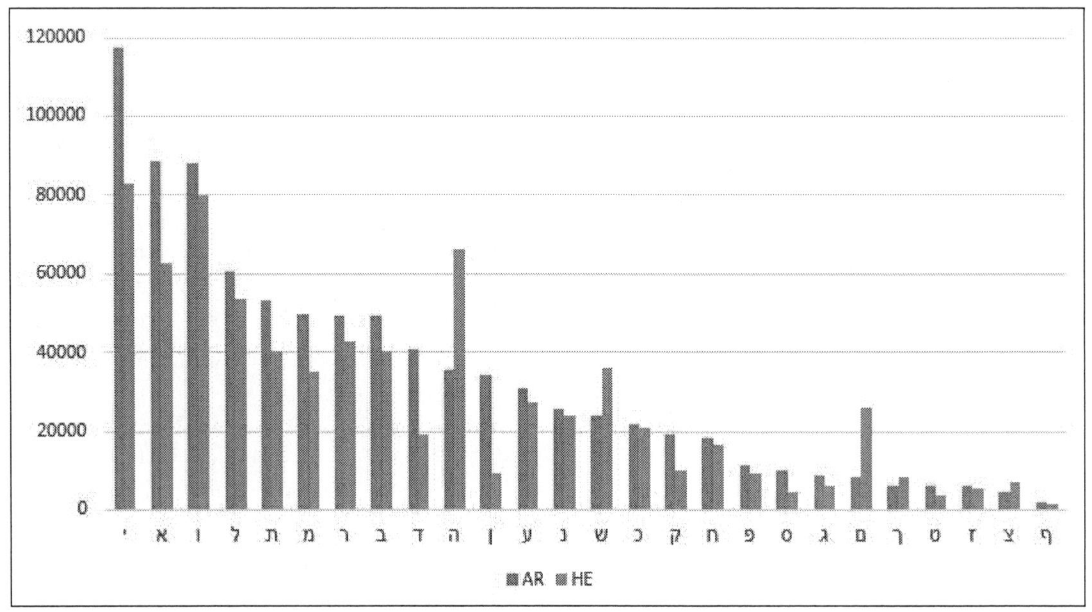

Figure 1: The frequency of the Aramaic and Hebrew letters.

Type	Measure	R	P	F1	Acc
HE-HE	Levenshtein	0.96	0.77	0.85	0.77
	Hamming	0.75	0.73	0.74	0.64
	Jaccard	0.8	0.9	0.85	0.8
	Jaro	0.89	0.83	**0.86**	**0.8**
	Word-level	0.65	0.9	0.75	0.71
AR-AR	Levenshtein	0.31	0.71	0.43	0.95
	Hamming	0.25	0.73	0.37	0.95
	Jaccard	0.41	0.5	0.45	0.94
	Jaro	0.41	0.72	**0.52**	**0.96**
	Word-level	0.19	0.26	0.22	0.92
AR-HE	Levenshtein	0.76	0.59	0.67	0.77
	Hamming	0.76	0.35	0.48	0.5
	Jaccard	0.65	0.72	0.69	0.82
	Jaro	0.69	0.8	**0.74**	**0.86**
	Word-level	0.49	0.79	0.61	0.81

Table 2: Performance of five string similarity measures for the three types of similarity

significant, there is very little precision increase and a dramatic recall drop. We concluded that the probability score is not sufficiently indicative to be used for filtering the initial lexicon and a different filtering scheme is required.

Threshold	RR	P	F1	Acc
0.1	0.85	0.798	0.823	0.711
0.2	0.758	0.789	0.773	0.648
0.3	0.634	0.8	0.708	0.585
0.4	0.533	0.823	0.647	0.54
0.5	0.498	0.819	0.619	0.516
0.6	0.33	0.852	0.476	0.425
0.7	0.291	0.846	0.433	0.397
0.8	0.273	0.838	0.412	0.383
0.9	0.251	0.826	0.385	0.366

Table 3: Baseline filtering approach with different probability thresholds

Table 4 compares the performance of our algorithmic scheme with that of the best baseline and the state-of-the-art IBM model 4. The state-of-the-art results corresponds to the baseline without any filtering. In other words, the IBM model classifies all the source-target pairs as positive. Therefore, its precision and accuracy are the same. Since we considered the correctly translated source-target pairs from its output as the full set of translated pairs, its relative-recall is 1.

Our algorithmic scheme increases both the F1 and the accuracy of the state-of-the-art IBM model by 5 points and 10 points, respectively. The baseline filtering does not improve the IBM model.

Method	RR	P	F1	Acc
Our Algorithmic Scheme	0.87	1	0.93	0.89
Baseline Filtering	0.85	0.8	0.82	0.7
State-of-the-art model	1	0.79	0.88	0.79

Table 4: Results Comparison

5.2.2. Error Analysis

We analyzed the classification errors of our algorithm. In Table 5, we present the classification confusion matrix. Each column of the matrix represents the instances in a predicted class while each row represents the instances in an actual class.

Predicted Actual	True	False
True	198	29
False	0	60

Table 5: The confusion matrix of our algorithm

All of the classification errors were due to incorrect classification of valid source-target pairs as invalid. In 34% of these incorrect classifications were cases where the translation appeared in a single morphology form. For example שמלתיו-כסותה (dress) and לאיש-לאנשא (to a man). The remainder of cases (66%) were classified incorrectly due to a low string similarity score. A low score was obtained in a few simple (ההר-טורא ,בהר (mountain)), mediocre (אחיו-לאחוהי ,אח (brother)) and more complex cases (החביאה-אטמרת ,נחבאת (hide)). We note that the string similarity measure can be improved by matching terminal letters to regular letters as in the incorrectly classified example of כשדימה-כסדאי ,כשדים (Chaldean (person)).

6. Conclusions and Future Work

We proposed a methodological algorithmic scheme to construct an Aramaic-Hebrew translation lexicon. First, by a state-of-the-art word alignment translation model, we generated an initial translation lexicon. We then filtered the initial lexicon using three types of string similarity measures. For each similarity type, we evaluated five string similarity measures. Our algorithmic scheme significantly increased both the accuracy of the F1 over the initial lexicon and a filtered lexicon based on word alignment probability scores. The scheme was investigated for Aramaic and Hebrew, but can be generically applied for other languages.

At some stage, during learning or in feature functions, all existing statistical machine translation (SMT) methods are using word alignments. Therefore, we plan to integrate our translation lexicon in a SMT scheme.

7. Bibliographical References

Adler, M. and Elhadad, M. (2006). An unsupervised morpheme-based hmm for hebrew morphological disambiguation. In *Proceedings of the 21st International Conference on Computational Linguistics and the 44th annual meeting of the Association for Computational Linguistics*, pages 665–672. Association for Computational Linguistics.

Brown, P. F., Pietra, V. J. D., Pietra, S. A. D., and Mercer, R. L. (1993). The mathematics of statistical machine translation: Parameter estimation. *Computational linguistics*, 19(2):263–311.

Chiang, D. (2007). Hierarchical phrase-based translation. *computational linguistics*, 33(2):201–228.

HaCohen-Kerner, Y., Kass, A., and Peretz, A. (2010). Haads: A hebrew aramaic abbreviation disambiguation system. *Journal of the American Society for Information Science and Technology*, 61(9):1923–1932.

HaCohen-Kerner, Y., Schweitzer, N., and Mughaz, D. (2011). Automatically identifying citations in hebrew-aramaic documents. *Cybernetics and Systems: An International Journal*, 42(3):180–197.

HaCohen-Kerner, Y., Kass, A., and Peretz, A. (2013). Initialism disambiguation: Man versus machine. *Journal of the American Society for Information Science and Technology*, 64(10):2133–2148.

Hamming, R. W. (1950). Error detecting and error correcting codes. *The Bell system technical journal*, 29(2):147–160.

Jaccard, P. (1901). Étude comparative de la distribution florale dans une portion des alpes et des jura. *Bull Soc Vaudoise Sci Nat*, 37:547–579.

Jaro, M. A. (1989). Advances in record-linkage methodology as applied to matching the 1985 census of tampa, florida. *Journal of the American Statistical Association*, 84(406):414–420.

Koehn, P., Och, F. J., and Marcu, D. (2003). Statistical phrase-based translation. In *Proceedings of the 2003 Conference of the North American Chapter of the Association for Computational Linguistics on Human Language Technology-Volume 1*, pages 48–54. Association for Computational Linguistics.

Koppel, M. and Schweitzer, N. (2014). Measuring direct and indirect authorial influence in historical corpora. *Journal of the Association for Information Science and Technology*, 65(10):2138–2144.

Levenshtein, V. I. (1966). Binary codes capable of correcting deletions, insertions, and reversals. In *Soviet physics doklady*, volume 10, pages 707–710.

Liebeskind, C., Dagan, I., and Schler, J. (2012). Statistical thesaurus construction for a morphologically rich language. In * *SEM 2012: The First Joint Conference on Lexical and Computational Semantics–Volume 1: Proceedings of the main conference and the shared task, and Volume 2: Proceedings of the Sixth International Workshop on Semantic Evaluation (SemEval 2012)*, pages 59–64.

Liebeskind, C., Dagan, I., and Schler, J. (2016). Semiautomatic construction of cross-period thesaurus. *Journal on Computing and Cultural Heritage (JOCCH)*, 9(4):22.

Liebeskind, C., Dagan, I., and Schler, J. (2019). An algorithmic scheme for statistical thesaurus construction in a morphologically rich language. *Applied Artificial Intelligence*, 33(6):483–496.

Moghaz, D., Hacohen-Kerner, Y., and Gabbay, D. (2019). Text mining for evaluating authors' birth and death years. *ACM Transactions on Knowledge Discovery from Data (TKDD)*, 13(1):7.

Mughaz, D., HaCohen-Kerner, Y., and Gabbay, D. (2017). Mining and using key-words and key-phrases to identify the era of an anonymous text. In *Transactions on Computational Collective Intelligence XXVI*, pages 119–143. Springer.

Och, F. J. and Ney, H. (2000). A comparison of alignment models for statistical machine translation. In *Proceedings of the 18th conference on Computational linguistics-Volume 2*, pages 1086–1090. Association for Computational Linguistics.

Och, F. J. and Ney, H. (2003). A systematic comparison of various statistical alignment models. *Computational linguistics*, 29(1):19–51.

Och, F. J., Tillmann, C., and Ney, H. (1999). Improved alignment models for statistical machine translation. In *1999 Joint SIGDAT Conference on Empirical Methods in Natural Language Processing and Very Large Corpora*.

Porat, E., Koppel, M., and Shmidman, A. (2018). Identification of parallel passages across a large hebrew/aramaic corpus. *Journal of Data Mining & Digital Humanities*.

Snyder, B. and Barzilay, R. (2008). Unsupervised multilingual learning for morphological segmentation. In *Proceedings of ACL-08: HLT*, pages 737–745, Columbus, Ohio, June. Association for Computational Linguistics.

Vogel, S., Ney, H., and Tillmann, C. (1996). Hmm-based word alignment in statistical translation. In *Proceedings of the 16th conference on Computational linguistics-Volume 2*, pages 836–841. Association for Computational Linguistics.

Zohar, H., Liebeskind, C., Schler, J., and Dagan, I. (2013). Automatic thesaurus construction for cross generation corpus. *Journal on Computing and Cultural Heritage (JOCCH)*, 6(1):4.

Proceedings of 1st Workshop on Language Technologies for Historical and Ancient Languages, pages 17–21
Language Resources and Evaluation Conference (LREC 2020), Marseille, 11–16 May 2020
© European Language Resources Association (ELRA), licensed under CC-BY-NC

Dating Ancient texts: an Approach for Noisy French Documents

Anaëlle Baledent[1,2], Nicolas Hiebel[1], Gaël Lejeune[1]
[1] Sorbonne University, STIH - EA 4509, Paris, France ;
[2] Normandie Univ, UNICAEN, ENSICAEN, CNRS, GREYC, 14000 Caen, France
anaelle.baledent@unicaen.fr, nicolas.hiebel@etu.sorbonne-universite.fr, gael.lejeune@sorbonne-universite.fr

Abstract

Automatic dating of ancient documents is a very important area of research for digital humanities applications. Many documents available via digital libraries do not have any dating or dating that is uncertain. Document dating is not only useful by itself but it also helps to choose the appropriate NLP tools (lemmatizer, POS tagger ...) for subsequent analysis. This paper provides a dataset with thousands of ancient documents in French and present methods and evaluation metrics for this task. We compare character-level methods with token-level methods on two different datasets of two different time periods and two different text genres. Our results show that character-level models are more robust to noise than classical token-level models. The experiments presented in this article focused on documents written in French but we believe that the ability of character-level models to handle noise properly would help to achieve comparable results on other languages and more ancient languages in particular.

Keywords: Old documents, Text Mining, Document Dating, Corpus, Digital Humanities, Textual Document Dating

1. Introduction

Nowadays, a large number of historical documents is accessible through digital libraries among which we can cite EUROPEANA [1] or GALLICA [2] among other Digital Humanities (DH) digitization projects. This allows libraries to spread cultural heritage to a large and various audience (academics, historians, sociologists among others). It is also a great opportunity to have such an amount of data usable in various projects including NLP projects.

However, exploiting these documents automatically can be difficult because of the their various quality, their imperfect digitization, the lack of metadata or the fact that they exhibit a great variety of languages (among which under-resourced languages). Many documents will be difficult to access for researchers since it is difficult to unite them in a corpus, to rely on consistent metadata or to use NLP tools if the data is too noisy.

In particular, it is difficult for DH researchers to use most of available data since the quality of the Optical Character Recognition (OCR) on ancient documents can make them impossible to process properly with classical NLP tools. Therefore, pre-processing and data cleaning is often mandatory to make them suitable for classical NLP pipelines. This need increases the cost of treating new corpora for DH researchers since choosing the appropriate NLP tools can even be difficult. The problems encountered can vary with respect to the languages used in the document or the period were the document has been printed but it remains an open problem. Therefore, the knowledge of the date of the document is not only useful by itself but also because it helps to choose the appropriate OCR configuration (Cecotti and Belaïd, 2005), the post-processing techniques after the OCR phase (Afli et al., 2016) or the appropriate NLP processing tools to use for a particular corpus (Sagot, 2019). Hence, we propose in this paper to investigate the problem of document dating in noisy documents.

The contribution of this paper is three fold : (I) we pro-

pose a corpus of around 8,000 ancient documents in French (published from 1600 to 1710), (II) we propose some methods to enrich the metadata and (III) we propose new ideas to evaluate the quality of digitized data in order to put the DH researcher in the center of the loop. In the experiments part we will focus on the document dating task but we believe that the corpus we developed and the rationale of our methods can be useful for other tasks.

In Section 2. we present related work on corpus construction and document dating. In Section 3. we present the corpus made available with the article and in section 4. we show some results on document dating on this corpus and compare our method with other state-of-the-art datasets. Finally in Section 5. we give some words of conclusion and present future orientations of this work.

2. Textual Document Dating

In this work we try to tackle the problem of document dating in the context of historical textual documents. One way to tackle this task is to define it as a classification task, each year (or another time granularity) being a class. (Niculae et al., 2014) proposed a text ranking approach for solving document dating. Temporal language models for document dating use mainly a token-level representation. (Popescu and Strapparava, 2013) develop the hypothesis that period changes come with topics changes and written information reflect these changes by used vocabulary. So, one can delimit epochs by observing the variation in word frequencies or word contexts like in recent works about semantic change (Hamilton et al., 2016).

In the same fashion, (de Jong et al., 2005) and (Kanhabua and Nørvåg, 2008) used probabilistic models: the authors assign each word a probability to appear in a time period. Semantic change is therefore leveraged to give a time stamp to a given document. Some authors proposed graph models to extract relationship between events related in the document in order to find the document focus time (Jatowt et al., 2013) or compute an appropriate time stamp for the document(Mishra and Berberich, 2016). Another interesting approach comes from (Stajner and Zampieri, 2013) who used

---

four stylistic features to find appropriate document dating: average sentence length, average word length, lexical density and lexical richness.

Several works on the subject of document dating involved preprocessing of texts (e.g. tokenization, morphosynctatic tagging or named-entity recognition) or external resources, like Wikipedia or Google Ngram in order to detect explicit features that can characterize the date of a document : named entities, neologisms or to the contrary archaic words ((Garcia-Fernandez et al., 2011); (Salaberri et al., 2015)) However, this implies to have access a clean plain text, or a text without too much OCR errors in order to apply data cleaning techniques. Indeed the majority of works exploits newspapers' articles, due to facility for collect them on web and a high precision for dating, and few works use digitized documents. In Section 3. we show how corpus construction can be an issue for these token-level models and why the corpus we wanted to process can be too noisy for them.

3. Corpus and Methodology

3.1. Corpus Construction

Corpus construction is a crucial aspect in Computational Linguistics (CL) and Digital Humanities (DH) fields: the corpus construction is one of the first steps in research. To obtain relevant results, the used corpora must meet specific criteria: genre, medium, topic among other criteria (see (Sinclair, 1996) or (Biber, 1993) for other criteria examples). It must also be adapted with research objectives: a classification task doesn't require same data that a literary analysis. Another question regarding corpus construction is the following: what NLP tools can be used for processing the corpus ?

With Internet one can easily access to a huge amount of texts and corpora. Despite this, researchers must be careful with the data sources : quality, authenticity, noisiness. Barbaresi (Barbaresi, 2015) mentions inherent problems with a web scrapper method to collect corpus: repeated and/or generated text, wrong machine-translated text, spam, multilanguage documents or empty documents. Documents exhibiting this kind of problems can impair the efficiency of classifiers or other NLP modules and force researchers to rebuild a new corpus or to clean the data manually.

Digital libraries provide many and various textual archives, easy to collect and often used in Digital Humanities in view of topics. Indeed, these corpora are also diversified that domains in Humanities and Social Sciences (HSS): 19th century newspapers, middle-age manuscripts or early modern prints,(Abiven and Lejeune, 2019).

However, these documents are not "born-digital" and are often available only in image format. The quality of the text one can extract from these images is far from perfect. So, OCR performances are lower than one can expect on a modern document and this deterioration has an impact on the usability of the data. Several works like (Traub et al., 2015) or (Linhares Pontes et al., 2019) showed that OCR errors has an important impact on NLP tools efficiency and subsequent expert analysis.

Therefore, correcting automatically OCR has become an important prior task to take more advantage of digitalized

Decade	# Docs (Ratio)	Mean size (± stdev)	
		Characters	Words
1600	389 (5%)	24117 (± 25449)	3702 (± 3698)
1610	649 (8%)	20861 (± 21421)	3248 (± 3223)
1620	926 (12%)	18979 (± 18437)	3033 (± 2727)
1630	917 (12%)	20691 (± 22471)	3304 (± 3339)
1640	815 (10%)	21692 (± 20791)	3558 (± 3271)
1650	583 (7%)	28877 (± 27754)	4725 (± 4306)
1660	552 (7%)	33739 (± 26172)	5698 (± 4266)
1670	489 (6%)	29887 (± 22052)	5150 (± 3655)
1680	630 (8%)	28355 (± 21519)	5023 (± 3677)
1690	802 (10%)	29554 (± 23751)	5276 (± 4106)
1700	791 (10%)	34302 (± 30191)	5928 (± 5030)
1710	427 (5%)	31620 (± 29799)	5461 (± 5151)
All	7970	26276 (± 24577)	4407 (± 3998)

Table 1: Statistics on the GALLICA dataset

corpora ((Barbaresi, 2016) (Rigaud et al., 2019)). Automation of this post-processing may reduce financial and temporal costs as compared to manual correction. It is a great challenge for Digital Humanities since these costs can in some cases constitute the biggest part of DH projects budget.

3.2. A Dataset for Document Dating

The corpus we mainly use for our experimentations has been collected on the French digital library GALLICA. From GALLICA it is possible to access to a large amount of digitized historical and various documents and we wanted to see how we can apply NLP techniques to old documents were the OCR makes a lot of errors. Some textual documents have also plain text access, in fact a non corrected OCR output.

On the GALLICA website, advanced search's tab allows a search with different filters like date of publication, language, type of document or theme. For this experiment, we selected all Latin and French documents with plain text access and dated between 1600 and 1720. It represents about 8,000 documents. With the search API we exported a research report in CSV format and transformed it in a JSON file. Each document has an unique identifier and has metadata among which title, author(s), editor, date and other descriptions[3].

We took advantage of this research report to download all the documents in HTML. We developed a tool that scrapes the text and sorts the documents according to different kinds of metadata[4]. Four versions for each text are extracted by this tool in order to fulfill different needs : (i) plain text with dates inside the documents; (ii) plain text where dates have been removed (with regular expressions); (iii) text with HTML tags and dates; (iv) text with HTML tags and without date. For assuring that we have the appropriate date for each document, we took advantage of the date indicated in HTML metadata. Documents for which the metadata exhibited an uncertain date like *16, 16??, 16..* or a time period (*1667-1669*) have been discarded.

Table 1 exhibits the statistics on the dataset we extracted

---

[3]Metadata present in the resource associated with this paper
[4]GITHUB repository to be made public

from GALLICA. In order to perform comparisons with other approaches we also used two other corpora of ancient French documents of another period (1800-1950) which had also OCR issues: Deft 2010 challenge on document dating (Grouin et al., 2010) where the objective was to give the good decade for a given text.

3.3. Training a Temporal model

We propose a method that takes advantage of noisy corpus to enrich metadata. The rationale of our method is to be as much independent of pre-processing steps because the lack of language dedicated resources (few NLP tools exist for ancient languages and their efficiency can be put into question). This can help DH researchers to process more easily new datasets since models robust to noise can avoid research projects to use too much resources in data preparation. For the GALLICA corpus we split the data into a training set (70%) and a test set (30%) and maintained the imbalance between the different classes. For the DEFT2010 corpora, the data was already separated between train and test so we kept it in order to ease comparisons with previous approaches.

We aim to find models suitable for noisy data so we got inspiration from recent works that showed that character-level models perform well for document dating (Abiven and Lejeune, 2019). We compare character-level representation to word-level representations in order to assess their respective advantages. We present our first results in Section 4..

4. Evaluation

In this Section, we first present results on the the Gallica dataset, then we use the exact same configuration to train a temporal model for the DEFT2010 challenge dataset.

4.1. Evaluation Metrics

For evaluation purposes, we use two different metrics. First, we use macro f-measure rather than micro f-measure to compare different models for document dating since the corpus we built from GALLICA is quite imbalanced. Then, since all the classification errors do not have the same impact, in other words when we have a document from 1650 it is better to predict 1640 than 1630, we wanted to have another measure. We chose to use a Gaussian similarity (here after Similarity), as defined by Grouin et $al.$ (Grouin et al., 2011) in order to measure how much there is a difference between the predicted decade and the real decade. It is computed as follows (with pd being the predicted decade and rd being the real decade):

$$Similarity(pd, rd) = e^{-\pi/10^2(pd-rd)^2}$$

This measure has the good property to highlight systems that produce smaller errors: an error of two decades is worst than two errors of one decade (see Table 2 for an excerpt of this similarity measure outcome).

4.2. Results on the GALLICA Dataset

Table 3 shows an extract of the results we obtained. It appeared that Decision Trees give good results and Random Forest (with 10 estimators) even better ones. Character 1-grams give good results and considering longer N-grams

$\lvert pd - rd\rvert$	0	1	2	3	4	5	6	
SIMILARITY	1	0.97	0.88	0.75	0.60	0.46	0.31	...

Table 2: Similarity measure between pd the predicted decade and rd the real decade

N-gram size	Decision Tree	Random Forest
$1 \leq N \leq 1$	F = 31.62	F = 35.32
	S = 0.851	S = 0.877
$1 \leq N \leq 2$	F = 51.23	F = 58.86
	S = 0.907	S = 0.931
$1 \leq N \leq 3$	F = 59.49	F = 66.436
	S = 0.926	S = 0.947
$1 \leq N \leq 4$	F = 64.6	**F = 71.43**
	S = 0.933	**S = 0.950**
$1 \leq N \leq 5$	**F = 65.1**	F = 69.8
	S = 0.933	S = 0.945
$2 \leq N \leq 2$	F = 51.17	F = 58.30
	S = 0.905	S = 0.928
$2 \leq N \leq 3$	F = 59.94	F = 67.16
	S = 0.927	S = 0.948
$2 \leq N \leq 4$	F = 64.06	F = 70.53
	S = 0.934	S = 0.948
$2 \leq N \leq 5$	F = 65.00	F = 70.87
	S = 0.934	S = 0.948

Table 3: Extract of the results obtained on the GALLICA dataset. Macro F-measure (F) and Similarity (S)

improves results until $N = 4$. With $N > 4$ there is no improvement and at some point the results get even worse, this observation is consistent with previous experiments with this kind of features (Brixtel, 2015). Longer N size seems to interfere with generalization. With a random forest classifier and token-level features (token n-grams with $1 <= N <= 3$) we obtained at the best 0.85 in similarity if we discard tokens that include non-alphanumeric characters and 0.93 if we do not discard them. This shows that punctuation, and in general short sequences of characters, are very useful for this kind of task even if they offer worse performances than character n-grams. Another interesting result is that this token-level model achieves only a 46.3% score in macro F-measure. These features exhibit more errors, resulting in a worse F-measure, but the errors are closer to the target.

Figure 1 exhibits the confusion matrix on the GALLICA dataset with our best classifier. One can see that most classification errors are low range errors, this is consistent with the high similarity score the classifier achieves. As presented before, this model outperforms the best token-level model (Figure 2) in F-measure but the difference in similarity is less significant. When comparing the first line of the two confusion matrices one can see that the number of true positives (first cell of the line) is logically higher with the character-level model. However, the false negatives (rest of the line) are in fact very close to the target class, the token-level model shows a bit less errors of 3 decades and more.

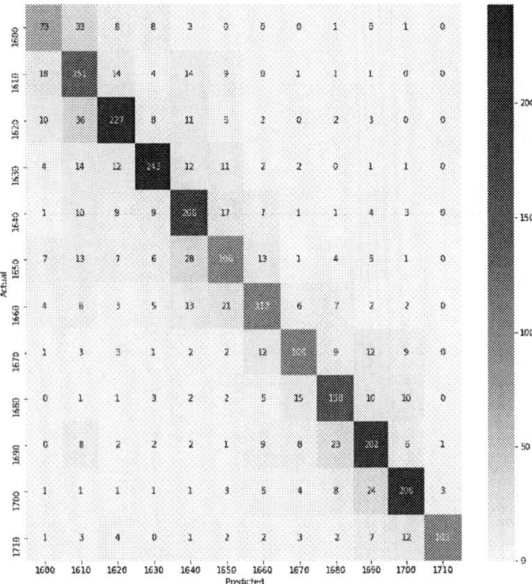

Figure 1: Character-level model (n-grams with $1 <= n <= 4$): confusion matrix for the best classifier (Random Forest with 10 trees) on the GALLICA corpus, F-measure= 71.43, Similarity =0.950

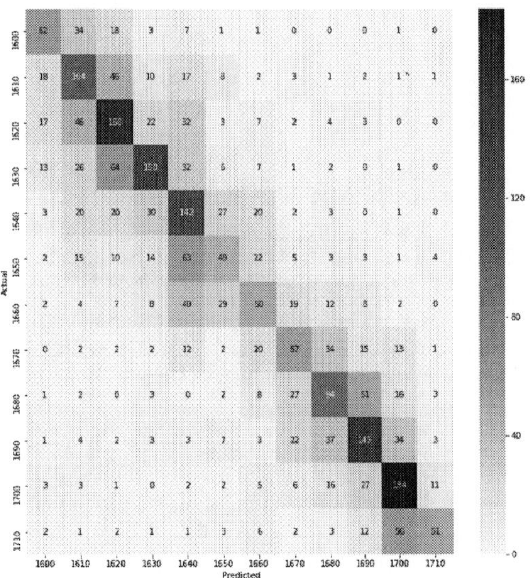

Figure 2: Token-level model (n-grams with $1 <= n <= 2$): confusion matrix for the best classifier (Random Forest with 10 trees) on the GALLICA corpus, F-measure= 46.27, Similarity =0.928

4.3. Results on the DEFT2010 dataset

In Figure 3 we present the results obtained with the same classifier trained and tested on the DEFT2010 dataset. With an F-measure of 32.8 its results are comparable to the best performer (F=33.8) for that challenge which is promising since we did not perform any kind of feature engineering dedicated to this dataset, we just used the same kind of features and the same classifier parameters. We can see

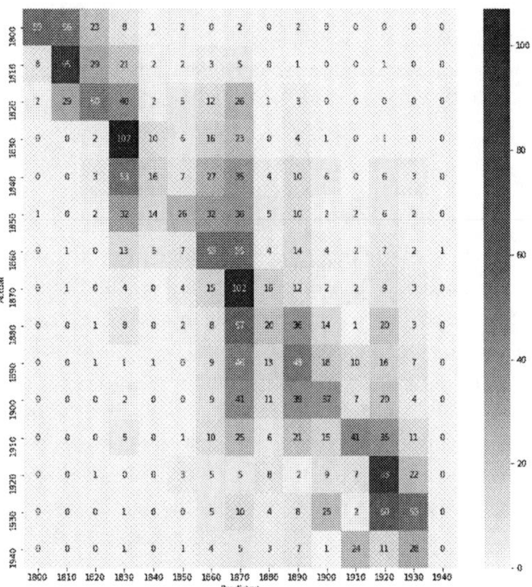

Figure 3: Character-level model (n-grams with $1 <= n <= 4$): confusion matrix for a Random Forest classifier with 10 trees trained and tested on the DEFT2010 dataset, F-measure= 32.81, Similarity =0.872

that most classification errors occur on the previous or next decade. Two interesting things occur however, the 1870 is the most prone to False Positives. It is interesting since this class represent the middle of the period. The 1940 decade does not contain any True Positive. This can be linked to a historical reason since most of the newspapers of this period were not authorized so that there is no clear tendency regarding the printing methods used during this period, illustrating a limit of the character-based models.

5. Conclusion and Perspectives

In this paper we proposed a dataset suited for ancient documents dating. This dataset contains more than 8k documents in French written between 1600 to 1710. The documents in this dataset exhibit a poor quality due to a bad and not post-corrected OCR. Our results show that this should not be a problem for document dating since noise in texts does not seen to impair document dating results. To the contrary, OCR errors seem to be good features to detect the printing time of the original document. We showed that a character-level model can take advantage of noise to improve classification results as compared to a classical token-level model. On a comparable dataset (DEFT2010) from a different time period (1800 to 1940) we show that the exact same features and classifier configuration achieved results close to the state-of-the-art. We believe this is an important result since post-correction of texts can be a very costly operation. This result shows that one can perform NLP task without requiring perfect datasets as input. In the future it would be interesting to see in a larger scope what is the impact of bad digitization on subsequent Natural Language Processing tasks.

6. Bibliographical References

Abiven, K. and Lejeune, G. (2019). Automatic analysis of old documents: taking advantage of an incomplete, heterogeneous and noisy corpus. *Recherche d'information, document et web sémantique*, 2(Numéro 1).

Afli, H., Qiu, Z., Way, A., and Sheridan, P. (2016). Using SMT for OCR error correction of historical texts. In *Proceedings of the Tenth International Conference on Language Resources and Evaluation (LREC'16)*, pages 962–966, Portorož, Slovenia, May. European Language Resources Association (ELRA).

Barbaresi, A. (2015). *Ad hoc and general-purpose corpus construction from web sources*. Theses, ENS Lyon, June.

Barbaresi, A. (2016). Bootstrapped OCR error detection for a less-resourced language variant. In Stefanie Dipper, et al., editors, *13th Conference on Natural Language Processing (KONVENS 2016)*, pages 21–26, Bochum, Germany, September.

Biber, D. (1993). Representativeness in corpus design. *Literary and Linguistic Computing*, 8(4):243–257, 01.

Brixtel, R. (2015). Maximal repeats enhance substring-based authorship attribution. In *Proceedings of the International Conference Recent Advances in Natural Language Processing*, pages 63–71, Hissar, Bulgaria, September. INCOMA Ltd. Shoumen, BULGARIA.

Cecotti, H. and Belaïd, A. (2005). Hybrid OCR combination approach complemented by a specialized ICR applied on ancient documents. In *8th International Conference in Document Analysis and Recognition - ICDAR'05*, pages 1045–1049, Seoul, Korea, August.

de Jong, F., Rode, H., and Hiemstra, D. (2005). Temporal language models for the disclosure of historical text. In *Humanities, computers and cultural heritage: Proceedings of the XVIth International Conference of the Association for History and Computing (AHC 2005)*, pages 161–168. Koninklijke Nederlandse Academie van Wetenschappen, 9.

Garcia-Fernandez, A., Ligozat, A.-L., Dinarelli, M., and Bernhard, D. (2011). Méthodes pour l'archéologie linguistique : datation par combinaison d'indices temporels. In *DÉfi Fouille de Textes*, pages –, Montpellier, France, July.

Grouin, C., Forest, D., Da Sylva, L., Paroubek, P., and Zweigenbaum, P. (2010). Présentation et résultats du défi fouille de texte DEFT2010 où et quand un article de presse a-t-il été écrit ? In *Actes de DEFT*, Montréal, QC, 23 juillet. TALN.

Grouin, C., Forest, D., Paroubek, P., and Zweigenbaum, P. (2011). Présentation et résultats du défi fouille de texte DEFT2011. quand un article de presse a-t-il été écrit ? à quel article scientifique correspond ce résumé ? In *Actes de DEFT*, Montpellier, France, 1er juillet. TALN.

Hamilton, W. L., Leskovec, J., and Jurafsky, D. (2016). Diachronic word embeddings reveal statistical laws of semantic change. In *Proceedings of the 54th Annual Meeting of the Association for Computational Linguistics (Volume 1: Long Papers)*, pages 1489–1501, Berlin, Germany, August. Association for Computational Linguistics.

Jatowt, A., man Au Yeung, C., and Tanaka, K. (2013). Estimating document focus time. In *CIKM*.

Kanhabua, N. and Nørvåg, K. (2008). Improving temporal language models for determining time of non-timestamped documents. volume 5173, pages 358–370, 09.

Linhares Pontes, E., Hamdi, A., Sidere, N., and Doucet, A. (2019). Impact of ocr quality on named entity linking. In Adam Jatowt, et al., editors, *Digital Libraries at the Crossroads of Digital Information for the Future*, pages 102–115, Cham. Springer International Publishing.

Mishra, A. and Berberich, K. (2016). Estimating time models for news article excerpts. In *CIKM*.

Niculae, V., Zampieri, M., Dinu, L., and Ciobanu, A. M. (2014). Temporal text ranking and automatic dating of texts. In *Proceedings of the 14th Conference of the European Chapter of the Association for Computational Linguistics, volume 2: Short Papers*, pages 17–21, Gothenburg, Sweden, April. Association for Computational Linguistics.

Popescu, O. and Strapparava, C. (2013). Behind the times: Detecting epoch changes using large corpora. In *IJCNLP*.

Rigaud, C., Doucet, A., Coustaty, M., and Moreux, J.-P. (2019). ICDAR 2019 Competition on Post-OCR Text Correction. In *15th International Conference on Document Analysis and Recognition*, Sydney, Australia, September.

Sagot, B. (2019). Development of a morphological and syntactic lexicon of Old French. In *26ème Conférence sur le Traitement Automatique des Langues Naturelles (TALN)*, Toulouse, France, July.

Salaberri, H., Salaberri, I., Arregi, O., and Zapirain, B. n. (2015). Ixagroupehudiac: A multiple approach system towards the diachronic evaluation of texts. In *Proceedings of the 9th International Workshop on Semantic Evaluation (SemEval 2015)*, pages 840–845, Denver, Colorado, June. Association for Computational Linguistics.

Sinclair, J. (1996). Preliminary recommendations on text typology. Technical report, EAGLES (Expert Advisory Group on Language Engineering Standards), June.

Stajner, S. and Zampieri, M. (2013). Stylistic changes for temporal text classification. In *TSD*.

Traub, M. C., van Ossenbruggen, J., and Hardman, L. (2015). Impact analysis of ocr quality on research tasks in digital archives. *SpringerLink*, pages 252–263, Sep.

Proceedings of 1st Workshop on Language Technologies for Historical and Ancient Languages, pages 22–27
Language Resources and Evaluation Conference (LREC 2020), Marseille, 11–16 May 2020
© European Language Resources Association (ELRA), licensed under CC-BY-NC

Lemmatization and POS-tagging process by using joint learning approach. Experimental results on Classical Armenian, Old Georgian, and Syriac

Chahan Vidal-Gorène, Bastien Kindt

École Nationale des Chartes-PSL, Université catholique de Louvain
65, rue de Richelieu (F-75002 Paris), Institut orientaliste - Place Blaise Pascal, 1 (B-1348 Louvain-la-Neuve)
chahan.vidal-gorene@chartes.psl.eu, bastien.kindt@uclouvain.be

Abstract

Classical Armenian, Old Georgian and Syriac are under-resourced digital languages. Even though a lot of printed critical editions or dictionaries are available, there is currently a lack of fully tagged corpora that could be reused for automatic text analysis. In this paper, we introduce an ongoing project of lemmatization and POS-tagging for these languages, relying on a recurrent neural network (RNN), specific morphological tags and dedicated datasets. For this paper, we have combine different corpora previously processed by automatic out-of-context lemmatization and POS-tagging, and manual proofreading by the collaborators of the GREgORI Project (UCLouvain, Louvain-la-Neuve, Belgium). We intend to compare a rule based approach and a RNN approach by using PIE specialized by Calfa (Paris, France). We introduce here first results. We reach a mean accuracy of 91,63% in lemmatization and of 92,56% in POS-tagging. The datasets, which were constituted and used for this project, are not yet representative of the different variations of these languages through centuries, but they are homogenous and allow reaching tangible results, paving the way for further analysis of wider corpora.

Keywords: POS-tagging, Lemmatization, Morphological Analysis, Classical Armenian, Old Georgian, Syriac

1. Introduction

Classical Armenian, Old Georgian and Syriac are still poorly digitally resourced. Some major corpora already exist, for instance the *Digital Syriac Corpus* (DSC) for Syriac; *Digilib*, *Arak29*, *Calfa* and *Titus* for Classical Armenian; and *Titus* and the *Georgian Language Corpus* for Georgian[1]. These corpora, when they are really specialized on the ancient state of these languages, are mainly composed of plain texts or texts analyzed out of context (all possible analyses are given for each token and polylexical[2] word-forms are not fully described). Accordingly, scholars are still waiting for corpora enhanced with complete and reliable linguistic tags. Concerning the modern state of these languages, the Universal Dependencies (UD) provide annotated corpora for Armenian and Georgian, with the same limitations as described above. Furthermore, the modern and the ancient states of each language are usually quite different, so that digital resources built for either are inadequate to process the other.

Usual techniques for the lemmatization of these corpora rely on sets of rules and dictionaries. Such a method is unable to handle unknown tokens, or to readily process data in context. We have initiated experimentations to complete these operations using a neural network (RNN) and purpose-built corpora dedicated to this very task (Dereza, 2018). The task is particularly complex for these aforenamed languages due to their wealth of polylexical forms. In this paper, we present experimental results achieved through the application of state-of-the-art technologies to these languages. This

research depends on the data and tools developed by both the GREgORI (henceforth GP)[3] and Calfa[4] projects. The texts all derive from the database of the GP, which consists of texts written in the main languages of the Christian East and already published in the form of critical editions.

The scope of this paper is limited to the three already quoted languages. The datasets described below have all previously undergone automatic out-of-context lemmatization, and manual proofreading (see *infra* 3. Data Structure).

2. Datasets

D-HYE: Classical Armenian is an Indo-European language. This dataset contains 66.812 tokens (16.417 of which are unique) originating from three different corpora: Gregory of Nazianzus (Coulie, 1994; Coulie and Sirinian, 1999; Sanspeur, 2007; Sirinian, 1999) (GRNA), the *Geography of the Indian World* (Boisson, 2014) (GMI), and the *Acta Pauli et Theclae* (Calzolari, 2017) (THECLA). GRNA gathers the text of the Armenian versions of Gregory of Nazianzus' *Discourses*, already published in the *Corpus Christianorum* series. Gregory of Nazianzus (†390 AD) is the author of 45 *Discourses*, more than 240 letters, as well as theological and historical works in verse.

The Armenian version is anonymous and dates from 500-550 AD; its style has been qualified as pre-Hellenophile

---

[1] We only quote here some freely available data.

[2] The word "polylexical" is used here as a very generic term (but relevant for the three mentioned languages), referring to word-forms combining more than one lexeme in a single graphical unit (e.g. agglutinated forms).

[3] The GP develops digital tools and resources aimed at producing tagged corpora, at first in Ancient Greek, but now also in the main languages of the Christian East. Tagged textual data are processed in order to publish lemmatized concordances and different kinds of indexes. These tools are based on a stable standard of lexical examination (Kindt, 2018).

[4] The Calfa project develops a complete database for Classical Armenian, as well as tools for corpora creation and annotation (crowdsourcing interface and OCR technology for historical languages) (Vidal-Gorène and Decours-Perez, 2020).

(Lafontaine and Coulie, 1983). THECLA contains the Armenian version of a group of texts relating to the legend of Thecla and the martyrdom of Paul (5th-14th c. AD), while GMI is a very small text written around 1120 AD, enumerating cities and trading posts of the Indian world. GMI contains a lot of unique tokens, such as toponyms and personal names. **D-HYE** primarily covers texts of the Hellenophile tradition, which entails a large number of neologisms and idiosyncratic syntactic constructions. As such, for the time being, it is not entirely representative of the Classical Armenian language (see *infra* 5. Perspectives).

D-KAT: Old Georgian is a Kartvelian language. It contains 150.869 tokens (30.313 unique) from one unique corpus, made up of the texts of the Georgian versions of Gregory of Nazianzus' *Discourses* already published in the *Corpus Christianorum* series (Coulie and Métrévéli, 2001; Coulie and Métrévéli, 2004; Coulie and Métrévéli, 2007; Coulie and Métrévéli, 2011; Métrévéli, 1998; Métrévéli, 2000). Several translations from Greek into Georgian are known. The most important of which are those by Euthymius the Hagiorite (10th c. AD) and Ephrem Mtsire (Black Mountain, near Antioch, 11th c. AD) (Haelewyck, 2017b).

D-SYC: Syriac is a Semitic language. This dataset contains 46.859 tokens (10.612 unique). It is the most heterogenous dataset of this study, since the texts it contains relate to a variety of topics: biblical, hagiographic, and historical texts, homilies, hymns, moral sayings, translations of Greek philosophical works, etc. These texts have been lemmatized by the collaborators of the GP: the Syriac version of *Discourses* I and XIII by Gregory of Nazianzus, translated from Greek in the 6th-7th c. AD (Haelewyck, 2011; Haelewyck, 2017b; Schmidt, 2002; Sembiante, 2017); the *Story of Zosimus*, translated no later than the 4th c. AD (Haelewyck, 2014; Haelewyck, 2015; Haelewyck, 2016; Haelewyck, 2017a); the *Syriac Sayings of Greek Philosophers* (6th-9th c. AD) (Arzhanov, 2018); the *Life of John the Merciful* (Venturini, 2019); and some other texts dating from the 4th to the 9th century, described on the GP's website.

Type	D-HYE	D-KAT	D-SYC
different tokens	66.812	150.869	46.859
unique tokens	16.417	30.313	10.612
unique lemmata	5.263	8.897	2.957

Table 1: Composition of the datasets

These datasets do not embrace the whole lexicon of these languages (as a reference, the Calfa dictionary contains around 65.000 entries for Classical Armenian). We discuss this shortcoming in parts 3. and 4.

3. Data Structure

The data have been prepared and analysed in the framework of the GP. For each corpus, the following processing steps were implemented:

1. Cleaning up the forms of the text (removal of uppercase, critical signs used by editors, etc.). These forms constitute the column "cleaned form" of the corpus (see figure 1);

2. Morpho-lexical tagging, i.e. identifying a lemma and a POS for every cleaned-up form (token) of the text. This task is conducted through automatic comparison of the clean forms of the texts to the linguistic resources of the GP: dictionaries of simple forms and rules for the analysis of polylexical forms (see *infra*);

3. Proofreading of the results, corrections and encoding of missing analyses;

4. Enrichment of the linguistic resources for future processing of other texts.

Syriac, Classical Armenian and Old Georgian contain a large quantity of polylexical forms, combining words with different prefixes (preposition or binding particle) and/or suffixes (postposition or determiner). These forms are systematically (and automatically) segmented in order to identify explicitly each of its components. The different lexical elements are separated by an @ sign and divided into the following columns: lemma, POS and morph (see table 4; displaying a short sentence from the *Inscription of the Regent Constantine of Paperōn* (Ouzounian et al., 2012)). The morpho-lexical tagging follows the rules laid out for each language by the collaborators of the GP (Coulie, 1996; Coulie et al., 2013; Coulie et al., 2020; Kindt, 2004; Haelewyck et al., 2018; Van Elverdinghe, 2018). This automated analysis does not take the context into account. The resulting data are proofread manually and the proofreaders add the morphology according to the context (see table 4, columns marked GP).

text form	cleaned form (token)	lemma	POS
զթ[ա]գ[աւոր]անայրն *zt'[a]g[awor]ahayrn*	զթագաւորանայրն *zt'agaworahayrn*	զ@թագաւորանայր@ն *z@t'agaworahayr@n*	I+Prep@N+Com@PRO+Dem
უძლოურებისათვს, *uẓlurebisatwis,*	უძლოურებისათვს *uẓlurebisatwis*	უძლოურებაჲ@თვს *uẓlurebaj@twis*	N+Com@I+Prep
ܘܕܡܠܟ. *wdmlkh.*	ܘܕܡܠܟ *wdmlkh*	ܘ@ܕ@ܡܠܟ *wa@d@malkh*	PART@PART@NOUN

Figure 1: Raw output from the GP system

4. Method and Experiments

Up until now, the annotation has depended on a set of rules and dictionaries, and the result has been manually corrected. The main flaw of this approach lies in the fact that this analysis only concerns the forms attested in the corpus and already included in the lexical resources (< 40% for a representative corpus of Classical Armenian like the NBHL (Vidal-Gorène et al., 2019)) on the one hand, and that it does not provide answers in case of lexical ambiguity on the other hand. We have, hence, initiated experimentations to complete the task of lemmatization and POS-tagging with a neural network.

At present, the choice has fallen on PIE (Manjavacas et al., 2019), which offers a highly modular architecture (using

Train	All token			Ambiguous token			Unknown token		
	D-ARM	D-KAT	D-SYC	D-ARM	D-KAT	D-SYC	D-ARM	D-KAT	D-SYC
accuracy	0.9307	0.9698	0.8877	0.9318	0.9354	0.8307	0.7210	0.8460	0.5914
precision	0.7067	0.8187	0.6475	0.5997	0.7104	0.5382	0.5350	0.7177	0.4131
recall	0.7076	0.8132	0.6503	0.6566	0.7367	0.5982	0.5361	0.7101	0.4094
f1-score	0.7071	0.8159	0.6489	0.6269	0.7233	0.5666	0.5355	0.7139	0.4117

Test	All token			Ambiguous token			Unknown token		
	D-ARM	D-KAT	D-SYC	D-ARM	D-KAT	D-SYC	D-ARM	D-KAT	D-SYC
accuracy	0.9044	0.9628	0.8817	0.8620	0.8235	0.8460	0.6864	0.8220	0.6274
precision	0.6630	0.784	0.6211	0.4411	0.4261	0.6106	0.5074	0.6775	0.4112
recall	0.6711	0.7761	0.6215	0.5211	0.4928	0.6591	0.5118	0.6702	0.4072
f1-score	0.6670	0.7800	0.6213	0.4778	0.4570	0.6339	0.5096	0.6738	0.4092

Table 2: 1. Best scores for the training step of the lemmatizer on **D-HYE**, **D-KAT** and **D-SYC**; 2. Evaluation of the lemmatizer on the **D-HYE**, **D-KAT** and **D-SYC** Test datasets

bidirectional RNN). PIE enables, in particular, to process ambiguous or unknown forms by integrating contextual information, and to increase accuracy of the lemmatizer and the POS-tagger (Egen et al., 2016). Even though PIE allows simultaneous annotation of lemmata and POS, we have decided here to conduct the tasks independently. We use the default hyper parameters proposed by Manjavacas and applied on twenty different corpora from UD, without tailoring them in any way to the dataset under consideration[5]. For the lemmatization task, we have followed the default structure provided by PIE. We are working at the char level, and we include the sentence context. We use an attention encoder-decoder.

For the POS-tagging task, we have compared the Conditional Random Field (CRF) provided by LEMMING (Müller et al., 2015) and the linear decoder implemented in PIE.

We have divided **D-HYE**, **D-KAT** and **D-SYC** into three sets: Train (80% of data), Validation (10%) and Test (10%). The distribution was implemented automatically on a sentence basis.

Results on lemmatization

The results achieved are consistent with the representativeness and the size of the corpora studied, and the results provided by Manjavacas on similar datasets (see *infra* 5. Perspectives). **D-HYE** is the most homogenous dataset, despite the numerous unique toponyms. Thus, there is little variation regarding vocabulary and expressions, which is why we achieve a very good accuracy during training, almost as good as with **D-KAT**, but for a corpus twice as small. By contrast, **D-SYC** is more representative of all the language state of Syriac.

The results on ambiguous and unknown tokens are quite low, however they make it possible to already process automatically a larger number of cases.

The train set for Armenian contains 17% of unknown tokens, due to the high proportion of proper nouns from GMI, whereas the proportion of unknown tokens is 14% in Georgian and 20% in Syriac, the latter being penalized twice, by its size and this proportion of unknown tokens. The confusion matrix reveals that mistakes are concentrated on homographic lemmata (e.g. *mayr* (mother) and *mayr* (cedrus)). Besides, these languages exhibit numerous polylexical forms: these are similar in form but they differ in their analysis. We had identified the homographs beforehand, in order to disambiguate them (e.g. իւր (իւրոց) and իւր (իւրեանց)), but the lack of data results in a more complex task for the network. Besides, 50% of mistakes are localized on polylexical forms, such as demonstrative pronouns or prepositions. This is made clear in table 4, where no pronoun has been predicted. The same applies for the task of POS-tagging.

Results on POS-tagging (crf / linear)

The Linear Decoder achieves better results for the task of POS-tagging, except for the task of tagging ambiguous and unknown tokens during training. Nevertheless, the linear decoder remains better than the CRF decoder (LEMMING) on the test datasets, except for unknow tokens in Old Georgian and Syriac. The issue of the ambiguous tokens is the same as for the task of lemmatization. The confusion matrix for **D-HYE** shows that mistakes are essentially concentrated on common nouns (21%, generally predicted as verbs) and verbs (12%, generally predicted as common nouns). Vocalic alternation in Classical Armenian appears to create ambiguities between declined and conjugated tokens.

As regards **D-KAT**, mistakes are essentially concentrated on common nouns (30%) and V+Mas (12%)[6], which are generally confused with each other.

In **D-SYC**, mistakes are more diversified: adjectives (11%), tokens composed by a particle followed by a name

---

[5]The hyperparameters we used are: batch size: 25; epochs: 100; dropout: 0.25; optimizer: Adam; patience: 3; learning rate: 0.001; learning rate factor: 0.75; learning rate patience: 2.

[6]The tag "V+Mas" ("Masdar Verb") is used for Georgian Infinitives corresponding to the conjugated verbs.

Train	All token			Ambiguous token			Unknown token		
	D-ARM	D-KAT	D-SYC	D-ARM	D-KAT	D-SYC	D-ARM	D-KAT	D-SYC
accuracy	0.9403 0.9485	0.9773 0.9769	0.9203 0.9126	0.9418 0.9435	0.9452 0.9424	0.9330 0.9088	0.7794 0.6594	0.8923 0.8854	0.6970 0.6594
precision	0.7704 0.7725	0.7057 0.6993	0.6424 0.6612	0.7473 0.7528	0.7771 0.7390	0.8011 0.7151	0.4207 0.4159	0.4417 0.3935	0.4369 0.4159
recall	0.7242 0.7408	0.6536 0.6733	0.6133 0.6456	0.7417 0.7215	0.7284 0.6938	0.8026 0.7445	0.4100 0.4029	0.4504 0.3764	0.4047 0.4029
f1-score	0.7466 0.7563	0.6787 0.6861	0.6275 0.6533	0.7445 0.7368	0.7520 0.7157	0.8018 0.7295	0.4153 0.4093	0.4460 0.3848	0.4202 0.4093

Test	All token			Ambiguous token			Unknown token		
	D-ARM	D-KAT	D-SYC	D-ARM	D-KAT	D-SYC	D-ARM	D-KAT	D-SYC
accuracy	0.9238	0.9718	0.8813	0.9145	0.8694	0.8775	0.7441	0.8632 0.8647*	0.6067 0.6463*
precision	0.6513	0.7604	0.5832	0.6306	0.5790	0.6516	0.2920	0.4215 0.4550*	0.3128 0.3433*
recall	0.6264	0.6979	0.5725	0.6501	0.5847	0.6884	0.3124	0.3991 0.4146*	0.3431 0.3495*
f1-score	0.6386	0.7278	0.5778	0.6402	0.5818	0.6695	0.3019	0.4100 0.4339*	0.3273 0.3464*

Table 3: 1. Best scores for the training step of the POS-tagger on **D-HYE**, **D-KAT** and **D-SYC** with a CRF decoder (a) and a Linear Decoder (b); 2. Evaluation of the POS-tagger (linear decoder) on the **D-HYE**, **D-KAT** and **D-SYC** Test datasets. For the "unknown token" on **D-KAT** and **D-SYC**, the CRF decoder (LEMMING) gives better results (displayed in the table*)

token	lemma GP	lemma pred.	POS GP	POS pred.	Morph. GP
շինեցաւ *šinec'aw*	շինեմ *šinem*	շինեմ *šinem*	V	V	BÎJ3s
տաճարս *tačars*	տաճար@ս *tačar@s*	տաճար *tačar*	N+Com@PRO+Dem	N+Com	Ns@ø
սուրբ *surb*	սուրբ *surb*	սուրբ *surb*	A	A	Ns
փրկչին *p'rkč'in*	փրկիչ@ն *p'rkič'@n*	փրկիչ *p'rkič'*	N+Com@PRO+Dem	N+Com	Gs@ø
եւ *ew*	եւ *ew*	եւ *ew*	I+Conj	I+Conj	ø
անապատս *anapats*	անապատ@ս *anapat@s*	անապատ *anapat*	A@PRO+Dem	A	Ns@ø
հրամանաւ *hramanaw*	հրաման *hraman*	հրաման *hraman*	N+Com	N+Com	Hs
եւ *ew*	եւ *ew*	եւ *ew*	I+Conj	I+Conj	ø
ծախիւք *caxiwk'*	ծախ *cax*	ծախ *cax*	N+Com	N+Com	Hp
թագաւորահաւրն *t'agaworahawrn*	թագաւորահայր@ն *t'agaworahayr@n*	թագաւորահայր *t'agaworahayr*	N+Com@PRO+Dem	N+Com	Gs@ø
կոստանդեայ *kostandeay*	կոստանդին *kostandin*	կոստանդեայ *kostandeay*	N+Ant	N+Ant	Gs

Table 4: Results of lemmatization and POS-tagging on a sentence from the *Inscription of the Regent Constantine of Paperōn* and comparison with expected values manually proofread by GP

(9%), verbs (6%) and proper nouns (6%). At the moment, tokens consisting of polylexical forms are the main cause for such results (e.g. table 4).

5. Perspectives

The problems affecting our results are due to two challenges posed by the structure and the source of our data. Firstly, the amount of data remains too small to ensure representativeness of the described languages. Secondly, the large number of polylexical tokens makes processing more challenging. We intend to integrate the OCR developed by Calfa for Syriac, Old Georgian and Classical Armenian with our process, in order to increase drastically our datasets. These data will be manually proofread and pre-tagged by the previous models for training.

As regards Classical Armenian, we intend to combine the data of the NBHL on Calfa — composed in particular of more than 1.3 million tokens (190.000 of which are unique) and representative of the Armenian literary production (compilation of several hundreds of classical and medieval sources) — and lemmatized forms from the Gospels. The NBHL has already been lemmatized and the proofreading is being finalized (Vidal-Gorène et al., 2019; Vidal-Gorène and Decours-Perez, 2020). Calfa also offers a database of more than 65.000 headwords for Classical Armenian and has generated a very large number of verbal and noun forms that will be integrated into the training. Furthermore, the GP is now producing a digital corpus of all the Armenian, Georgian and Syriac texts published in the *Corpus Scriptorum Christianorum Orientalium* series.

The results presented here are a first step in the development of a lemmatizer and a POS-tagger for these languages. In particular, we only provide the results of one single neural network, but we intend to conduct a comparison with state-of-the-art technologies and rule-based approches, and to include contextual tagging at the morphological level.

We already reach a mean accuracy of 91,63% in lemmatization (84,28% for ambiguous tokens and 71,93% for unknown tokens), and of 92,56% in POS-tagging (88,71% for ambiguous tokens and 75,17% for unknown tokens). Nevertheless, these results are not robust on a wide variety of texts: resolving issue constitutes the chief objective of our upcoming experiments.

6. Bibliographical References

Arzhanov, Y. (2018). *Syriac Sayings of Greek Philosophers: A Study in Syriac Gnomologia with Edition and Translation*. Corpus Scriptorum Christianorum Orientalium, 669. Subsidia, 138. Peeters, Leuven.

Boisson, P. (2014). Précis de géographie du monde indien à l'usage des commerçants: édition et traduction annotée. In A. Mardirossian, et al., editors, *Mélanges Jean-Pierre Mahé*, Travaux et Mémoires, 18, pages 105–126. Association des Amis du Centre d'Histoire et Civilisation de Byzance, Paris.

Calzolari, V. (2017). *Acta Pauli et Theclae, Prodigia Theclae, Martyrium Pauli*. Corpus Christianorum. Series Apocryphorum, 20. Apocrypha Armeniaca, 1. Brepols, Turnhout.

Coulie, B. and Métrévéli, H. (2001). *Sancti Gregorii Nazianzeni Opera. Versio Iberica. III. Oratio XXXVIII*. Corpus Christianorum. Series Graeca, 45. Corpus Nazianzenum, 12. Brepols, Turnhout.

Coulie, B. and Métrévéli, H. (2004). *Sancti Gregorii Nazianzeni Opera. Versio Iberica. IV. Oratio XLIII*. Corpus Christianorum. Series Graeca, 52. Corpus Nazianzenum, 17. Brepols, Turnhout.

Coulie, B. and Métrévéli, H. (2007). *Sancti Gregorii Nazianzeni Opera. Versio Iberica. V. Orationes XXXIX et XL*. Corpus Christianorum. Series Graeca, 58. Corpus Nazianzenum, 20. Brepols, Turnhout.

Coulie, B. and Métrévéli, H. (2011). *Sancti Gregorii Nazianzeni Opera. Versio Iberica. VI. Orationes XI, XXI, XLII*. Corpus Christianorum. Series Graeca, 78. Corpus Nazianzenum, 26. Brepols, Turnhout.

Coulie, B. and Sirinian, A. (1999). *Sancti Gregorii Nazianzeni Opera. Versio armeniaca. III. Orationes XXI, VIII. Oratio VII*. Corpus Christianorum. Series Graeca, 38. Corpus Nazianzenum, 7. Brepols, Turnhout.

Coulie, B., Kindt, B., and Pataridze, T. (2013). Lemmatisation automatique des sources en géorgien ancien. *Le Muséon*, 126:161–201.

Coulie, B., Kindt, B., and Kepeklian, G. (2020). Un jeu d'étiquettes morphosyntaxiques pour le traitement automatique de l'arménien ancien. *Études Arméniennes Contemporaines*. in press.

Coulie, B. (1994). *Sancti Gregorii Nazianzeni Opera. Versio armeniaca. I. Orationes II, XII, IX*. Corpus Christianorum. Series Graeca, 28. Corpus Nazianzenum, 3. Brepols, Turnhout.

Coulie, B. (1996). La lemmatisation des textes grecs et byzantins : une approche particulière de la langue et des auteurs. *Byzantion*, 66:35–54.

Dereza, O., (2018). *Lemmatization for Ancient Languages: Rules or Neural Networks?: 7th International Conference, AINL 2018, St. Petersburg, Russia, October 17–19, 2018, Proceedings*, pages 35–47. Springer, Jan.

Egen, S., Gleim, R., and Mehler, A. (2016). Lemmatization and morphological tagging in German and Latin: A comparison and a survey of the state-of-the-art. In *Proceedings of the Tenth International Conference on Language Resources and Evaluation*.

Furlani, G. (1933). *Le Categorie e gli Ermeneutici di Aristotele nella versione siriaca di Giorgio delle Nazioni*. Serie VI. Vol. V. Fasc. 1. Reale Accademia Nazionale dei Lincei, Rome.

Haelewyck, J.-C., Kindt, B., Schmidt, A., and Atas, N. (2018). La concordance bilingue grecque - syriaque des Discours de Grégoire de Nazianze. *Babelao*, 7:51–80.

Haelewyck, J.-C. (2011). *Sancti Gregorii Nazianzeni Opera. Versio Syriaca V. Orationes I, II, III*. Corpus Christianorum. Series Graeca, 77. Corpus Nazianzenum, 25. Brepols, Turnhout.

Haelewyck, J.-C. (2014). Historia Zosimi De Vita Beatorum Rechabitarum ; Édition de la version syriaque brève. *Le Muséon*, 127:95–147.

Haelewyck, J.-C. (2015). La version syriaque longue de l'Historia Zosimi De Vita Beatorum Rechabitarum ; Édition et traduction. *Le Muséon*, 128:295–379.

Haelewyck, J.-C. (2016). *Histoire de Zosime sur la vie des Bienheureux Réchabites. Les versions orientales et leurs manuscrits*. Corpus Scriptorum Christianorum Orientalium, 664. Subsidia, 135. Peeters, Leuven.

Haelewyck, J.-C. (2017a). Histoire de Zosime sur la Vie des Bienheureux Réchabites. Les trois recensions syriaques. Édition de la version résumée. *Parole de l'Orient*, 43:175–194.

Haelewyck, J.-C. (2017b). Les versions syriaques des Discours de Grégoire de Nazianze: un processus continu de révision. *Babelao*, 6:75–124.

Kindt, B. (2004). La lemmatisation des sources patristiques et byzantines au service d'une description lexicale du grec ancien. *Byzantion*, 74:213–272.

Kindt, B. (2018). Processing Tools for Greek and Other Languages of the Christian Middle East. *Journal of Data Mining & Digital Humanities*, Special Issue on Computer-Aided Processing of Intertextuality in Ancient Languages.

Kondratyuk, D., Gavenčiak, T., Straka, M., and Hajič, J. (2018). LemmaTag: Jointly tagging and lemmatizing for morphologically rich languages with BRNNs. In *Proceedings of the 2018 Conference on Empirical Methods in Natural Language Processing*, pages 4921–4928, Brussels, Belgium, October-November. ACL.

Lafontaine, G. and Coulie, B. (1983). *La version arménienne des discours de Grégoire de Nazianze*. Corpus Scriptorum Christianorum Orientalium, 446. Subsidia, 67. Peeters, Leuven.

Manjavacas, E., Kádár, Á., and Kestemont, M. (2019). Improving lemmatization of non-standard languages with joint learning. In *Proceedings of the 2019 Conference of the North American Chapter of the Association for Computational Linguistics: Human Language Technologies, Volume 1 (Long and Short Papers)*, pages 1493–1503, Minneapolis, Minnesota. Association for Computational Linguistics.

Métrévéli, H. (1998). *Sancti Gregorii Nazianzeni Opera. Versio Iberica. I. Orationes I, XLV, XLIV, XLI*. Corpus Christianorum. Series Graeca, 36. Corpus Nazianzenum, 5. Brepols, Turnhout.

Métrévéli, H. (2000). *Sancti Gregorii Nazianzeni Opera. Versio Iberica. II. Orationes XV, XXIV, XIX*. Corpus Christianorum. Series Graeca, 42. Corpus Nazianzenum, 9. Brepols, Turnhout.

Müller, T., Cotterell, R., Fraser, A., and Schütze, H. (2015). Joint lemmatization and morphological tagging with lemming. In *Proceedings of the 2015 Conference on Empirical Methods in Natural Language Processing*, pages 2268–2274, Lisbon, Portugal. Association for Computational Linguistics.

Ouzounian, A., Goepp, M., and Mutafian, C. (2012). L'inscription du régent Constantin de Paperōn (1241). redécouverte, relecture, remise en contexte historique. *Revue des Études Arméniennes*, 34:243–287.

Peshiṭta Institute. (1977). *The Old Testament in Syriac according to the Peshiṭta Version*. Peshitta. The Old Testament in Syriac. Brill, Leiden.

Sanspeur, C. (2007). *Sancti Gregorii Nazianzeni Opera. Versio Armeniaca. IV. Oratio VI*. Corpus Christianorum. Series Graeca, 61. Corpus Nazianzenum, 21. Brepols, Turnhout.

Schmidt, A. (2002). *Sancti Gregorii Nazianzeni Opera. Versio Syriaca. II. Orationes XIII, XLI*. Corpus Christianorum. Series Graeca, 47. Corpus Naizanzenum, 15. Brepols, Turnhout.

Sembiante, A. (2017). Appunti sulla tradizione siriaca delle opere di Gregorio Nazianzeno. *Koinonia*, 10:607–634.

Sirinian, A. (1999). *Sancti Gregorii Nazianzeni Opera. Versio armeniaca. II. Orationes IV et V*. Corpus Christianorum. Series Graeca, 37. Corpus Nazianzenum, 6. Brepols, Turnhout.

Van Elverdinghe, E. (2018). Recurrent Pattern Modelling in a Corpus of Armenian Manuscript Colophons. *Journal of Data Mining & Digital Humanities*, Special Issue on Computer-Aided Processing of Intertextuality in Ancient Languages.

Venturini, G. (2019). *La versione siriaca della vita di Giovanni il Misericordioso di Leonzio di Neapolis*. Corpus Scriptorum Christianorum, 679. Scriptores Syri, 263. Peeters, Leuven.

Vidal-Gorène, C. and Decours-Perez, A. (2020). Languages resources for poorly endowed languages : The case study of Classical Armenian. In *Proceedings of the Twelfth International Conference on Language Resources and Evaluation (LREC 2020)*. in press.

Vidal-Gorène, C., Decours-Perez, A., Queuche, B., Ouzounian, A., and Riccioli, T. (2019). Digitalization and Enrichment of the Nor Baṙgirkʿ Haykazean Lezui: Work in Progress for Armenian Lexicography. *Journal of the Society of Armenian Studies*, 27. in press.

7. Language Resource References

American University of Armenia. (1999). *Digital Library of Armenian Literature*.

Arak29. (2002). *Arak29*.

Calfa. (2014). *Calfa - Enriched Dictionaries of Classical and Modern Armenian*.

J. Gippert. (2003). *TITUS Project*. Johann Wolfgang Goethe University.

Ilia State University. (2009). *Georgian Language Corpus*.

Université catholique de Louvain. (1990). *GREgORI Project - Softwares, linguistic data and tagged corpus for ancient GREek and ORIental languages*.

J. E. Walters. (2004). *Digital Syriac Corpus*.

Proceedings of 1st Workshop on Language Technologies for Historical and Ancient Languages, pages 28–36
Language Resources and Evaluation Conference (LREC 2020), Marseille, 11–16 May 2020
© European Language Resources Association (ELRA), licensed under CC-BY-NC

Computerized Forward Reconstruction for Analysis in Diachronic Phonology, and Latin to French Reflex Prediction

Clayton Marr, David Mortensen
Carnegie Mellon University, Carnegie Mellon University
Pittsburgh PA 15213 USA, Pittsburgh PA 15213 USA
cmarr@andrew.cmu.edu, dmortens@cs.cmu.edu

Abstract

Traditionally, historical phonologists have relied on tedious manual derivations to calibrate the sequences of sound changes that shaped the phonological evolution of languages. However, humans are prone to errors, and cannot track thousands of parallel word derivations in any efficient manner. We propose to instead automatically derive each lexical item in parallel, and we demonstrate *forward reconstruction* as both a computational task with metrics to optimize, and as an empirical tool for inquiry. For this end we present DiaSim, a user-facing application that simulates "cascades" of diachronic developments over a language's lexicon and provides diagnostics for "debugging" those cascades. We test our methodology on a Latin-to-French reflex prediction task, using a newly compiled dataset *FLLex* with 1368 paired Latin/French forms. We also present, *FLLAPS*, which maps 310 Latin reflexes through five stages until Modern French, derived from Pope (1934)'s sound tables. Our publicly available rule cascades include the baselines *BaseCLEF* and *BaseCLEF**, representing the received view of Latin to French development, and *DiaCLEF*, build by incremental corrections to *BaseCLEF* aided by DiaSim's diagnostics. DiaCLEF vastly outperforms the baselines, improving final accuracy on FLLex from 3.2%to 84.9%, and similar improvements across FLLAPS' stages. .

Keywords: diachronic phonology, computerized forward simulation, regular sound change, Romance linguistics, French, Latin, DiaSim

1. Introduction

When reconstructing the phonological history of a language, linguists usually operate under the Neogrammarian assumption that sound change operates on an input defined by its phonetic characteristics, can be conditioned based on its phonetic context, and results in a predictable output, with no exceptions (excluding non-phonologically motivated phenomena such as analogy, homophony avoidance, hyper correction, et cetera). This paradigm operationalizes sound change as a classical function: an input maps to a unique output. Aggregated, the ordered sequence ("cascade") of these sound change functions forms an algorithm. Such an algorithmic phenomenon naturally lends itself to automated simulation. There are ample theoretical underpinnings for using simulations – or *computerized forward reconstruction* (Sims-Williams, 2018) (*CFR*) – to test the accuracy of the cascade implied by any given understanding of a language's phonological history. However, for reasons discussed in depth in 1.2., it failed to achieve widespread usage. Instead, current work has tended to analyse at high resolution the specifics of certain types of sound changes cross-linguistically, and rarely explicitly and holistically tackles how they fit together in the whole of any one language's phonological history. To verify our understanding of that latter "bigger picture", the diachronic phonologist would have to either write or memorize the effects of thousands of rules operating over millennia, mapping the forms of thousands of reflexes. No wonder, then, that current work prefers to "zoom in" on one phenomenon.

These typological discussions are greatly useful, but must remain grounded by understanding the histories of the languages in question. The phonological histories of the majority of the world's languages, which likely will not survive the next century, remain mysterious, and work on them would certainly be more efficient if aided by computers.

While it could take months for a human to map thousands of etyma across millennia, a computer can do so in seconds. CFR furthermore greatly facilitates thorough coverage of the lexicon. Building on the example of earlier now abandoned projects discussed in section 1.2., we present *DiaSim*, a generalizable transparent forward reconstruction application which offers various diagnostic capabilities, hoping to improve the present situation.

We present our work in using *DiaSim* to "debug" the received understanding of French phonological history, as represented by Pope (1934). We additionally present our newly compiled datasets *FLLex* and *FLLAPs* (described in 5.), with which we demonstrate the utility of CFR using DiaSim. We present results on the measured performance of baseline (derived from Pope (1934)) rule cascades *Base-CLEF* and *BaseCLEF**, and the "debugged" cascade *Dia-CLEF*. While the baseline model was 3.2%accuracy (without "uninteresting errors", 30.3%), the corrected ruleset achieved 84.9%accuracy, with the biggest improvement observed in the (largely unattested) Gallo-Roman stage, as discussed at length in section 7..

All of these resources are made publicly available for use, at the DiaSim github repo.

1.1. Related Work

1.1.1. French Phonological History

Romance philology is typically considered founded by François-Juste Raynouard (Posner, 1996, p. 3), and formalized by Diefenbach (1831) and Diez (1836), followed by a work on work on French propelled by Neogrammarianism (Thurot, 1881; Meyer-Lübke, 1899; Suchier, 1893; Marchot, 1901; Nyrop, 1914); foundational early 20th century work includes Fouché (1961), Martinet (1970), Brunot and Charlier (1927), and, of course, Pope (1934). Of the extensive subsequent work, we specifically note Adams (2007)'s work on regional ("Popular") Latin inscriptions, work on French historical sociolinguistics (Lodge, 2013; Lodge and others, 2004; Lusignan, 1986), French orthographical history, and "protofrançais" (Noske, 2011; Banniard, 2001). Traditional methodology balanced Neogrammarian inquiry with the principle that, as Pope (1934) describes it, "the history of a language should be related as closely as possible to the study of texts". Such methodology often involved tracing changes in spelling as it represented certain sounds and morphemes ("flexion") and taking the remarks of historical writers (especially grammarians) as objective evidence. We, like other recent researchers (Posner, 2011; Fouché, 1961), take a more sceptical look at these writings, viewing them not as descriptions of reality but rather prescriptions for how French subjectively *should* be pronounced. We offer an alternative to relying on these voices: the empirical methodology described in section 3..

Since the beginning, work in French diachronic phonology has functioned more or less to calibrate what is in effect the diachronic *cascade* of French, with Pope's meticulous 1934 opus still considered the "invaluable" (Posner and others, 1997, p. 3) baseline against which new theories in French are being presented as improving upon (Short, 2013). Our aim in this work is twofold. Alongside the goal of demonstrating the power of CFR, we also aim to, like Pope before us, provide a holistic account of French diachrony. Ultimately, our vision is a publicly available cascade for every language of interest that may be improved upon whenever a correction becomes accepted in the field.

1.2. Computerized Forward Reconstruction

Not long after the mid-20th century emergence (Dunn, 2015) of computational historical linguistics (Jäger, 2019) with the works of scholars like Swadesh and Gleason (Swadesh, 1952; Gleason, 1959), the first published CFR (coarsely) derived 650 Russian words from Proto-Indo-European (Smith, 1969); the next derived Old French from Latin in 1976 (Burton-Hunter, 1976). Others looked at Medieval Ibero-Romance (Eastlack, 1977), Latin from Proto-Indo-European (Maniet, 1985), Old Church Slavonic from PIE (Borin, 1988), Bantu (Hombert et al., 1991), and Polish from Proto-Slavic (Kondrak, 2002). These systems were not intended to be generalizable, lacked sufficiently expressive rule formalisms, and used orthography rather than underlying phones (Piwowarczyk, 2016), having "no notion of phonology" (Kondrak, 2002). Generalizable rule formalisms have in fact been presented in related topics, such as learning *synchronic* sound rules (Gildea and Jurafsky, 1995).

Phono, a phonologically-motivated and phoneme-mediated forward reconstruction, appeared in 1996 and was applied to Spanish and Shawnee (Hartman, 2003; Muzaffar, 1997), but as far as we know, no further work using Phono was published. Despite computational modeling seeing an "explosion"[1] in other diachronic fields (Dunn, 2015) alongside rapid improvements in computing, CFR fell out of fashion by the late 20th century (Lowe and Mazaudon, 1994), and

old CFR systems are now incompatible with modern computers (Kondrak, 2002). Reasons for this decline are varied, including dissent Neogrammarianism, and an unfortunate association with supposedly "unprofessional" enterprises (Sims-Williams, 2018).

2. Contributions

We aim to show that a sufficiently generalizable CFR system is a useful and professional research tool for diachronic phonology. It is recognized (Sims-Williams, 2018) that human cognition simply has insufficient working memory to track all the (likely millions of) implied calculations while mapping sound rule functions spanning centuries or millennia across a language's entire inherited lexicon. Ensuring the accuracy of the tedious human calculations in this scenario is itself extremely onerous and error-prone. On the other hand, the task is trivial for a computer. Information attained in this much more efficient and rigorous manner can then be leveraged to improve our diachronic understanding of the languages in question, revealing new sound laws and analogical patterns, refining existing ones, and revealing new reflexes and cognates, all while ensuring holistic coverage rather than cherry-picking for validation. This improved efficiency and rigor could be crucial for advancing our critical understanding for less well studied and especially endangered language families — especially where phylogeny, which often relies on diachronic phonology, is concerned.

This paper contributes the following:

- DiaSim, an application that performs *transparent*[2] CFR for rule cascades over any lexicon, offering accuracy metrics and a diagnostics for analysis

- FLLex, a dataset pairing 1368 Latin etyma with their known ("gold") inherited French reflexes.

- FLLAPS, a dataset mapping gold reflexes of 310 Latin etyma across five attested stages

- Two cascades based on the received understanding of Latin > French sound change, and a "debugged" cascade built using DiaSim with PATCH

- PATCH, a guideline for using CFR for inquiry

3. PATCH

We recommend PATCH as an empirically sound way to utilize CFR for scientific inquiry in "debugging" rule cascades. PATCH is described in the following prose, and summarized in figure 1.

The baseline cascade ideally should reflect the latest available, but conservative, "least common denominator" for which there is consensus. For French, such a baseline is easily identifiable — and explicitly used as such still in current research (Short, 2013) — as Pope (1934). In this way, our inquiry can independently support or challenge findings in subsequent literature.

PATCH is then performed on the "working cascade", which starts out as a copy of the baseline before it is progressively

---

[1] Including analogous work in closely related topics, such as learning FST-based *synchronic* sound rules (Gildea and Jurafsky, 1995)

[2] See section 4.1.

Figure 1: The PATCH process, summarized.

1. "Debug" the working cascade[3] by repeating the following steps:

  (a) (P)inpoint – Isolate a source of error

  (b) (A)mend – Try various solutions; choose the one with the best accuracy, preferring simplicity where there are statistical ties

  (c) (T)est – is the selection justifiable?

    i. If a new sound change is being added, preferably ensure that it can be motivated typologically/theoretically

    ii. Ensure there are no adverse side effects

    iii. Consult any relevant existing work, and relevant data as appropriate: philology, dialectology, loans, etc.

  (d) CHoose – If the proposal remains plausible, commit it to the working cascade. Otherwise recalibrate it, or redact it entirely.

modified. We hold that when using CFR, a linguist should initially make fixes based solely on Neogrammarian empiricism, not prior knowledge (neither topical nor typological). Thus the *Pinpoint* stage is performed "blind" regarding any information not drawn from CFR results. Automated statistical assistance such as DiaSim's diagnostics is often useful to pinpoint the source of error.

One likewise performs the second stage (*Amend*) "blinded" of outside info: the researcher comes up with all reasonable possible solutions to the problem identified in *Pinpoint*, implements them on the working cascade, and records the effects on performance. Of these, (s)he chooses the one with the best performance; in cases where there is no significant difference in performance, choose the fix that is the "simplest". By "simplicity", we do not necessarily mean "the least rules possible and the least specifications on each rule", although in practice the two are often similar. Instead, "simplicity" here refers to the simplest possible way to explain the data. These are different, because leaving numerous lexemes with plausibly related developments unexplained by any single rule is to be considered simpler *only* if we have a "simple" and ideally *single* explanation, such as systematic analogy, interference, or identifiable sociolinguistic effects. On the other hand, leaving them with no explanation at all implies a "default" that they each have lexically explanations – which is the exact opposite of "simplicity", and to be avoided[4]. Then, implement the chosen "fix" by amending the cascade at the proper point.

It is only in the third stage, *Test*, that outside info is weighed against other factors, before a binding decision is made in the final stage *Choose*, to either enshrine the solution in the working cascade, enshrine a modified version, or redact it

entirely. Then, to find more fixes, the linguist iteratively repeats this process.

We tried our best to follow PATCH building DiaCLEF. However, we do not advocate brittle literal adherence to PATCH, but rather suggest it as a guideline; we additionally suggest some specific exceptions to its use. Firstly, at the end of the *Choose* stage, if other fixes become clear with the synthesis of data from the simulation and from other sources (such as dated attested forms), they can also be fixed at the time, as long as there is (a) robust corroboration in coverage, and (b) no adverse side effects when checked with the entire dataset. Secondly, fixing baseline rules so that they obtain their stated intended effects when otherwise they clearly do not [5] is exempt from PATCH. Lastly, fixing rules that have already been changed (or moved), or have been created anew by prior iterations of PATCH can be done without the entire process, because this is really a revision of the re-calibration aspect of *Choose*.

4. DiaSim

4.1. Transparent Large-Scale Cascade Simulation

DiaSim transparently simulates a specified rule cascade for every lexeme in parallel. The user must input at minimum (1) a lexicon file, and (2) a cascade. The lexicon file includes the input forms to forward reconstruction, and optionally gold reflex forms for the final or intermediate results of CFR. Each rule in the cascade is written in the conventional SPE format (Chomsky and Halle, 1968). DiaSim implements the subset of the SPE rule formalism that (Johnson, 1972) and (Kaplan and Kay, 1981) showed to be formally equivalent to finite state transducers (FSTs), while enabling users to explicitly modify sound laws in terms of conventional notation rather than computer code[6].

DiaSim can capture any and all regular relations between strings in the specified symbol alphabet, whether that alphabet is the provided IPA default, or another supplied by the user. In between rules, the user may flag a stage, at which the simulation state can be stored and retrieved. Flagged stages may also be used as *pivots* during evaluation to help detect long-distance interactions between rules.

Being able to observe the iterative realization of cascade *transparently* (effects of each rule being "visible") is quite useful for illuminating relationships between involved processes. One can see how the preconditions for later rules may emerge, or be perturbed, or how they fail to do so when expected. For such "transparency", DiaSim can retrieve each time an etyma was changed (shown in figure 2), its new form and by what rule, or all effects of any rule.

---

[4]We except from this cases that are known to be predictably lexically specific: homophony avoidance, onomatopoeia, and spelling pronunciations.

[5]I.e. the baseline source states one outcome but the rule formalism does not produce it. When using DiaSim, a quick way to check this is to check the printouts of etymon-wise *transparent* mutations for the sound change in question.

[6]DiaSim's sound rule "grammar" handles all IPA except for clicks and tones, can support all SPE notations including complicated alpha functions, disjunction, and nested parenthetical optional segments, and adds "@" for "any single phone" (anything but the word bound #).

```
#m,ən'at͡sə# | R534 : t͡sʲ > t͡s
#m,ə̃ŋ'at͡sə# | R628 : [+syl,-front] > [+nas] / __ [+nas,-syl]
#m,ə̃ŋ'asə# | R648 : [+delrel] > [+cont]
#m,ə̃ŋ'asə# | R653 : {ɔ̃;.ə̃} > {ə;.ə}
#m,əŋ'a:sə# | R706 : [-round,+syl] > [+long] / __ s ə #
#m,əŋ'a:sə̰# | R708 : ə > [-syl] / __ #
#m,əŋ'ɑ:sə̰# | R715 : [+lo,+long] > [+back]
#m,əŋ'ɑ:s# | R736 : ə̰ > ø
#məŋɑ:s# | R753 : [+stres] > [-stres]
#məŋɑs# | R754 : [+syl,+long] > [-long]
```

Figure 2: Derivation of *menace* (< Latin MINACIA).

```
Success: now making subsample with filter 'a [+ant,+strid,-cont] a
(Pivot moment name: pivot@R633)
Filter seq : 'a [+ant,+strid,-cont] a
Size of subset : 7;
0.507% of whole
Accuracy on subset with sequence 'a [+ant,+strid,-cont] a in pivot@R633 : 0.0%
Percent of errors included in subset: 3.431372549019608%
```

Figure 3: A context autopsy, one of DiaSim's diagnostics. Here the error is likely related to following /t͡s/.

4.2. Performance Metrics

For either the entire lexicon or a chosen subset, DiaSim can supply the word-wise accuracy, the accuracy within one or two phones, the word-wise average Levenshtein distance between result and gold form (normalized for gold length, hence forth *mPED*[7]), and the word-wise average length-normalized *feature edit distance* (Mortensen et al., 2016; Kondrak, 2003) *(mFED)* between result and gold forms. Future work should incorporate a measure of *implied complexity*[8].

These metrics offer different information. Accuracy indicates how much of the lexicon the rule cascade renders correct. On the other hand, mPED gives how wrong we are if we treat phones as discrete tokens, whereas mFED indicates mean phonetic result/gold distance between in terms of phone-wise feature vector distance — on average, how different is each wrong phone from the correct one?

4.3. Diagnostics

Aside from failure to consider how the rule cascade could affect every word in the lexicon, significant sources of error could be missed, especially where rules interact, given the multiplicity of all the factors at play. Additionally, what is actually observed as one relatively acute error could actually be a sign of a much larger pattern of errors. To help overcome these factors, DiaSim offers a suite of diagnostics. If interactive mode is flagged at command line, at the end of the simulation, and also any flagged gold stage, DiaSim halts, gives basic performance metrics, and queries if the user would like to run any diagnostic options. These diagnostics, including correlation of error with the presence of segments at the same or different stages (the "context autopsy" diagnostic presented in 3 being an example), identification of particularly common correspondences between errant and gold phones, among others, are enumerated in more detail in the diagnostics README contained in the package.

Wherever phone-wise errors is involved, an alignment algorithm based on minimizing feature edit distance (Mortensen et al., 2016) measures phone-wise error. DiaSim's diagnostics aims to help pinpoint where in the sequence of realized shifts the critical error occurred. For example, the final stage error correlated to a particular phone measures how much error arises from failure to properly generate it or its effects on neighbors. The same statistic observed for an earlier pivot stage would instead indicate how much inaccuracy comes from errant handling of its future reflexes and their behavior. Meanwhile, error correlated with the resulting phone for an earlier "pivot" stage could instead reveal the degree of error propagation caused by errant generation of the said phone at the pivot stage. Likewise, when analyzing specific errors between the gold and the result, DiaSim can pinpoint for the user if the type of error happens to be particularly common in certain contexts.

These sorts of diagnostics can be useful for identifying the regularity of the contexts of a phenomenon that may have otherwise appeared sporadic or inexplicable. Given that DiaSim, unlike previous models, is explicitly modeled using phonological features, it is well-equipped to identify phonological regularity that humans could easily miss. For example, the traditional paradigm for French (Pope, 1934) holds that the voicing of Latin initial /k/ to Gallo-Roman /g/ was simply sporadic, but as we demonstrate in section 7.1., we were able to detect a plausible new regular rule to explain them collectively.

4.4. Theoretical Grounding

DiaSim was constructed to be faithful to longstanding theory while maintaining flexibility. It is built on the premise that words consist of token instances of a bounded set of phone types (alongside juncture phonemes), and that phones are uniquely defined by value vectors for each of a constant feature set (Chomsky and Halle, 1968; Hall, 2007; Hock, 2009). Each feature can be assigned one of three values : positive (+), negative (-) or unspecified (0). Which features are relevant for phonemic distinctions vary by language. DiaSim allows the user to use a custom set of feature-defined phones and/or of phone-defining features, while providing holistic default sets for each.

5. Datasets

The dataset FLLex[9] consists of 1368 Latin etyma paired with their inherited modern French reflexes. These include all 1061 inherited etyma in French (excluding some verb forms) that are used in Pope (1934), as well as 307 etyma recruited from Rey (2013) and from the online French philological resource, *Trésor de la Langue Française informatisé* (TLFi) ATILF (2019a).

For inclusion, lexemes had to have been in continuous usage throughout the relevant sixteen centuries. Words affected by non-phonologically motivated phenomena such as analogy, folk etymology, etc were excluded, but words with apparent irregularity that could not be attributed to such processes (such as cases of sporadic metathesis) remained included. Each entry was checked with multiple sources (Pope, 1934; Rey, 2013; ATILF, 2019a) to ensure it was indeed an etymon

---

[7](m)ean (P)honeme (E)dit (D)istance

[8]Considering the explicit cascade and the "implicit" complexity of exception cases made for words considered *non-regular* and thus excluded from calculation of all (other) provided metrics

[9](F)rench from (L)atin (Lex)icon

with continuous usage from Latin to French, unaffected by non-phonologically motivated interference.

The period-indexed dataset FLLAPS[10] is recruited from Pope (1934)'s sound tables. FLLAPS has an intentional degree of balance in phonological coverage, as Pope designed her sound tables to have at least one etymon that was affected by each notable sound change (FLLex, meanwhile, is more proportionally representative of the overall phonemic frequencies of the French language). FLLAPS offers gold forms derived from Pope's philological work for each of the four intermediate stages, including Late Latin in Gallia (dated to circa 400 CE), Old French I (EOFdate), Old French II (circa 1325 CE), and Middle French (circa 1550 CE). A few corrections were made in order to adapt the set for this task. For example, as Pope did not foresee this use of her work, she sometimes omits finer distinctions (such as lax/tense distinctions). When these concern segments that are not of interest to the specific sound changes being demonstrated, the sound changes described elsewhere in her work for the period in question were regularly applied and consistency enforced.

6. Rule cascades

In order to demonstrate both how DiaSim simulates long-term and holistic Neogrammarian sound change, we designed our baseline cascade, **BaseCLEF** [11] to include all regular sound changes posited in (Pope, 1934), which represents the received view of French phonological history, and remains the "indispensible"(Short, 2013) work that others in the field build off of. The **DiaCLEF**[12] cascade was then built from a copy of BaseCLEF by exhaustively correcting non-sporadic errors detected using DiaSim's simulation and evaluation functionalities.

We built BaseCLEF to include all regular sound changes posited in (Pope, 1934), in the order specified. Where Pope's writing is ambiguous, the benefit of the doubt is given as a general policy (that is, we assume the reading that gives the correct output). There are numerous cases where literal interpretation of Pope's treatise leads to "non-interesting" errors, mere omissions and the like because at the time of writing were not essential, perhaps because Pope didn't foresee her work being converted into an explicit rule cascade. For example, Pope states that modern French lacks any phonemic length differences, but never states when it was lost. To handle this, we made an additional ruleset, *BaseCLEF**, where these trivial omissions are corrected.

7. Results

As seen in table 1, the increase in accuracy obtained by "debugging" via DiaSim is striking, with raw accuracy going from 3.2%to 84.9%. The improvement in average feature edit distance, a decrease from 0.518to 0.056, is also large, even when we consider the baseline to be BaseCLEFstar (with "uninteresting" errors already corrected as discussed in section 6.), with 30.3%accuracy and 0.380mean FED.

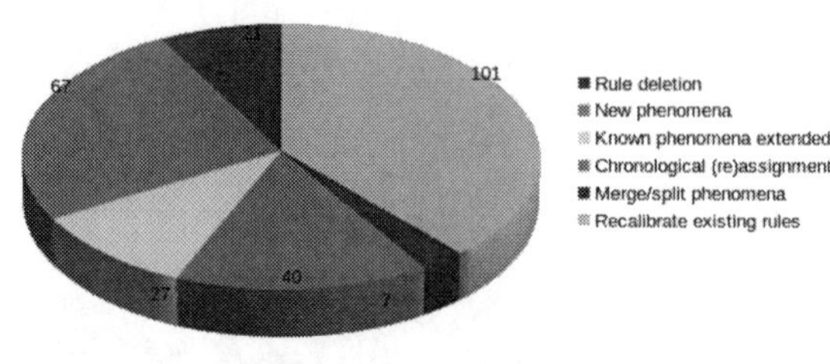

Figure 4: Breakdown of "fixes" in DiaCLEF

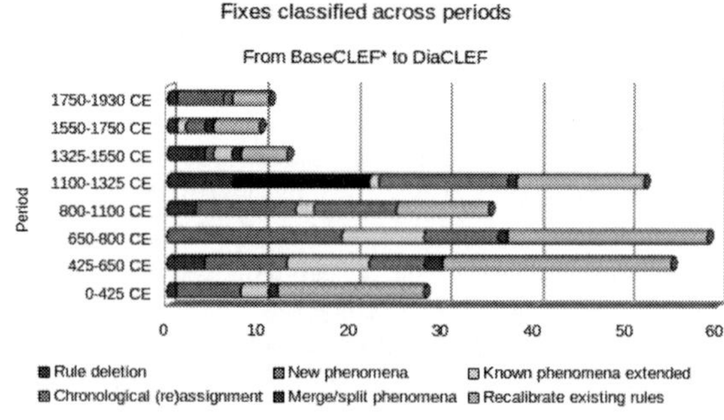

Figure 5: Differences between different periods in number and type of edits made to the cascade

In table 4, we see a breakdown of the sorts the corrections that were done for DiaCLEF (excluding those also handled in BaseCLEF*). The more radical sorts of changes include *rule deletion*, *rule creation*, and re-orderings, constituted 48.7% of changes, leaving the rest to less radical amendments such as extension of acknowledged phenomena, recalibration of rule contexts, and mergers and splits of existing rules.

As displayed in figure 5, the biggest volume of changes occur in the Gallo-Roman and Old French periods. There were notable differences with regard to where changes that fundamentally challenge Pope's understanding of French diachronology led to meaningful improvements. This is also true of re-orderings, which are broken down by period and type in figure 6. On the other hand, few changes were necessary for the transition from Classical Latin to Late Latin, and even fewer were necessary for early modern French.

This should come as no surprise. The Gallo-Roman period (except in its very latest stages) is by far the least well-attested – and therefore, the most like what we would be dealing with if we were working with an understudied indigenous language.

Many of these new insights are discussed at length in (Marr and Mortensen, 2020); we present just one here at length in section 7.1. to demonstrate the empirical use of CFR with PATCH.

Metric	BaseCLEF	BaseCLEF*	DiaCLEF
Accuracy	3.2%	30.3%	84.9%
Accuracy within 1 phone	26.3%	55.7%	94.8%
Accuracy within 2 phones	56.7%	79.9%	99.1%
Avg Normalized Levenshtein Edit Distance	0.518	0.380	0.056
Avg Normalized Feature Edit Distance	0.673	0.392	0.061

Table 1: Performance on FLLex

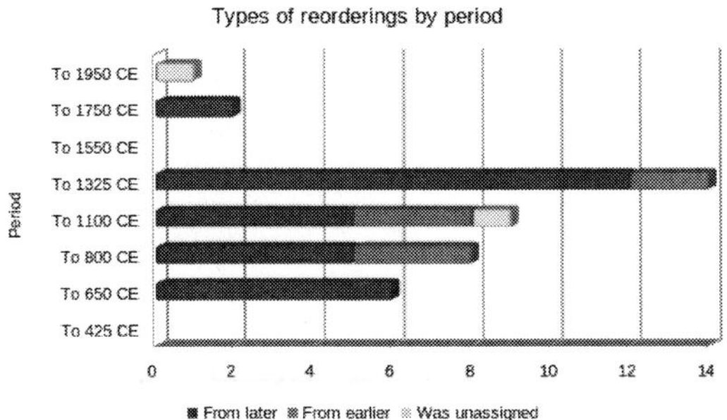

Figure 6: Corrections of ordering by period.

```
Result phones most associated with error:
0: /k/ with rate 2.3333333333333335,    Rate present in mismatches : 24.13:
1: /p/ with rate 1.4444444444444444,    Rate present in mismatches : 14.94:
2: /s/ with rate 0.5645161290322581,    Rate present in mismatches : 40.22!
3: /æ̃/ with rate 0.5,    Rate present in mismatches : 1.1494252873563218
Gold phones most associated with error:
0: /p/ with rate 1.5555555555555556,    Rate present in mismatches : 16.09:
1: /k/ with rate 1.4444444444444444,    Rate present in mismatches : 14.94:
Focus point phones most associated with error:
0: /a/ with rate Infinity,    Rate present in mismatches : 1.1494252873560
1: /t̪ʰ/ with rate 1.0,  Rate present in mismatches : 1.1494252873563218
...
Most common distortions:
....
Distortion 1: k for g
% of errant words with this distortion : 8.0459%
Most common predictors of this distortion:
No constant features for pre prior
No particularly common pre prior phones.
Percent word bound for prior: 100.0
posterior phone constant features: -syl -nas -sg -cg -lab -hi -lo -front -i
Most common posterior phones: /ʁ/ (85.7%)
post posterior phone constant features: -cons -lat -nas -strid -sg -cg -an:
Most common post posterior phones: /ɑ/ (71.4%)
....
Distortion 2: e for ɛ
% of errant words with this distortion : 6.8965%
```

Figure 7: DiaSim's Confusion Prognosis

7.1. Regular Explanation for "Sporadic" Onset /k/ Voicing

We use the simple yet striking example of the plausible regularity of Early Old French initial velar stop voicing to demonstrate the use of CFR with PATCH to propose and validate new rules. In this case, we are unable to find any work in the past century and a half of research that treats this plausible regularity as a unified phenomenon, instead giving a number of unrelated explanations for affected etyma.

We begin our investigation (*Find* in PATCH) with DiaSim's *Confusion Prognosis* (figure 7). In the top left, we see the phones which have the highest ratio of occurrence in error cases to correct cases, and in top right we see the overall prevalence in error cases. In the bottom part of the Confusion Prognosis, the most significant correspondences between specific errant and gold phones ("distortions") are displayed.[13]

Here, the most problematic distortion is /k/:/g/, where we find /k/ for what should be /g/, comprising 8% of all errors. Furthermore, /k/ is the phone most correlated with error. 100% of /k/:/g/ distortions occur immediately after the word onset, 86% of cases have the uvular fricative /ʁ/ immediately after, and for 71% of cases, the next phone is /ɑ/. This suggests to the linguist that behind this error, a regular rule may be hiding, and those statistics give an idea of what its conditioning context likely is.

Clearly we are dealing with a case of onset voicing. French fricative /ʁ/ reflects historic sonorant /r/, which is significant, as French lenition likewise happened regularly in Gallo-Roman intervocalic consonant + sonorant clusters. However, because we are consciously choosing to ignore what we think we know about French (per PATCH), we ignore this fact at this point so as not to bias our search, and as seen we will end condition our rule not on specifically sonorant consonants but instead simply on consonants.

This suggests that an onset velar voicing happened at some point in the history of French, but we don't know when. We next aim to isolate the problem by filtering out "noise", identified with the help of our statistics, to get a "noise"-less subset. In our case, we set the *focus point*[14] as the input form from Classical Latin, and use a *filter sequence* "# k @ [+lo]"[15].

The user can then access a list of the resulting subset's errors, which include (with correct forms second) /kle/:/glɛv/, /klɑ/:/glɑ/, /kʁɑs/:/gʁɑs/, /kʁaj/:/gʁij/, and so on. Viewing this list, it is apparent that /k/ in all the error cases lies between the word onset and a consonant. We no longer have to rely on prior knowledge because all the words which end up with uvular /ʁ/ still have alveolar /r/ at our *focus point*. However, because we never observe a non-sonorant consonant having a different effect, we continue to condition our rule on consonants, not sonorants, because we seek the least specific rule possible. If we assert a low vowel after the onset cluster, we perfectly predict the /k/:/g/ distortion, with one exception[16].

The subset of data filtered for etyma with the Latin sequence "# k [+cons] [+lo]" has well under 50% accuracy. Examining the specific non-error cases among this subset, they all have changed the original ᴀ into a non-low vowel, and in all of these cases, the ᴀ had primary stress and was in an open syllable. The same is true of only one of the error cases[17].

---

[13] These calculations are done on the back of an alignment algorithm that aligns phones so as to minimize *Feature Edit Distance* (Mortensen et al., 2016).

[14] The time step at which a subset is made using the *filter sequence*

[15] onset k, any single phone ("@"), then a low vowel

[16] The ⟨clef⟩/⟨clé⟩ doublet, reflexes of ᴄʟᴀ̄ᴠᴇᴍ, with a low vowel

[17] namely, ⟨glaive⟩, whose exact history is unclear

```
k l 'ɑː r ɑ m
#kl'ɑrɑm# | Rule 58  : [+syl,+long] > [-long,-splng]
#kl'ɑrɑ#  | Rule 74  : [+nas,+cons] > ø / [-stres] ___ #
#kl'ɑːrɑ# | Rule 116 : [+prim] > [+long] / ___ [+cons] [-cons]
#kl'ɑːrɑ# | Rule 205 : [+lo] > [+front,-back]
#kl'ae̯rɑ# | Rule 420 : {'aː;'eː;'oː;'ɛː} > {'a e̯;'e j;'o w;'i e̯}
#kl'ae̯rə# | Rule 447 : a > ə / [+syl] ( [-syl] )* ___
#kl'eːrə# | Rule 554 : {a e̯;,a e̯;'a e̯} > {eː;,eː;'eː}
#kl'ɛːrə# | Rule 612 : {'eː;'e} > {'ɛː;'ɛ} / ___ [+cons] [+syl]
```

Figure 8: Derivation of CLĀRAM >·· ·>⟨*claire*⟩.

```
In: delete & filter by input
Out: delete & filter at current output
Gold: delete & filter by current gold
U: delete and also delete filter
R#: right before rule with index number <#>(you can find rule indices with option 3
Please enter the appropriate indicator.
R461
On rule number 0
On rule number 100
On rule number 200
On rule number 300
On rule number 400
Size of subset : 7;
0.508% of whole
Accuracy on subset with sequence # k [+cons] [+lo] in pivot@R461 : 0.0%
```

Figure 9: We isolate our error by setting our focus point right after the last *bleeding* rule, to find a subset with zero accuracy.

This pattern points us toward our next objective — to propose a solution (*Amend* in PATCH). Now that we have determined our rule's conditioning, we want to pin down where it should be placed in the cascade. To locate when the vocalic changes that *bled* (Kiparsky and Good, 1968) our proposed rule occurred, we examine the derivations of affected cases. In the derivation for CLĀRAM >·· ·>⟨*claire*⟩ (figure 8) we see the bleeding rule at rule 554: /ae̯/ > /eː. This explains not only why we have ⟨*claire*⟩ and not ⟨*glaire*⟩, but also the cases of of CLĀRUM and CLĀVEM. The printout derivation of CLĀVUM >·· ·>⟨*clou*⟩ likewise reveals an earlier bleeding effect as /aw/ passed to / w/. Our proposed rule must thus be placed after these bleeding rules.

Now that we have a proposed rule, its conditioning, and its relative date, we must next justify it (*Test* in PATCH). First, we want to make sure that this is really what the data supports.

As demonstrated in figure 9, in DiaSim we do this by setting our focus point to time step 555, to exclude the words affected by bleeding rules. As expected, our accuracy on that subset is zero. Now that we have zeroed in on the source of error, and inserted a corrective rule (figure 2) at a specified time, the proposal will be validated if our accuracy dramatically improves.

(2) k > g / # ___ $\begin{bmatrix} +\text{cons} \end{bmatrix}$ $\begin{bmatrix} +\text{lo} \end{bmatrix}$

Surely enough, we achieve perfect accuracy for all etyma in the subset except one.[18]

Since we have added a new rule, per PATCH we also justify it. It is easy to see this phenomenon in the context of ear-lier lenition processes in French, as well as most Western Romance and British Celtic languages, whereby stops that were either intervocalic or in an intervocalic stop + sonorant cluster were voiced, often as a precursor to spirantization. Although in French, the process ceased being productive without diachronic affects on onset consonants, in both Ibero-Romance and Insular Celtic, it continues to operate across word boundaries (Martinet, 1952); the general tendency toward weak word boundaries is known in French is well known, and is realized in sandhi phenomena such as liaison (Cerquiglini, 2018). At the same time, our proposed rule is dated right around the time that the deletion of final consonants was beginning, meaning that many onset clusters would newly become intervocalic where previously they weren't.[19] There is evidence suggesting a related synchronic phenomenon that was once broader in coverage, such as attested k > g substitution in initial /klo-/ (Pope, 1934, p. 96).

It is at this point that one consults other relevant lexical data to corroborate their simulation-guided proposal. In this case, we are supported by philological data from the Old French corpus. Replacement of initial ⟨c⟩ with ⟨g⟩ in these effected words, is first attested in early 12th century Old French, which is after both bleeding effects on stressed /a/.[20]

Despite this evidence from the early 12th century, the traditional view in the literature has been that such voicing was only a sporadic "tendency" that occurred at the *Gallo-Roman* stage (Pope, 1934, p. 96). Meanwhile, the involved words have been assigned a number of unrelated and often rather convoluted explanations by the scholarship: ⟨*glas*⟩ *alone* is said to be affected by "*assimilation du c initial à la consonne sonore suivante*" (ATILF, 2019c), while analogy is proposed for ⟨*gras*⟩ (ATILF, 2019g), which supposedly cascaded onto ⟨*graisse*⟩ (ATILF, 2019d). The explanation of ⟨*glaive*⟩ relies on both of two proposed language contact effects holding true (ATILF, 2019b), while the voicing in the case of *grille* is not explained at all. Bourciez (1971, p. 146) in fact notes a large subset of our filtered set and includes ⟨*gratter*⟩, from Frankish ⟨*kratton*⟩, a relevant lexeme that agrees with our analysis but was outside our dataset. But, tantalizingly, he does not investigate an explanation using regular sound change, instead attributing the case of *gras* to analogy from *gros*, and leaving the others unexplained.

However, the conditioning and timing we found perfectly divides affected words from all other words with an initial /k/ in Latin which were unaffected, except for CAVEŌLA > *geole* and Celtic *CAMBITU-, which are separately explained by Bourciez (1971, p. 134,142) anyways. Furthermore, our findings were supported by words outside our dataset, such as ⟨*grappe*⟩ and ⟨*gratter*⟩. Thus, for the *Choose* stage of

---

[18]The exception is CRĀTĪCULAM > ⟨*grille*⟩, due to irregular hiatus behavior after the loss of the interdental fricative /ð/, reflex of /t/. The only other words with EOF sequence /ˌað'i/ show different but also irregular behavior. See also CLADĒBON >·· ·>⟨*glaive*⟩ and TRĀDITOR >·· ·>⟨*traitre*⟩, which are similarly nearby a vanishing /ð/, and also display irregularity. These suggest there something *else* to fix, not that our otherwise well corroborated proposal is wrong.

[19]Specific lexemes that tend to precede nouns are especially relevant here: the conjunction ET (</eθ/), the prepositions ⟨*à*⟩ (< /aθ/), the articles ⟨*ce*⟩ (< ⟨*cel*⟩), ⟨*ceci*⟩ and ⟨*ci*⟩ (< /t͡six/), and ⟨*cela*⟩ (*ce* + *là* < /lax/).

[20]The reflex of Latin CRASSIA is still attested as ⟨*craisse*⟩ in 1100 but is attested as ⟨*graisse*⟩ in 1150 (ATILF, 2019d), thus falling into line with ⟨*grappe*⟩ (1121) (ATILF, 2019e; ATILF, 2019f), ⟨*glaive*⟩ (1121) (ATILF, 2019b), ⟨*glas*⟩ (1140) (ATILF, 2019c) and so forth.

PATCH, we uphold our proposed fix.

Pope (Pope, 1934, p. 69) is likely correct that there was at one point a *synchronic* tendency of such form, the *diachronic* effect became phonologized later, late enough to be bled by the loss of /a/ in both of our bleeding cases, hence why we nevertheless have ⟨*clou*⟩ (< CLAVUM), ⟨*clore*⟩ (< CLAUDERE), ⟨*claire*⟩ < CLĀRAM, and so forth.

A possible criticism is that we could in fact be "overfitting" specifications on a sound law to the data. One may note that there would be a double standard in the application of this critique, because the traditional view has enshrined into the academic canon a large number of highly specific sound laws, or even sets of sound laws that explain only a few words, in this case and others[21] To reply, we in turn ask, "what is more likely"? According to the current view in the French diachronic literature, each one of these words is explained by different, highly specific, and sometimes rather elaborate explanations. What is more likely, that each of these words was the result of a different obscure effect perhaps involving two stages of language contact, or that an easily explained shift that we demonstrate here that leaves no exceptions gives a single, simple, and unified explanation?

Nevertheless, it is also difficult to conclusively "disprove" this critique. We do agree that future work should incorporate a measure of *overall complexity* as discussed in section 4.2., but even without this, we maintain that our method actually favors the simplest and most likely explanation much more than the traditional method, because it focuses on finding new rules that correct large numbers of derivations simultaneously whereas the traditional method not only tolerates but turns a blind eye to the proliferation of lexically specific explanations. As such, we propose that adopting CFR alongside traditional methods would in fact work against "overfitting".

8. Conclusion

We maintain that we have clearly demonstrated the utility of computerized forward simulation (CFR) for calibrating diachronic rule cascades. The magnitude of improvement, from a baseline accuracy of 3.2% up to an improved accuracy of 84.9%, was far better than we expected. Equally important however is that applying the PATCH methodology with CFR not only reproduces conclusions in literature coming after Pope (1934), but also contributes new insights even for a language as well studied as French. That the epoch with, by far, the highest density of corrections was Gallo-Roman demonstrates the utility of our method for less well-studied languages, because Gallo-Roman is the only era without a substantial attested corpus.

The next step for CFR with PATCH is to take it out of the lab and into the field. We strongly advise the adoption of transparent computerized forward reconstruction, for the clear advantages it offers in efficiency, accuracy, accountability, and coverage. Furthermore, for the overwhelming majority of the world's languages which remain vastly understudied, our method offers a way to speed up research into diachronic phonology and by extension phylogeny, allowing us to advance our knowledge further before the majority of them likely become moribund in the next century.

9. Bibliographical References

Adams, J. N. (2007). *The regional diversification of Latin 200 BC-AD 600*. Cambridge University Press.

ATILF. (2019a). `http://atilf.atilf.fr/`. Accessed December 16 2018.

ATILF. (2019b). glaive. `https://www.cnrtl.fr/definition/glaive/`. Accessed August 29, 2019.

ATILF. (2019c). glas. `https://www.cnrtl.fr/definition/glas/`. Accessed August 29, 2019.

ATILF. (2019d). graisse. `https://www.cnrtl.fr/definition/graisse/`. Accessed August 29, 2019.

ATILF. (2019e). grappe. `https://www.cnrtl.fr/definition/grappe/`. Accessed August 29, 2019.

ATILF. (2019f). Grappe : Attestation dans frantext. `http://atilf.atilf.fr/scripts/dmfAAA.exe?LGERM_FORMES_LEMME;FLEMME=GRAPPE1;FRANTEXT=1;XMODE=STELLa;FERMER;ISIS=isis_dmf2015.txt;MENU=menu_dmf;OUVRIR_MENU=1;ONGLET=dmf2015;001=2;002=1;003=-1;s=s133936ac;LANGUE=FR;FERMER`. Accessed December 23, 2019.

ATILF. (2019g). gras. `https://www.cnrtl.fr/definition/gras/`. Accessed August 29, 2019.

Banniard, M. (2001). Causes et rythmes du changement langagier en occident latin (iiie-viiie s.)(causes and rhythms of language change in the latin occident [3rd-8th centuries]). *Travaux Neuchatelois de Linguistique (Tranel)*, 34(35):85–99.

Borin, L. (1988). A computer model of sound change: An example from Old Church Slavic. *Literary and Linguistic Computing*, 3(2):105–108.

Bourciez, E. (1971). Phonétique française.

Brunot, F. and Charlier, G. (1927). Histoire de la langue française des origines à 1900, t. vii. la propagation du français en france jusqu'à la fin de l'ancien régime. *Revue belge de Philologie et d'Histoire*, 6(1):326–330.

Burton-Hunter, S. K. (1976). Romance etymology: A computerized model. *Computers and the Humanities*, 10(4):217–220.

Cerquiglini, B. (2018). *Une langue orpheline*. Minuit.

Chomsky, N. and Halle, M. (1968). *The Sound Pattern of English*. Harper& Row, New York.

Diefenbach, L. (1831). *Ueber die jetzigen romanischen Schriftsprachen, die spanische, portugiesische, rhätoromanische, in der Schweiz, französische, italiaänische nd dakoromaische, in mehren Ländern des östlichen Europa, mit Vorbemerkungen über Entstehung, Verwandtschaft usw dieses, Sprachstammes*. Ricker.

Diez, F. (1836). Grammatik der romanischen sprachen, 3 vols. *Bonn: Weber (3rd ed. 1870–1872)*.

---

[21]Indeed, ⟨*glas*⟩ is supposedly explained by a lexically specific rule that only affected other words indirectly through sporadic analogy, despite that rule working better as a broader and regular rule, as we have just demonstrated. This, plus all the other lexically specific explanations, is not in line with Occam's razor at all.

Dunn, M. (2015). Language phylogenies. In *The Routledge handbook of historical linguistics*, pages 208–229. Routledge.

Eastlack, C. L. (1977). Iberochange: a program to simulate systematic sound change in Ibero-Romance. *Computers and the Humanities*, 11(2):81–88.

Fouché, P. (1961). *Phonétique historique du français: Les consonnes et index général*, volume 3. Klincksieck.

Gildea, D. and Jurafsky, D. (1995). Automatic induction of finite state transducers for simple phonological rules. In *Proceedings of the 33rd annual meeting on Association for Computational Linguistics*, pages 9–15. Association for Computational Linguistics.

Gleason, H. A. (1959). Counting and calculating for historical reconstruction. *Anthropological Linguistics*, pages 22–32.

Hall, T. A. (2007). Segmental features. *The Cambridge handbook of phonology*, pages 311–334.

Hartman, L. (2003). Phono (version 4.0): Software for modeling regular historical sound change. In *Actas: VIII Simposio Internacional de Comunicación Social: Santiago de Cuba*, pages 20–24.

Hock, H. H. (2009). *Principles of historical linguistics*. Walter de Gruyter.

Hombert, J.-M., Mouele, M., and Seo, L.-W. (1991). Outils informatiques pour la linguistique historique bantu. *Pholia*, page 131.

Jäger, G. (2019). Computational historical linguistics. *Theoretical Linguistics*, 45(3-4):151–182.

Johnson, C. D. (1972). *Formal aspects of phonological description*. Mouton & Co. NN.

Kaplan, R. M. and Kay, M. (1981). Phonological rules and finite-state transducers. In *Linguistic Society of America Meeting Handbook, Fifty-Sixth Annual Meeting*, pages 27–30.

Kiparsky, P. and Good, J. (1968). Linguistic universals and language change. *Universals in linguistic theory*, pages 170–202.

Kondrak, G. (2002). *Algorithms for language reconstruction*. Ph.D. thesis, University of Toronto.

Kondrak, G. (2003). Phonetic alignment and similarity. *Computers and the Humanities*, 37(3):273–291.

Lodge, R. A. et al. (2004). *A sociolinguistic history of Parisian French*. Cambridge University Press.

Lodge, R. A. (2013). *French: From dialect to standard*. Routledge.

Lowe, J. B. and Mazaudon, M. (1994). The reconstruction engine: a computer implementation of the comparative method. *Computational Linguistics*, 20(3):381–417.

Lusignan, S. (1986). *Parler vulgairement: les intellectuels et la langue française aux XIIIe et XIVe siècles*, volume 1. Librairie philosophique J. Vrin; Montréal: Presses de l'Université de Montréal.

Maniet, A. (1985). Un programme de phonologie diachronique: de l'«indo-européen» au latin par ordinateur; version définitive. *Cahiers de l'Institut de linguistique de Louvain*, 11(1-2):203–243.

Marchot, P. (1901). *Petite phonétique du français prélittéraire (VIe-Xe siècles)*. B. Veith.

Marr, C. and Mortensen, D. (2020). Large-scale computerized forward reconstruction yields new perspective in french diachronic phonology. unpublished.

Martinet, A. (1952). Celtic lenition and Western Romance consonants. *Language*, 28(2):192–217.

Martinet, A. (1970). Economie des changements phonétiques.

Meyer-Lübke, W. (1899). *Grammatik der romanischen Sprachen*, volume 1. Georg Olms Verlag.

Mortensen, D. R., Littell, P., Bharadwaj, A., Goyal, K., Dyer, C., and Levin, L. (2016). PanPhon: A resource for mapping ipa segments to articulatory feature vectors. In *Proceedings of COLING 2016, the 26th International Conference on Computational Linguistics: Technical Papers*, pages 3475–3484.

Muzaffar, T. B. (1997). *Computer simulation of Shawnee historical phonology*. Ph.D. thesis, Memorial University of Newfoundland.

Noske, R. (2011). L'accent en proto-français: arguments factuels et typologiques contre l'influence du francique. In *Congrès Mondial de Linguistique Française 2008*, pages 307–320. Institut de Linguistique Française, Paris.

Nyrop, K. (1914). *Grammaire historique de la langue française*, volume 1. Gyldendal.

Piwowarczyk, D. (2016). Abstract: A computational-linguistic approach to historical phonology. *New Developments in the Quantitative Study of Languages*, page 70.

Pope, M. K. (1934). *From Latin to Modern French with especial consideration of Anglo-Norman: Phonology and morphology*. Manchester University Press.

Posner, R. et al. (1997). *Linguistic change in French*. Oxford University Press.

Posner, R. (1996). *The Romance languages*. Cambridge University Press.

Posner, R. (2011). 'phonemic overlapping and repulsion revisited. *General and Theoretical Linguistics*, 7:235.

Rey, A. (2013). *Dictionnaire historique de la langue française*. Le Robert.

Short, I. R. (2013). *Manual of Anglo-Norman*, volume 8. Anglo-Norman Text Society.

Sims-Williams, P. (2018). Mechanising historical phonology. *Transactions of the Philological Society*, 116(3):555–573.

Smith, R. N. (1969). A computer simulation of phonological change. *ITL-Tijdschrift voor Toegepaste Linguistiek*, 5(1):82–91.

Suchier, H. (1893). *Altfranzösische Grammatik*. M. Niemeyer.

Swadesh, M. (1952). Lexico-statistic dating of prehistoric ethnic contacts: with special reference to North American Indians and Eskimos. *Proceedings of the American philosophical society*, 96(4):452–463.

Thurot, C. (1881). *De la prononciation française depuis le commencement du XVIe siècle: d'après les témoinages des grammairiens*, volume 1. Impr. nationale.

Using LatInfLexi for an Entropy-Based Assessment of Predictability in Latin Inflection

Matteo Pellegrini
Università di Bergamo
piazza Rosate 2 – 24129 Bergamo (BG) – Italia
matteo.pellegrini@unibg.it

Abstract

This paper presents LatInfLexi, a large inflected lexicon of Latin providing information on all the inflected wordforms of 3,348 verbs and 1,038 nouns. After a description of the structure of the resource and some data on its size, the procedure followed to obtain the lexicon from the database of the Lemlat 3.0 morphological analyzer is detailed, as well as the choices made regarding overabundant and defective cells. The way in which the data of LatInfLexi can be exploited in order to perform a quantitative assessment of predictability in Latin verb inflection is then illustrated: results obtained by computing the conditional entropy of guessing the content of a paradigm cell assuming knowledge of one wordform or multiple wordforms are presented in turn, highlighting the descriptive and theoretical relevance of the analysis. Lastly, the paper envisages the advantages of an inclusion of LatInfLexi into the LiLa knowledge base, both for the presented resource and for the knowledge base itself.

Keywords: Lexicon, Morphology, Paradigm, Predictability, Entropy

1. Introduction

This paper presents LatInfLexi, an inflected lexicon of Latin verbs and nouns, and shows its place in the larger field of resources for the Latin language in general, and its usefulness in allowing for an entropy-based analysis of predictability in verb inflection in particular.

In studies on morphological theory, inflected wordforms are often considered to be composed of smaller, meaningful units, morphemes. Such an approach to word structure has been called 'constructive' by Blevins (2006; 2016). In this perspective, the goal is analyzing how exactly the relevant units are assembled in order to realize different Morphosyntactic Property Sets (MPS) for a given lexical item, in a 'syntagmatic' (Boyé and Schalchli, 2016), 'exponence-based' (Stump, 2015) fashion. Conversely, a different line of research, finding its roots in work on the implicative structure of paradigms within the framework of Natural Morphology (Wurzel, 1984), takes full inflected wordforms as the starting point, with smaller units possibly inferred only *a posteriori*, in an 'abstractive' (Blevins, 2006; Blevins, 2016) perspective. Similar approaches can be defined as implicative, in Stump (2015)'s terms, and 'paradigmatic', in Boyé and Schalchli (2016)'s terms: the focus is on implicative relations between wordforms, allowing to infer the content of a given paradigm cell assuming knowledge of the content of other cells.

This task has been stated in the question that Ackerman et al. (2009) call the 'Paradigm Cell Filling Problem' (PCFP): «What licenses reliable inferences about the inflected (and derived) surface forms of a lexical item?». In the last decade, this question has received remarkable attention in the morphological literature, especially within two related but different frameworks. A set-theoretic approach is represented by Stump and Finkel (2013)'s Principal Part Analysis, that aims at finding sets of inflected wordforms ('Principal Part Sets') from which the content of the whole paradigm of a lexeme can be inferred. Another way of tackling the PCFP is quantifying the contri-

bution of each inflected wordform to predictability, estimating the uncertainty in guessing the content of individual cells, rather than trying to fill the whole paradigm as in Principal Part Analysis. This second possibility has been modelled in information-theoretic terms, using conditional entropy (Ackerman et al., 2009). In this way, it is also possible to weigh the impact of different inflectional patterns according to their type frequency (Bonami and Boyé, 2014; Beniamine, 2018).

However, this presupposes the availability of large, representative inflected lexicons for the languages under investigation. Indeed, similar resources are being increasingly developed for modern Indo-European languages: see, among else, the CELEX database (Baayen et al., 1996) for Dutch, English, and German, Flexique (Bonami et al., 2014) and GLÀFF (Hathout et al., 2014) for French, Morph-it! (Zanchetta and Baroni, 2005) and GLÀFF-IT (Calderone et al., 2017) for Italian. The availability of inflected lexicons is much more limited for historical languages like Latin, despite the growing amount of resources and NLP tools developed for such languages in the last years (Piotrowski, 2012; Bouma and Adesam, 2017), among which also lexical resources, like the derivational lexicon Word Formation Latin (Litta et al., 2016). As for inflected lexicons, the only easily available resource is the one provided within the Unimorph[1] project (Sylak-Glassman et al., 2015). However, the data of this resource display issues of lack of homogeneity and systematicity, due to the collaborative design of the source from which they are taken, namely Wiktionary. On the other hand, it would be possible to obtain an inflected lexicon without such shortcomings semi-automatically, using the information contained in morphological analyzers such as *Words*,[2] *Morpheus*,[3] *LatMor*,[4] and the PROIEL Latin morphology

---

[1] http://unimorph.org/.
[2] http://archives.nd.edu/words.html.
[3] https://github.com/tmallon/morpheus.
[4] http://cistern.cis.lmu.de.

system.[5]

This paper details, in Section 2., the procedure that was followed to exploit one of these morphological analyzers – namely, the recently renewed Lemlat 3.0 (Passarotti et al., 2017) – in order to obtain LatInfLexi, a paradigm-based inflected lexicon of Latin. Section 3. shows how the data in LatInfLexi allow for a quantitative, entropy-based analysis of predictability in Latin verb inflection that on the one hand recovers traditional notions such as Principal Parts on a more solid ground, on the other hand sheds new light on Latin paradigm structure, revealing patterns of inter-predictability between wordforms that are less trivial than the ones that are usually identified. Section 4. discusses the possible use of LatInfLexi to enhance the LiLa knowledge base (Passarotti et al., 2019), providing information not only on wordforms that are attested in the texts included therein, but also on unattested, but nevertheless possible wordforms, also highlighting the advantages for LatInfLexi itself of a connection with the textual resources in LiLa. In conclusion, Section 5. summarizes the main points of the paper.

2. The Resource: LatInfLexi

This section is devoted to a careful description of LatInflexi, starting in 2.1. from a few words on its design and overall structure. Some quantitative data on the size of the resource and its coverage of the Latin lexicon are then given in 2.2.. In 2.3., the procedure followed to generate inflected wordforms from the information provided in Lemlat 3.0 is detailed, regarding both verbs and nouns. Lastly, 2.4. explains and motivates the choices made in the resource for cases of non-canonical filling of paradigm cells, namely defectiveness and overabundance.

2.1. Design

The overall structure of LatInfLexi is based on lexemes and paradigm cells, rather than on attested wordforms. This means that for each nominal and verbal[6] lexeme, we list all the paradigm cells, providing the following information for each of them:

- the lexeme to which the cell refers, notated through the citation form used in Lemlat;

- its PoS-tag and the MPS realized by the cell, notated through Petrov et al. (2011)'s 'Universal Part-Of-Speech Tagset' and the features used in the Universal Dependencies[7] project (Nivre et al., 2016);

- the inflected wordform filling the cell, in both orthographical and phonological, IPA, transcription;

- its frequency according to Tombeur (1998)'s *Thesaurus Formarum Totius Latinitatis*, across different epochs: *Antiquitas*, from the origins to the end of the 2nd century A.D.;

Aetas Patrum, from the 2nd century to 735; *Medium Aeuum*, from 736 to 1499; *Recentior Latinitas*, from 1500 to 1965.

2.2. Size

The selection of lexemes is frequency-based. LatInfLexi contains all the 3,348 verbs reported in the *Dictionnaire fréquentiel et Index inverse de la langue latine* (Delatte et al., 1981). Regarding nouns, only those with a frequency of 30 or more are kept, for a total of 1,038.

For each noun, a 12-cells paradigm is given, as generated by various combinations of different values of the inflectional categories of number – singular vs. plural – and case – nominative, genitive, dative, accusative, vocative, ablative. In the currently distributed version of LatInfLexi, the locative case is not considered because of its marginality, being attested almost only in names of towns and small islands. This exclusion is due to practical reasons: since the resource was originally conceived to allow for a quantitative analysis of predictability, for a cell attested in so few lexemes it would not have been possible to obtain significant results. However, the plan is to add the locative too, to make the resource more complete.

As for verbs, the provided paradigms are made up of 254 cells, generated by the combinations of values of tense-aspect (present, perfect, future, imperfect, pluperfect, future perfect), mood (indicative, subjunctive, imperative, infinitive), voice (active vs. passive), person and number. They include also nominal and adjectival forms inflected for case and (only the adjectival ones) for gender, for instance gerunds and participles. On the other hand, paradigm cells that are always filled analytically by means of a periphrasis, rather than with a dedicated, synthetic inflected wordform, are excluded: for instance, there is no cell PRF.PASS.IND.1SG, since passive perfective cells are always realized by means of a periphrasis composed by the perfect participle of the relevant verb and the appropriately inflected form of the verb 'to be', e.g. *amātus sum* 'I was loved'.

Table 1 summarizes some data on the overall size of the lexicon.

	verbs	nouns
lexemes	3,348	1,038
paradigm cells	850,392	12,456
wordforms	752,537	12,355
distinct wordforms	434,040	7,307

Table 1: The size of LatInfLexi

The number of wordforms does not match the number of cells because there are cells that are marked as defective (#DEF#) in LatInfLexi: they do not contain any inflected wordform. Further details on such cases can be found in 2.4. On the other hand, the difference between the sheer number of wordforms and the number of distinct wordforms is due to cases of more or less systematic syncretism, where the same surface wordform appears in different cells: for instance, in nominal inflection the dative and ablative plural are always realized in the same way. It is interesting to compare the number of distinct wordforms in our resource to the ones reported in the very extensive database of Tombeur (1998), that lists all the

---

[6] Adjectives have not been included in the current version because LatInfLexi was originally conceived to allow for an entropy-based analysis of verb and noun inflection, but the plan for the near future is to add adjectives too.

[7] http://universaldependencies.org/u/feat/index.html.

forms attested in a very large corpus of Latin, also providing information on their frequency in different epochs (see above, 2.1.). Out of the 554,828 wordforms attested in Tombeur (1998), 183,579 are present also in LatInfLexi, that thus cover for about one third of the forms of Tombeur (1998). This proportion is remarkable, especially considering that LatInfLexi only contains verbs and nouns, systematically excluding other lexical categories, even open ones like adjectives and adverbs. Furthermore, it should be noticed that LatInfLexi, thanks to its previously mentioned paradigm-based design, also contains many inflected wordforms (257,768 distinct wordforms) that are not attested in the texts on which Tombeur (1998) is based.

2.3.   Generation of Wordforms

The database of Lemlat 3.0, a large and recently renewed morphological analyzer for Latin, was exploited to generate full paradigms for all the lexemes of our sample. For each lemma, Lemlat reports one or more 'LExical Segment(s) (LES), roughly corresponding to the stem(s) appearing in the various inflected wordforms. Every LES is equipped with a CODLES, from which plenty of information can be inferred, for instance on the subset of paradigm cells where the CODLES can be used and on the inflectional endings that are compatible with it. As an example, for the verb STO 'stay', Lemlat lists the LESs and CODLESs given in Table 2 below.

LES	CODLES
st	v1i
ist	v1i
stet	v7s
stat	n41
stat	n6p1
statūr	n6p2

Table 2: LESs and CODLESs of STO 'stay'

The CODLES 'v1i' is used for LESs that correspond to the stem traditionally labelled as 'present stem', appearing in the so-called 'present system' – i.e., in imperfective cells – in intransitive ('i') 1ˢᵗ conjugation ('1') verbs ('v'). The CODLES 'v7s' instead marks LESs that correspond to the 'perfect stem', appearing in the 'perfect system' – i.e., in perfective cells. The remaining CODLESs identify stems used in nominal forms ('n'), namely the supine ('n41') and the perfect ('n6p1') and future ('n6p2') participle, corresponding to what Aronoff (1994) calls the 'third stem', and other stems derived from it, like the one of the future participle.

The first step of the procedure consists in extracting all LESs and CODLESs for each of the selected lexemes and matching them to the stems used in the principal parts provided by Latin dictionaries – in particular, Lewis and Short (1879), that is used as the primary source of information, due to its easy availability in machine-readable format. On the one hand, this allows to decide what LES should be selected in cases – like the one of Table 2 – where more than one LES with the same CODLES is present in Lemlat. For instance, the principal parts of STO in Lewis and Short (1879) are *stō*, *stetī* and *statum*, filling the cells PRS.ACT.IND.1SG, PRF.ACT.IND.1SG and SUP.ACC,

respectively. Therefore, between the two LESs with CODLES 'v1i' given in Table 2, only the first one is kept, since it corresponds to the stem appearing in the wordform used as principal part, while the second one is in Lemlat only because it is reported in dictionaries as a marginal variant sometimes attested in texts. On the other hand, the information that can be inferred from the principal parts of Lewis and Short (1879) and other dictionaries is more detailed than the one in Lemlat regarding the phonological shape of the stems, since there is also a coding of vowel length and of the distinction between the vowels /i/, /u/ (<i>, <u>) and the semivowels /j/, /w/ (<j>, <v>). Since our lexicon aims to be as surface-true as possible, the LESs of Lemlat are enhanced with this additional information. This also allows to automatically obtain phonological transcriptions in IPA notation.

After the extraction of LESs, by attaching the endings of the 1ˢᵗ conjugation to the ones with CODLES 'v1i', the imperfective forms of the present system are generated – but not the passive ones, that are defective because the verb is intransitive, except for the ones referring to the third-person singular, attested in an impersonal usage (e.g. *stātur* 'one stays'). The LESs with CODLES v7s can be used to generate perfective forms of the perfect system, again by attaching the appropriate endings, that are the same for all conjugations. The other LESs are used to generate supine and participial wordforms, adding the relevant nominal/adjectival endings. The procedure is illustrated in Table 3 below.

LES	CODLES	cell	wordform
st	v1i	PRS.ACT.IND.1SG	*st-ō*
		PRS.ACT.IND.3SG	*st-at*
		PRS.PASS.IND.1SG	#DEF#
		PRS.PASS.IND.3SG	*st-ātur*
		…	…
stet	v7s	PRF.ACT.IND.1SG	*stet-ī*
		PRF.ACT.IND.3SG	*stet-it*
		…	…
stat	n41	SUP.ACC	*stat-um*
		SUP.ABL	*stat-ū*
stat	n6p1	PRF.PTCP.NOM.M.SG	*stat-us*
		…	…
statūr	n6p2	FUT.PTCP.NOM.M.SG	*statūr-us*
		…	…

Table 3: Generation of some inflected wordforms of STO 'to stay'

The procedure followed for nouns was very similar, the only difference being that for a given lexeme there are not multiple LESs with different CODLESs to be used in different sections of the paradigm, but only one (or more) LES with a CODLES corresponding to the inflectional (sub)class. In most cases, all the inflected wordforms can be generated from the LES and CODLES alone. For instance, Table 4 and Table 5 illustrate the generation of some wordforms of the 1ˢᵗ declension noun ROSA 'rose' and of the 5ᵗʰ declension noun RES 'thing', respectively.

On the other hand, in 3ʳᵈ declension nouns and in some 2ⁿᵈ declension nouns, a different stem allomorph appears in some cells, namely NOM.SG and VOC.SG in masculine and feminine nouns and ACC.SG too in neuter nouns, where this cell is systematically syncretic with NOM.SG and VOC.SG.

LES	CODLES	cell	wordform
ros	n1	NOM.SG	*ros-a*
		GEN.SG	*ros-ae*
		ACC.SG	*ros-am*
		…	…

Table 4: Generation of some inflected wordforms of ROSA 'rose'

LES	CODLES	cell	wordform
r	n5	NOM.SG	*r-ēs*
		GEN.SG	*r-eī*
		ACC.SG	*r-em*
		…	…

Table 5: Generation of some inflected wordforms of RES 'thing'

Differently than what happens for verbs, the shape of this allomorph is not explicitly coded with a dedicated LES and a specific CODLES. However, in Lemlat, for all lemmas, under the heading LEM, information on how to produce the citation form is provided. Since the citation form used for nouns is exactly NOM.SG, and the other cells are syncretic with NOM.SG whenever they display a different allomorph, this information was exploited to fill the cells displaying stem allomorphy in our resource, as illustrated below in Table 6 by the allomorphic 2nd declension noun APER 'boar' and in Table 7 by the 3rd declension noun AGMEN 'multitude (of men/animals)'.

LES	CODLES	LEM	cell	wordform
apr	n2	aper	NOM.SG	*aper*
			GEN.SG	*apr-ī*
			ACC.SG	*apr-um*
			…	…

Table 6: Generation of some inflected wordforms of APER 'boar'

LES	CODLES	LEM	cell	wordform
agmin	n3	agmen	NOM.SG	*agmen*
			GEN.SG	*agmin-is*
			ACC.SG	*agmen*
			…	…

Table 7: Generation of some inflected wordforms of AGMEN 'multitude (of men/animals)'

2.4. Defectiveness and Overabundance

As was hinted above, LatInfLexi aims at providing full paradigms for all its lexemes. Therefore, every paradigm cell is filled with a wordform, whenever this is possible. This choice is reasonable, since in the usual, 'canonical' (Corbett, 2005) situation each paradigm cell is expected to be realized by exactly one inflected wordform.

However, it is a well-known fact that there are non-canonical cases of defectiveness (Sims, 2015), i.e. empty cells, for which the corresponding inflected wordform is not only unattested, but indeed non-existent. For instance, in Latin intransitive verbs are defective of passive wordforms, except for the third-person singular that can be used with an impersonal meaning (cf. above, 2.3., Table 3). Conversely, deponent verbs (Grestenberger, 2019) are always defective of morphologically active wordforms. Impersonal verbs only display third-person singular wordforms, as well as infinitives, gerunds and participles, but are systematically defective in all other cells. Regarding nouns, *pluralia tantum* do not have singular wordforms. In all such cases, the defective paradigm cells are not filled with a wordform, but simply marked as such (#DEF#) in LatInfLexi. In verb paradigms, also cells for which the stem that should be used to generate the corresponding wordform is not reported in Lemlat are marked as defective: for instance, for the verb ALBEO 'to be white', only the LES corresponding to the present stem is reported in Lemlat, thus perfective forms and the nominal forms based on the third stem are marked as #DEF#.

Another non-canonical phenomenon concerning paradigms is overabundance – multiple filling of the same cell by different wordforms (Thornton, 2019). In the current version of LatInfLexi, each non-defective cell contains exactly one wordform. In cases where more than one wordform could potentially be generated for the same paradigm cell – either because more than one LES with the same CODLES is available, or because different endings would be compatible with a given LES – a choice was made on which wordform to keep and which one(s) to discard, based on the principal parts reported in dictionaries in the former case (as showed above in 2.3.), while in the latter case the wordforms outputted in the inflectional tables of the Collatinus toolkit[8] are used.

3. An Entropy-Based Assessment of Predictability in Latin Verb Paradigms

This section illustrates how the data of LatInfLexi can be used for a quantitative, entropy-based analysis of predictability in Latin verb inflection. After an explanation, in 3.1., of the procedure that was followed, the results obtained on Latin verb paradigms are presented in 3.2., first focusing on predictions from one form (3.2.1.) and then extending the investigation to predictions from more than one form (3.2.2.).

3.1. The Method

In general, entropy (H) is a measure of uncertainty about the outcome of a random variable: the more the uncertainty, the higher the entropy value. Entropy increases with the number of possible outcomes: for instance, the entropy of a coin flip, with two possible outcomes, is higher than the entropy of rolling a dice, where the possible outcomes are six. Conversely, entropy decreases if the different outcomes are not equiprobable: the entropy of a coin flip is lower if the coin is rigged to always or often come up heads. Bonami and Boyé (2014) propose a method to estimate the uncertainty in predicting one cell from another one by means of conditional entropy – $H(A|B)$, a measure of the uncertainty about the outcome of a random variable A, given the value of another random variable B. To illustrate

---

their procedure, let us consider in Table 8 the phonological shape of the inflected wordforms filling the paradigm cells PRS.ACT.IND.1SG and PRS.ACT.IND.2SG for Latin verbs belonging to different conjugations, explaining how the conditional entropy of guessing the latter given the former can be computed.

lexeme	conj.	PRS.ACT. IND.1SG	PRS.ACT. IND.2SG
AMO 'love'	1st	amoː	amaːs
MONEO 'warn'	2nd	moneoː	moneːs
SCRIBO 'write'	3rd	skriːboː	skriːbis
CAPIO 'take'	mix.[9]	kapioː	kapis
VENIO 'come'	4th	wenioː	weniːs

Table 8: PRS.ACT.IND.1SG and PRS.ACT.IND.2SG of Latin verbs of different conjugations

The first step of Bonami and Boyé (2014)'s methodology consists in extracting alternation patterns between the wordforms, and contexts where such alternation patterns can be applied, as the second column of Table 9 illustrates. The second step is a classification of lexemes according to the patterns that can potentially be applied, based on the phonological makeup of the patterns themselves and of the extracted contexts. The outcome of this classification is given in the third column of Table 9. Verbs of the 1st and 3rd conjugation are in the same class, because patterns 1 and 3 can both be applied to a PRS.ACT.IND.1SG ending in /oː/ preceded by a consonant; similarly, verbs of the 4th and mixed conjugation are in the same class, because faced with a PRS.ACT.IND.1SG ending in /ioː/ preceded by a consonant, both pattern 4 and pattern 5 can be applied.

lexeme	pattern/context (1SG ↔ 2SG)	applicable patterns	n. verbs
AMO	1. _oː ↔ _aːs / C_#	A. (1,3)	1,332
MONEO	2. _eoː ↔ _eːs / C_#	B. (2)	298
SCRIBO	3. _oː ↔ _is / C_#	A. (1,3)	1,152
CAPIO	4. _oː ↔ _s / i_#	C. (4,5)	132
VENIO	5. _ioː ↔ _iːs / C_#	C. (4,5)	169

Table 9: Information used to compute $H(PRS.ACT.IND.2SG|PRS.ACT.IND.1SG)$

Given these two cross-cutting classifications and information on the number of verbs in which the various alternation patterns occur (given in the last column of Table 9 with data taken from LatInfLexi), it is possible to compute the conditional entropy of guessing PRS.ACT.IND.2SG from PRS.ACT.IND.1SG in each of the classes based on applicable patterns, using the type frequency of alternation patterns as an estimate of their probability of application. In class B (see (1), b.) there is no uncertainty: given a PRS.ACT.IND.1SG in /eoː/, the PRS.ACT.IND.2SG cannot but be in /eːs/.[10] In classes A and C (cf. (1), a. and c.) there are competing patterns (1 vs. 3 and 4 vs. 5), and

therefore there is some uncertainty, whose impact can be quantified by means of the number of verbs in which each pattern occurs. The results regarding the different classes can then be put together – again weighing them on the basis of type frequency, as is shown in (1)d. – to obtain a single entropy value, estimating the uncertainty in guessing the content of PRS.ACT.IND.2SG knowing the wordform filling PRS.ACT.IND.1SG. This value is called 'implicative entropy' by Bonami (2014).

(1) $H(PRS.ACT.IND.2SG|PRS.ACT.IND.1SG)$

   a. Class A:
$$H = -\left(\left(\tfrac{1{,}332}{2{,}484} \times log_2 \tfrac{1{,}332}{2{,}484} \right) + \left(\tfrac{1{,}152}{2{,}484} \times log_2 \tfrac{1{,}152}{2{,}484} \right) \right) = 0.996$$

   b. Class B:
$$H = -(1 \times log_2 1)$$

   c. Class C:
$$H = -\left(\left(\tfrac{132}{301} \times log_2 \tfrac{132}{301} \right) + \left(\tfrac{169}{301} \times log_2 \tfrac{161}{309} \right) \right) = 0.989$$

   d. Overall:
$$H = \left(\tfrac{2{,}484}{3{,}083} \times 0.996 \right) + \left(\tfrac{298}{3{,}083} \times 0 \right) + \left(\tfrac{301}{3{,}083} \times 0.989 \right) = 0.899$$

This procedure has two crucial advantages with respect to other entropy-based quantitative measurements of inflectional predictability proposed in the literature (cf. e.g. Ackerman et al. (2009) and subsequent work). Firstly, this methodology takes the type frequency of different patterns into account, rather than relying on the simplifying assumption that all inflection classes are equiprobable. Secondly, it does not require a pre-existing classification of inflection classes, since alternation patterns and contexts can simply be inferred from the surface phonological shape of the inflected wordforms.

3.2. Applying the Method to Latin Verb Paradigms

Thanks to the freely available Qumin[11] toolkit (Beniamine, 2018), it is possible to automatically perform implicative entropy computations according to Bonami and Boyé (2014)'s procedure on all the inflected wordforms of LatInfLexi, obtaining the results that will be presented in the following sub-sections.

3.2.1. Predicting from One Form: Zones of Interpredictability in Latin Verb Inflection

To have a first overall picture of predictability in Latin verb paradigms, implicative entropy values are computed for each pair of cells. A first relevant fact that should be noticed is that for a lot pairs of cells (A,B) the entropy values of both $H(A|B)$ and $H(B|A)$ are null, meaning that knowing one of the two inflected wordforms involved, the other one can be predicted with no uncertainty, since they are in systematic covariation: for instance, given the present active infinitive of a verb, the cells of the imperfect active subjunctive can always be obtained by adding personal endings to it, no matter how irregular the infinitive, and vice-versa, as is shown in (2).

---

[9]The conjugation of CAPIO is called 'mixed', as in Dressler (2002), because it displays the endings of the 3rd conjugation in some cells and the endings of the 4th conjugation in other cells.

[10]For the sake of simplicity, in this example we disregard highly irregular verbs, as well as verbs whose PRS.ACT.IND.1SG ends in /eoː/ that belong to the 1st conjugation

and thus have PRS.ACT.IND.2SG in /eaːs/ (e.g. CREO 'create', PRS.ACT.IND.1SG *creō*, PRS.ACT.IND.2SG *creās*).

[11]`https://github.com/XachaB/Qumin`

(2) PRS.ACT.INF X ↔ PRS.ACT.SBJV.1SG X*m*

   a. AMO 'love':
      PRS.ACT.INF *amāre* ↔ PRS.ACT.SBJV.1SG *amārem*

   b. FERO 'bring':
      PRS.ACT.INF *ferre* ↔ PRS.ACT.SBJV.1SG *ferrem*

Similar categorical implicative relations can be exploited to obtain a mapping of the Latin verbal paradigm in zones of full interpredictability: within such zones, all cells can be predicted from one another with no uncertainty. This mapping is sketched in Table 10 (for active[12] verbal forms) and Table 11 (for nominal and adjectival forms) below, with cells that belong to the same zone sharing the same color and index (Z1-15), and different shades of the same color used to visualize zones that are closer to one another in terms of mutual predictability.

ACT	1SG	2SG	3SG	1PL	2PL	3PL
IPRF.IND	Z1	Z1	Z1	Z1	Z1	Z1
IPRF.SBJV	Z2	Z2	Z2	Z2	Z2	Z2
PRS.IMP		Z3			Z2	
PRS.IND	Z4	Z5	Z6	Z2	Z2	Z7
FUT.IMP		Z2	Z2		Z2	Z7
FUT.IND	Z8	Z8	Z8	Z8	Z8	Z8
PRS.SBJV	Z9	Z9	Z9	Z9	Z9	Z9
PRF.IND	Z10	Z10	Z10	Z10	Z10	Z10
PLUPRF.IND	Z10	Z10	Z10	Z10	Z10	Z10
FUTPRF.IND	Z10	Z10	Z10	Z10	Z10	Z10
PRF.SBJV	Z10	Z10	Z10	Z10	Z10	Z10
PLUPRF.SBJV	Z10	Z10	Z10	Z10	Z10	Z10

Table 10: Zones of interpredictability in Latin verb paradigms: verbal forms (active only)

				GDV	PRS. PTCP	PRF. PTCP	FUT. PTCP
PRS.INF.ACT	Z2	NOM.SG		Z12	Z13	Z14	Z15
PRS.INF.PASS	Z11	GEN		Z12	Z12	Z14	Z15
PRF.INF.ACT	Z10	DAT		Z12	Z12	Z14	Z15
GER.GEN	Z12	ACC		Z12	Z12	Z14	Z15
GER.DAT	Z12	VOC.N.SG		Z12	Z13	Z14	Z15
GER.ACC	Z12	VOC.M/F.SG		Z12	Z12	Z14	Z15
GER.ABL	Z12	ABL		Z12	Z12	Z14	Z15
SUP.ACC	Z14	NOM.PL		Z12	Z12	Z14	Z15
SUP.ABL	Z14	VOC.PL		Z12	Z12	Z14	Z15

Table 11: Zones of interpredictability in Latin verb paradigms: nominal and adjectival forms

Therefore, although the sheer number of cells in Latin verb paradigms is very high, in many cases the presence of different wordforms does not contribute to uncertainty in the PCFP, since such wordforms can be predicted from other wordforms in the same zone. In this way, the 254-cells paradigm of LatInfLexi can be reduced to only 15 zones between which there is not full interpredictability. To go into some more detail, Z10 corresponds to what traditional descriptions call the 'perfect system', containing cells based on the perfect stem. The cells that Aronoff

---

^[12] Passive wordforms can be inferred from their active counterpart with no uncertainty, and they are therefore not reported in Table 10 for reasons of space.

(1994) identifies as based on the 'third stem' correspond to two different zones (Z14 and Z15) in our mapping because there actually are a few cases where the future participle is based on a different stem than the perfect participle and supine (e.g. PRF.PASS.PTCP.NOM.SG *mortu-us* vs. FUT.ACT.PTCP.NOM.M.SG *morit-ūrus*). As for what traditional descriptions label the 'present system', containing imperfective wordforms based on the present stem, it proves to be split between several (13) zones. This happens because with the adopted methodology not only the uncertainty generated by stem allomorphy is taken into account, but also the impact of the opacity of some endings with respect to inflection class assignment – witness the example provided above in Table 8, where the endings of PRS.ACT.IND.1SG are partly uninformative on the inflectional behavior of PRS.ACT.IND.2SG, because the ending -$ō$ is ambiguous between the 1st and 3rd conjugation, and the ending -$iō$ between the 4th and mixed conjugation.

It is interesting to observe that, if compared with the picture that would emerge by only considering the role of stem allomorphy, the mapping of the paradigm summarized in Table 10 and Table 11 is much more similar to the situation found in Romance verb inflection, with several zones of interpredictability, as shown e.g. by Bonami and Boyé (2003) for French, Pirrelli and Battista (2000) and Montermini and Bonami (2013) for Italian, Boyé and Cabredo Hofherr (2006) for Spanish. For instance, Table 10 shows that the cells PRS.ACT.IND.1SG and PRS.ACT.IND.3PL are very distant from the other present active indicative cells in terms of interpredictability. Thus, the overall picture is similar to the one produced by what Maiden (2018, pp. 84 ff.) calls 'U-pattern' in Romance languages. This suggests that there might be more continuity from Romance to Latin regarding paradigm structure than is usually assumed in diachronic accounts of this topic, like e.g. Maiden (2009).

Having identified these 15 zones of interpredictability, it is possible to take advantage of them to obtain a more compact version of the Latin paradigm, where only one cell per zone is kept. This allows to focus on the cases where there is some uncertainty and compare the different levels of predictability of different zones. To this aim, for each selected cell X, the values of average cell predictability – i.e., the average implicative entropy of predicting cell X knowing each of the other chosen cells – and average cell predictiveness – i.e., the average implicative entropy of predicting each of the other cells knowing cell X – are computed and given in Table 12a-b, sorted by decreasing entropy values. It can be observed that while the values of predictability are in a narrower range, the various zones display remarkable differences in their predictiveness: in particular, Z4 (the zone of the first-person singular of the present indicative) has a very low predictiveness, because of the above-mentioned opacity of the endings of that cell, that is poorly informative on the overall inflectional behavior of the lexemes (see again Table 8 above).

3.2.2. Predicting from More than One Form: (Near) Principal Parts

In the previous sub-section, the implicative entropy of guessing the content of one cell given knowledge of in-

a			b	
zone	average cell predictability		zone	average cell predictiveness
Z13	0.208271		Z8	0.079394
Z1	0.229066		Z7	0.089352
Z4	0.231378		Z9	0.127819
Z12	0.240871		Z2	0.130643
Z11	0.244131		Z3	0.13107
Z14	0.255304		Z5	0.166161
Z15	0.263901		Z11	0.189036
Z6	0.269721		Z15	0.257111
Z9	0.302484		Z14	0.266108
Z8	0.309003		Z1	0.3122
Z7	0.311636		Z12	0.348084
Z3	0.315026		Z6	0.355214
Z5	0.315126		Z13	0.370468
Z2	0.342413		Z10	0.442993
Z10	0.343957		Z4	0.916636

Table 12: Average cell predictability and predictiveness

dividual wordforms – what Bonami and Beniamine (2016) call 'unary implicative entropy' – was used in order to obtain an overall assessment of predictability in Latin verb paradigms. However, Bonami and Beniamine (2016) argue that, in languages with large paradigms, in many cases speakers are exposed to more than one inflected wordform of a lexeme without being exposed to all of them: therefore, it is reasonable to extend the investigation to predictions from more than one wordform, using what Bonami and Beniamine (2016) call 'n-ary (binary, ternary etc.) implicative entropy'. Table 13 compares average unary implicative entropy – i.e., the entropy of guessing paradigm cells from one another, averaged across all pairs of cells – with average n-ary implicative entropy at different cardinalities – i.e., using combinations of n forms as predictors. These results show that knowledge of multiple wordforms reduces uncertainty in the PCFP drastically: already with two predictors, the average implicative entropy value drops below 0.1, and with five predictors uncertainty is virtually eliminated.

cardinality	average implicative entropy
1	0.28
2	0.06
3	0.03
4	0.02
5	0.01

Table 13: Average n-ary implicative entropy

The idea of predictions from more than one form is what stands behind the traditional notion of principal parts and their contemporary and more principled recovery by Stump and Finkel (2013): in an entropy-based perspective, principal parts are sets of inflected wordforms knowing which the entropy of guessing the content of all the remaining cells of the paradigm – what Bonami and Beniamine (2016) call 'residual uncertainty' – is exactly 0. As can be seen from Table 14 below, in Latin verb inflection there are no principal part sets composed of two or three paradigm cells. The smallest combinations of cells that work as principal parts are composed of four cells: there are 56 combinations of

four cells that allow to eliminate residual uncertainty. If five predictors are used, there are more principal part sets, both in absolute terms and in percentage on the number of possible combinations of cells.

cardinality	principal parts	
	n.	%
2	0	0
3	0	0
4	56	4.1%
5	336	11.2%

Table 14: Principal part sets at different cardinalities

This confirms on a more empirically-based ground the descriptions of Latin grammars and dictionaries, where the four principal parts are PRS.ACT.IND.1SG, PRS.ACT.IND.2SG, PRF.ACT.IND.1SG and, lastly, PRF.PASS.PTCP.NOM.M.SG or SUP.ACC, depending on the choices made by different authors.[13] Our results are also in line with the findings obtained by Finkel and Stump (2009) with a different, set-theoretic rather than information-theoretic, methodology: also in their study, four principal parts prove to be sufficient in order to be able to guess the rest of the paradigm with no uncertainty. An advantage of the information-theoretic methodology is that it makes it possible to take into consideration not only categorical principal parts, but also what Bonami and Beniamine (2016) call 'near principal parts', i.e., sets of cells that allow to infer the rest of the paradigm with very low – but not null – residual uncertainty. In Table 15, the threshold of residual uncertainty is set at 0.001 and 0.01, and the number and percentage of near principal parts at different cardinalities is reported.

cardinality	near principal parts			
	$H < 0.001$		$H < 0.01$	
	n.	%	n.	%
2	0	0	15	14.3%
3	15	3.3%	196	43.1%
4	122	8.9%	834	61.1%
5	471	15.7%	2,190	72.9%

Table 15: Near principal part sets at different cardinalities

It can be observed that already with the very low threshold of 0.001, there are sets of near principal parts composed of three cells. If the threshold is set at 0.01, there are even combinations of two cells that work as near principal parts; furthermore, almost half of the available combinations of three cells, more than half of the combinations of four cells, and the relevant majority of combinations of five cells allow to infer the rest of the paradigm with a residual uncertainty of less than 0.01. This means that knowledge of a limited number of cells yields a very relevant reduction of uncertainty in the PCFP, giving further confirmation to Ackerman and Malouf (2013)'s 'low entropy conjecture', according to which the surface complexity of the inflectional patterns of languages with a rich morphology – like Latin – does not make unpredictability in such systems so great as to make them hard to learn and master for speakers.

---

[13]Lewis and Short (1879) use only three principal parts, but only because the conjugation is stated explicitly.

4. Inclusion of LatInfLexi into the LiLa Knowledge Base

The topic of this section is a discussion of the perspectives opened by the planned inclusion of the data of LatInfLexi into the LiLa knowledge base (Passarotti et al., 2019). The goal of the LiLa (Linking Latin) project[14] is to connect and make interoperable the wealth of digital resources – like corpora and lexicons – and NLP tools – like lemmatizers, morphological analyzers and dependency parsers – that are already available for Latin. To this aim, LiLa makes use of a set of Semantic Web and Linguistic Linked Open Data standards, among which here at least the ontology used for lexical resources (Lemon, Buitelaar et al. (2011), Ontolex[15]) should be mentioned, that is based on the 'Lexical Entry' to which all the relevant forms can be associated. The architecture of LiLa thus has the 'lemma' as its core. A lemma is defined as an inflected 'form' that is conventionally chosen as the citation form of a lexical entry. Lemmas are then directly linked to 'tokens' – i.e., actual occurrences in textual resources. Both forms and tokens can be analyzed by NLP tools.

Within this architecture, it would be useful to make the coverage of LatInfLexi more systematic – adding also the nouns with less than 30 occurrences in Delatte et al. (1981) and including adjectives – and incorporate the wordforms reported in LatInfLexi in the knowledge base. Both LatInfLexi and the Lila knowledge base would benefit greatly from such interaction, due to their different design. The LiLa knowledge base takes a concrete perspective, including only wordforms that are either attested in corpora, or reported in lexical resources that are in turn based on actual usage in texts, like for instance Tombeur (1998). Conversely, we have seen in 2.1. that in LatInfLexi a much more abstract perspective drives the selection of different inflected wordforms: for each lexeme, the content of all non-defective paradigm cells is given, regardless of the actual attestation of the generated wordforms in actual texts. Therefore, the inclusion of the data of LatInfLexi into the LiLa knowledge base would greatly enrich the latter: lemmas would be linked to all their possible inflected wordforms, rather than only to attested ones. The relevance of such enrichment would be more relevant than one could think, since recent quantitative work on the attestation of inflected wordforms in large paradigms (Chan, 2008; Bonami and Beniamine, 2016; Blevins et al., 2017) shows that, even using very large corpora, 'saturation' – i.e., the situation in which all the inflected wordforms of a lexeme occur in a given corpus (Chan, 2008) – is reached only for a handful of very frequent lexemes, while in all other cases only some cells are actually filled by a wordform, and for many lexemes only a couple of wordforms are attested, or even only one. On the other hand, LatInfLexi too would benefit from being included into LiLa, because the linking of the possible wordforms of the former to the real occurrences in the lemmatized (and sometimes, e.g. in treebanks, even equipped with fine-grained morphosyntactic analyses) texts of the latter would allow for a more accurate assessment of the frequency of wordforms,[16] and thus for a more careful discrimination between forms that are possible but are not attested and those that actually occur in texts. This could also be useful in order to have a more satisfactory, corpus-based treatment of overabundance, where the marginality of a 'cell-mate' (Thornton, 2019) with respect to the other one(s) is not decided according to lexicographical sources, but rather on the basis of the actual usage of the competing wordforms in texts.

5. Conclusions

This paper has presented LatInfLexi, a large, freely available, paradigm-based inflected lexicon of Latin verbs and nouns, detailing how the wordforms have been generated starting from the information provided in the morphological analyzer Lemlat 3.0.

It has then illustrated the usefulness of such a lexicon, firstly to perform a quantitative analysis of predictability in inflectional morphology by means of the information-theoretic notion of implicative entropy. From this analysis, by means of unary implicative entropy a mapping of the verbal paradigm in 15 zones of complete interpredictability has been proposed: this picture is less straightforward than the traditional one, based on the three different stems appearing in the paradigm, and therefore more similar to the situation found in Romance verb paradigms, suggesting that there is more continuity from Latin to Romance than is traditionally assumed, at least if patterns of inter-predictability are considered. Secondly, n-ary implicative entropy has been used to recover the traditional notion of principal parts on more solid grounds, confirming the analysis of grammars and dictionaries in this respect, as well as results recently obtained for Latin verb inflection with Finkel and Stump (2009)'s Principal Part Analysis, but also highlighting the usefulness of extending the investigation to non-categorical 'near principal parts', that allow for a relevant – although not complete – reduction of residual uncertainty regarding other paradigm cells.

Lastly, another possible use of the resource that has been discussed in this paper is its inclusion in the LiLa knowledge base, that in this way would be enhanced with possible inflected wordforms that can be linked to lemmas, besides the ones attested in textual resources, while LatInfLexi would benefit from this interaction in that it would have access to more detailed frequency data.

6. Availability of Data and Tools

The data and tools used in this study are freely available online, allowing for an easy replication of the presented results. LatInfLexi can be found at `https://github.com/matteo-pellegrini/LatInfLexi`. The Qumin toolkit that was used to automatically perform entropy computations can be freely downloaded at `https://github.com/XachaB/Qumin`.

---

[14] `https://lila-erc.eu/`.

[15] `https://www.w3.org/community/ontolex/`.

[16] As we have seen in 2.1., LatInfLexi provides information on frequency, but with the same shortcomings of the source from which it takes it, Tombeur (1998), where there is no disambiguation of wordforms with multiple possible analyses. For a more detailed discussion of the issues related to frequency data in LatInfLexi, the reader is referred to Pellegrini and Passarotti (2018).

7. Bibliographical References

Ackerman, F. and Malouf, R. (2013). Morphological organization: The low conditional entropy conjecture. *Language*, 89(3):429–464.

Ackerman, F., Blevins, J. P., and Malouf, R. (2009). Parts and wholes: Patterns of relatedness in complex morphological systems and why they matter. In James P Blevins et al., editors, *Analogy in grammar: Form and acquisition*, pages 54–82. Oxford University Press, Oxford.

Aronoff, M. (1994). *Morphology by itself: Stems and inflectional classes*. MIT press, Cambridge.

Baayen, R. H., Piepenbrock, R., and Gulikers, L. (1996). The CELEX lexical database (cd-rom). University of Pennsylvania.

Beniamine, S. (2018). *Classifications flexionnelles. Étude quantitative des structures de paradigmes*. Ph.D. thesis, Université Sorbonne Paris Cité-Université Paris Diderot.

Blevins, J. P., Milin, P., and Ramscar, M. (2017). The zipfian paradigm cell filling problem. In Ferenc Kiefer, et al., editors, *Perspectives on Morphological Organization*, pages 139–158. Brill, Leiden-Boston.

Blevins, J. P. (2006). Word-based morphology. *Journal of Linguistics*, 42(3):531–573.

Blevins, J. P. (2016). *Word and paradigm morphology*. Oxford University Press, Oxford.

Bonami, O. and Beniamine, S. (2016). Joint predictiveness in inflectional paradigms. *Word Structure*, 9(2):156–182.

Bonami, O. and Boyé, G. (2003). Supplétion et classes flexionnelles. *Langages*, 37(152):102–126.

Bonami, O. and Boyé, G. (2014). De formes en thèmes. In Florence Villoing, et al., editors, *Foisonnements morphologiques. Études en hommage à Françoise Kerleroux*, pages 17–45. Presses Universitaires de Paris-Ouest, Paris.

Bonami, O., Caron, G., and Plancq, C. (2014). Construction d'un lexique flexionnel phonétisé libre du français. In *Congrès Mondial de Linguistique Française — CMLF 2014*, volume 8, pages 2583–2596. EDP Sciences.

Bonami, O. (2014). La structure fine des paradigmes de flexion. études de morphologie descriptive, théorique et formelle. Mémoire d'habilitation à diriger des recherches. Université Paris Diderot (Paris 7).

Bouma, G. and Adesam, Y. (2017). *Proceedings of the NoDaLiDa 2017 Workshop on Processing Historical Language*. Linköping University Electronic Press, Gothenburg.

Boyé, G. and Cabredo Hofherr, P. (2006). The structure of allomorphy in spanish verbal inflection. *Cuadernos de Lingüística del Instituto Universitario Ortega y Gasset*, 13:9–24.

Boyé, G. and Schalchli, G. (2016). The status of paradigms. In Andrew Hippisley et al., editors, *The Cambridge handbook of morphology*, pages 206–234. Cambridge University Press, Cambridge.

Buitelaar, P., Cimiano, P., McCrae, J., Montiel-Ponsoda, E., and Declerck, T. (2011). Ontology lexicalization: The lemon perspective. In *Proceedings of the Workshops-9th International Conference on Terminology and Artificial Intelligence (TIA 2011)*.

Calderone, B., Pascoli, M., Sajous, F., and Hathout, N. (2017). Hybrid method for stress prediction applied to GLÀFF-IT, a large-scale Italian lexicon. In *International Conference on Language, Data and Knowledge*, pages 26–41, Cham. Springer.

Chan, E. (2008). *Structures and distributions in morphology learning*. Ph.D. thesis, University of Pennsylvania.

Corbett, G. G. (2005). The canonical approach in typology. In Zygmunt Frajzyngier, et al., editors, *Linguistic diversity and language theories*, pages 25–49. John Benjamins, Amsterdam.

Delatte, L., Evrard, É., Govaerts, S., and Denooz, J. (1981). *Dictionnaire fréquentiel et index inverse de la langue latine*. LASLA, Liège.

Dressler, W. U. (2002). Latin inflection classes. In A Machtelt Bolkestein, et al., editors, *Theory and description in Latin linguistics*, pages 91–110. Brill, Leiden-Boston.

Finkel, R. and Stump, G. (2009). What your teacher told you is true: Latin verbs have four principal parts. *Digital Humanities Quarterly*, 3(1).

Grestenberger, L. (2019). Deponency in morphology. In *Oxford Research Encyclopedia of Linguistics*. Oxford University Press.

Hathout, N., Sajous, F., and Calderone, B. (2014). GLÀFF, a large versatile French lexicon. In *Proceedings of the Ninth International Conference on Language Resources and Evaluation (LREC '14)*, pages 1007–1012.

Lewis, C. and Short, C. (1879). *A Latin Dictionary*. Clarendon, Oxford.

Litta, E., Passarotti, M., and Culy, C. (2016). Formatio formosa est. Building a word formation lexicon for Latin. In *Proceedings of the Third Italian Conference on Computational Linguistics (CLiC-it 2016)*, pages 185–189.

Maiden, M. (2009). From pure phonology to pure morphology: the reshaping of the romance verb. *Recherches linguistiques de Vincennes*, 38:45–82.

Maiden, M. (2018). *The Romance verb: Morphomic structure and diachrony*. Oxford University Press, Oxford.

Montermini, F. and Bonami, O. (2013). Stem spaces and predictability in verbal inflection. *Lingue e linguaggio*, 12(2):171–190.

Nivre, J., De Marneffe, M.-C., Ginter, F., Goldberg, Y., Hajic, J., Manning, C. D., McDonald, R., Petrov, S., Pyysalo, S., Silveira, N., et al. (2016). Universal dependencies v1: A multilingual treebank collection. In *Proceedings of the Tenth International Conference on Language Resources and Evaluation (LREC '16)*, pages 1659–1666.

Passarotti, M., Budassi, M., Litta, E., and Ruffolo, P. (2017). The Lemlat 3.0 package for morphological analysis of Latin. In Gerlof Bouma et al., editors, *Proceedings of the NoDaLiDa 2017 Workshop on Processing Historical Language*, pages 24–31. Linköping University Electronic Press, Gothenburg.

Passarotti, M. C., Cecchini, F. M., Franzini, G., Litta, E., Mambrini, F., and Ruffolo, P. (2019). The LiLa knowledge base of linguistic resources and NLP tools for latin.

In *2nd Conference on Language, Data and Knowledge (LDK 2019)*, pages 6–11. CEUR-WS. org.

Pellegrini, M. and Passarotti, M. (2018). LatInfLexi: an inflected lexicon of Latin verbs. In *Proceedings of the Fifth Italian Conference on Computational Linguistics (CLiC-it 2018)*.

Petrov, S., Das, D., and McDonald, R. (2011). A universal part-of-speech tagset. *ArXiv*, pages 2089–2096.

Piotrowski, M. (2012). Natural language processing for historical texts. *Synthesis lectures on human language technologies*, 5(2):1–157.

Pirrelli, V. and Battista, M. (2000). The paradigmatic dimension of stem allomorphy in italian verb inflection: 2628. *Italian Journal of Linguistics*, 12(2):307–380.

Sims, A. D. (2015). *Inflectional defectiveness*. Cambridge University Press, Cambridge.

Stump, G. and Finkel, R. A. (2013). *Morphological typology: From word to paradigm*. Cambridge University Press, Cambridge.

Stump, G. (2015). *Inflectional paradigms: Content and form at the syntax-morphology interface*. Cambridge University Press, Cambridge.

Sylak-Glassman, J., Kirov, C., Post, M., Que, R., and Yarowsky, D. (2015). A universal feature schema for rich morphological annotation and fine-grained cross-lingual part-of-speech tagging. In *International Workshop on Systems and Frameworks for Computational Morphology*, pages 72–93, Cham. Springer.

Thornton, A. M. (2019). Overabundance: a canonical typology. In Francesco Gardani, et al., editors, *Competition in inflection and word-formation*, pages 223–258. Springer, Berlin.

Tombeur, P. (1998). *Thesaurus formarum totius Latinitatis: a Plauto usque ad saeculum XXum; TF.[2]. CETEDOC Index of Latin forms: database for the study of the vocabulary of the entire Latin world; base de données pour l'étude du vocabulaire de toute la latinité*. Brepols, Turnhout.

Wurzel, W. U. (1984). *Flexionsmorphologie und Natürlichkeit: ein Beitrag zur morphologischen Theoriebildung*. Akademie-Verlag, Berlin.

Zanchetta, E. and Baroni, M. (2005). Morph-it!: A free corpus-based morphological resource for the Italian language. In *Proceedings of corpus linguistics, http://dev.sslmit.unibo.it/ linguistics/morph-it.php*. Citeseer.

Proceedings of 1st Workshop on Language Technologies for Historical and Ancient Languages, pages 47–51
Language Resources and Evaluation Conference (LREC 2020), Marseille, 11–16 May 2020

A Tool for Facilitating OCR Postediting in Historical Documents

Alberto Poncelas, Mohammad Aboomar, Jan Buts, James Hadley, Andy Way

ADAPT Centre, School of Computing, Dublin City University, Ireland
Trinity Centre for Literary and Cultural Translation, Trinity College Dublin, Ireland
{alberto.poncelas, jan.buts andy.way}@adaptcentre.ie
{ABOOMARM, HADLEYJ}@tcd.ie

Abstract

Optical character recognition (OCR) for historical documents is a complex procedure subject to a unique set of material issues, including inconsistencies in typefaces and low quality scanning. Consequently, even the most sophisticated OCR engines produce errors. This paper reports on a tool built for postediting the output of Tesseract, more specifically for correcting common errors in digitized historical documents. The proposed tool suggests alternatives for word forms not found in a specified vocabulary. The assumed error is replaced by a presumably correct alternative in the post-edition based on the scores of a Language Model (LM). The tool is tested on a chapter of the book *An Essay Towards Regulating the Trade and Employing the Poor of this Kingdom* (Cary, 1719). As demonstrated below, the tool is successful in correcting a number of common errors. If sometimes unreliable, it is also transparent and subject to human intervention.

Keywords: OCR Correction, Historical Text, NLP Tools

1. Introduction

Historical documents are conventionally preserved in physical libraries, and increasingly made available through digital databases. This transition, however, usually involves storing the information concerned as images. In order to correctly process the data contained in these images, they need to be converted into machine-readable characters. This process is known as optical character recognition (OCR). Converting a book from image into text has obvious benefits regarding the identification, storage and retrieval of information. However, applying OCR usually generates noise, misspelled words and wrongly recognised characters. It is therefore often necessary to manually postedit the text after it has undergone the automatic OCR process. Usually, the errors introduced by the OCR tool increase with the age of the document itself, as older documents tend to be in worse physical condition. The circumstances of digitization, e.g. the quality of the scan and the mechanical typeset used, also impact the outcome of the OCR procedure. This paper proposes a tool for automatically correcting the majority of errors generated by an OCR tool. String-based similarities are used to find alternative words for perceived errors, and a Language Model (LM) is used to evaluate sentences. This tool has been made publicly available.[1]

The performance of the tool is evaluated by correcting the text generated when using OCR with the book *An Essay Towards Regulating the Trade and Employing the Poor of this Kingdom* (Cary, 1719).

2. Related Work

To improve the outcome of OCR, one can either focus on the processing of images in the scanned book, or on editing the output of the OCR tool. For either stage, several approaches have been proposed.

The approaches involving image-processing perform modifications on the scanned book that make the OCR perform better. Examples of these approaches include adding noise, as through rotation, for augmenting the training set (Bieniecki et al., 2007), reconstructing the image of documents in poor condition (Maekawa et al., 2019), clustering similar words so they are processed together (Kluzner et al., 2009) or jointly modeling the text of the document and the process of rendering glyphs (Berg-Kirkpatrick et al., 2013).

Techniques for increasing accuracy by performing post-OCR corrections can be divided into three sub-groups. The first group involves lexical error correction, and consists of spell-checking the OCR output using dictionaries, online spell-checking (Bassil and Alwani, 2012), and using rule-based systems for correcting noise (Thompson et al., 2015). The second group of strategies for correcting OCR output is context-based error correction, in which the goal is to evaluate the likelihood that a sentence has been produced by a native speaker by using an *n*-gram LM to evaluate the texts produced by the OCR (Zhuang et al., 2004), and to use a noisy-channel model (Brill and Moore, 2000), or a Statistical Machine Translation engine (Afli et al., 2016) to correct the output of the OCR. A final approach proposes using several OCR tools and retrieving the text that is most accurate (Volk et al., 2010; Schäfer and Weitz, 2012).

3. OCR Challenges for Historical Document

Performing OCR is a challenging task. Although ideally the procedure should successfully generate the text represented in an image, in practice the tools often produce errors (Lopresti, 2009). In addition, when older documents are converted into text further difficulties arise that cause the performance of the OCR tools to decrease. One of the problems of historical documents is that the quality of the print medium has often degraded over time. The quality of the paper also impacts the output, as in some cases the letters on the reverse side of a page are visible in the scanned image, which adds noise to the document.

---

[1] `https://github.com/alberto-poncelas/tesseract_postprocess`

Figure 1: Example of the scan of the book *An Essay Towards Regulating the Trade*.

Furthermore, OCR systems are generally best suited to contemporary texts, and not built to handle the typefaces and linguistic conventions that characterize older documents. In Figure 1 we show a small extract of a scan of the book *An Essay Towards Regulating the Trade* to illustrate some of the problems frequently encountered. One may notice the following particularities of the text:

- Some words such as *especially*, *whose* and *spent* contain the "ſ" or long "s", an archaic form of the letter "s" which can easily be confused with the conventional symbol for the letter "f".

- Some words, such as *Poor* and *Profits*, are capitalized even though they occur mid-sentence. This would be unusual in present-day English.

Piotrowski (2012) categorizes variations in spelling as uncertainty (digitization errors), variance (inconsistent spelling) and difference (spelling that differs from contemporary orthography). In our work we focus on the latter. Spelling issues compound the general challenges touched upon before, such as the quality of the scan (e.g. the word "us" in Figure 1 is difficult to read even for humans). Further issues include the split at the end of the line (e.g. the word "especially" or "generally").

4. Proposed Tool

This paper introduces a tool that automatically edits the main errors in the output of an OCR engine, including those described in Section 3.. The method retains, next to the edited text, the material that has been automatically replaced. Thus, the human posteditor has the agency to approve or discard the changes introduced by the tool. The aim of automating the initial replacement procedure is to shorten the overall time spent on post-editing historical documents.

In order to execute the tool, run the command `ocr_and_postprocess.sh $INPUT_PDF $OUT $INITPAGE $ENDPAGE`. In this command, `$INPUT_PDF` contains the path of the *pdf* file on which OCR will be performed, and `$OUT` the file where the output will be written. `$INITPAGE` and `$ENDPAGE` indicate from which page until which page the OCR should be executed.

The output is a file consisting of two columns (tab-separated). The first column contains the text after OCR is applied and the errors have been corrected. In the second column, we include the list of edits performed by our tool, so that a human post-editor can easily identify which words have been replaced.

The pipeline of this approach is divided into three steps, as further explained in the subsections below. First, the OCR is executed (Section 4.1.). Subsequently, words that are unlikely to exist in English are identified and replacement words are sought (Section 4.2.). Finally, the word-alternatives are evaluated within the larger sentence in order to select the best alternative (Section 4.3.).

4.1. Perform OCR

The first step is to extract part of the *pdf* and convert it into a list of *png* images (one image per page). These images are fed to an OCR engine and thus converted into text. The line-format in the text will conform to the shape of the image, meaning that word forms at the end of a line ending on an "-" symbol need to be joined to their complementary part on the following line to ensure completeness.

4.2. Get alternative words

As the output of the OCR tool is expected to contain errors, this text is compared to a list of English vocabulary referred to as *recognized words*.

Once the text is tokenized and lowercased, some of the words can be replaced by alternatives that fit better within the context of the sentence. The words that we want to replace are those that are not included in the list of *recognized words* or contain letters that are difficult to process by the OCR tool (as in the case of confusion between the letters "ſ" and "f" mentioned in Section 3.). For each of these words we construct a list of candidates for a potential replacement. This list is built as follows:

1. Even if a word seems to be included in the list *recognized words*, it still may contain errors, as some letters are difficult for the OCR to recognize. As per the above, "f" can be replaced with "s", and the resultant word can be added as a replacement candidate if it is a *recognized word*.

2. If the word is not in the list *recognized words*, we proceed along the following lines:

   (a) The word is split into two subwords along each possible line of division. If both items resulting from the split are recognized words, the pair of words is added as an alternative candidate.

   (b) Similar words in the vocabulary are suggested using a string-distance metric. The 3 closest words, based on the *get_close_matches* function of python's *difflib* library, are included.

After this step, for a word w_i we have a list of potential replacements $w_i, w_i^{(1)}, w_i^{(2)}...w_i^{(r_i)}$, where r_i is the number of alternatives for w_i. Note also that the original word is included as an alternative.

4.3. Replace words with their alternatives

Once we have obtained a list of alternatives, we proceed to evaluate which of the alternatives fits best within the context of the sentence. This means that given a sentence consisting of a sequence of N words $(w_1, w_2...w_N)$, the word

w_i is substituted in the sentence with each of its replacement candidates, and a set of sentences is obtained as in (1):

$$\{(w_1 \ldots w_i \ldots w_N),$$
$$(w_1 \ldots w_i^{(1)} \ldots w_N), \tag{1}$$
$$\ldots$$
$$(w_1 \ldots w_i^{(r_i)} \ldots w_N)\}.$$

The perplexity of an LM trained on an English corpus is used to evaluate the probability that a sentence has been produced by a native English speaker. Given a sentence consisting of a sequence of N words as $w_1, w_2 \ldots w_N$, the perplexity of a language model is defined as in Equation (2):

$$PP = 2^{-\frac{1}{n} P_{LM}(w_1 \ldots w_N)} \tag{2}$$

Note that the LM evaluation is performed with lowercased sentences. Once the sentence with the lower perplexity has been selected, the case is reproduced, even if the word has been replaced. This is relevant in the case of capitalization conventions, as related to words such as *Poor* or *Profits* in Figure 1.

5. Experiments

5.1. Experimental Settings

In order to evaluate our proposal, we use the Tesseract[2] Tool (Smith, 2007) to apply OCR to the book *An Essay Towards Regulating the Trade*. Specifically, we convert into text a scan of the chapter *An Act for Erecting of Hospitals and Work-Houses within the City of Bristol, for the better Employing and Maintaining the Poor thereof* (pages 125 to 139).

The list of *recognized words* consists of the vocabulary of the python package nltk[3], expanded with a list of 467K words[4] (DWYL, 2019). For each word that is not included in the vocabulary list we search for the closest 3 alternatives (based on a string-distance metric).

In order to evaluate which word-alternative is the most plausible in the sentence we use a 5-gram LM built with KenLM toolkit (Heafield, 2011), trained on the Europarl-v9 corpus (Koehn, 2005).

5.2. Results

The text obtained after applying OCR consists of 576 lines. These lines are usually short, containing about 7 words per line.

In Figure 2 we show an extract of the scanned book. The text obtained after OCR is given in Table 1 (in the first column). Comparing the resultant text with the original, one can easily spot errors mentioned in Section 3.,such as retrieving "fuch" instead of "such", and further irregularities, such as interpreting "time as" as a single word.

Figure 2: Extract from the test set.

Original	Edited	Changes
{uch timeas the faid Twenty Guardians fhall	{uch times the said Twenty Guardians shall	timeas $\rightarrow$ times; faid $\rightarrow$ said; fhall $\rightarrow$ shall
fo defire ; and on his Refutal, the faid	so desire; and on his Refutal, the said	fo $\rightarrow$ so; defire $\rightarrow$ desire; faid $\rightarrow$ said
Deputy-Governor for the time being, on fuch	Ex-governor for the time being, on such	Deputy-Governor $\rightarrow$ Ex-governor; fuch $\rightarrow$ such
fignification, fhall be Bound, and is hereby	fignification, shall be Bound, and is hereby	fhall $\rightarrow$ shall
ikewife Enjoyned and Required to Call and	likewise Enjoined and Required to Call and	ikewife $\rightarrow$ likewise; Enjoyned $\rightarrow$ Enjoined

Table 1: Example of postedited line

Table 1 also presents the text after being processed with our tool (second column). In the third column we include the substitution performed (this information is also retrieved by the tool). We observe that 66% of the lines contain at least one correction. Each line has a minimum of 0 and a maximum of 3 corrections.

The tool is generally successful in correcting the words in which the letter "f" and "f" were previously confused. Most frequent in this regard are word-initial errors for "shall", "so" and "said", but word-internal mistakes, as in "desire" (see second row), are not uncommon.

In the first row we observe that the word "timeas" is not recognized as part of the vocabulary. The tool finds that the item can be split into the English words "time" and "as". However, the tool also finds other options, and opts to render "times", thus requiring human intervention and illustrating the necessity of transparency in the automated procedure. In the last row, a non-existent word has been corrected as "likewise" because it is similar in terms of string-distance and is plausible according to the LM.

Table 2 presents some of the words that could not be found in the vocabulary (first column) and their respective candidates for replacement. The tool replaced these words by the

---

[2]https://github.com/tesseract-ocr/tesseract
[3]https://www.nltk.org/
[4]https://github.com/dwyl/english-words/blob/master/words.zip

Unrec. word	Alternatives
"faid"	"fai", "f aid", "fid", "fa id", "said", "fraid"
"timeas"	"timias", "tim eas", "time as", "tineas", "ti meas", "times"
"ikewife"	"likewise", "ike wife", "piewife", "kalewife"

Table 2: Example of replacement dictionaries

most plausible alternative, employing th LM to evaluate the resulting sentence.

Despite numerous successful corrections, Table 1 also shows some of the limitations of the tool. For example, the word "fignification" has not been properly replaced by a correct alternative. Other words have been incorrectly replaced, such as "Deputy-Governor", which now occurs as "Ex-Governor".

In our experiments, we observe that around 63% of the errors are corrected by our tool. Most of the corrections are made in frequent words such as the word "shall" mentioned in Table 1.

6. Conclusion and Future Work

In this paper we have presented a tool to postprocess errors in the output of an OCR tool. As the problems addressed mainly pertains to historical documents, the tool was illustrated with reference to the early 18th-century text *An Essay Towards Regulating the Trade*. In order to achieve a more accurate representation of the original document than is commonly attained in image-text conversion, we constructed a system that identifies words that have potentially been incorrectly recognised and which suggests candidates for replacement. In order to select the best candidate, these alternatives are evaluated within the context of the sentence using an LM.

In this study we have manually stated which characters are misrecognized by the OCR system. In the future, we hope to develop a method for automatically identifying such characters.

We did not find large amounts of good-quality data from around 1700. Further research would benefit from LM models built on data from the same period as the test set, which could also be used to select appropriate sentences (Poncelas et al., 2016; Poncelas et al., 2017).

The tool could also be expanded to address related issues of textual organization, such as the automatic separation of side notes from a body of text. Overall, OCR technology is a fundamental factor in the dissemination of knowledge in the digital age, and to refine its output is essential.

7. Acknowledgements

The QuantiQual Project, generously funded by the Irish Research Council's COALESCE scheme (COALESCE/2019/117).

This research has been supported by the ADAPT Centre for Digital Content Technology which is funded under the SFI Research Centres Programme (Grant 13/RC/2106).

8. Bibliographical References

Afli, H., Qiu, Z., Way, A., and Sheridan, P. (2016). Using SMT for OCR error correction of historical texts. In *Proceedings of the Tenth International Conference on Language Resources and Evaluation*, pages 962–966, Portorož, Slovenia.

Bassil, Y. and Alwani, M. (2012). Ocr post-processing error correction algorithm using google's online spelling suggestion. *Journal of Emerging Trends in Computing and Information Sciences*, 3(1).

Berg-Kirkpatrick, T., Durrett, G., and Klein, D. (2013). Unsupervised transcription of historical documents. In *Proceedings of the 51st Annual Meeting of the Association for Computational Linguistics (Volume 1: Long Papers)*, pages 207–217.

Bieniecki, W., Grabowski, S., and Rozenberg, W. (2007). Image preprocessing for improving ocr accuracy. In *2007 International Conference on Perspective Technologies and Methods in MEMS Design*, pages 75–80. IEEE.

Brill, E. and Moore, R. C. (2000). An improved error model for noisy channel spelling correction. In *Proceedings of the 38th annual meeting on association for computational linguistics*, pages 286–293, Hong Kong. Association for Computational Linguistics.

Heafield, K. (2011). KenLM: Faster and smaller language model queries. In *Proceedings of the Sixth Workshop on Statistical Machine Translation*, pages 187–197, Edinburgh, Scotland.

Kluzner, V., Tzadok, A., Shimony, Y., Walach, E., and Antonacopoulos, A. (2009). Word-based adaptive OCR for historical books. In *2009 10th International Conference on Document Analysis and Recognition*, pages 501–505.

Koehn, P. (2005). Europarl: A parallel corpus for statistical machine translation. *Proceedings of the 10th Machine Translation Summit (MT Summit)*, pages 79–86.

Lopresti, D. (2009). Optical character recognition errors and their effects on natural language processing. *International Journal on Document Analysis and Recognition (IJDAR)*, 12(3):141–151.

Maekawa, K., Tomiura, Y., Fukuda, S., Ishita, E., and Uchiyama, H. (2019). Improving OCR for historical documents by modeling image distortion. In *Digital Libraries at the Crossroads of Digital Information for the Future: 21st International Conference on Asia-Pacific Digital Libraries, ICADL 2019*, volume 11853, pages 312–316, Kuala Lumpur, Malaysia.

Piotrowski, M. (2012). Natural language processing for historical texts. *Synthesis lectures on human language technologies*, 5(2):1–157.

Poncelas, A., Way, A., and Toral, A. (2016). Extending feature decay algorithms using alignment entropy. In *International Workshop on Future and Emerging Trends in Language Technology*, pages 170–182, Seville, Spain. Springer.

Poncelas, A., Maillette de Buy Wenniger, G., and Way, A. (2017). Applying n-gram alignment entropy to improve feature decay algorithms. *The Prague Bulletin of Mathematical Linguistics*, 108(1):245–256.

Schäfer, U. and Weitz, B. (2012). Combining ocr outputs

for logical document structure markup: technical background to the acl 2012 contributed task. In *Proceedings of the ACL-2012 Special Workshop on Rediscovering 50 Years of Discoveries*, pages 104–109, Jeju, Republic of Korea.

Smith, R. (2007). An overview of the tesseract OCR engine. In *Ninth International Conference on Document Analysis and Recognition (ICDAR 2007)*, volume 2, pages 629–633, Curitiba, Brazil.

Thompson, P., McNaught, J., and Ananiadou, S. (2015). Customised OCR correction for historical medical text. In *2015 Digital Heritage*, volume 1, pages 35–42.

Volk, M., Marek, T., and Sennrich, R. (2010). Reducing ocr errors by combining two ocr systems. *ECAI 2010*, page 61.

Zhuang, L., Bao, T., Zhu, X., Wang, C., and Naoi, S. (2004). A chinese OCR spelling check approach based on statistical language models. In *2004 IEEE International Conference on Systems, Man and Cybernetics*, volume 5, pages 4727–4732, The Hague, Netherlands.

9. Language Resource References

Cary, J. (1719). *An Essay Towards Regulating the Trade and Employing the Poor of this Kingdom: Whereunto is Added an Essay Towards Paying Off the Publick Debts.*

DWYL. (2019). `https://github.com/dwyl/english-words/blob/master/words.zip`.

Proceedings of 1st Workshop on Language Technologies for Historical and Ancient Languages, pages 52–58
Language Resources and Evaluation Conference (LREC 2020), Marseille, 11–16 May 2020

Integration of Automatic Sentence Segmentation and Lexical Analysis of Ancient Chinese based on BiLSTM-CRF Model

CHENG Ning[1], LI Bin[1,2], XIAO Liming[1], XU Changwei[1], GE Sijia[1], HAO Xingyue[1], FENG Minxuan[1]

1.School of Chinese Language and Literature, Nanjing Normal University, Nanjing, Jiangsu 210097, China
2. Institute for Quantitative Social Science, Harvard University, Cambridge, MA 02138, USA
chengninmo@foxmail.com, libin.njnu@gmail.com, lmxiao1leo@gmail.com, changweixu36@gmail.com, sijiage007@gmail.com, haoxingyue@hotmail.com, fengminxuan@njnu.edu.cn

Abstract

The basic tasks of ancient Chinese information processing include automatic sentence segmentation, word segmentation, part-of-speech tagging and named entity recognition. Tasks such as lexical analysis need to be based on sentence segmentation because of the reason that a plenty of ancient books are not punctuated. However, step-by-step processing is prone to cause multi-level diffusion of errors. This paper designs and implements an integrated annotation system of sentence segmentation and lexical analysis. The BiLSTM-CRF neural network model is used to verify the generalization ability and the effect of sentence segmentation and lexical analysis on different label levels on four cross-age test sets. Research shows that the integration method adopted in ancient Chinese improves the F1-score of sentence segmentation, word segmentation and part of speech tagging. Based on the experimental results of each test set, the F1-score of sentence segmentation reached 78.95, with an average increase of 3.5%; the F1-score of word segmentation reached 85.73%, with an average increase of 0.18%; and the F1-score of part-of-speech tagging reached 72.65, with an average increase of 0.35%.

Keywords: sentence segmentation of ancient Chinese, word segmentation, part-of-speech tagging, BiLSTM-CRF, ancient Chinese information processing

1.   Introduction

Lexical analysis is the most basic task of Chinese information processing, including automatic word segmentation, part of speech tagging, and named entity recognition. Besides the above tasks, the basic task of information processing in ancient Chinese also includes automatic sentence segmentation. Chinese ancient books have a vast number of texts, and most of them are unpunctuated, which brings great difficulties for readers to read and study. The use of advanced natural language processing technology for automatic sentence segmentation and lexical analysis of ancient Chinese can not only facilitate readers to read, but also of great significance to the arrangement of ancient books, the development of ancient Chinese and the intelligent application of ancient Chinese.

Most of the research on information processing in ancient Chinese is focused on a specific subtask, such as automatic sentence segmentation and word segmentation, part of speech tagging and named entity recognition. To complete the basic task of ancient Chinese information processing, most scholars adopt different research methods and techniques, and each subtask need to be completed in turn, which greatly affects the processing efficiency of the machine. Moreover, using sentence segmented by machine to go on doing word segmentation and part of speech tagging are easy to result in multi-level diffusion of tagging errors, which affects the accuracy of overall tagging task.

In this paper, a tagging system integrating automatic sentence segmentation and lexical analysis in ancient Chinese is designed and completed. BiLSTM-CRF model is used to joint learn sentence segmentation, word segmentation and part of speech information. Due to the relative shortage of tagged ancient Chinese corpus, most of the previous studies were conducted according to a special book, and the corpus scales were relatively small, so the training model could not be well applied to other types of ancient Chinese texts. Based on the existing resources, this paper constructs four kinds of annotated corpus written in different ages, and verifies the effect of the integrated annotation on different test sets by using the neural network model.

2.   Model introduction

RNN model and its variants, which are suitable for sequence tagging, have greatly changed the research methods of natural language processing. RNN can be regarded as a multiple overlay structure of the same network. It performs the same operation for each element in the sequence, and each operation depends on the previous calculation results. In theory, RNN can use any length of sequence information, but in practice, only some previous steps can be reviewed. LSTM neural network is a kind of special RNN. Based on the original RNN model, input gate, forgetting gate and output gate are added. Neurons will selectively forget the useless information for current output. It inherits the advantage that RNN can keep the preorder's information, and overcomes the problem that RNN can't really capture the long-distance dependency in the text.

BiLSTM is a model put forward by Schuster in 1997 to solve the problem that LSTM can't retain the post information. The main idea of the model is to set up two LSTM structures in the front and back direction of the training sequence. By splicing the LSTM in two directions to capture the preorder and post order's information, the information in the whole training sequence can be retained to the greatest extent.

The BiLSTM-CRF model structure used in this paper was first proposed by Huang et al. The output of BiLSTM layer is a probability matrix, which is calculated by BiLSTM based on the optimal result of each moment. In this way, the output tag doesn't consider the influence of the previous tag. For example, the word "孟子" appears in the input sequence "孟子 *(name)* 卒 *(die)* 继室 *(second wife)* 以 *(a conjunction)* 馨子 *(name)*", in which "孟" is the first character and "子" is the last character. The model may predict both "孟" and "子" as the first character, such situation should be avoided in the lexical analysis task of ancient Chinese. CRF is a framework for an undirected graph model that can be used to define the joint probability distribution of a tag sequence in a situation that a set of observed sequences need to be tagged. Assume that X is the random variable of the data sequence to be annotated, and Y is the random variable of the corresponding tag sequence. For example, X is the set of sentences in natural language, and Y is the part of speech set that used to mark these sentences. Random variables X and Y are jointly distributed and a conditional model P(Y|X) is constructed according to the pairs of observation sequence and label sequence. The CRF layer is matched with the output layer of BiLSTM, so that the output sequence of BiLSTM becomes the observation sequence of CRF, and then CRF calculates the optimal solution of the whole sequence in probability without ignoring the interaction between sequence element tags.

3.　Construction of corpus

Ancient texts were selected according to different historical stages, and the corpus with the same size was extracted from the traditional version of *Tso Chuan* (左傳, Han dynasty, 722BC~468BC), *Brush Talks from Dream Brook* (夢溪筆談, Song dynasty, AD1086~AD1093), *Fantastic Tales by Ji Xiaolan* (閱微草堂筆記, Qing dynasty, language style is more colloquial, AD1789~AD1798), and *Documents of History of Qing Dynasty* (清史稿, Republic of China, AD1914~AD1927) as the experimental data set of this paper. The purpose of constructing a corpus by age is to explore the generalization ability of the model for text annotation in different ages after training based on mixed corpus of different ages. The data set is manually proofread on the basis of machine-assisted word segmentation and POS tagging. Kappa was used for labeling consistency test and the Kappa value was higher than 0.8, indicating a higher degree of labeling consistency. The specification of POS tags refers to Ancient Chinese Corpus published by LDC[1], totaling 21 tags. The experimental data set is divided into training set, development set and test set according to the ratio of 8:1:1. Among them, the training set is a mixed corpus composed of 80% of the corpus in *Tso Chuan*, *Brush Talks from Dream Brook*, *Fantastic Tales by Ji Xiaolan*, and *Documents of History of Qing Dynasty*. Based on this mixed corpus, this paper discusses the annotation ability of the model to texts of various ages. The experimental corpus set "：，。；！？" six kinds of punctuation as sentence breaks, and each text sequence divided by two sentence breaks is treated as a sentence, with all other punctuation ignored. Table 1 is a general overview of the experimental data set.

4.　Integrated word position tag design

Xue is the first to put forward a character-based learning method of sequential annotation, who uses four kinds of tags, which is LL(stands for left boundary of a word), LR(stands for monosyllabic word), MM(stands for the middle of a word) and RR(stands for the right boundary of a word), to express the segmentation and annotation information of characters, thus it translates word segmentation task into serialized annotation task formally for the first time.

The data set	The training set			The development set			The test set		
	#character	#word	#sentence	#character	#word	#sentence	#character	#word	#sentence
Tso Chuan	75,000	65,000	15,000	9136	7755	1917	9280	7738	2046
Brush Talks from Dream Brook	81,000	63,000	13,000	9483	8384	1662	9825	8378	1643
Fantastic Tales by Ji Xiaolan	81,000	69,000	14,000	9722	8699	1745	9789	8680	1784
Documents of History of Qing Dynasty	81,000	57,000	12,000	10248	8851	1651	9991	8159	1432
Total	32,400	25,400	54,000	38,000	34,000	6975	38,000	33,000	6905

Table 1 : Experimental data set

This paper uses this method of character annotation to construct an ancient Chinese integrated-analysis annotation system. For this model, the problem is actually a tag multi-classification problem, where each character needs to be assigned to a specific tag type.

Word segmentation layer (WS): Using B, I, E, S four tags. B means that the current character is at the beginning of a multi-character word. I means that the current character is at the middle of a multi-character word. E means that the current character is at the ending of a multi-character word. S represents the current character is a one-character word. After transforming the character annotation sequence, the sentence segmentation results can be calculated out. For example:

Character annotation: 九 B 月 E ，S 晉 B 惠 I 公 E 卒 S 。S 懷 B 公 E 立 S ，S
After the transformation: 九月 *(September)* ，晉惠公 卒 *(die)* 。懷公 立 *(ascend the throne)* ，

POS tagging layer (POS): Tagging the part of speech of the word to which each character belongs. Meanwhile, incorporating physical tags (personal name *nr*, place name *ns*) into POS. Then, adding POS on the basis of WS so that each character can corresponds to its position in the word

---

[1] LDC Ancient Chinese Corpus

https://catalog.ldc.upenn.edu/LDC2017T14

and the part of speech it represents or entity information it has.

九 B-t 月 E-t ，S-w 晉 B-nr 惠 I-nr 公 E-nr 卒 S-v 。S-w 懷 B-nr 公 E-nr 立 S-v ，S-w

Each character is tagged word segmentation tag and POS tag, connected by "-".Take "晉 B-nr 惠 I-nr 公 E-nr" as example, "晉" is the first character of a personal name, "惠" is a character in the middle of a personal name, "公" is the last character in a personal name, so that "晉惠公" can be segmented and recognized to a person's name, whose reality tag is represented as "nr".

Sentence segmentation layer (SS): Tagging whether a character is at the end of a sentence. Adding SS layer on the basis of WS and POS, so that each character can be corresponded with three layers, i.e., word segmentation, part of speech and sentence segmentation.

九 B-t-O 月 E-t-L 晉 B-nr-O 惠 I-nr-O 公 E-nr-O 卒 S-v-L 懷 B-nr-O 公 E-nr-O 立 S-v-L

If a character in the corpus is at the break of a sentence, such as "月", "卒" and "立" in the sentence, then tag "L" will be put after the part of speech tag, otherwise, tag "O" will be put after the part of speech tag.

During the process of corpus preprocessing, three-layers tags categories (WS, POS, SS) can be processed in different ways:

WS+POS+SS (e.g., 卒 S-v-L) is a three-layers tag. Under this annotation level, the annotation effect of each subtask, such as sentence segmentation (SS), can be calculated.

There is WS+POS (e.g., 卒 S-v) in two-layers tags. Under this annotation level, the effects of word segmentation (WS) and POS tagging (WS+POS) can be calculated.

There is WS (e.g., 卒 S) and SS (e.g., 卒 L) in one-layer tags. The effect of sentence segmentation or word segmentation can be calculated.

5.　Evaluation indexes

The experimental training set is used for feature learning and training of the model, and the test set is used to verify the results of automatic tagging. For the evaluation of automatic tagging results, F1-score (harmonic mean), the most commonly used evaluation index in sequence tagging, is used to measure the effect of the model. F1-score is calculated from P(precision) and R(recall), and the calculation formula is:

$$F1 = \frac{2 * P * R}{P + R}$$

The calculation of Precision is as follows:

$$P = \frac{\text{Correct number of tags}}{\text{Number of machine tags}}$$

The calculation of Recall is as follows:

$$R = \frac{\text{Correct number of tags}}{\text{Number of all tags in the corpus}}$$

Based on the above evaluation metrics, sentence segmentation, word segmentation, part of speech tagging

results are calculated. Sentence segmentation calculation is based on sentence rather than characters, that is, according to the label "L". If both machine and manual tagging results are "L", it is correct. Word segmentation and part of speech are calculated on the basis of words rather than characters. Taking POS tagging as example, it is assumed that the word 孟子(Mencius) is predicted as "孟S-nr子S-nr". Although the model gets a correct part of speech based on characters, however, the word segmentation is wrong, and the correct answer should be "孟B-nr子E-nr". To determine whether a word belongs to the correct part of speech, whether the character is correctly divided into words should be determined first, that is, determination should be based on the correct word segmentation.

6.　Experimental design and result analysis

The results of Experiment 1 are the super parameters obtained by manual parameter adjustment on the development set, and the results of Experiment 2, Experiment 3 and Experiment 4 are obtained on the test set.

Experiment 1 will verify the necessity of adding word vectors into the integration analysis of ancient Chinese and investigate the effect of word vectors of different dimensions on the results of integrated annotation. Generally speaking, the higher the dimension of the word vector, the more semantic features it contains, but they are not absolute positively correlated. Based on nearly 1.5 billion characters of traditional ancient Chinese raw corpus (from Imperial Collection of Four and other ancient Chinese corpus), selecting word2vec as the tool, CBOW (Continuous Bag of-Words Model) as the model, we carry out character vector pretraining. The experiment sets the word vector dimension to 50, 100, 128 and 200 respectively, selects *Tso Chuan* test set as the test corpus, and adopts "WS+ POS+ SS" as its tagging layer, which is a tagging method of integrating sentence segmentation and lexical analysis. By manually adjusting parameters on the development set, the final hyper-parameter adopted is shown in Table 2.

Word vector dimension	50/100/128/200
Number of hidden layers	1
Number of hidden units	200
Minimum number of samples	64
Dropout rate dropout	0.5
The optimizer	Adam
Learning rate	0.001

Table 2: Experimental hyper-parameter setting

In the BiLSTM-CRF structure, based on experiments on the development set, it is found that the number of layers in BiLSTM had little influence on the precision, so the number of hidden layers in the model, namely the number of layers in BiLSTM, is set as 1. The number of hidden nodes in the sequence tagging task is usually from 200 to 600, and 200 is taken as the parameter here. The minimum sample size is set to 64, with each sample size controlled between 50 and 60. The optimization of the model adopts the "Adam" algorithm, which has a good effect in the sequence tagging task. The Dropout method is used to reduce overfitting. A Dropout with a parameter of 0.5 is added between the BiLSTM layer and the full connection layer, which can weaken the excessive interaction between various features caused by the small amount of data, so that the model has the optimal generalization ability and the lowest degree of overfitting. The experimental results are shown in Table 3.

Word vector dimension	Sentence segmentation	Word segmentation	POS tagging
No word vector	82.16	88.23	78.36
50 dimensions	83.07	89.39	79.53
100 dimensions	83.89	90.19	80.59
128 dimensions	**84.11**	**90.24**	**80.88**
200 dimensions	83.58	89.83	80.42

Table 3: The F1-score of integration of sentence segmentation and lexical analysis(unit %)

As can be seen in table 3, the addition of word vector is necessary for sentence segmentation and lexical analysis tasks in ancient Chinese, especially for POS tagging tasks, which increased by 2.5 percentage points. In the word vector dimension setting, the experiment shows that 128 dimensions is the best for the integrated automatic tagging of ancient Chinese. In order to verify the training effect of the word vector under this dimension, cosine similarity is used to calculate the semantic correlation between the two word vectors: Assume word vector A=(A1,A2,…,An), B=(B1, B2,…,Bn), the formula for cosine similarity is as follows:

$$\cos \theta = \frac{\sum_1^n (Ai \times Bi)}{\sqrt{\sum_{i=1}^n (Ai)^2} \times \sqrt{\sum_{i=1}^n (Bi)^2}}$$

i represents the dimension of the vector, and Ai represents the specific value of the i-dimension of the character A. Taking characters 也 *(modal particle)* and 曰 *(say)* as examples, the calculation results are as follows in Table 4:

The most semantically relevant word of 也	The most semantically relevant word of 曰
矣 *(modal particle)* 0.662	云 *(say)* 0.696
之 *(modal particle)* 0.659	謂 0.584
乎 *(modal particle)* 0.658	也 0.514
謂 *(say)* 0.652	言 *(say)* 0.500
非 *(be not)* 0.593	問 *(ask)* 0.465
歟 *(modal particle)* 0.584	耶 0.434
耶 *(modal particle)* 0.571	荅 *(answer)* 0.415
哉 *(modal particle)* 0.563	答 *(answer)* 0.413
以 *(with)* 0.525	為 *(do)* 0.412

Table 4: Semantic relevancy calculation results

In experiment 2, for testing the performance of BiLSTM-CRF model in tagging ancient texts, we used IDCNN (Iterated Dilated Convolutions) and non-CRF-layer BiLSTM model to compare with it. DCNN (Dilated Convolutions) was first proposed by (Yu et al., 2015) and applied to image semantic classification. IDCNN model structure is generated based on DCNN. Drawing on the advantages of CNN and RNN, IDCNN takes into account the parallel processing and breadth of context feature extraction, so it is also widely used in sequence tagging tasks. In this experiment, *Tso Chuan* is chosen as test set, and tagged in the method of integrating sentence segmentation and lexical analysis. Keeping other experimental variables (e.g., training corpus, word vector dimension) consistent, we investigate tagging effect of different models in the word segmentation task under integrated tagging layer. The experimental results are shown in Table 5.

Neural network models	*Tso Chuan* testing set (unit %)		
	P	R	F1
IDCNN	88.25	89.28	88.76
BiLSTM	**89.39**	90.05	89.71
BiLSTM-CRF	89.37	**91.13**	**90.24**

Table 5: Word segmentation performance of different models on *Tso Chuan*

The results of comparative experiments show that in ancient Chinese word segmentation task, the precision of BiLSTM-CRF model is only 0.02% lower than BiLSTM model, which is almost not different, and the recall is 1.08% higher than non-CRF-layer BiLSTM model, and F1-score is 1.48% higher than IDCNN and 0.53% higher than BiLSTM. As a result, BiLSTM-CRF model's performance is generally higher than IDCNN model and BiLSTM model in ancient Chinese word segmentation task.

This experiment was not carried out in the other three books, but the effects should be good because of the BiLSTM-CRF's advantage compared to the other two models.

The third set of experiments focuses on four kinds of texts, including *Tso Chuan*, *Brush Talks from Dream Brook*, *Fantastic Tales by Ji Xiaolan*, and *Documents of History of Qing Dynasty*. In each text's in-domain experiment, the training and testing corpus we used are both from the same text. The purposes of experiment 3 is to explore the modeling ability of the model that integrates sentence segmentation and lexical analysis applying to various texts, and to compare the result with experiment 4 which based on mixed corpus.

Tagging layer in the experiment is "WS+POS+SS", i.e., the tagging method of integrating sentence segmentation and lexical analysis. The experimental parameters are consistent with the previous ones. The experimental results are shown in Table 6.

Tagging layers		Tso Chuan			Brush Talks from Dream Brook			Fantastic Tales by Ji Xiaolan			Documents of History of Qing Dynasty		
		P	R	F1	P	R	F1	P	R	F1	P	R	F1
integration	sentence segmentation	85.8	83.0	84.4	72.4	67.4	69.8	70.2	71.7	71.0	87.7	87.0	**87.4**
	word segmentation	89.9	92.1	**90.9**	86.8	84.8	85.8	85.8	87.9	86.8	82.8	77.3	80.0
	POS tagging	81.0	83.0	**82.0**	66.7	65.1	65.9	71.1	72.9	72.0	72.7	68.0	70.3

Table 6: Experimental results of BiLSTM-CRF model applying to various texts under "WS+POS+SS" layer (unit %)

Because of the differences in the age and genre of the four texts, the experimental results of the model for each corpus are quite different. By comparing the F1-score of word segmentation task, POS tagging task and sentence segmentation task, we found that in word segmentation task, *Tso Chuan* performances best, *Fantastic Tales by Ji Xiaolan* ranks the second, *Documents of History of Qing Dynasty* is the worst; in POS tagging task, *Tso Chuan* and *Fantastic Tales by Ji Xiaolan* have the same rank as last task, but *Brush Talks from Dream Brook* is the worst; in sentence segmentation task, *Tso Chuan* and *Documents of History of Qing Dynasty*'s effects are relatively good, far more accurate than *Fantastic Tales by Ji Xiaolan* and *Brush Talks from Dream Brook*. After analyzing the model tagging errors, we found that *Brush Talks from Dream Brook* contains a large number of non-repetitive professional terms in various disciplines, for example, in sentence "南呂調皆用七聲*(scales)*：下五、高凡、高工、尺、高一、", the words "下五", "高凡" are proper names related to music. The relatively sparse data of proper names makes it difficult for the model to learn the relevant features, which is the main reason that *Brush Talks from Dream Brook* performances worse in POS tagging task.

Experiment 4 is designed from two dimensions: (1) in the horizontal dimension, the experiment discusses the differences of model based on mixed corpus, tagging in different ages' corpus under a same tagging layer, and investigates the models' generalization ability considering the result of experiment 3; (2) in the vertical dimension, the experiment compares the tagging differences of same testing corpus under different tagging layers. The performance of the joint model is almost unaffected by the mixed corpus, so the experiment can verify the effectiveness of the integrated tagging method of word segmentation, POS tagging and sentence segmentation.

The experiment selects BiLSTM-CRF as model, mixed corpus as training corpus, and 128-word vector dimensions. The experimental results are shown in Table 7.

Tagging layers		Tso Chuan			Brush Talks from Dream Brook			Fantastic Tales by Ji Xiaolan			Documents of History of Qing Dynasty		
		P	R	F1	P	R	F1	P	R	F1	P	R	F1
only sentence segmentation		83.6	79.5	81.5	69.0	64.4	66.6	68.1	68.7	68.4	86.8	83.9	85.3
only word segmentation		88.8	91.4	90.0	87.4	85.8	86.6	85.8	87.1	86.4	81.2	77.2	79.2
POS	word segmentation	88.9	91.2	90.0	86.9	86.2	86.6	85.5	86.8	86.1	82.1	77.4	**79.7**
	POS tagging	79.2	81.2	80.2	67.6	65.6	**66.6**	72.2	73.2	72.7	71.8	67.7	69.7
integration	sentence segmentation	86.5	81.9	**84.1**	72.0	71.1	**71.5**	73.7	73.0	**73.3**	85.2	88.8	**86.9**
	word segmentation	89.4	91.1	**90.2**	87.6	85.9	**86.8**	86.3	87.0	**86.6**	81.7	77.0	79.3
	POS tagging	80.1	81.7	**80.9**	67.4	65.4	66.4	72.5	72.9	**72.7**	72.8	68.6	**70.6**

Table 7: Experimental results of BiLSTM-CRF model based on mixed corpus applying to various corpus under different tagging layers

After comparing model's tagging results of each testing set under different tagging layers, there are 4 conclusions:

(1) By observing the F1-score of each testing set in the same tagging layer, it is found that taking mixed corpus as training set, tagging results of the model applying to various testing corpus are not balanced, which are similar to experiment 3's result. By comparing the results under the layer that integrates sentence segmentation and lexical analysis with experiment 3, we found that *Brush Talks from Dream Brook*'s performance in sentence segmentation, word segmentation and POS tagging tasks are 0.7, 1.0, 0.5 percentage points higher respectively; *Fantastic Tales by Ji Xiaolan*'s performance in sentence segmentation and POS tagging tasks are 2.3, 0.7 percentage points higher respectively; *Tso Chuan* declines slightly in all tasks. This result indicates that the integration model based on mixed corpus has learnt some homogeneity features of each corpus, which improves some testing sets' tagging performances. However, in the meantime, the differences among corpus interferes with the comprehensive judgment of the model, resulting in some testing sets' performance degradation. Therefore, the generalization ability of the integrated tagging model applying to different ages' texts needs to be improved.

(2) By observing the F1-score of each testing set's word segmentation task under different tagging layers, the layer

that integrates sentence segmentation and lexical analysis performances best in its entirely. Regardless of which testing set, the F1-score of the tagging layer that only segments word is lower than the integrated layer, which means that integrated tagging method of sentence segmentation and lexical analysis can improve word segmentation task in ancient Chinese.

(3) By observing the F1-score of each testing set's sentence segmentation task under different tagging layers, the layer that integrates sentence segmentation and lexical analysis performances best in its entirely, which shows that integrated tagging method can improve sentence segmentation task in ancient Chinese. Taking *Tso Chuan* as example, the F1-score of sentence segmentation under integrated tagging layer is 2.6 percentage higher than the layer only segment sentence. Similar improvement happens in other testing sets, reflecting that in automatic sentence segmentation task of ancient Chinese, integration of sentence segmentation and lexical analysis is better than step-by-step tagging method.

(4) Comparing the layer of integrated tagging and the layer of POS tagging, we can find that the F1-score of integrated tagging in most testing sets is higher than POS tagging layer. Taking *Tso Chuan* as example, the performance of word segmentation and part-of-speech tagging under integrated tagging layer is 0.2 and 0.7 percentage higher than the POS tagging layer respectively. This result verifies that the integration of sentence segmentation and lexical analysis performances better in word segmentation task and POS tagging task than those methods without adding information of sentence break.

A comprehensive analysis based on (2), (3), (4) can find that the sentence segmentation, word segmentation, and POS tagging tasks have improvement because of the integrated annotation system, and the promotion(F1-score) is not limited to one kinds of testing set. The concrete conditions are shown in Table 8.

Tagging tasks	Tso Chuan	Brush Talks from Dream Brook	Fantastic Tales by Ji Xiaolan	Documents of History of Qing Dynasty
sentence segmentation	+2.6	+4.9	+4.9	+1.6
word segmentation	+0.2	+0.2	+0.2	+0.1
POS tagging	+0.7	-0.2	+0	+0.9

Table 8: The promotion of F-score in each task after using the integrated annotation system

Although the integrated tagging method has limit in task promotion, the experiment proves the feasibility of it. It can avoid multi-level spread of tagging errors in single task. For example, if performing tasks step-by-step, we need segment sentence first, and then perform word segmentation task and POS tagging task, which will cause erroneous multi-level accumulation, and the whole performance is not as good as the integrated method. What's more, the tagging method of integrating sentence segmentation and lexical analysis can greatly improve the efficiency of processing words and sentences in ancient Chinese.

7. Conclusion

This paper designs and implements the annotation systerm of integrating sentence segmentation and lexical analysis of ancient Chinese. Based on BiLSTM-CRF neural network model, we verify the intergrated tagging model's generalization ability on different ages' texts, as well as the model's effects on sentence segmentation, word segmentation and part of speech tagging of ancient Chinese under different tagging layers on four different historical testing sets, including *Tso Chuan, Brush Talks from Dream Brook, Fantastic Tales by Ji Xiaolan* and *Documents of History of Qing Dynasty*. The results appeal that the integrated tagging method performs better among tasks of sentence segmentation, word segmentation and POS tagging. The F1-score of sentence segmentation reached 78.95, with an average increase of 3.5%; the F1-score of word segmentation reached 85.73%, with an average increase of 0.18%; and the F1-score of part-of-speech tagging reached 72.65, with an average increase of 0.35%.

Future research will expand the scale of corpus and improve the model. Focusing on the design of deep learning model in the context of large-scale cross era corpus, the model will include *attention* system and transfer learning method to explore the adaptability of model to different times' texts. Finally, we will develop an integrated analysis system of ancient Chinese with better performance across the ages and styles.

8. Acknowledgements

Supported by the project for Jiangsu Higher Institutions& Excellent Innovative Team for Philosophy and Social Sciences.

A Project Funded by the Priority Academic Program Deve lopment of Jiangsu Higher Education Institutions.

National Language Committee Project of China (YB135-61).

Researches of Building Syntactic Chinese-English Parallel Corpus and Humanities Computing Based on Ancient Classics Index(NO. 71673143) national natural science foundation of China.

9. Bibliographical References

Chen J, Weihua L I, Chen J I, et al. Bi-directional Long Short-term Memory Neural Networks for Chinese Word Segmentation[J]. Journal of Chinese Information Processing, 2018, 32(2):29-37.

HAN X, WANG H, Zhang S, et al. Sentence Segmentation for Classical Chinese Based on LSTM with Radical Embedding[J]. The Journal of China Universities of Posts and Telecommunications, 2019, 26(2):1-8.

Hochreiter S, Schmidhuber, Jürgen. Long Short-Tern Memory[J]. Neural Computation, 1997, 9(8):1735-1780.

Kaixu Z, Yunqing X, Hang Y. CRF-based approach to sentence segmentation and punctuation for ancient

Chinese prose[J]. Journal of Tsinghua University (Science and Technology), 2009(10):1733-1736.

Mikolov T, Chen K, Corrado G, et al. Efficient estimation of word representations in vector space[J]. arXiv preprint arXiv: 1301.3781, 2013.

Min S, Bin LI, Xiaohe C. CRF Based Research on a Unified Approach to Word Segmentation and POS Tagging for Pre-Qin Chinese[J]. Journal of Chinese Information Processing, 2010, 24(2):39-46.

Rumelhart D E, Hinton G E, Williams R J. Learning representations by back-propagating errors[J]. Nature, 1986, 323(6088):533-536.

Strubell E, Verga P, Belanger D, et al. Fast and Accurate Entity Recognition with Iterated Dilated Convolutions[C] // Proceeding of the 2017 Conference on Empirical Methods in Natural Language.

Wang B, Shi X, Tan Z, et al. A sentence segmentation method for ancient Chinese texts based on NNLM// Proceedings of CLSM. Singapore, 2016: 387-396.

XUE N. Chinese word segmentation as character tagging [J]. Computational Linguistics and Chinese Language Processing, 2003, 8(1): 29-48.

Yao Y, Huang Z. Bi-directional LSTM Recurrent Neural Network for Chinese Word Segmentation[C]// Conference on Empirical Methods in Natural Language Processing. 2016:1197-1206.

Yu F, Koltun V. Multi-Scale Context Aggregation by Dilated Convolutions[J]. arXiv preprint arXiv:1511.07122, 2015.

Yun-Tian F, Hong-Jun Z, Wen-Ning H, et al. Named Entity Recognition Based on Deep Belief Net[J]. Computer Science, 2016, 43(4):224-230.

Zheng X, Chen H, Xu T. Deep Learning for Chinese Word Segmentation and POS Tagging[C] // Proceedings of the 2013 Conference on Empirical Methods in Natural Language Processing. 2013:647-657.

10. Language Resource References

Ancient Chinese Corpus. (2017). Linguistic Data Consortium. Chen, Xiaohe, et al., 1.0, ISLRN 924-985-704-453-5.

Proceedings of 1st Workshop on Language Technologies for Historical and Ancient Languages, pages 59–67
Language Resources and Evaluation Conference (LREC 2020), Marseille, 11–16 May 2020
© European Language Resources Association (ELRA), licensed under CC-BY-NC

Automatic Semantic Role Labeling in Ancient Greek Using Distributional Semantic Modeling

Alek Keersmaekers

KU Leuven/Research Foundation - Flanders
Blijde Inkomststraat 21, 3000 Leuven
alek.keersmaekers@kuleuven.be

Abstract

This paper describes a first attempt to automatic semantic role labeling in Ancient Greek, using a supervised machine learning approach. A Random Forest classifier is trained on a small semantically annotated corpus of Ancient Greek, annotated with a large amount of linguistic features, including form of the construction, morphology, part-of-speech, lemmas, animacy, syntax and distributional vectors of Greek words. These vectors turned out to be more important in the model than any other features, likely because they are well suited to handle a low amount of training examples. Overall labeling accuracy was 0.757, with large differences with respect to the specific role that was labeled and with respect to text genre. Some ways to further improve these results include expanding the amount of training examples, improving the quality of the distributional vectors and increasing the consistency of the syntactic annotation.

Keywords: Semantic Role Labeling, Ancient Greek, distributional semantics

1. Introduction

In the last couple of years there has been a large wave of projects aiming to make the large and diachronically diverse corpus of Ancient Greek linguistically searchable. Some large treebanking projects include the Ancient Greek Dependency Treebanks (Bamman, Mambrini, and Crane, 2009), the PROIEL Treebank (Haug and Jøhndal, 2008), the Gorman Trees (Gorman, 2019) and the Pedalion Treebanks (Keersmaekers et al., 2019). Altogether (also including some smaller projects) the Greek treebank material already contains more than 1.3 million tokens – and it is still growing – offering a solid basis for corpus-linguistic research. There have also been recent efforts to automatically annotate an even larger body of text using natural language processing techniques: see Celano (2017) and Vatri and McGillivray (2018) for the literary corpus and Keersmaekers (2019) for the papyrus corpus. However, despite this large amount of *morphologically* and *syntactically* annotated data, *semantic* annotation for Ancient Greek is far more limited. A label such as "ADV" (adverbial) in the Ancient Greek Dependency Treebanks, for instance, refers to a large category of adverbials that do not necessarily have much in common: e.g. expressions of time, manner, place, cause, goal, and so on. While there have been some smaller scale initiatives for semantic role annotation in Greek, these only amount to about 12500 tokens (see section 2). This can be explained by the fact that manual annotation is a time-intensive task. Therefore this paper will present a first attempt to automatic semantic role labeling in Ancient Greek, using a supervised machine learning approach.

This paper is structured as follows: after introducing the data used for this project (section 2), section 3 will describe the methodology. Section 4 will give a detailed overview and analysis of the results, which are summarized in section 5.

2. The data

Devising a definite list of semantic roles for Ancient Greek is not a trivial task. Looking at semantic annotation projects of modern languages, we can also see a wild amount of variation in the number of roles that are annotated, ranging from the 24 roles of *VerbNet* (Kipper Schuler, 2005) to the more than 2500 roles of *FrameNet* (Baker, Fillmore, and Lowe, 1998). Obviously learning 2500 semantic roles is not feasible in a machine learning context (and even the 39 roles in the *Ancient Greek Dependency Treebanks* are a little on the high side considering the amount of training data we have, see below). Therefore I decided to make use of the roles of the *Pedalion* project (Van Hal and Anné, 2017). These are based on semantic roles that are commonly distinguished both in cross-linguistic typological frameworks and in the Greek linguistic tradition (in particular Crespo, Conti, and Maquieira 2003, although their list is more fine-grained). The 29 Pedalion roles I used for this project (see table 1) are a reasonable enough amount to be automatically learned through machine learning, and they are also specifically relevant for Ancient Greek, in the sense that no role of this list is expressed by the exact same set of formal means as any other role: e.g. while both an instrument and a cause can be expressed with the dative in Greek, a cause can also be expressed by the preposition ἕνεκα (*héneka*: "because of") with the genitive while an instrument cannot.

For this task I limited myself to nouns and other nominalized constructions, prepositional groups and adverbs, depending on a verb. I excluded a number of constructions from the data (on a rule-based basis), either due to a lack of semantic annotation in the data I used (see below) or because they did not express any of the semantic roles listed in table 4 (e.g. appositions): nominatives, vocatives, accusatives when used as an object, infinitive and participial clauses (they are still included when nominalized with an article, see e.g. sentence 1 below), and words with a syntactic relation other than ADV (adverbial), OBJ (complement) or PNOM (predicate nominal).[1] ADV is used for optional modifiers (e.g. "**Yesterday** I gave him a book"), while OBJ is used for obligatory arguments of non-copula verbs (e.g. "Yesterday I gave **him** a book") and PNOM for obligatory arguments of copula verbs (e.g. "I was **in Rome**").

---

[1] While I am planning to include nominatives and accusatives in future versions of the labeler, this was not possible at this moment because none of the projects I included annotated them.

I took semantically annotated data from the following sources:

(1) The **Ancient Greek Dependency Treebanks** (AGDT) (Bamman, Mambrini, and Crane 2009), which has semantic data from the *Bibliotheca* of Pseudo-Apollodorus, Aesop's *Fables* and the Homeric *Hymn to Demeter* (1119 semantically annotated tokens in total).[2] The annotation scheme is described in Celano and Crane (2015): since it was more fine-grained (39 unique roles) than the one this project uses, some of their categories needed to be reduced (e.g. "relation", "connection", "respect" and "topic" to "respect"). Additionally, there are two other projects that are not included in the AGDT but use the same annotation scheme: a treebank of **Apthonius' Progymnasmata** (Yordanova, 2018, 752 tokens in total) and of the **Parian Marble** (Berti, 2016, annotated by Giuseppe G. A. Celano, 61 tokens in total).

(2) The **Harrington Trees** (Harrington, 2018), consisting of *Susanna* from the Old Testament, the first part of Lucian's *True Histories* and the *Life of Aesop* (Vita G): in total 1118 semantically annotated tokens. While their annotation scheme is quite compatible with the Pedalion scheme, their role set is a little smaller (22 unique roles), so I manually checked their data and disambiguated some roles (in particular "extent", "orientation" and "indirect object"). Syntactically its annotation scheme does not make a distinction between obligatory (OBJ) and non-obligatory (ADV) modifiers, so they were also disambiguated manually.

(3) The **Pedalion Treebanks** (Keersmaekers et al., 2019), annotated by a group of people involved at the University of Leuven in the annotation scheme described in this paper (syntactically, they are annotated in the same way as the AGDT). This is the largest amount of data this project uses (9446 semantically annotated tokens, or 76% of the total) and contains a wide range of classical and post-classical authors.

In total this data includes 12496 tokens of 29 roles, as described in table 4 at the end of this paper.

3.   Methodology

Next, I used this dataset of 12496 annotated roles as training data for a supervised machine learning system. Traditionally, automated approaches typically make use of formal features such as part-of-speech tags and morphology, syntactic labels, lemmas and sometimes encyclopedic knowledge such as lists of named entities (see e.g. Gildea and Jurafsky, 2002; Màrquez et al., 2008; Palmer, Gildea, and Xue, 2010), essentially excluding semantic information. This seems counter-intuitive, but was necessary at the time due to a lack of good methods to represent lexical semantics computationally. Recently, however, due to the rise of so-called distributional semantic models (or "vector space models") and word embeddings, it has become possible to computationally represent the meaning of a word as a vector, with words that are similar in meaning also having mathematically similar vectors. This methodology has been highly successful for several natural language processing tasks, including semantic role labeling (e.g. Zhou and Xu, 2015; He et al., 2017; Marcheggiani and Titov, 2017).

Therefore one of the crucial features used for this task was a distributional vector of both the verb and the argument that bears the semantic relationship to the verb. The method of computing these distributional vectors is explained in more detail in Keersmaekers and Speelman (to be submitted). In short, they are calculated by computing association values (with the PPMI "positive pointwise mutual information" measure) of a given target lemma with its context elements, based on a large (37 million tokens) automatically parsed corpus of Ancient Greek (see Turney and Pantel, 2010 for a more detailed explanation of this methodology). These context elements are lemmas with which the target lemma has a dependency relationship (either its head or its child).[3] Next, these vectors are smoothed and their dimensionality is reduced by a technique called latent semantic analysis (LSA). This technique (using so-called Singular Value Decomposition) enables us to retrieve vectors with a lower dimensionality, where the individual elements do not directly correspond to individual contexts but the 'latent meaning'[4] contained in several context elements (see Deerwester et al., 1990 for more detail). Experimentally I found that reducing the vector to only 50 latent dimensions was sufficient for this task, with no significant improvements by increasing the number of dimensions.[5]

Apart from the distributional vector of both the verb and its argument, the following additional features were included:

- The form of the construction, subdivided into three features: the preposition (or lack thereof), the case form of its dependent word and a feature that combines both; e.g. for ἀπό+genitive (*apó*: "from") these features would be {ἀπό,genitive,ἀπό+genitive}. Combinations that did occur less than 10 times were set to "OTHER" (179 in total).

- The lemma of both the verb and its argument. For verbs or arguments that occurred less than 50 times, the value of this feature was set to "OTHER". Only 26 argument lemmas and 25 verb lemmas occurred more than 50 times; however, altogether these lemmas account for 34% of all tokens for the arguments and 34% of all tokens for the verbs as well.

---

[2] While the AGDT treebank is also available in the Universal Dependencies project, I used their original version (in the style of the Prague Dependency Treebank) to ensure compatibility with the other projects included.

[3] This is the *DepHeadChild* model in the Keersmaekers and Speelman (to be submitted) paper.

[4] This "latent meaning" simply refers to the fact that several context features tend to be highly correlated: e.g. a word such as ἐξέρχομαι (*exérkhomai*) and ἀπέρχομαι (*apérkhomai*) "go away" would typically be used with similar nouns. These "latent meanings" can therefore be seen as generalizations over several correlated features.

[5] I used the function *svds* from the *R* package *RSpectra* (Qiu et al., 2019).

- The syntactic relation between verb and argument, which was either "OBJ" (complement), "ADV" (adverbial) or "PNOM" (predicate nominal).
- Animacy data, taken from an animacy lexicon coming from several sources: the PROIEL project (Haug and Jøhndal, 2008) as well as data annotated at the University of Leuven (see Keersmaekers and Speelman, to be submitted). It categorizes nouns into the following groups: *animal, concrete object, non-concrete object, group, person, place* and *time*. For 5249 (42%) arguments a label from this category could be assigned; the others were set to "unknown".
- The part-of-speech of the argument to the verb: *adjective, article, demonstrative pronoun, indefinite pronoun, infinitive, interrogative pronoun, noun, numeral, participle, personal pronoun and relative pronoun.*
- Morphological features of the argument and of the verb: *gender* and *number* for the argument and *number, tense, mood* and *voice* for the verb.

I trained a *Random Forest* classifier on this data, using *R* (R Core Team 2019) package *randomForest* (Breiman et al., 2018), building 500 classification trees[6] – this classifier turned out to perform better than any other machine learning model I tested. The results were evaluated using 10-fold cross-validation (i.e. by dividing the data in 10 roughly equally sized parts as test data, and training 10 models on each of the other 9/10 of the data).

4. Results and analysis

Overall labeling accuracy was 0.757, or 9460/12496 roles correctly labeled.[7] However, there were large differences among specific roles, as visualized in table 1. These results are calculated by summing up the errors for each of the 10 test folds.

	Precision	Recall	F1
agent (364)	0.875	0.712	0.785
beneficiary (715)	0.649	0.691	0.669
cause (753)	0.728	0.681	0.704
companion (424)	0.870	0.682	0.765
comparison (198)	0.882	0.455	0.600
condition (5)	(never used)	0.000	0.000
degree (295)	0.745	0.793	0.768
direction (1006)	0.809	0.874	0.840
duration (221)	0.821	0.665	0.735
experiencer (259)	0.742	0.444	0.556
extent of space (67)	0.917	0.164	0.278
frequency (78)	0.704	0.487	0.576
goal (282)	0.696	0.422	0.525
instrument (507)	0.628	0.673	0.650
intermediary (16)	1.000	0.688	0.815
location (1436)	0.702	0.808	0.752
manner (1596)	0.745	0.809	0.775
material (22)	1.000	0.727	0.842
modality (17)	0.385	0.294	0.333
possessor (127)	0.781	0.701	0.739
property (6)	0.000	0.000	0.000
recipient (1289)	0.879	0.942	0.909
respect (800)	0.708	0.733	0.720
result (15)	0.667	0.133	0.222
source (803)	0.724	0.885	0.797
time (943)	0.805	0.752	0.777
time frame (45)	0.786	0.489	0.603

Table 1: Precision, recall and F1 scores for each semantic role (number of instances between brackets)

In general low recall scores for a specific role can be explained by a lack of training examples: roles that had very little training data such as condition (only 5 instances), property (6 instances) and result (15 instances) expectedly had very low recall scores (0 for condition and property, and 0.133 for result). Figure 1 plots the recall score of each role as a function of the (logarithmically scaled) token frequency of the role in the training data, showing that the amount of training examples is one of the main factors explaining the performance of each role. Figure 2 shows a confusion matrix detailing how often each role ("Reference") got labeled as another role ("Prediction").

Next, we can estimate the effect of each variable by testing how well the classifier performs when leaving certain variables out of the model.[8] As can be inferred from table 2, there were only two features that had a substantial effect on the overall model accuracy: the word vectors (-8% accuracy when left out) and the syntactic label (-2.4% accuracy when left out). Lemmas, morphology, animacy and part-of-speech were less essential, as the accuracy decreases less than half a percentage point when either of them (or all of them) is left out. Probably the information that is contained in the lemma, animacy and part-of-speech features is already largely contained in the word vectors,

---

[6] This is the default setting for the *randomForest* package, but this amount can be decreased to as low as 250 without having a large negative effect on labeling accuracy (0.756, or -0.1%).

[7] While this set of roles is quite fine-grained, a reduction in the number of roles did not have a large effect on accuracy: when I merged some less frequent roles with more frequent ones ('condition' to 'respect', 'extent of space' to 'location', 'frequency' and 'time frame' to 'time', 'intermediary' and 'value' to 'instrument', 'material' to 'source', 'modality' to 'manner', 'property' to 'possessor' and 'result' to 'goal', reducing the amount of roles to 19 from 29), accuracy only increased with 1.1% point (0.768). This is probably because these roles, while semantically quite similar, typically use other formal means in Greek to express them (e.g. 'time frame' is typically expressed by the genitive, but 'time' by the dative).

[8] I did not test leaving out the three variables indicating the form of the construction since I considered them essential for the classification task. The variable importances calculated by the random forest also indicate that these variables are by far the most important (in the order "combined preposition/case" > "preposition" > "case"). While including a feature "combined preposition/case" might seem superfluous, considering that the regression trees are able to model the interaction between them natively, when it is excluded there is a relatively big drop in accuracy, from 0.757 to 0.726 (-3.1%). Presumably due to the low amount of training data and the large feature space, the data often gets partitioned into too small groups during the construction of the tree so that this interaction effect is not modelled (see also Gries, 2019, who argues that adding such combined features in a Random Forest can be beneficiary for regression as well).

while most morphological features are not that important for semantic role labeling. [9]

	Accuracy
Overal accuracy	0.757
Excluding word vectors	0.677 (-8.0%)
Excluding syntactic label	0.734 (-2.3%)
Excluding lemmas	0.759 (+0.2%)
Excluding morphology	0.754 (-0.3%)
Excluding animacy class	0.758 (+0.1%)
Excluding part-of-speech	0.756 (-0.1%)
Excluding lemmas, morphology, animacy class and part-of-speech	0.754 (-0.3%)

Table 2: Accuracy when leaving out certain features

As for part-of-speech differences, interrogative pronouns (accuracy 0.893; however, 3/4 of examples are the form τί *tí* "why"), adverbs (0.822) and personal pronouns (0.807) did particularly well, while relative pronouns (0.528), articles (0.616), numerals (0.629, but only 35 examples) and infinitives (0.667) did rather badly. The results of relative pronouns are not particularly surprising, since they are inherently anaphoric: therefore it would likely be better to model them by the vector of their antecedent (which is directly retrievable from the syntactic tree) rather than the "meaningless" vector of the lemma ὅς (*hós*: "who, which"). As for infinitives, the issue might be that they are modelled with the same vectors as nouns, while their usage is quite different: in sentence (1), for instance, whether the lemma of the infinitive is θολόω (*tholóō*: "disturb") or any other lemma is irrelevant, and the causative meaning is instead inferred from the verb ἐμέμφετο (*emémpheto*: he reproached) combined with the ἐπί + dative (*épi*: "because of") infinitive construction (in the future it might therefore be better to model infinitive arguments with a singular vector generalizing over all occurrences of an infinitive). Similarly, articles are modelled with the vector of the lemma ὁ (*ho*: "the"), which covers all usages of this lemma, while the (dominant) attributive usage is quite different from its pronominal usage (as a verbal argument): therefore restricting the vector of ὁ to pronominal uses might also help performance.

(1) ἐμέμφετο ἐπὶ τῷ
     emémpheto *epí* *tōi*
     reproach.3SG.IMPF for the.DAT

     τὸν ποταμὸν θολοῦν
     tón *potamón* *tholoũn*
     the.ACC river.ACC disturb.INF.PR

He reproached [him] **for disturbing the river**

Finally, there were some genre differences, as can be seen in table 3.

	Accuracy
Religion	0.838 (932/1112)
Documentary	0.809 (1332/1646)
History	0.765 (1439/1881)
Drama	0.751 (1091/1453)
Narrative	0.751 (2019/2689)
Rhetorical	0.723 (1086/1503)
Philosophy	0.714 (1076/1506)
Epic and lyric poetry	0.687 (485/706)

Table 3: Accuracy per genre

Unsurprisingly, the texts that did well are quite repetitive in nature, have a large amount of training examples and use an everyday, non-abstract language: religious and documentary texts. On the other side of the spectrum are poetic texts, which often express their semantic roles with other formal means than prose texts (which are the majority of the training data), and philosophical and rhetorical texts, which use relatively abstract language (see also below).

Moving towards a more detailed analysis of the results, the following will give a short overview of the specific problems associated with some roles that turned out to be especially problematic. As for **condition**, **property**, **result** and **modality**, which all had recall scores of less than 0.3, there are simply not enough training tokens in the data to make any conclusions about the performance of these roles (5, 6, 15 and 17 respectively). **Intermediary** and **material** did perform relatively well, on the other hand (recall of 0.688 and 0.727), even though they do not have that many training examples either (16 and 22 respectively). However, they are rather uniformly represented in the training data: each example of "intermediary" that was classified correctly was encoded by διά + genitive (*diá*: "through") and had either the verb γράφω (*gráphō*: "write"), κομίζω (*komízō*: "bring") or πέμπω (*pémpō*: "send") with it, while every single example of "material" that was classified correctly was a genitive object of either πίμπλημι (*pímplēmi*) or ἐμπίμπλημι (*empímplēmi*) "fill". Because of this large level of uniformity, their relatively high performance with respect to their token frequency is not particularly surprising.

Extent of space, on the other hand, did quite bad even when its frequency of 67 training examples is taken into account, as can be seen on figure 1. From the confusion matrix in figure 2, we can see that it was, unsurprisingly, most commonly misclassified as "location" (almost half of all cases) and, to a much lower extent, "direction" and "cause". One of the difficulties is that most expressions that can be used to express this role can also express a location: e.g. διά with the genitive (*diá*: "through"), ἐπί with the accusative (*epí* "at, to"), κατά with the accusative (*kata*: "along") and so on (sometimes this role was also misclassified as "location" in the data, which obviously did not help the learning or evaluation process). As an additional difficulty, the lemmas used with this role do not

---

[9] In the variable importances, *gender* and *number* of the argument of the verb were considered to be the most important, while in particular *person*, *number* and *voice* of the verb ranked lower than any other feature (including any of the 100 vector elements). As for *voice* of the verb, this can probably be explained because I did not label subjects, making the number of roles where this would be a factor relatively limited (mainly "agent" and possibly "experiencer").

substantially differ from the lemmas typically used for the role "location" (e.g. lemmas such as ἀγορά *agorá* "market", γῆ *gē* "land" etc.). Instead it is typically an interaction of the meaning of the verb and the form of the construction that determines that the semantic role should not be "location" but "extent of space", which is likely too difficult to learn with the limited amount of training examples for this role. Similar problems arise for the roles **time frame** and **frequency**, which are often expressed with the same argument lemmas as "time" and therefore are often confused with this role: however, the degree of confusion is less than with "extent of space", likely because the formal means to express these roles are quite different from the ones used to express "time" (e.g. time frame is mostly expressed with the genitive, while time is rarely so; frequency uses several adverbs such as πολλάκις *pollákis* "frequently", δίς *dís* "twice" etc. that can only express this role). More training examples would probably be beneficial in these cases: while **source** and **direction**, for instance, are also often used with the same arguments as "location", their recall scores are quite high, likely because they have many training examples to learn from (803 and 1006 respectively).

Moving to the more frequent roles, there were three roles in particular that received a wrong classification quite frequently even with a relatively high amount of training examples: **comparison**, **experiencer** and **goal**. As for **comparison**, one problem is that there are a wide range of formal means to express this role: 21 in total, which is on the high side, considering that the median role only has 12 formal means and that there is only an average amount of training examples for this role (198 in total). Another problem is that unlike for roles such as "time" and "location", the argument of the verb can be almost any lemma (and, when it is used in an adverbial relationship, the verb itself as well): if we look at sentence 2, for instance, neither the verb ἔχω (*ékhō:* "have") nor the noun ἄνθρωπος (*ánthrōpos:* "human") is particularly useful to identify the role of ἀντί (*antí:* "instead"): instead ἀντί functions more as a "mediator" between κυνοκέφαλος (*kunoképhalos:* "baboon") and ἄνθρωπος. Involving not only the verb but also its dependents would help in this case, but since the comparative construction can refer to any element in the sentence this problem is rather complicated (and might be more appropriate to solve at the parsing stage).

(2)
τίς	αὐτὸν	θελήσει
tís	*autón*	*thelḗsei*
who.NOM	he.ACC	want.3SG.FUT
ἀγοράσαι	καὶ	κυνοκέφαλον
agorásai	*kaí*	*kunoképhalon*
buy.INF.AOR	and	baboon.ACC
ἀντὶ	**ἀνθρώπου**	**ἔχειν;**
antí	**anthrṓpou**	**ékhein?**
instead.of	**human.GEN**	**have.INF.PR**

Who will want to buy him and have a baboon **instead of a human**?

The **experiencer** role is most often confused with the beneficiary/maleficiary role. This happens in particular when this role receives the label ADV "adverbial" (recall 0.173) rather than OBJ "complement" (recall 0.817). In this case both "beneficiary" and "experiencer" refer to a person who is affected in some way by the action of the main verb, and the difference between being advantaged or disadvantaged by an action and being affected by it is often only subtle (and sometimes also inconsistently annotated). In sentence 3, for instance, σοί (*soí* "for you") has been labeled as an experiencer, but might also be considered a beneficiary: "the rest is according to your wishes **for your benefit**". In general verbs that denote an action that have clear results (e.g. ποιέω *poiéō* "make", παρασκευάζω *paraskeuázō* "prepare" etc.) would be more likely to have a beneficiary rather than an experiencer adverbial, but more training data is likely needed to learn this subtle difference.

(3)
εἰ	(...)	τὰ	λοιπά
ei		*tá*	*loipá*
if		the.ACC.PL	rest.ACC.PL
σοί	*ἐστιν*	*κατὰ*	*γνώμην,*
soí	*estin*	*katá*	*gnṓmēn,*
you.DAT	be.3SG	according	will.ACC
ἔχοι	*ἂν*	*καλῶς*	
ékhoi	*án*	*kalõs*	
have.3SG.PR.OPT	PTC	good	

If (…) the rest is according to your wishes **for you**, it would be good.

Finally, as for **goal**, its large amount of confusion with roles such as "cause" or "respect" is not very surprising, as they are expressed by similar argument lemmas. However, the role is also frequently confused with roles such as "direction" and "location" (to a lesser extent). While the same formal means are often used to express goals and directions (e.g. εἰς/κατά/ἐπί/πρός + accusative), one would expect directions to be used predominantly with concrete objects and goals with non-concrete objects. However, in general non-concrete objects do perform quite badly: their accuracy is only 0.655, as opposed to 0.744 for all nouns in general. This might suggest that these nouns are not that well modelled by their distributional vector (which we also found to some extent in Keersmaekers and Speelman to be submitted), although other explanations (e.g. non-concrete objects typically receiving roles that are harder to model in general) are also possible. Other than that, there was also a large influence of the syntactic label: the recall of goals that had the label ADV was 0.493 while it was only 0.111 for the label OBJ – and 35/48 of the goals that were misclassified as direction had the label "OBJ": this is consistent with the fact that goals predominantly have the ADV label (80%) while directions predominantly have OBJ (83%), and some of the goals that were classified as OBJ were in fact misclassifications.

5. Conclusion

This paper has described a first approach to automatic semantic role labeling for Ancient Greek, using a Random Forest classifier trained with a diverse range of features.

While the amount of training data was relatively low (only about 12500 tokens for 29 roles), the model was still able to receive a classification accuracy of about 76%. The most helpful features were distributional semantic vectors, created on a large corpus of 37 million tokens, while other features (lemmas, morphology, animacy label, part-of-speech) did not contribute as much. Probably it is exactly this small amount of training samples that explains why these vectors are so important: since there are a large amount of lemmas in the training data (about 2700 argument lemmas and 1900 verb lemmas), the model is able to reduce this variation by assigning similar vectors to semantically similar lemmas. The distinctions that features such as morphology are able to make (e.g. the role *agent* as expressed by *ὑπό hupó* "by" with the genitive is rare with active verbs) might be too subtle, on the other hand, to be statistically picked up by the model with the relatively low training examples we have, and therefore these features would perhaps be more helpful when there is more data to learn from.

An in-depth error analysis reveals a number of ways for further improvement. First of all, the most important step would be expanding the amount of training data, since there is an obvious correlation between the amount of training examples and the performance of each role. Secondly, while the distributional semantic approach works well for most words, some categories (e.g. relative pronouns, infinitives) are not modelled that well and might require a special treatment. Thirdly, non-concrete words turned out to be particularly problematic, and need to be investigated in more detail (particularly by examining if their meaning is modelled well by their semantic vector). Finally, the syntactic relation (adverbial or complement) was also relatively influential in the model, and some wrongly classified instances had in fact received the wrong syntactic label. Therefore improving the syntactic data with regards to this distinction would also likely improve results, especially when moving from manually disambiguated syntactic data (as used in this paper) to automatically parsed data.

The semantic role labeling system used in this paper, as well as the training data on which the system was trained (including all modifications of existing treebanks) is available on GitHub.[10] Hopefully this will encourage corpus annotators to add a semantic layer to their project (since there is already an automatically annotated basis to start from), so that their data can also be integrated in the system and results can be further improved.

6.   Abbreviations used in interlinear glosses

ACC	accusative
AOR	aorist
DAT	dative
FUT	future
GEN	genitive
IMPF	imperfect
INF	infinitive
NOM	nominative
OPT	optative
PL	plural
PR	present

---

[10] https://github.com/alekkeersmaekers/PRL

PTC	particle
SG	singular

7.   Acknowledgements

The present study was supported by the Research Foundation Flanders (FWO) [grant number: 1162017N]. Some preliminary work was carried out by Colin Swaelens (whose master thesis I supervised). I would like to thank my PhD supervisors (Toon Van Hal and Dirk Speelman), as well as three anonymous reviewers for their detailed and helpful feedback.

8.   Bibliographical references

Baker, C.F., Fillmore, C.J. and Lowe, J.B. (1998). The Berkeley FrameNet Project. In Proceedings of the 17th International Conference on Computational Linguistics Volume 1, pages 86–90, Montreal, Quebec, Canada, august. Association for Computational Linguistics.

Bamman, D., Mambrini, F. and Crane, G. (2009). An Ownership Model of Annotation: The Ancient Greek Dependency Treebank. In Marco Passarotti, Adam Przepiórkowski, Savina Raynaud, Frank Van Eynde, editors, Proceedings of the Eighth International Workshop on Treebanks and Linguistic Theories (TLT 8), pages 5–15, Milan, Italy, december. EDUCatt.

Berti, M. (2016). The Digital Marmor Parium. Presented at the Epigraphy Edit-a-thon. Editing Chronological and Geographic Data in Ancient Inscriptions, Leipzig.

Breiman, L., Cutler, A., Liaw, A., and Wiener, M. (2018). randomForest: Breiman and Cutler's Random Forests for Classification and Regression. https://CRAN.R-project.org/package=randomForest.

Celano, G.G.A. and Crane, G. (2015). Semantic Role Annotation in the Ancient Greek Dependency Treebank. In Marcus Dickson, Erhard Hinrichs, Agnieszka Patejuk, Adam Przepiórkowski, editors, Proceedings of the Fourteenth International Workshop on Treebanks and Linguistic Theories (TLT14), pages 26–34, Warsaw, Poland, december. Institute of Computer Science, Polish Academy of Sciences.

Crespo, E., Conti, L., and Maquieira, H. (2003). Sintaxis Del Griego Clásico. Madrid: Gredos.

Deerwester, S., Dumais, S.T., Furnas, G.W., Landauer, T.K., and Harshman, R. (1990). Indexing by Latent Semantic Analysis. *Journal of the American Society for Information Science*, 41(6):391–407.

Gildea, D. and Jurafsky, D. (2002). Automatic Labeling of Semantic Roles. *Computational Linguistics*, 28(3):245–288.

Gries, S. (2019). On Classification Trees and Random Forests in Corpus Linguistics: Some Words of Caution and Suggestions for Improvement. *Corpus Linguistics and Linguistic Theory*.

Haug, D.T.T. and Jøhndal, M. (2008). Creating a Parallel Treebank of the Old Indo-European Bible Translations. In Caroline Sporleder and Kiril Ribarov (Conference Chairs), et al., editors, Proceedings of the Second Workshop on Language Technology for Cultural Heritage Data (LaTeCH 2008), pages 27–34, Marrakech,

Morocco, may. European Language Resource Association (ELRA).

He, L., Lee, K., Lewis, M., and Zettlemoyer, L. (2017). Deep Semantic Role Labeling: What Works and What's next. In Regina Barzilay, Min-Yen Kan, editors, Proceedings of the 55th Annual Meeting of the Association for Computational Linguistics (Volume 1: Long Papers), pages 473–483, Vancouver, Canada, july-august. Association for Computational Linguistics.

Keersmaekers, A. (2019). Creating a Richly Annotated Corpus of Papyrological Greek: The Possibilities of Natural Language Processing Approaches to a Highly Inflected Historical Language. *Digital Scholarship in the Humanities*.

Keersmaekers, A., Mercelis, W., Swaelens, C., and Van Hal, T. (2019). Creating, Enriching and Valorizing Treebanks of Ancient Greek. In Marie Candito, Kilian Evang, Stephan Oepen, Djamé Seddah, editors, Proceedings of the 18th International Workshop on Treebanks and Linguistic Theories (TLT, SyntaxFest 2019), pages 109–117, Paris, France, august. Association for Computational Linguistics.

Keersmaekers, A. and Speelman, D. (to be submitted). Applying Distributional Semantic Models to a Historical Corpus of a Highly Inflected Language: The Case of Ancient Greek.

Kipper Schuler, K. (2005). VerbNet: A Broad-Coverage, Comprehensive Verb Lexicon. Dissertation in Computer and Information Science. University of Pennsylvania.

Marcheggiani, D. and Titov, I. (2017). Encoding Sentences with Graph Convolutional Networks for Semantic Role Labeling. In Martha Palmer, Rebecca Hwa, Sebastian Riedel, editors, Proceedings of the 2017 Conference on Empirical Methods in Natural Language Processing, pages 1506–1515, Copenhagen, Denmark, september. Association for Computational Linguistics.

Màrquez, L., Carreras, X., Litkowski, K.C., and Stevenson, S. (2008). Semantic Role Labeling: An Introduction to the Special Issue. *Computational Linguistics*, 34(2):145–159.

Palmer, M., Gildea, D., and Xue, N. (2010). Semantic Role Labeling. Morgan & Claypool.

Qiu, Y., Mei, J., Guennebaud, G., and Niesen, J. (2019). RSpectra: Solvers for Large-Scale Eigenvalue and SVD Problems. https://CRAN.R-project.org/package=RSpectra.

R Core Team. (2019). R: A language and environment for statistical computing. R Foundation for Statistical Computing. https://www.R-project.org/

Turney, P.D. and Pantel, P. (2010). From Frequency to Meaning: Vector Space Models of Semantics. *Journal of Artificial Intelligence Research*, 37:141–188.

Van Hal, T. and Anné, Y. (2017). Reconciling the Dynamics of Language with a Grammar Handbook: The Ongoing Pedalion Grammar Project. *Digital Scholarship in the Humanities*, 32(2):448–454.

Vatri, A. and McGillivray, B. (2018). The Diorisis Ancient Greek Corpus. *Research Data Journal for the Humanities and Social Sciences*, 3(1):55–65.

Zhou, Y. and Xu, W. (2015). End-to-End Learning of Semantic Role Labeling Using Recurrent Neural Networks. In Chengqing Zong, Michael Strube, editors, Proceedings of the 53rd Annual Meeting of the Association for Computational Linguistics and the 7th International Joint Conference on Natural Language Processing (Volume 1: Long Papers), pages 1127–1137, Beijing, China, july. Association for Computational Linguistics.

9.   Language Resource References

Giuseppe G. A Celano. (2017). Lemmatized Ancient Greek Texts. 1.2.5. https://github.com/gcelano/LemmatizedAncientGreekXML.

Vanessa Gorman. (2019). Gorman Trees. 1.0.1. https://github.com/vgorman1/Greek-Dependency-Trees.

Matthew J. Harrington. (2018). Perseids Project - Treebanked Commentaries at Tufts University. https://perseids-project.github.io/harrington_trees/.

Polina Yordanova. (2018). Treebank of Aphtonius' Progymnasmata. https://github.com/polinayordanova/Treebank-of-Aphtonius-Progymnasmata.

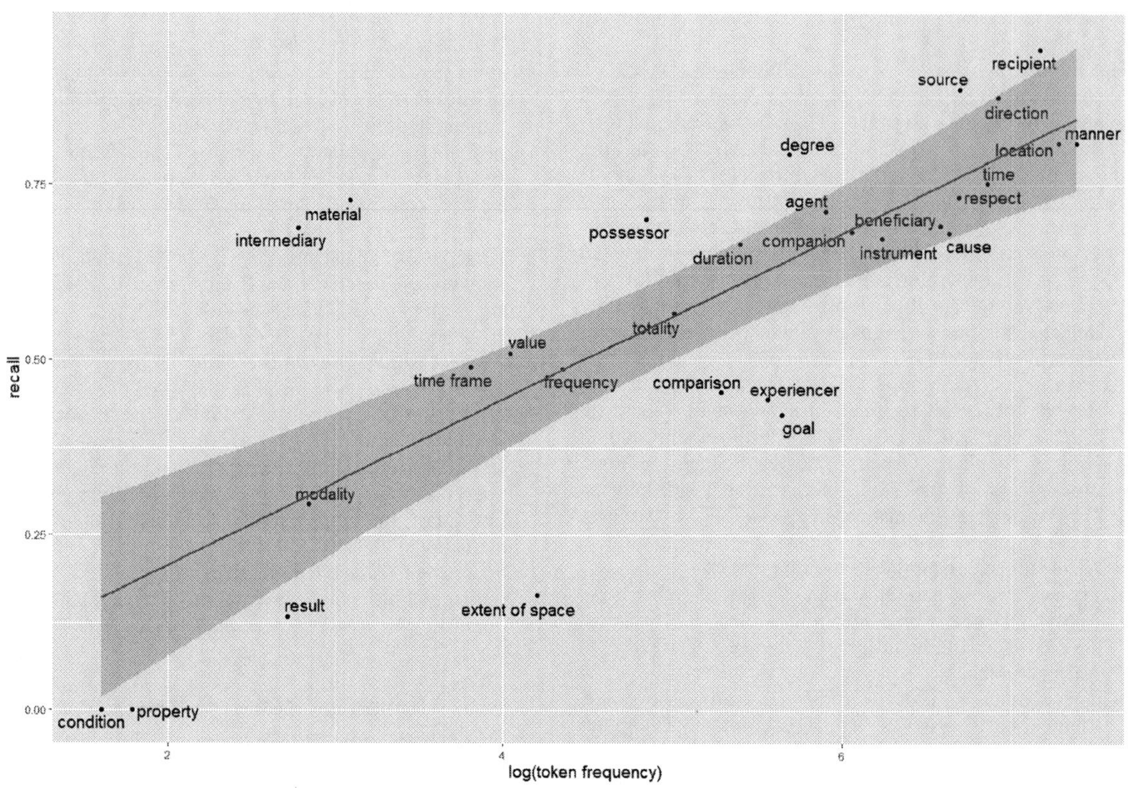

Figure 1: Recall scores for semantic roles as a function of their logarithmically scaled token frequency

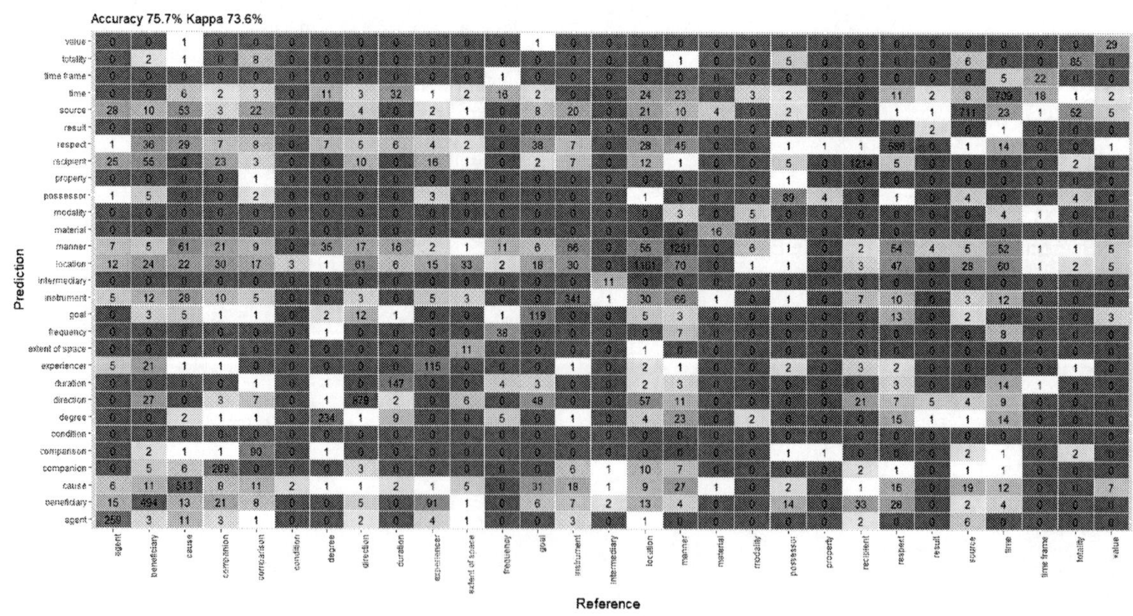

Figure 2: Confusion matrix of semantic roles

Role	Example
Agent (364 instances)	δύο δὲ παῖδες **ὑπὸ μητρὸς** τρεφόμενοι "Two children being raised **by their mother**"
Beneficiary/Maleficiary[11] (715 instances)	**ὑπὲρ τῆς πατρίδος** ἀποθανεῖν δυνήσομαι "I will be able to die **for my native land**"
Cause (753 instances)	ἐκπλαγὼν **διὰ τὸ παράδοξον τῆς** ὄψεως "Being struck **by the incredibility of the sight**"
Companion (424 instances)	τοῦτον **μετὰ Σιτάλκους** ἔπινον τὸν χρόνον "During that time I was drinking **with Sitalces**"
Comparison (198 instances)	πάντα ἐοικότες **ἀνθρώποις** πλὴν τῆς κόμης "Completely looking **like humans** except for their hair"
Condition (5 instances)	κελεύοντος **ἐπ' αὐτοφώρῳ** τὸν μοιχὸν κτείνεσθαι "Commanding that an adulterer should be killed **in case he is caught**"
Degree (295 instances)	ξεῖνε **λίην** αὐχεῖς ἐπί γαστέρι "Stranger, you are boasting **too much** about your belly"
Direction (1006 instances)	**εἰς Θετταλίαν** αὐτοὺς ἀγαγὼν "Bringing them **to Thessaly**"
Duration (221 instances)	εὐφράνθη **ἐφ' ἡμέρας τέσσαρες** "She was happy **for four days**"
Experiencer (259 instances)	σὺ δέ **μοι** δοκεῖς αἰτιᾶσθαι τὸν γάμον "You seem **to me** to defend marriage"
Extent of space (67 instances)	**διὰ Καϋστρίων πεδίων** ὁδοιπλανοῦντες "Wandering **through Castrian plains**"
Frequency (78 instances)	ἀποθνήσκομεν ὅτι οὐ βλέπομέν σε **καθ' ἡμέραν** "We are dying because we do not see you **every day**"
Goal (282 instances)	ὥσπερ **ἐπὶ δεῖπνον** ἀποδεδημηκὼς εἰς Θετταλίαν "As if going to Thessaly **for a banquet**"
Instrument (507 instances)	**τοῖς δακτύλοις** τῶν ἑαυτοῦ βλεφάρων ἡπτόμην "I felt my own eyelids **with my fingers**"
Intermediary (16 instances)	ἔπεμψά σοι ἐπιστολὴν **διὰ τοῦ ἀρτοκόπου** "I've sent you a letter **by the baker**"
Location (1436 instances)	**ἐν Βυζαντίῳ** διατρίβειν δυναμένοις "Being able to stay **in Byzantium**"
Manner (1596 instances)	ἐάν τις τῷ **εὖ** λέγοντι μὴ πείθηται "If someone does not believe the person who speaks **well**"
Material/Content (22 instances)	ἔπλησεν τόν ἀσκόν **ὕδατος** "He filled the sack **with water**"
Modality (17 instances)	**ἴσως** οἶδας τί σοι ἔγραψα "**Perhaps** you know what I've written to you"
Possessor (127 instances)	ἔσται **τῇ Σαρρα** υἱός "**Sara** will have a son" (lit. "There will be a son to Sara")
Property (6 instances)	ὅ ἦν **ἀγαθοῦ βασιλέως** "What is typical **of a good king**"
Recipient (1289 instances)	τὰ ἱμάτια αὐτοῦ ἔδωκεν **τῷ Αἰσώπῳ** "He gave **Aesop** his clothes"
Respect (800 instances)	μήτε ἀλγεῖν **κατὰ σῶμα** μήτε ταράττεσθαι **κατὰ ψυχήν** "Neither having pain **in the body** neither being disturbed **in the soul**"
Result (15 instances)	φαίνῃ **εἰς μανίαν** ἐμπεπτωκέναι "You seem to be fallen **into madness**"
Source (803 instances)	ῥίπτει δὲ αὐτὸν **ἐξ οὐρανοῦ** Ζεὺς "Zeus threw him **from Heaven**"
Time (943 instances)	**τετάρτῳ τε καί εἰκοστῷ τῆς βασιλείας ἔτει** νόσῳ διεφθάρη "He died from disease **in the twenty-fourth year of his reign**"
Time frame (45 instances)	μηδ' εἰληφέναι μηθὲν **ἐνιαυτοῦ** "Not receiving anything **over the course of the year**"
Totality (150 instances)	ἐπιλαμβάνεται **τῆς χειρὸς αὐτῆς** "He took her **by the hand**"
Value (57 instances)	**ἑξήκοντα δηναρίων** τοῦτον ἠγόρακα "I've bought him **for sixty denarii**"

Table 4: Pedalion semantic roles

---

[11] I combined these two roles because they were not distinguished in the data, but since some prepositions (e.g. ὑπέρ + genitive) can only be used for a beneficiary, while others (e.g. κατά + genitive) only for a maleficiary, in the future it might be better to keep them apart.

Proceedings of 1st Workshop on Language Technologies for Historical and Ancient Languages, pages 68–73
Language Resources and Evaluation Conference (LREC 2020), Marseille, 11–16 May 2020
© European Language Resources Association (ELRA), licensed under CC-BY-NC

A Thesaurus for Biblical Hebrew

Miriam Azar, Aliza Pahmer, Joshua Waxman
Department of Computer Science
Stern College for Women, Yeshiva University
New York, NY, United States
mtazar@mail.yu.edu, apahmer@mail.yu.edu, joshua.waxman@yu.edu

Abstract

We build a thesaurus for Biblical Hebrew, with connections between roots based on phonetic, semantic, and distributional similarity. To this end, we apply established algorithms to find connections between headwords based on existing lexicons and other digital resources. For semantic similarity, we utilize the cosine-similarity of tf-idf vectors of English gloss text of Hebrew headwords from Ernest Klein's A Comprehensive Etymological Dictionary of the Hebrew Language for Readers of English as well as from Brown-Driver-Brigg's Hebrew Lexicon. For phonetic similarity, we digitize part of Matityahu Clark's Etymological Dictionary of Biblical Hebrew, grouping Hebrew roots into phonemic classes, and establish phonetic relationships between headwords in Klein's Dictionary. For distributional similarity, we consider the cosine similarity of PPMI vectors of Hebrew roots and also, in a somewhat novel approach, apply Word2Vec to a Biblical corpus reduced to its lexemes. The resulting resource is helpful to those trying to understand Biblical Hebrew, and also stands as a good basis for programs trying to process the Biblical text.

Keywords: Corpus (Creation, Annotation, etc.), Less-Resourced/Endangered Languages, Lexicon, Lexical Database, Phonetic Databases, Phonology, Tools, Systems, Applications, graph dictionary, semantic similarity, distributional similarity, Word2Vec

1. Introduction

Biblical Hebrew is the archaic form of Hebrew in which the Hebrew Bible is primarily written. Its syntax and vocabulary differ from later Rabbinic Hebrew and Modern Hebrew. Hebrew is a highly inflected language, and the key to understanding any Hebrew word is to identify and understand its root. For example, the first word in the Bible is בראשית / *bereishit* / 'in the beginning'. The underlying three-letter root is ראש / *rosh* / 'head, start'. By adding vowels and morphology to a root, one can produce derived forms, or lexemes. The lexeme ראשית / *reishit* / 'beginning' is derived from the root ראש. Finally, the prefix letter ב / *be* introduces the preposition 'in'.

Many scholars have developed resources for understanding these Hebrew roots. While we do not intend to provide a comprehensive list, we will mention a few notable resources. *A Hebrew and English Lexicon of the Old Testament*, developed by Brown, Driver and Briggs (1906), is one such standard dictionary. *The Exhaustive Concordance of the Bible*, by Strong (1890), is an index to the English King James Bible, so that one can look up an English word (e.g. "tree") and find each verse in which that word occurs. Strong's Concordance also includes 8674 Hebrew lexemes, and each verse occurrence includes the corresponding Hebrew lexeme number. Some versions of Brown-Driver-Briggs are augmented with these Strong numbers. For example, Sefaria, an open-source library of Jewish texts, includes such an augmented dictionary as part of their database. Another concordance is that of Mandelkern (1896), *Veteris Testamenti Concordantiæ Hebraicae Atque Chaldaicae*, a Hebrew-Latin concordance of the Hebrew and Aramaic words in the Bible, also organized by root.

Another notable dictionary is that of Clark (1999), *Etymological Dictionary of Biblical Hebrew: Based on the Commentaries of Samson Raphael Hirsch*. Rabbi Samson Raphael Hirsch developed a theory, which is expressed through his Biblical commentary (Hirsch, 1867), in which roots which are phonologically similar are also semantically related. This theory is founded on the well-grounded idea, accepted by many scholars, that Hebrew's triliteral roots are often derived from an underlying biliteral root. Thus, the third letter added to the true biliteral root modifies that underlying root's meaning. For instance, Jastrow's dictionary (1903) lists √אב / *`av* is a biliteral root, and derived triliteral roots include אבב / *`avav* / 'to be thick, to be heavy, to press; to surround; to twist; to be warm, glow etc.'; אבד / *`avad* / 'to be pressed, go around in despair', אבר / *`avar* / 'to be bent, pressed, thick', and others. Within Hirsch's system, specific added letters often convey specific connotations.

When comparing roots, alternations between letters within the same or similar place of articulation often carry similar meanings. For instance, in the entry for אבב / *`avav* (listed above), Jastrow notes the connection between it and other biliteral roots, such as קב / *qav*, כב / *kav*, גב / *gav*, חב / *hav*, and עב / *`av*. The first letter of אבב, an *aleph*, is a guttural, as is the *ayin* of עב and the *het* of חב. The entry for the triliteral root חבב / *havav*, which is an expansion of the biliteral root חב, includes the gloss to 'embrace (in a fight), to wrestle'. This clearly bears a related meaning to the √אב roots in the previous paragraph, which involved pressing and surrounding. These related meanings might be termed phonemic cognates.

Within the triliteral root system are what might be called gradational variants. At times, there are only two unique letters in a root. For instance, in the root רדד / *radad* / 'flattening down or submitting totally', the two unique letters are the ר / *r* and the ד / *d*. The geminated triliteral root can be formed by gemination of the second letter (as here, the ד / *d* was repeated, to form רדד / *radad*). Alternatively, a hollow triliteral root can be formed by employing a י / *y*, ו / *w*, ה / *h* in one of the three consonant positions. These three letters, *yud, vav,* and *heh* are called *matres lectiones*. They sometimes function in Hebrew as full consonants and sometimes function to indicate the presence of a specific associated vowel. The hollow roots include רדה / *radah* / 'ruling or having dominion over', ירד / *yarad* / 'going down', and רוד / *rod* / 'humbling'. Within Hirsch's system, these gradational variants in general are semantically related to one another, just as is evident in the present case.

While these phenomena have been observed by other scholars, Hirsch made these ideas central to his Biblical commentary and greatly expanded the application of these rules, to analyze many different Hebrew roots. His commentary on the first verse, and indeed the first word, of Genesis, is typical. In explaining the root ראש / *rosh* / 'head, start' (which has the guttural *aleph* in the middle position), he notes two other words, רעש / *ra'ash* / 'commotion, earthquake' (with a guttural *'ayin* in that position) and רחש / *rahash* / 'moving, vibrating, whispering' (with a guttural *het* in that position). Hirsch explains that the core phonemic meaning is movement, with ראש / *rosh* being the start of movement, רעש / *ra'ash* as an external movement, and רחש / *rahash* as an internal movement.

Clark arranged these analyses into a dictionary, and applied the principle in an even more systematic manner. For each headword, he provides a cognate meaning (a generic meaning shared by each specific cognate variant), and discusses all phonemic and gradational variants. In an appendix, he establishes a number of phonemic classes, in which he groups related words which follow a specific phonemic pattern. For instance, he lists phonemic class A54, which is formed by a guttural (א / *aleph*, ה / *heh*, ח / *het*, ע / *ayin*) followed by two instances of the Hebrew letter ר / *resh*. The roots ארר / *'arar*, הרר / *harar*, and ערר / *'arar* mean 'isolate' and חרר / *harar* means 'parch'. These all share a general phonemic cognate meaning of 'isolate'. (To relate the last root, perhaps consider that a desert is a parched, isolated place; perhaps they are not related at all.) A less clear-cut example is A60, which is formed by a guttural, the Hebrew letter ד / *dalet*, and then a sibilant, with a cognate meaning of 'grow'. The roots involved are הדס / *hadas* / 'grow', חדש / *hadash* / 'renew', עדש / *'adash* / 'grow', and עטש / *'atash* / 'sneeze'. There is sometimes a level of subjective interpretation to place these words into their phonemic cognate classes, but some true patterns seem to emerge.

Another noteworthy dictionary is that of Klein (1987), *A Comprehensive Etymological Dictionary of the Hebrew Language for Readers of English*. It focuses not only on Biblical Hebrew, but on Post-Biblical Hebrew, Medieval Hebrew, and Modern Hebrew as well. His concern includes the etymology of all of these Hebrew words, and he therefore includes entries on Biblical Hebrew roots. Klein's dictionary was recently digitized by Sefaria (2018) and made available on their website and their database. Other important digital resources include the Modern Hebrew WordNet project, by Ordan and Wintner (2007), as well as the ETCBC dataset, from Roorda (2015), which provides in-depth linguistic markup for each word in each verse of the Biblical corpus.

Our aim was to create a new digital resource, namely a graph dictionary / thesaurus for the roots (or lexemes) in Biblical Hebrew, in which headwords are nodes and the edges represent phonetic, semantic, and distributional similarity. This captures connections not drawn in earlier efforts. We have thereby created a corpus and tool for Biblical philologists to gain insight into the meaning of Biblical Hebrew roots, and to consider new, possibly unappreciated connections between these roots. The digital resource – a graph database and a Word2Vec model – can also aid in other NLP tasks against the Biblical text – for example, as a thesaurus in order to detect chiastic structures.

2. Method

We sought to create our graph dictionary for Biblical Hebrew in three different ways, creating several different subgraphs. In future work, we plan to merge these subgraphs.

Our first approach was to look for semantic similarities between headwords. Our source data was Ernest Klein's *A Comprehensive Etymological Dictionary of the Hebrew Language for Readers of English*, using Sefaria's (2018) MongoDB database. This dictionary has headwords for both roots (*shorashim*) and derived forms, for Biblical Hebrew as well as many later forms of Hebrew. We first filtered out all but the Biblical roots. Non-root entries have vowel points (called *niqqud*) and non-Biblical Hebrew words are often marked with a specific language code, such as PBH for post-Biblical Hebrew. We calculated the semantic similarity between headwords as the cosine similarity of the tf-idf vectors of the lemmatized words in their English gloss. Thus, אמר / *'amar* and דבר / *dabier* share the English definition 'say', and a cosine similarity of about 0.35. Function words, such as "to" or "an", will have a low tf-idf score in these vectors and would not contribute much to the cosine similarity metric. We therefore set a threshold of 0.33 in creating the "Klein" graph. We applied this approach to Brown-Driver-Briggs' lexicon of lexemes, which had been digitized by Sefaria as well, for the sake of having a comparable graph (for lexemes instead of roots) with semantic relationships calculated in the same manner.

Our second approach was to consider phonetic similarity between headwords. One data source for this was Matityahu Clark's *Etymological Dictionary of Biblical Hebrew*. We digitized a portion of Clark's dictionary, namely his 25-page appendix which contains the listing of phonemic classes containing phonemic cognates with their short glosses. We created a separate graph from this data, linking Clark's headwords to their phonemic class (e.g. ארר to A54) as well as shared short gloss, e.g. ארר / *'arar* to הרר / *harar* based on a shared gloss of 'isolate'.

Aside from that standalone Clark graph, we introduced phonetic relationships on the Klein graph as well. We connected each combination of words which Clark had listed as belonging to the same phonemic class. Additionally, we computed gradational variants for each triliteral root in the Klein dictionary as follows. We treated each triliteral root as a vector of three letters. We checked if the vector matched the pattern of a potential gradational root. If the root contained a potential placeholder letter (י / *yud* in the first position, ו / *vav* or י / *yud* in the middle position, or ה / *heh* in the final position), or if the final letter was a repetition of the middle letter, then it was a potential gradational variant. We then generated all possible gradational variant candidates for this root, and if a candidate also appeared in Klein's dictionary as a headword, we connected the two headwords.

We also looked for simpler, single-edit phonemic connections between headwords in Klein's dictionary. That is, we took the 3-letter vectors for triliteral roots and, in each position, if the letter was a sibilant, we iterated through all Hebrew sibilant letters in that position. We checked whether the resulting word was a headword and, if so, established a phonemic relationship between the word pair. We similarly performed such replacement on other phonetic groups, namely dentals, gutturals, labials and velars.

Our third approach was based on distributional criteria. Our source data was the ETCBC dataset, from Roorda (2015). We first reduced the text of the Bible to its lexemes, using ETCBC lex0 feature. These lexemes were manually produced by human expects. As discussed above, the Hebrew lexeme is often more elaborate than the Hebrew root. Many of the lexemes in this dataset are also triliteral roots (such as ראש / rosh / 'head', and אור / *'or* / 'light'), but

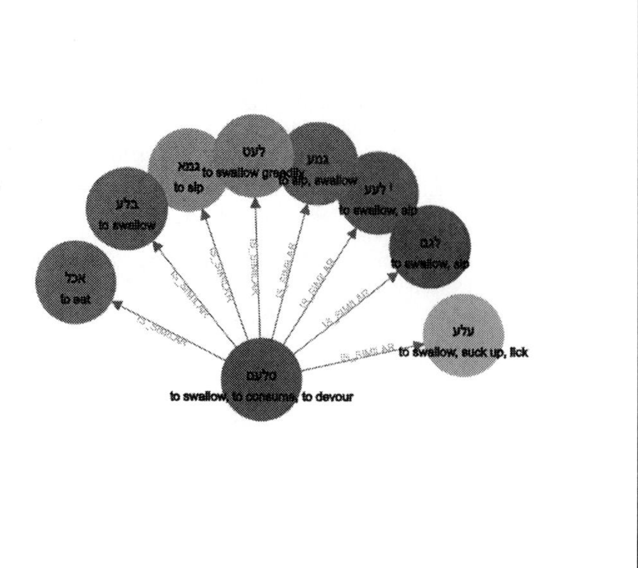

The figure's left panel reproduces a dictionary entry:

Shoresh: סלעם

Meaning: to swallow, to consume, to devour. was swallowed, was destroyed.

Similar words:

גמא to sip. he sipped, swallowed. was sipped, swallowed. he swallowed. he gave to drink. was given to drink.

אכל to eat. he ate, devoured, consumed, destroyed. was eaten, was devoured, was consumed. he digested, consumed, burned. was digested, was consumed, was burnt. was digested, was consumed. he caused to eat, gave to eat, fed, nourished; he caused to devour. was fed, was nourished.

לעע ' to swallow, sip. he swallowed, sipped (a hapax legomenon in the Bible, occurring Oba. verse 16). he swallowed the wrong way, he choked.

גמע to sip, swallow. he sipped, swallowed, gulped, drank. was sipped, was swallowed. he sipped, swallowed, gulped, drank. he gave to drink. was given to drink.

לגם to swallow, sip. he swallowed, sipped. was swallowed, was sipped.

לעט to swallow greedily. he swallowed greedily. he made to swallow (a hapax legomenon in the Bible, occurring Gen. 25:30 in the form הלעיטני = let me swallow); he stuffed, fattened. was stuffed, was fattened.

בלע to swallow. he swallowed, devoured, ate up; he absorbed. was swallowed up, was devoured; was absorbed; was assimilated (grammar). he destroyed. was destroyed. was destroyed; was assimilated (grammar). he caused to swallow; he assimilated (grammar). was swallowed, was devoured; was absorbed; was syncopated, was assimilated (grammar).

עלע to swallow, suck up, lick. he swallowed, licked, sucked up (a hapax legomenon in the Bible, occurring Job 39:30 in the form יעלעו).

Figure 1: Klein entry for סלעם / *sal'am* / 'to swallow, to consume, to devour'

there are also quite a number of lexemes that would not be considered roots (such as ראשית / *reishit* /'beginning' and מאור / *ma`or* / 'luminary').

We represented each lexeme A as a V-length vector, where V is the vocabulary size (of 6,466). Each position in the vector corresponded to a different lexeme B, and recorded positive pointwise mutual information (PPMI) values. PPMI values of lexeme A and lexeme B were computed as follows:

$$PPMI(A, B) = \max\left(0, log \frac{p(A, B)}{p(A)p(B)}\right)$$

The joint probability p(A, B) is computed as the frequency of lexeme B occurring within a window of the 10 previous and 10 following words of each occurrence of lexeme A, and the individual distributions p(A) and p(B) as the frequencies of lexemes A and B, respectively, within the Biblical corpus.

We then calculated the cosine similarity of each combination of PPMI vectors. Word pairs which exceeded a threshold (again, of 0.33) were considered related. This yielded word pairs such as טוב / *tov* / 'good' and ישר / *yashar* / 'upright' which indeed seem semantically related.

As an additional way of relating words by distributional criteria, we took the same lexeme-based Biblical corpus and trained a Word2Vec model. This is a slightly novel approach to Word2Vec, in that we are looking at the surrounding context of lexemes, rather than the (often highly inflected) full words. The results are promising. For instance, the six most distributionally similar words to ארץ / *`eretz* / 'land' include גוי / *goy* / 'nation', אדמה / *`adamah* / 'earth', and ממלכה / *mamlacha* / 'kingdom', which captures the elemental, geographical, and political connotations of the word 'land'. We filtered by a relatively high threshold of similarity, of 0.9.

We pushed all of these graphs to a Neo4j database and wrote a presentation layer using the D3 JavaScript library. Some of the resulting graphs can be seen at http://www.mivami.org/dictionary, and are also available as a download in GRAPHML file format.

3. Results

By applying our method, we have produced four graphs. Table 1 describes the number of nodes and edges in each graph.

Graph	Nodes	Connections
Klein's Dictionary	3,287 roots	7,472 semantic ; 1,509 phonemic class ; 2,329 phonemic edits
Brown-Driver-Briggs lexicon	8,674 lexemes	12,759 semantic
Clark's Etymological Dictionary	1,926 roots	Grouped into 388 phonemic classes
Distributional Criteria / ETCBC	6,466 lexemes	5773 Word2Vec ; 12,561 PPMI

Table 1: Corpora and Connections Established

At the moment, these different types of connections are in different graphs, and the headword types slightly differ from one another, and so we do not perform a comprehensive inter-graph analysis. However, in the evaluation section, we evaluate the quality of each individual graph, and in this results section, we present some individual interesting subgraphs. We examine the connections between nodes and find that there are some meaningful connections being established.

For instance, Figure 1 depicts the hyperlinked list of related words, from the Klein's dictionary graph, for the root סלעם / *sal'am* / 'to swallow, to consume, to devour'. (In all cases for these graphs, the colors are just the styling provided by the D3 JavaScript visualization library.)

Although the connection to other entries is based on semantic similarities (e.g. sipping, swallowing, gulping), there are some obvious phonological connections between

The following box (Figure 2 content):

Shoresh: דבר¹

Meaning: to speak. (used only in the act. part. דובר, 'saying, speaking', and in the pass. part. דָבוּר, 'said, spoken'). (pl.) they spoke to one another, talked; was said, was spoken. he spoke of; he spoke to or with. was spoken; was stipulated, was agreed. he spoke, talked; he came to an agreement.

Similar words:

דבב ‡ to speak, whisper. he spoke, whispered. he caused to speak; he spoke, whispered. he spoke; he caused to speak, interviewed. he was made to speak.

ברגז to not be on speaking terms with (slang). he was not on speaking terms.

פוץ ‡ to speak. he opened his mouth, spoke, said (used only in the perf. and in the part.).

סח to talk, say. talked, said. he talked, said, spoke.

לאט ‖ to speak softly, whisper. he spoke softly, whispered (a hapax legomenon in the Bible, occurring Job 15:11).

שיח to speak, talk, converse. he spoke, talked, conversed; he mused, meditated. he talked. , he spoke, talked conversed; tr. v. he caused to speak, caused to talk.

לוז ‖ to speak evil, slander. he spoke evil of, slandered.

נום ‖ to speak. he spoke, said.

חטם ‖ to speak through the nose. he spoke through the nose. (of s.m.).

מלל ¹ to speak, say, utter. he spoke, said, uttered. was spoken, was said, was uttered. he spoke with.

Figure 2: Klein hyperlinked entry for דבר

these roots. In particularly, the letters לע / *lamed-'ayin* appear in many words, as well as גמ / *gimel-mem* and לג / *lamed-gimel*. Sounding out each of these words, they all feel quite onomatopoetic, imitative of the sound of sipping and swallowing.

The connections in the Klein graph can, more generally, function as a thesaurus, providing insight into the inventory of similar words conveying a concept. Someone using Klein's print dictionary could look up the word דבר / *dabeir*, and discover that it means 'speak'. However, what similar words could the Biblical author have employed? Figure 2 shows the hyperlinked list of 'speak' words:

Interestingly, the common word אמר / *'amar* / 'say' does not appear in this list, because 'say' did not appear in the entry for דבר, only 'speak'. It is, however, in the two-step neighborhood of דבר, because it is a neighbor of the root מלל / *maleil* / 'to speak, say, utter'.

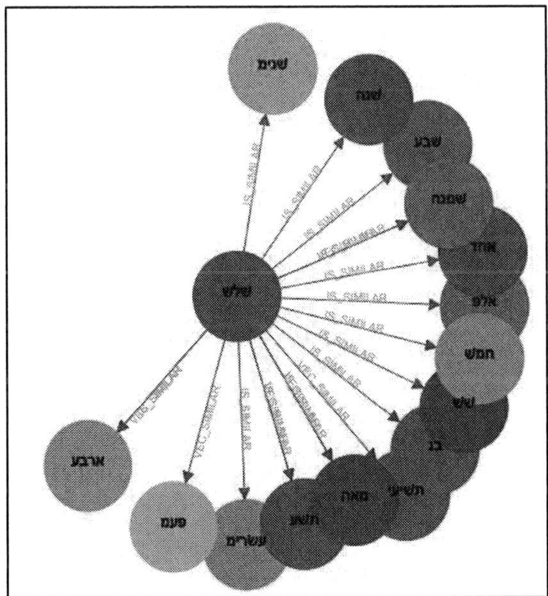

Figure 3: Distributional entry for the word שלש / *shalosh*

Meanwhile, an examination of sample entries in the distributional graph reveals real connections between words. For instance, Figure 3 displays the graph for the word שלש / *shalosh* / 'three'. The connected entries are for many other numbers, such as אחד / *'ehad* / 'one', שבע / *sheva'* / 'seven', and אלף / *'eleph* / 'thousand', as well as the word פעם / *pa'am* / 'occurrence' and שנה / *shanah* / 'year'. Some of these connections are based on Word2Vec, some on PPMI vector similarities, and some on both.

Finally, the present version of the Clark graph simply shows roots linked to their phonemic classes, as well as connections between roots whose short translation is identical. Since the connections are essentially manually crafted, the graph is exactly as we would expect. Figure 4 shows the graph for the Clark entry of המר / *hamar* / 'heap'.

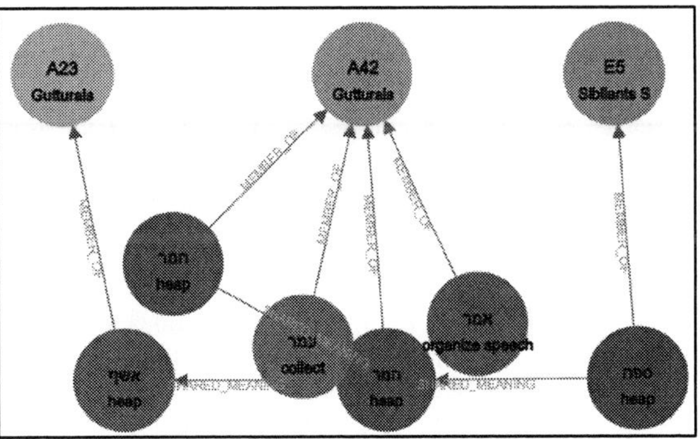

Figure 4: Clark entry for המר / *hamar*

If we had examined the same entry המר / *hamar* in Klein's dictionary, the gloss would be 'to bet, enter a wager'. This might be an example where Clark's decision as to the proper definition of המר / *hamar* was influenced by a desire to structure all A42 phonemic cognates into related words. When interpreting a specific instance of the word, one would need to carefully consider the Biblical usage, in context.

Consider how אמר / *'amar*, usually rendered as 'say', here is explained as 'organized speech', so that it works well with other roots which mean 'heap' and 'collect'. This root is placed in the phonemic class A42, which appears to be formed by a guttural as the first letter, followed by מ / *mem* and ר / *resh*. The subgraph also shows other roots, from other phonemic classes, with a shared meaning (namely "heap"), along with the phonemic class of those roots. This is a fitting way of exploring words within the context of their phonemic cognates.

4. Evaluation

To evaluate the precision of the semantic connections that we discovered within the Klein dictionary, we outputted and analyzed all connections between headwords that exceeded our 0.33 threshold of cosine similarity.

Among the 3287 Klein dictionary roots, 2728 were connected to another root, and we established 7472 such semantic relationships, for an average of 2.73 connections per word. However, a closer examination of the graphs reveals a number of tightly connected subgraphs or even cliques. That is, the graph contains several subgraphs in which a large number of semantically related roots link to each another. For instance, אגד / *'agad* contains a number of word senses including 'to bind, tie, join together, unite, amalgamate'. It is connected to 15 other roots, including אחד / `eḥad / 'to be one, to unite' – also a phonetically related word, אסר / `asar / 'to bind, tie, imprison', and חבר / ḥabar / 'to be united, be joined'. The first listed word אחד / `eḥad, is connected to 4 other words, 3 of which have the 'join' meaning. The word אסר / `asar is connected to 10 other words, all of which have the 'tie / bind' meaning. And the last word, חבר / ḥabar is connected to 8 words, which all have the 'join / attach' meaning.

We submitted the Klein root connections to human experts for judgement, to determine if the headwords indeed had semantic similarity. Of the 7472 connections, 6793 were deemed correct, for a precision of 0.91. We examined the 9% mistaken connections and found that the vast majority (539 out of 679, or 79%) were the result of three filtering errors particular to our dataset. Namely, often the gloss for a root was simply that this was a "base" (that is, a root) for a different non-root headword, that we should "see" the definition in another headword, or that the word was a "hapax legomenon", that is, a word which occurs only once in the Biblical corpus and can therefore only be guessed at based on context. The vectors for these glosses were similar, but not based on real semantic content. A fix would entail filtering out such null-glossed words, and linking the cross-references.

Most of the remaining erroneous connections were due to homonyms and homographs within the stemmed English gloss words. For instance, "tear" can either be a droplet from the eye or the act of ripping something, "left" can either be the opposite of right or the act of going away, and "leave" might refer to the act of going away or to a tree leaf. A few errors were due to non-essential function words, e.g. "to cut *off*" and "to hollow *out*". A fix might entail including part of speech disambiguation in the vectors, or comparison with a similar dictionary in another language.

We performed similar analysis among the lexemes in the Brown-Driver-Briggs lexicon, and found similar results to our results for Klein's Dictionary. Among the 8674 lexemes, 5047 were connected to another lexeme. We established 12,760 semantic relationships, for an average of 2.52 connections per word. We subjected 500 of these relationships to human judgement, which yielded a precision of 0.76. Among the correctly discovered relationships, we discovered some tightly connected subgraphs.

We analyzed the errors and could not find ready explanations for the vast majority of them. The corpus is quite different from Klein's dictionary. While Klein has headwords as roots, with what might be considered lexemes grouped together into a single entry, Brown-Driver-Briggs separates these lexemes into different entries. Each entry includes fewer words and English synonyms. Brown-Driver-Briggs also contains entries for Biblical personages, with a discussion of the etymology of their name, plus that they were the son, daughter, father, or mother of some other person. This has the effect of linking etymologies with familial relationships, and unrelated etymologies together by way of the familial relationships – that is, it introduces a good deal of noise. A fix would entail filtering out these Biblical names, but perhaps vector similarity is not as suited for shorter gloss entries.

We performed a similar analysis for the PPMI vector-based distributional approach applied to lexemes from the ETCBC dataset, where the threshold of cosine similarity of the vectors was 0.33. Of the 6466 lexemes, 4478 were connected to another lexeme. We established 12,561 connections, for an average of 2.80 connections per lexeme. A sample of 200 connections were reviewed by a human expert, where any relationship between the two lexemes (and not just synonymy) was deemed correct. The precision was 0.82. The majority of relationships found (67%) were between names of people or places, appearing for instance in Biblical genealogical lists or descriptions of borders, since these names occur rarely and only in context of each other. There were meaningful connections found. For instance, עדשה / `adašaha / 'lentil' is mentioned in II Samuel 17:28 among other places, and connections are made to the other grains and foodstuffs listed in the verse, but not to the beds, basins, and earthen vessels.

We similarly evaluated our Word2Vec approach. We set a relatively high similarity threshold of 0.9. We connected 1209 lexemes to one another, establishing 5772 connections, or about 4.8 connections per lexeme. Human evaluation of 200 such connections yielded a precision of 0.98. While a majority were again person and place names, those which were not were highly related to one another, e.g. the ordinal numbers, antonyms such as "light" and "darkness", and synonyms such as types of grass. As is typical of Word2Vec, by lowering the threshold, we encounter more connections which are more tangential but still related. In general, for all of these graphs, further exploration is needed regarding where to set the threshold parameter.

Our assessment of the precision of phonetic relationships on the Klein graph was performed programmatically, by checking whether the semantic similarity of the tf-idf vectors exceeded the 0.33 threshold. Table 2 shows the precision for each type of connection.

Connection Type	# Connections	Precision
Cognate Class	1509	0.03
Gradational Variant	275	0.11
Guttural replacement	582	0.07
Velar replacement	208	0.02
Sibilant replacement	168	0.24
Labial replacement	398	0.02
Dental replacement	698	0.01

Table 2: Connections for Phonological Relationships

Certain phonetic relationships – most notably sibilant replacement at 24% and gradational variants at 11% – seem to be borne out and valuable. Other relationships – such as dental replacement and belonging to the same phonemic class defined by Clark, do not seem to be borne out.

This might demonstrate that these phonetic connections and phonemic classes were an overreach, the result of trying to globally impose a system that works between certain word pairs but does not hold in the general case. Alternatively, the theory of phonemic classes – that there is a basic cognate meaning, with individual letter choices modifying this basic meaning in particular directions – involves a different approach to describing the word's meaning, one which is not captured by an English gloss which does not carry such concerns. For instance, עדש / `adash is the root of lentil (as above), which is something that grows. Clark connects it to other growing / renewal words, but he would not expect Klein to mention growing, rather than lentils, in his gloss. Similarly, Hirsch would not be at all surprised that a standard dictionary would not relate ראש / *rosh* / 'head' to רעש / *ra`ash* / 'earthquake' and רחש / *rahash* / 'vibrate'. Perhaps some of these relationships could be reproduced by considering a lower semantic similarity threshold, by considering Word2Vec distributional similarity, or by a WordNet ontology, but perhaps not.

Additionally, we would note that the low precision in some types of transformation simply indicates that while phonetically related words might be semantically related, this is not necessarily systematic, for all possible combination of gutturals (or velars, etc.) and for all letter positions. Additional exploration of the phonetic transformations with the greatest semantic value is necessary.

5. Future Work

We would like to develop a heuristic to stem the lex0 features in the ETCBC dataset to be roots rather than lexemes, so as to consider distributional criteria of roots, as well as to be able to create these connections on the Klein graph, which works with roots. We would like to similarly reduce entries in the Brown-Driver-Briggs lexicon to such roots, again to create a unified graph to enable a valid, apples-to-apples, quantitative evaluation.

With all these connections in place, we hope to apply machine learning, to discover which types of letter substitutions are likely to yield related terms, and to give a measure of the phonemic relatedness of two root entries.

Also, at the moment, within semantic similarities, we are primarily finding synonyms. We would like to expand the types of connections between entries, to find antonyms and hypernyms. There has been some recent work on finding such relationships using Word2Vec vectors, and so we could find such relationships based on our distributional graph. For the semantic similarity graphs, we could harness an English resource such as WordNet applied to the English gloss text of the Klein entries.

There are a few Digital Humanities projects that we look forward to implementing using the corpus as it presently stands. One such project involves detection of chiastic structure in the Biblical text, and the parallel words we need to detect are often synonyms rather than exact repetition of the root. Finally, we would look to duplicate this thesaurus construction process for other Semitic languages, such as Arabic or Aramaic and consider cross-lingual connections.

6. Acknowledgments

We would like to thank the Drs. Phyllis & Abraham S. Weissman Summer Student Research Fund in STEM at Stern College for Women for providing the initial funding for the research, from which the present project developed.

7. Bibliographical References

Brown, F., Driver, S.M., Briggs, C.A. (1906). A Hebrew and English Lexicon of the Old Testament, England.

Clark, M. (1999). Etymological Dictionary of Biblical Hebrew: Based on the Commentaries of Samson Raphael Hirsch. Feldheim, Nanuet, NY.

Hirsch, S. (1867 – 1878). Uebersetzung und Erklärung des Pentateuchs, 5 vols. Frankfurt-on-Main, Germany.

Klein, E. (1987). A Comprehensive Etymological Dictionary of the Hebrew Language for Readers of English. Carta, Jerusalem, Israel.

Mandelkern, S. (1896). Veteris Testamenti Concordantiæ Hebraicae Atque Chaldaicae. Veit et Comp., New York

Ordan, N., Wintner, S. (2007). Hebrew WordNet: a test case of aligning lexical databases across languages. International Journal of Translation 19(1):39-58, 2007.

Roorda, D. (2015). The Hebrew Bible as Data: Laboratory - Sharing – Experiences, https://arxiv.org/pdf/1501.01866.pdf

Sefaria, 2018. New Releases: Jastrow and Klein Dictionaries https://blog.sefaria.org/blog/2018/11/12/jastrow-and-klein-dictionaries

Strong, J. (1894). The Exhaustive Concordance of the Bible. Hunt and Eaton, New York.

8. Language Resource References

Eep Talstra Centre for Bible and Computer. (2015). ETCBC Dataset

Sefaria (2018). The Sefaria MongoDB.

Proceedings of 1st Workshop on Language Technologies for Historical and Ancient Languages, pages 74–78
Language Resources and Evaluation Conference (LREC 2020), Marseille, 11–16 May 2020

Word Probability Findings in the Voynich Manuscript

Colin Layfield[*], Lonneke van der Plas[†], Michael Rosner[‡], John Abela[*]
University of Malta
[*] Department of Computer Information Systems
[†] Institute of Linguistics and Language Technology
[‡] Department of Artificial Intelligence
Msida MSD2080, Malta
{colin.layfield, lonneke.vanderplas, mike.rosner, john.abela}@um.edu.mt

Abstract

The Voynich Manuscript has baffled scholars for centuries. Some believe the elaborate 15th century codex to be a hoax whilst others believe it is a real medieval manuscript whose contents are as yet unknown. In this paper, we provide additional evidence that the text of the manuscript displays the hallmarks of a proper natural language with respect to the relationship between word probabilities and (i) average information per subword segment and (ii) the relative positioning of consecutive subword segments necessary to uniquely identify words of different probabilities.

Keywords: Voynich Manuscript, Word Probabilities, Segment Information, Uniqueness Point

1. Introduction

The Voynich Manuscript (VM) is a codex or bound manuscript whose name derives from Wilfrid Michael Voynich, an antiquarian book dealer who purchased it in 1912 from the Jesuit Villa Mondragone in Frascati, near Rome. Recent radiocarbon tests at the University of Arizona have reliably dated the vellum to 1404-1438. The ink and colours used, although difficult to date directly, are not inconsistent with the time period nor suspicious (Stolte, 2011). It currently resides in the Beinecke Rare Book and Manuscript Library at Yale University as 'MS408'.

The physical manuscript is fairly modest upon first inspection, measuring about 10 inches high, 7 inches wide and about 2 inches thick (slightly larger than a typical modern paperback book). There is no indication of a title or an author for the work. The manuscript itself is made up of 116 numbered folios mostly of 2 pages with the exception of 10 foldouts of up to 6 pages most of which include both illustrations and text. VM comprises a total of about 35,000 words 170,000 characters written using between 24 and 30 letters of the unique VM alphabet[1], so it is clearly a very small corpus by modern standards (Zyats et al., 2016; Prinke and Zandbergen, 2017). An example of a page from the Herbal section, showing both the unusual text as well as drawings, can be found in Figure 1. Apart from these relatively concrete facts, very little is known about VM. The combination of illustrations and careful penmanship have led some researchers to suggest that VM is divided into sections devoted to astrology, cosmology, biology, pharmacology, herbs, and recipes (consisting of mostly text with star like 'bullet point' illustrations). Others have suggested that its overall purpose is to convey secrets of magic and alchemy. In short, there is no shortage of research that attempts or purports to unlock the secrets of this manuscript, but this does not fall into any coherent pattern of enquiry and is often of a highly speculative and/or subjective nature.

The authors believe that in order to make progress it is

Figure 1: Page 16v from the Manuscript - Herbal Section (from Beinecke Library, accessed from https://archive.org/details/voynich)

necessary to adopt a clearly articulated scientific approach in which goals, methodology and evidence are all clearly delimited. The present paper is a first step in that direction which provides some further evidence against theories which claim that VM is a hoax.

---

[1]There is some debate around the number of individual char-

acters since there appears to be some ligatures.

2. Background and Other Works

Mary D'Imperio, in her opening remarks at an early seminar on VM (when interest in it was renewed in the 1970s (Prinke and Zandbergen, 2017)) made the important observation that there was little agreement on the real nature of the document. She noticed that presenters classified it in one of five ways (D'Imperio, 1976):

- a natural language - not enciphered or concealed in any way but written in an unfamiliar script.

- a form of natural language but enciphered in some way.

- not a natural language at all, but rather a code or a synthetic language, like Esperanto, using a made up alphabet for further concealment.

- an artificial fabrication containing randomly generated meaningless padding, i.e. a hoax.

- completely meaningless doodling, produced by either a disturbed or eccentric person(s).

Knowledge of these classes provides some perspective for positioning research that has been carried out since. Thus the first 3 categories imply that the text has meaning and purpose, motivating attempts to "crack the Voynich code", whilst the last 2 negate the rationale for such efforts. Research that has been carried out can be roughly characterised under one or more of the following themes:

1. Character-level mapping

2. Word-level mapping and sentence interpretation

3. Investigations on statistical characteristics

4. Hoax-related investigations

The first theme is covered by work which aims to establish character-level correspondences with known writing systems or sounds. For example Bax (2014) exploited the fact that VM contains several examples of plant names adjacent to associated images. Through detailed micro-analysis matching sounds to symbols he proposed mappings for fourteen of the Voynich symbols used in ten words. Cheshire's work (Cheshire, 2019) not only proposes mappings for a larger set (33) of Voynich symbols but ventures into theme 2 by suggesting word mappings for certain sentences which are used to offer an unparalleled level of interpretation. The main problems here are that the samples are highly selective and justification for many of the assertions made is partial at best.

Work covering the third theme is often used to provide evidence for or against the fourth theme which is itself connected to the 5-way classification of VM mentioned earlier (e.g. if it is a fabrication it is also a hoax).

Experts are unsure whether the Voynich manuscript is written in some unknown language or is a hoax. Rugg (2004) claimed that the manuscript could have been written by constructing words from a grid of word prefixes, stems, and suffixes by means of a simple device known as a *Cardan grille* - an encryption tool used in the 16th century. Other researchers have proposed other hoax hypotheses.

Schinner (2007) attempted to show that the text was, statistically, consistent with stochastic text generation techniques similar to those proposed by Rugg. Not everyone agrees with Rugg and Schinner. Montemurro and Zanette (2013) conducted a study that shows that the text in the Voynich manuscript has similar word frequency distributions to text in natural languages. The authors claim that *"Here we analyse the long-range structure of the manuscript using methods from information theory. We show that the Voynich manuscript presents a complex organization in the distribution of words that is compatible with those found in real language sequences. These results together with some previously known statistical features of the Voynich manuscript, give support to the presence of a genuine message inside the book."*

Rugg and Taylor (2016) countered by stating than an "elaborate language" such as that in the Voynich manuscript can easily be created by using simple coding methods. At the moment there is disagreement on whether the Voynich manuscript is an elaborate hoax or whether it is a meaningful text in some code. This remains a hotly-debated topic amongst the experts.

Over the past 100 years or so, various researchers have applied a gamut of statistical analysis techniques. Many of these were used to find evidence that either supported or rejected the hoax hypothesis. Apart from Rugg, Montemurro, and Schinner, other researchers have used computational techniques to analyse, decipher, interpret, and to try to ultimately understand the manuscript.

In Mary D'Imperio's highly-cited book (D'Imperio, 1978), *The Voynich Manuscript: An Elegant Enigma*, she collected, analysed, and curated most of the research available up to that time.

Reddy and Knight (2011) investigated the VM's linguistic characteristics using a combination of statistical techniques and probabilistic models at page, paragraph, word and character levels. They found, *inter alia*, that VM characters within words were relatively more predictable than for English, Arabic, and Pinyin. Additional character-level analysis was performed by Landini (2001) and Zandbergen (2020) exploring topics such as entropy and spectral analysis of the text.

In 2015, McInnes and Wang (2015) published a comprehensive report on the application of statistical methods and data mining techniques that they used in order to discover linguistic features, relationship, and correlations in the Voynich text. The authors created an extensive, and comprehensive Wiki (Abbott, 2015) with all the results. A year later, Hauer and Kondrak (2016) proposed a suite of unsupervised techniques for determining the source language of text that has been enciphered with a monoalphabetic substitution cipher. The best method in the suite achieved an accuracy of 97% on the Universal Declaration of Human Rights in 380 languages. In the same paper the authors also present a novel approach to decoding anagrammed substitution ciphers that achieved an average decryption accuracy of 93% on a set of 50 ciphertexts. Where these methods were applied to the Voynich manuscript the results suggested Hebrew as the source language of the manuscript. This work has been criticised for not being scientifically rigorous enough (Hauer and Kondrak, 2018).

As recently as June 2019, Zelinka et al. (2019) applied somewhat unorthodox, albeit very interesting, techniques to analyse the text in the manuscript. They concluded that their results indicated that the manuscript was likely written in a natural language since its fractal dimension was similar to that of Hemingway's novel, *The Old Man and the Sea*. The authors also reported that *complex network maps* (CNMs) generated from the Voynich manuscript were different from CNMs generated from random texts.

3. Motivation and Objectives

The main motivation for the programme of work we propose is to take stock of the diverse approaches towards the VM that have been taken so far and to investigate whether consistent application of solidly motivated computational techniques will advance our understanding in measurable ways.

The work reported in this paper focuses on theme 3, with implications for theme 4 as it shows further evidence for the claim that the VM has several characteristics of a natural language. The main novelty is the nature of the metric. King and Wedel (2020) have shown that there are certain patterns in the sequences of sounds and their position within word boundaries that are shared across a dataset of diverse languages. In particular, they demonstrate that less-probable words not only contain more sounds, they also contain sounds that convey more disambiguating information overall, and this pattern tends to be strongest at word-beginnings, where sounds can contribute the most information. We reproduced their experiments on the VM and found similar patterns.

4. Method

4.1. Data Used

The dataset used for the experiment is a transliteration file using the EVA (Extensible Voynich Alphabet) alphabet representation in the IVTFF (Intermediate Voynich Transliteration File Format). Version '1b' of the 'ZL' version of the file was used with version 1.5 of the IVTFF[2]. Only words that have been transcribed with a high degree of certainty were kept for our experiments (words with uncertain characters, character sequences or uncertain spaces were omitted). In total the transcription file contains 36,249 words of which 32,216 were retained for the work done here and, of those, 7,283 were unique (René Zandbergen, 2017).

It is noteworthy, at this point, to observe that the transliteration files available are evolving documents. These transliterations of the Voynich text are constantly being improved and modified to better reflect the content in the manuscript.

4.2. Approach

In order to investigate whether the relation between segment information and word probability follows a pattern similar

to that found by King and Wedel (2020) across a large number of natural languages, we first computed the context-free word probabilities for all words retained from the transcription file, by dividing the counts for a given word by the total number of words as seen in Equation 1

$$p(word) \quad = \quad \frac{count(word)}{\sum_{word'} count(word')} \tag{1}$$

We also computed mean segment information for each word form up until the *uniqueness point* (Marslen-Wilson and Welsh, 1978) for that given word, that is, the point at which it is the only remaining word in the cohort starting with same sequence of segments. For example the Voychanese 'word' ⟨qokeedy⟩ has a uniqueness point of ⟨qoke⟩ (5) as no other word in the Voychanese lexicon begins with those characters (in fact, the only other word, appearing once, that starts with the same 4 characters is ⟨qokol⟩).

The mean segment information calculation itself (token based) is calculated as seen in Equation 2:

$$h^{*}(seg_n) = -\log_2 \frac{count(seg_1 \ldots seg_n) - count(word)}{count(seg_1 \ldots seg_{n-1}) - count(word)} \tag{2}$$

It can be seen that the information for each segment of length n is the count of the first n segments (Voychanese characters) minus the total count of the word over the count of the segment that is one letter shorter minus the count of the word. The count of the word is removed to eliminate the correlation that the frequency of an entire word contributes to the calculation of the information of its segments.

5. Results

In Figure 2, we see the best-fit regression lines for mean token-based segment information by word probability, for word lengths four to eight[3], for corpora in five languages in addition to the VM[4]. The VM follows the same pattern as the other five natural languages in that it shows that less probable words contain more informative segments.

Figure 3, shows linear regression models predicting the relative position of the uniqueness-point for the words in the given corpora. Less probable words have significantly earlier uniqueness points for all four word lengths in VM. Also here, VM shares characteristics of the natural languages presented in the study by King and Wedel (2020).

6. Discussion

As explained in Section 2., previous work used statistical methods to research whether the Voynich manuscript behaves like a natural language. Some focus on word level

---

[2]A good reference site, as well as detailed information and download links for transliteration versions of the Voynich Manuscript, can be found on René Zandbergen's excellent website dedicated to the manuscript http://www.voynich.nu/.

[3]We follow King and Wedel (2020) in their selection of this range in word length, and note that 84% of the total word occurrences in the VM lie within the word length range from four to eight

[4]Due to space limitations we show the graphs for 5 languages, varied in terms of their language families and morphological complexity, focussing on the Indo-European language family because of their relevance for the VM in terms of the location in which they are spoken (for comparison with another 15 languages see King and Wedel (2020))

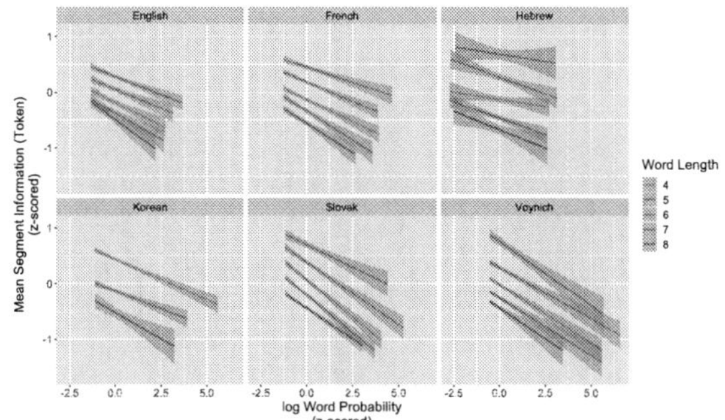

Figure 2: Relationship between log word probability and mean token-based segment information for words of length 4-8

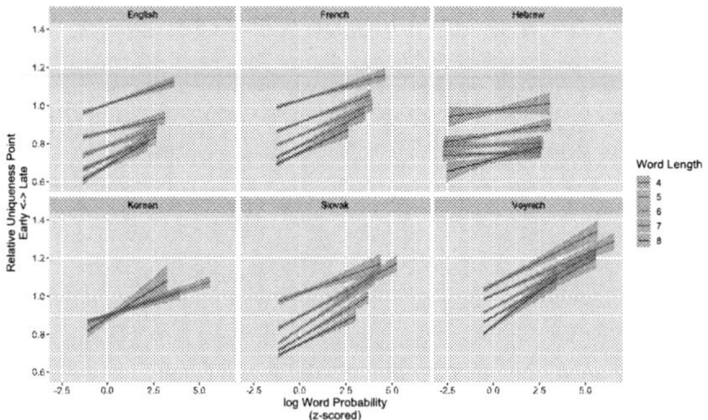

Figure 3: Relationship between log word probability and relative position of uniqueness-point for words of length 4-8

(Montemurro and Zanette, 2013; Zelinka et al., 2019) and find positive results.

The results above show several indications that not only at word level but also at the level of segments, VM shares characteristics with other natural languages. However, others, such as Zandbergen (2020) and Landini (2001) performed character-level analysis and show mixed results.

Landini's spectral analysis points in the same direction as our results, namely that the VM is a natural language, but it is hard to compare their results to ours, because of the different nature of their analysis.

Reddy and Knight (2011) compare the unigram and bigram predictability of VM characters with those of English, Arabic and Pinyin. Especially at bigram-level, VM is more predictable than English and Arabic, more closely resembling Pinyin.

This result is consistent with Zandbergen (2020) who shows that the entropy of characters in the VM is lower than for many other languages and in particular Indo-European languages. However, he also notes that the results differ depending on the position of the character. Characters at the 1st and 2nd position are more predictable than in Latin, but the 3rd and 4th characters are less predictable.

These works emphasise the difference between VM and other Indo-European languages, but also show the impor-

tance of character position. In contrast, our experiments show that when focusing on the relationship between word probability and character information, both on average and based on position (cf. Figure 2 and Figure 3), the same type of relation is found in the VM as in other text corpora.

A couple of caveats are needed: The comparisons in this paper are between VM and contemporary languages and larger corpora, in general. A better comparison would be between languages from roughly the same time period and corpora of the same size. Also, we do not have phonemic transcriptions of the VM and based these on the written characters.[5]

7. Conclusions and Future Work

In this paper, we showed more support for the claim that the VM is written in a natural language and therefore is not a hoax. Although several scholars have found statistical evidence pointing in the same direction, more evidence is needed, particularly to establish whether there is a known language family to which VM can plausibly be assigned. In future work, we would like to compare the results from VM with corpora from the same period that are also similar in size.

8. Acknowledgements

The authors extend their gratitude to Adam King who kindly assisted us and answered questions on the approach he used besides providing some code used to generate his results for comparison purposes. We would also like to thank the reviewers for their helpful comments and suggestions.

---

[5]Previous work (Mahowald et al., 2018) has used orthographics as a proxy for phonetics.

9.   Bibliographical References

Abbott, D. (2015). Cracking the Voynich Code 2015 - Final Report. `https://www.eleceng.adelaide.edu.au/personal/dabbott/wiki/index.php/Cracking_the_Voynich_Code_2015_-_Final_Report`. [Online; accessed 19-February-2020].

Bax, S. (2014). A Proposed Partial Decoding of the Voynich Script. `http://stephenbax.net/wp-content/uploads/2014/01/Voynich-a-provisional-partial-decoding-BAX.pdf`. [Online; accessed 19-February-2020].

Cheshire, G. (2019). The Language and Writing System of MS408 (Voynich) Explained. *Romance Studies*, 37(1):30–67.

M. D'Imperio, editor. (1976). *New Research on the Voynich Manuscript: Proceedings of a seminar.*

D'Imperio, M. (1978). *The Voynich Manuscript: An Elegant Enigma.* National Security Agency, US.

Hauer, B. and Kondrak, G. (2016). Decoding Anagrammed Texts Written in an Unknown Language and Script. *Transactions of the Association for Computational Linguistics*, 4:75–86.

Hauer, B. and Kondrak, G. (2018). AI didn't decode the cryptic Voynich manuscript — it just added to the mystery. *The Verge*, 1st February, 2018.

King, A. and Wedel, A. (2020). Greater Early Disambiguating Information for Less-Probable Words: The Lexicon Is Shaped by Incremental Processing: Early Information for Low-Probability Words. *Open Mind*, To appear.

Landini, G. (2001). Evidence of linguistic structure in the Voynich manuscript using spectral analysis. *Cryptologica*, 25(4).

Mahowald, K., Dautriche, I., Gibson, E., and Piantadosi, S. T. (2018). Word forms are structured for efficient use. *Cognitive Science*, 42(8):3116–3134.

Marslen-Wilson, W. and Welsh, A. (1978). Processing interactions and lexical access during word recognition in continuous speech. *Cognitive psychology*, 10(1):29–63.

McInnes, A. and Wang, L. (2015). *Statistical Analysis of Unknown Written Language: The Voynich Manuscript - Project Group 31.* University of Adelaide, Australia.

Montemurro, M. A. and Zanette, D. H. (2013). Keywords and Co-occurence Patterns in the Voynich Manuscript: An Information-Theoretic Analysis. *Plos One*, 8(6).

Prinke, R. T. and Zandbergen, R., (2017). *The Voynich Manuscript*, chapter The Unsolved Enigma of the Voynich Manuscript, pages 15–40. Watkins Publishing.

Reddy, S. and Knight, K. (2011). What We Know About The Voynich Manuscript. In *Proceedings of the 5th ACL-HLT Workshop on Language Technology for Cultural Heritage, Social Sciences, and Humanities*, pages 78–86, Portland, OR, USA, June. Association for Computational Linguistics.

Rugg, G. and Taylor, G. (2016). Hoaxing statistical features of the Voynich Manuscript. *Cryptologia*, 41(3):247–268.

Rugg, G. (2004). The Mystery of the Voynich Manuscript. *Scientific American*, 291(1):104–109.

Schinner, A. (2007). The Voynich Manuscript: Evidence of the Hoax Hypothesis. *Cryptologia*, 31(2):95–107.

Stolte, D. (2011). UA Experts Determine Age of Book 'Nobody Can Read'. *UA News*. https://uanews.arizona.edu/story/ua-experts-determine-age-of-book-nobody-can-read.

Zandbergen, R. (2020). Voynich MS. `http://www.voynich.nu/extra/sol_ent.html`. Online; accessed 27 March, 2020.

Zelinka, I., Zmeskal, O., Windsor, L., and Cai, Z. (2019). Unconventional Methods in Voynich Manuscript Analysis. *MENDEL*, 25(1):1–14.

Zyats, P., Mysak, E., Stenger, J., Lemay, M.-F., Bezur, A., and Driscoll, D., (2016). *The Voynich Manuscript*, chapter Physical Findings, pages 23–37. Yale University Press.

10.   Language Resource References

René Zandbergen. (2017). *ZL Transliteration of Voynich Manuscript.* http://www.voynich.nu/transcr.html, 1b, 1.5 IVTFF, 2017/09/24.

Proceedings of 1st Workshop on Language Technologies for Historical and Ancient Languages, pages 79–83
Language Resources and Evaluation Conference (LREC 2020), Marseille, 11–16 May 2020

Comparing Statistical and Neural Models for Learning Sound Correspondences

Clémentine Fourrier, Benoît Sagot

Inria - ALMAnaCH

2 rue Simone Iff, 75012 Paris, France

{clementine.fourrier, benoit.sagot}@inria.fr

Abstract

Cognate prediction and proto-form reconstruction are key tasks in computational historical linguistics that rely on the study of sound change regularity. Solving these tasks appears to be very similar to machine translation, though methods from that field have barely been applied to historical linguistics. Therefore, in this paper, we investigate the learnability of sound correspondences between a proto-language and daughter languages for two machine-translation-inspired models, one statistical, the other neural. We first carry out our experiments on plausible artificial languages, without noise, in order to study the role of each parameter on the algorithms respective performance under almost perfect conditions. We then study real languages, namely Latin, Italian and Spanish, to see if those performances generalise well. We show that both model types manage to learn sound changes despite data scarcity, although the best performing model type depends on several parameters such as the size of the training data, the ambiguity, and the prediction direction.

Keywords: Cognate prediction, Proto-form prediction, Statistical models, Neural models

1. Introduction

Since the works of the Neogrammarians (Osthoff and Brugmann, 1878), it is assumed that the lexicon of a language evolves diachronically according to regular sound changes, notwithstanding morphological phenomena, lexical creation and borrowing mechanisms.

The regularity of sound change can be modelled as follows. If, at a given "point" in time, a phone (or phoneme) in a given word changes into another phone (or phoneme), then all occurrences of the same phon(em)e in the same context change in the same way.[1] Such a global change is modelled as a *sound law*. The phonetic history of a language from an earlier to a later stage can then be modelled as an ordered sequence of sound laws. Sound laws are usually identified by studying *cognates*: given two languages with a common ancestor, two words are said to be cognates if they are an evolution of the same word from said ancestor, called their *proto-form*.[2,3] Therefore, the phonological differences between two cognates, which can be modelled as a sequence of *sound correspondences*, capture some of the differences between the phonetic evolution of the languages.

Most methods for sound correspondences identification start by aligning sequences of characters or phones, to which they then apply statistical models, clustering methods, or both (Mann and Yarowsky, 2001; Inkpen et al., 2005; List et al., 2017; List et al., 2018; List, 2019) with the notable exception of Mulloni (2007), who uses Support Vector Machines. However, this task presents a number of similarities with machine translation (MT), as they

both involve modelling sequence-to-sequence cross-lingual correspondences,[4] yet state-of-the-art neural network techniques used in MT (Bahdanau et al., 2015; Sutskever et al., 2014; Luong et al., 2015) have only been used once for sound correspondence prediction, with disappointing results (Dekker, 2018).

Our goal in this paper is to study under which conditions either a neural network or a statistical model performs best to learn sound changes between languages, given the usually limited available training data.[5] We first compare the performances of these two types of models in an ideal setting. To do that, we generate an artificial phonetised trilingual lexicon between a proto-language and two daughter languages, use it to train each model with varying hyperparameters and compare the results. We observe that statistical models perform better on small data sizes and neural models on cases of ambiguity. We then present the results of preliminary experiments, reproducing the same study under real life conditions, using a trilingual cognate dataset from Romance languages. We observe that both models learn different kind of information, but that it is too early to conclude; experiments need to be extended with better and bigger datasets.

2. Data

2.1. Artificial Data Creation

In order to compare how both model types perform on the task of sound correspondence learning in an ideal setup, we create an artificial lexicon, composed of a proto-language and its reflect in two artificially defined daughter languages. Using artificial data for such a proof of concept offers several advantages: we can investigate the minimum number

---

[1]For example, the sequence [ka] in Vulgar Latin changed into [tʃa] in Old French, then to [ʃa] in French. This is illustrated by *chat* [ʃa] 'cat' < Vulg. Lat. *cattus* *[kat.tʊs] and *blanche* [blɑ̃ʃ] 'white (fem.)' < *blanca* *[blan.ka].

[2]For example, Pol. *być* 'to be', Cz. *být* 'id.' and Lith. *būti* 'id.' are cognates as they share the same Proto-Balto-Slavic ancestor.

[3]The term 'cognate' is sometimes used with broader definitions that are tolerant to morphological differences between the proto-forms of both words and/or to morphological restructurings in the history of the languages.

[4]MT generally process sequences of (sub)words, whereas we process sequences of phon(em)es.

[5]Such a method could also be applied to learn orthographic correspondences between close languages, provided said correspondences are regular enough; however, this is not the point of this paper as we focus on an historical linguistic application.

of word pairs required to successfully learn sound correspondences, as well as control the different parameters constraining the proto-language (number of phonemes, phonotactics) and its transformation into the daughter languages (e.g. number of sound changes). However, the artificial data must be realistic, to not impair the linguistic validity of the experiment; the proto-language must have its own realistic phonology, obey phonetic and phonotactic rules, and its daughter languages must have been generated by the sequential application of plausible sound changes.

Creating a Proto-Language We create an algorithm which, given a phone inventory and phonotactic constraints[6], generates a lexicon of a chosen size.[7]
For our experiments, we draw inspiration from Latin and Romance languages. More precisely, we use:

- The phone inventories of Romance languages: each lexicon generated uses all the phones common to all Romance languages, as well as a randomly chosen subset of less common Romance phones.[8]

- The phonotactics of Latin, as detailed in the work of Cser (2016): each word is constructed by choosing a syllable length in the distribution, and its syllables are then constructed by applying a random set of the corresponding positional phonotactic rules.

Generating a Daughter Language Given the proto-language, we create a daughter language by, first, randomly choosing a set of sound changes, then consecutively applying each chosen sound change to all words in the lexicon. Among the main possible sound changes for Romance languages are apocope, epenthesis, palatalisation, lenition, vowel prosthesis and diphtongisation. The dataset generated for this paper used two sets, each of 15 randomly chosen sound changes, to generate two daughter languages. Two examples from our generated dataset are [stra] > [isdre], [estre] and [ʒolpast] > [ʒolbes], [ʒolpes].

2.2. Real Dataset Extraction

Our second goal being to study how our results in an artificial setting generalise to a real-life setting, we need to gather a dataset of related real languages, from a well known direct ancestor language to two closely related but different daughter languages. We choose to study Latin (LA) as the ancestor language, with Italian (IT) and Spanish (ES) as its daughter languages.

Raw Data Extraction EtymDB 2.0 (Fourrier and Sagot, 2020) is a database of lexemes (i.e. triples of the form ⟨language, lemma, meaning expressed by English glosses⟩), which are related by typed etymological relations, including the type "inherited from." To generate the cognate dataset from EtymDB, we followed the inheritance etymological paths between words; two words form a cognate pair if they share a common ancestor[9] in one of their common parent languages (Old Latin, Proto-Italic, or Proto-Indo-European for LA-IT and LA-ES, Vulgar Latin, Latin, and the previous languages for IT-ES).

Phonetisation and filtering The phonetisation of the real data is done using Espeak, an open source multilingual speech synthesiser (Duddington, 2007 2015), which can also convert words or sequence of words into their IPA representations. We phonetise each word independently, then add to each phonetised word a start-of-sentence token indicating their language and a generic end-of-sequence token (EOS), following Sutskever et al. (2014).[10] When faced with competing pairs, i.e. pairs whose source word is the same but whose target words differ, we only retain the pair with the lowest Levenshtein edit distance (method with the strongest cognate recall according to List et al. (2018)).

2.3. Datasets properties

The artificial dataset contains 20,000 unique word triples containing a proto-language (PL) word and its reflects in the two daughter languages (DL1 and DL2). Samples of various sizes are then randomly drawn from this dataset.
The real-life dataset contains 605 cognate triples for LA-ES-IT (1/3-2/3 split in training and test set) as well as 388 additional cognate pairs for LA-IT, 296 for LA-ES, and 1764 for IT-ES, all extracted from EtymDB-2.0 (see above). Early experiments on real-life data have shown that, to compensate for noise, monolingual data must be used to constrain the encoder and decoder of each language to learn what can be plausible phone sequences in a word. We therefore extract 1000 words for each language.

3. Experimental Setup

Task Description For each dataset available, we want to compare how well the statistical and neural models learn sound correspondences between related languages. We define the corresponding task as the translation of phonetised cognates from one language to another.
However, we expect said translation tasks to vary considerably in terms of difficulty: since several proto-forms can give the same daughter form, going from a daughter language to a mother language should be harder than the opposite. To account for this ambiguity, we predict 1, 2, and 3-best answers with each model.

Statistical Model Moses is the reference (open source) tool for statistical MT (Koehn et al., 2007). We first tokenise and align the bilingual data using GIZA++ (Och and Ney, 2003), then train a 3-gram language model of the output (Heafield, 2011), a phrase table that stores weighted correspondences between source and target phonemes (we use 80% of our training data) and a reordering model. The relative weights of the language model, the phrase table and the reordering model are then tuned (we use MERT) on development data, the remaining 20% of our training data. For a given input, the decoder can then find the highest scoring equivalent(s) of an source word in the target language.

---

[6]Phonotactics govern which phonemes sequences are allowed.

[7]Code available at https://github.com/clefourrier/PLexGen

[8]For example, vowels common to all Romance languages are [a] [e] [i] [o] [u], and a subset of extra vowels could be [ɔ] [ɛ] [ɪ]

[9]Said ancestors are those present in the database, not an exhaustive list of all possible cases

[10]In the decoding phase of the model, everything predicted after an EOS token is discarded.

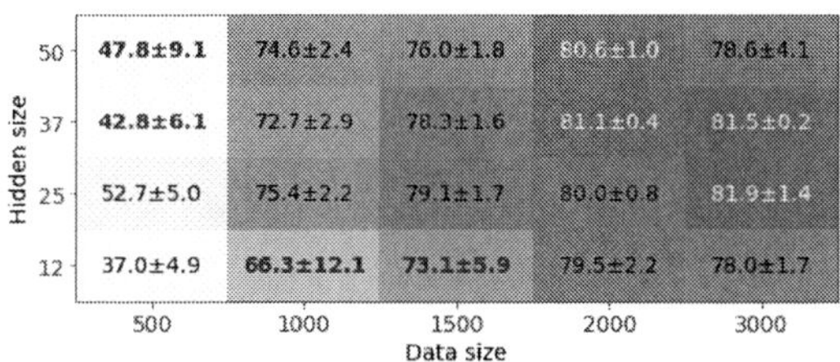

Figure 1: BLEU scores for MEDeA, function of the data size and hidden dimension, for the PL→DL1 pair.

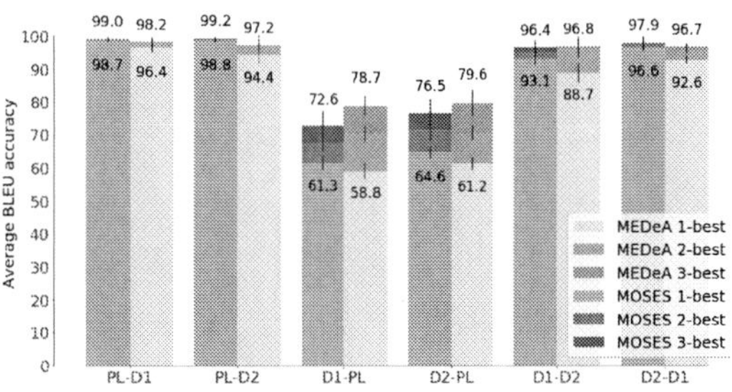

Figure 2: BLEU scores averaged over all runs for all training data sizes (except 500).[15] The bottom part of each bar represents the BLEU score of the most probable predicted word for each input word. The mid (resp. top) part of each bar corresponds to the gain in BLEU obtained by also considering the second-best (resp. third-best) ranked prediction for each input word.

Neural Model MEDeA (Multiway Encoder Decoder Architecture) is our implementation of one of the classical approaches in neural MT: the sequence-to-sequence encoder-decoder model with attention (Bahdanau et al., 2015; Luong et al., 2015).[11] We use an architecture with a specific single layer encoder and a specific single layer decoder for each source and each target language. We use an attention mechanism specific to each decoder (and not encoder-dependent). For a given multilingual lexicon the model learns on all possible language pairs,[12] which constrains the hidden representation to a single space. For all experiments, each phone is embedded as a vector of length 5,[13] and MEDeA is trained with batches of size 30, a batch dropout of 0.2, no layer or attention dropout, and Adam optimisation with a 0.01 learning rate.

Evaluation Metric We use BLEU as an evaluation metric.[14] BLEU is based on the proportion of 1- to 4-grams in the prediction that match the reference. This is extremely interesting for our task, as sound changes can affect several succeeding phones: this score gives us, not only the character error rate computed by the 1-gram, but also the errors in the phone successions computed by the 2- to 4-grams in BLEU. A major criticism of the BLEU score for MT is that it can under-score correct translations not included in its reference set. This does not apply in our case, since there is only one possible "translation" of a word into its cognate in another language.

In order to use BLEU even when we produce $n>1$ "translations", we compute BLEU scores by providing the n-best results as the reference, and our input word as the output.

4. Experiments on Artificial Data

4.1. Model Parameters

For all our experiments on artificial languages, we train the models on our multilingual artificial lexicon.

MEDeA learns a single model for all possible language pairs, on 50 epochs. We train it with hidden dimensions of 12, 25, 37, and 50, training set sizes of 500, 1000, 1500, 2000, and 3000 triplets of words, for 1, 2 or 3 best results. To limit the impact of train/test set separation, we repeat these experiments using three different shuffling seeds.

MOSES is trained on the same data splits as MEDeA, shuffled in the same order, to predict 1 to 3 best results. However, we have to do one run for each language pair, as MOSES can only learn on bilingual data.

4.2. Impact of the Hidden Dimension on Neural Models

We study the impact of the hidden dimension on the performance of MEDeA. No matter the data size, we observe in Figure 1 that a hidden dimension of 12 is consistently too small to learn as well as the rest, and very sensitive to instability (see the std in blue). A hidden dimension of 50 only performs well with big enough data sets, and is very sensitive to instability below 1000 pairs of words. On average, the hidden dimension which achieves the best performance for the data sizes we have is 25, as it represents a good balance between a high enough complexity of representation and a small enough number of weights to learn with. For this reason, in the rest of the paper, we will only introduce the results corresponding to a hidden dimension of 25 for the neural network.

4.3. Model Independent Observations

This analysis focuses on data sizes of 1000 and above, as the impact of very small datasets (500 word pairs per language) on the prediction BLEU scores of both MOSES and MEDeA will be specifically discussed in the next section. Across all experiments and models, we observe in Figure 2 that the easiest situation to learn is the predict from the proto language (PL) to its daughters (98 BLEU), then from one daughter language to the other (92-95 BLEU), and that, finally, the hardest task by far is to go from a daughter language to its mother (60-75 BLEU): there is a difference of 20 points between the best results from mother to daughter and the best from daughter to mother.

---

[11] Code available at https://github.com/clefourrier/MEDeA

[12] For example, for a bilingual Spanish-Italian lexicon, the model will learn on Spanish to itself, Italian to itself, Spanish to Italian and vice versa.

[13] The embedding size was chosen in preliminary experiments, and was the best choice between 2, 5 and 10. This seems adequate relative to the total vocabulary size, of less than 100 items

[14] We use SacreBLEU, Post (2018)'s implementation

[15] Results obtained with a data size 500 skew the average considerably, being several standard deviations apart from the others, for reasons discussed in Section 4.2., and were thus removed.

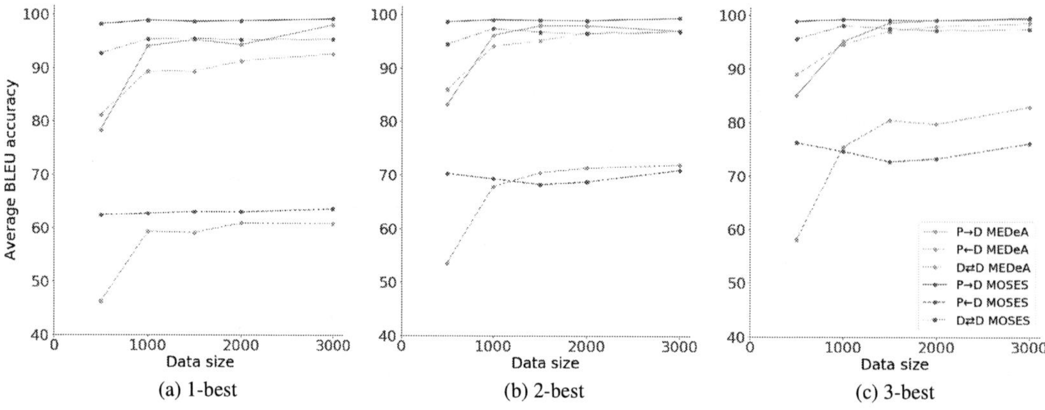

Figure 3: BLEU scores for the n-best prediction, for all experiments.

Along the same lines, we also observe that using 2 or 3 best experiments barely improves the result for the first two situations (adds 2 to 5 points from 1-best to 3-best on average), when it considerably increases the BLEU score for the prediction from daughter to mother language (20 to 25 points for MEDeA, 10 to 15 points for MOSES). This difference, due to ambiguity, was expected, and described in the experimental setup.

4.4. Comparison Between Models

Both models can learn to predict in all directions, but they perform well under different circumstances (Figure 3).

1-best Experiments On 1-best experiments, the statistical model consistently outperforms the neural model, though not by far when reaching data sizes of 2000 and above.

n-best Experiments With very little data (500 word pairs), the statistical model is significantly better; the neural model overfits on too little data. However, with a lot of data (2000 word pairs per language and above), the neural model outperforms the statistical model. This difference in performance seems to come from the better modelling of language structure by the neural model, as will be discussed in Section 5.2..

With 1000 and 1500 training pairs, the performance is roughly equivalent between the two models for 2 and 3 best (the statistical model is slightly better on 1000 word pairs, the neural network slightly better on 1500 word pairs).

5. Preliminary Experiments on Real Data

5.1. Model Parameters

To assess whether our results transfer to real world data, we carried out preliminary experiments on our real datasets. We expect both models to perform worse than on artificial data, since real data can contain noise, both from extraction errors and linguistic phenomena.

MEDeA is trained with the real dataset, on all language combinations possible (IT, ES, LA) at once, with early stopping at 50 epochs. We train it for 3 shuffling seeds, comparing a hidden size of 12 to 50, and 1, 2 or 3 best results, this time using all the data we have.

MOSES is trained on pairs of language combinations separately. We provide it with the same data splits, with the exception of monolingual data, removed from its training set. The triplets of manually corrected data is treated as several sets of pairs, for the same reasons.

Impact of Data Size on Neural Network Optimal Hyperparameters As mentioned in the data descriptions, not all language pair datasets are the same size. There are about 600 word pairs for ES-LA, 700 for IT-LA, and 2.5 times that for ES-IT. We observe that for low resource pairs, the corresponding best hidden size is 25, when for almost 2000 pairs, the best hidden size is 50, confirming what was observed in artificial data experiments. We will systematically investigate in further work the impact of data size on the best hidden dimension for learning.

5.2. Results

General Comparison We observe that, on this set of real data, the statistical model systematically outperforms the neural network, by on average 15 points. Neural networks are highly sensitive to noise and data inconsistencies when trained with too little data, especially without layer dropout.

Impact of the Data Size For our smallest dataset, ES-LA, BLEU scores ranges from 18 to 33 for MEDeA, and from 29 to 47 for MOSES (1-best to 3-best); for our biggest dataset, ES-IT, BLEU scores ranges in both direction from 40 to 54 for MEDeA, and 50 to 64 for MOSES (1-best to 3-best). Even for MOSES, there is a size threshold under which learning is significantly difficult.

What Are the Models Learning? When looking at the respective 3-best predictions of the two models, we observe that the statistical model learns sound correspondence patterns when the neural network learns the underlying structure of the data. For example, for IT→LA, the neural network consistently predicts several forms as possible words translations: [rustiko] 'rustic', coming from [rʊstɪkʊs] 'of the country', is predicted as [rʊstɪkʊs] (masc.), [rʊstɪkʊm] (neut.), and [rʊstɪkss] (nonsense) by MEDeA, vs [rʊkʊstɪ], [rʊɪkɔst] and [ʊsrtɪkwʊs], three meaningless forms by

MOSES.[16] It even allowed us to identify errors in our data: [ramo] 'branch' < [ramʊs] 'branch', erroneously related to Latin [radɪks] 'root' (cognate with [ramʊs]) in our dataset, was predicted by MEDeA as [ramʊs] (masc.), [ramʊ], [ramʊm], and by MOSES as [mʊr], [rɛam], and [raɛm].

6. Conclusion

Through this paper, we studied the respective performances of a statistical and a neural model, in two different settings, to produce the directly related correspondent of a source language word in a related, target language (i.e. to predict the cognate of a source word in a sister language of the source language, the etymon of a source word in a parent language, or the reflex of a source word in a daughter language). Our experiments with artificial data allowed us to study both models in a controlled setting. We observed that statistical models perform considerably better when trained on very little datasets, but that neural networks produce better predictions when both more data is available and models are used to produce more than one output in order to account for the intrinsic ambiguity of some of the language pairs. In preliminary experiments on real data, we observed that, on small and noisy datasets, the statistical model performs consistently better than the neural model, but that the neural model seems to have learned higher level morphological information. Further experiments need to be done, both with less noisy, bigger real datasets (e.g. manually curated) and with more complex artificial data, with more sound changes and added noise separating the proto-language from its daughter languages.

7. Bibliographical References

Bahdanau, D., Cho, K., and Bengio, Y. (2015). Neural machine translation by jointly learning to align and translate. In *3rd International Conference on Learning Representations, ICLR 2015, San Diego, CA, USA, May 7-9, 2015, Conference Track Proceedings*.

Cser, A. (2016). *Aspects of the phonology and morphology of Classical Latin*. Ph.D. thesis, Pázmány Péter Katolikus Egyetem.

Dekker, P. (2018). Reconstructing language ancestry by performing word prediction with neural networks. *Master. Amsterdam: University of Amsterdam*.

Duddington, J. (2007-2015). espeak text to speech. `http://espeak.sourceforge.net/index.html`.

Fourrier, C. and Sagot, B. (2020). Methodological Aspects of Developing and Managing an Etymological Lexical Resource: Introducing EtymDB-2.0. In *Twelfth International Conference on Language Resources and Evaluation (LREC 2018)*, Marseilles, France. (to appear).

Heafield, K. (2011). KenLM: Faster and smaller language model queries. In *Proceedings of the Sixth Workshop on Statistical Machine Translation*, pages 187–197, Edinburgh, Scotland, July. Association for Computational Linguistics.

Inkpen, D., Frunza, O., and Kondrak, G. (2005). Automatic identification of cognates and false friends in french and english. In *Proceedings of the International Conference Recent Advances in Natural Language Processing*, volume 9, pages 251–257.

Koehn, P., Hoang, H., Birch, A., Callison-Burch, C., Federico, M., Bertoldi, N., Cowan, B., Shen, W., Moran, C., Zens, R., et al. (2007). Moses: Open source toolkit for statistical machine translation. In *Proceedings of the 45th annual meeting of the association for computational linguistics companion volume proceedings of the demo and poster sessions*, pages 177–180.

List, J.-M., Greenhill, S. J., and Gray, R. D. (2017). The potential of automatic word comparison for historical linguistics. *PLOS ONE*, 12(1):1–18, 01.

List, J.-M., Walworth, M., Greenhill, S. J., Tresoldi, T., and Forkel, R. (2018). Sequence comparison in computational historical linguistics. *Journal of Language Evolution*, 3(2):130–144, 07.

List, J.-M. (2019). Automatic inference of sound correspondence patterns across multiple languages. *Computational Linguistics*, 45(1):137–161.

Luong, T., Pham, H., and Manning, C. D. (2015). Effective approaches to attention-based neural machine translation. In *Proceedings of the 2015 Conference on Empirical Methods in Natural Language Processing*, pages 1412–1421, Lisbon, Portugal, September. Association for Computational Linguistics.

Mann, G. S. and Yarowsky, D. (2001). Multipath translation lexicon induction via bridge languages. In *Proceedings of the Second Meeting of the North American Chapter of the Association for Computational Linguistics on Language Technologies*, NAACL '01, pages 1–8, Pittsburgh, Pennsylvania. Association for Computational Linguistics.

Mulloni, A. (2007). Automatic prediction of cognate orthography using support vector machines. In *Proceedings of the ACL 2007 Student Research Workshop*, pages 25–30, Prague, Czech Republic, June. Association for Computational Linguistics.

Och, F. J. and Ney, H. (2003). A systematic comparison of various statistical alignment models. *Computational Linguistics*, 29(1):19–51.

Osthoff, H. and Brugmann, K. (1878). *Morphologische Untersuchungen auf dem Gebiete der indogermanischen Sprachen*. Number 1 in Morphologische Untersuchungen auf dem Gebiete der indogermanischen Sprachen. Hirzel.

Post, M. (2018). A call for clarity in reporting BLEU scores. In *Proceedings of the Third Conference on Machine Translation: Research Papers*, pages 186–191, Belgium, Brussels, October. Association for Computational Linguistics.

Sutskever, I., Vinyals, O., and Le, Q. V. (2014). Sequence to sequence learning with neural networks. *CoRR*, abs/1409.3215.

---

[16]Since the algorithms have to predict n different answers for n-best prediction (when only one answer might be correct), it is expected that in each set of predicted words, some will be nonsensical; we present here words ordered by algorithm confidence.

Proceedings of 1st Workshop on Language Technologies for Historical and Ancient Languages, pages 84–93
Language Resources and Evaluation Conference (LREC 2020), Marseille, 11–16 May 2020
© European Language Resources Association (ELRA), licensed under CC-BY-NC

Distributional Semantics for Neo-Latin

Jelke Bloem, Maria Chiara Parisi, Martin Reynaert, Yvette Oortwijn and Arianna Betti
Institute for Logic, Language and Computation, University of Amsterdam
{j.bloem, m.w.c.reynaert}@uva.nl, {mariachiara.paris, yvette.oortwijn, ariannabetti}@gmail.com

Abstract

We address the problem of creating and evaluating quality Neo-Latin word embeddings for the purpose of philosophical research, adapting the Nonce2Vec tool to learn embeddings from Neo-Latin sentences. This distributional semantic modeling tool can learn from tiny data incrementally, using a larger background corpus for initialization. We conduct two evaluation tasks: definitional learning of Latin Wikipedia terms, and learning consistent embeddings from 18th century Neo-Latin sentences pertaining to the concept of *mathematical method*. Our results show that consistent Neo-Latin word embeddings can be learned from this type of data. While our evaluation results are promising, they do not reveal to what extent the learned models match domain expert knowledge of our Neo-Latin texts. Therefore, we propose an additional evaluation method, grounded in expert-annotated data, that would assess whether learned representations are conceptually sound in relation to the domain of study.

Keywords: distributional semantics, evaluation, small data, philosophy, digital humanities, Neo-Latin

1. Introduction

Christian Wolff (1679-1754)'s philosophical ideas on the so-called 'mathematical method' are deemed greatly influential upon 18th century thinking about science (Frängsmyr, 1975, 654-55). An interesting research question is whether the influence of Wolff's ideas can be more precisely assessed by using a mixed (quantitative, qualitative and computational) approach along the lines of Betti et al. (2019) and Ginammi et al. (2020). In addressing this question, we want to link concepts and terms used to express them using computational techniques, including query expansion based on distributional semantics, information retrieval as a downstream task, and meaning shift analysis built upon this.

The endeavour involves several challenges, starting with (i) building a high-quality, multi-author 18th century philosophy corpus with distinctive characteristics including Neo-Latin texts; and (ii) getting satisfactory distributional semantics models for Neo-Latin. In this paper we report results on (ii), and describe initial steps towards (i). As to (ii), our goal is to evaluate Neo-Latin (word) embeddings learned from tiny data (very small data, i.e. a few sentences, following Herbelot and Baroni (2017)) from the specific domain of philosophy, adapting methods known to work well for this data type, but previously applied to English only (Herbelot and Baroni, 2017; Bloem et al., 2019). We perform two evaluation tasks: 1. compare embeddings learned from a single Vicipaedia definitional sentence to Word2vec (Mikolov et al., 2013) embeddings learned from the full Vicipaedia corpus, and 2. test the consistency of embeddings trained on tiny amounts of topic-specific 18th century Neo-Latin data, initialized using different background corpora.

2. Background

Advances in natural language processing and expanding digital archives have made it possible to analyse old texts in new ways (Hinrichs et al., 2019). Distributional semantics (DS) (Turney and Pantel, 2010; Erk, 2012; Clark, 2015) has emerged as an effective way to computationally represent words and sentences in a way that appears to represent their semantic properties. Along with its prevalence in present-day natural language processing, this aspect makes DS a promising family of techniques for application in text-based fields. The application of DS models to historical languages is however challenging, as large amounts of training data are required (Bengio et al., 2003), while relatively little new digital text is being produced online, in comparison with living languages. Artefacts from digitization processes such as Optical Character Recognition (OCR) may also pose problems. At the same time, philosophers who are interested in Latin texts make accurate studies of concepts and expect high accuracy from the digital tools they use. Application of DS models in this context therefore demands the use of specific methods suited to low-resource languages, small corpus sizes and domain-specific evaluation.

2.1. Latin word embeddings

Latin is a highly inflectional language with words taking many forms depending on features such as case and gender, and language models tend to perform worse on inflectional languages. This effect is greater in n-gram models (Cotterell et al., 2018) due to how each word form is represented separately, leading to a large vocabulary. Word2vec also represents words in this way.

DS models of Latin have only been explored to a limited extent, and never for Neo-Latin texts. In contrast to the more numerous and larger-sized Latin corpora of the so-called *Latinitas Romana*, or Classical Latin (7th cent. B.C.-6th cent. A.D.), Latin corpora of the so-called *Latinitas Nova*, or Neo-Latin (15th cent. A.D.-21st cent. A.D.), also called New Latin when referring specifically to the language, are usually smaller in size,[1] and they often present linguistic variations or new word types in comparison to Classical Latin corpora. For example, the terms *analyticus* (analytic) or *syntheticus* (synthetic) are present only in Neo-Latin, and not in Classical Latin. Various Latin corpora are available. Vicipaedia, the Latin Wikipedia, contains 10.7M tokens of text that has been written in recent years. The Latin Library (16.3M to-

---

[1] For example, in the LatinISE historical corpus v2.2 (McGillivray and Kilgarriff, 2013), the subcorpus Historical_era_Romana (8,069,158 tokens) is considerably bigger than the Historical_era_Nova one (1,985,968 tokens)

kens) is available in plain text format[2], containing texts from all time periods. There are a few manually annotated treebanks: the Index Thomisticus Treebank (Passarotti, 2019) (354k tokens, 13th century, the works of Thomas Aquinas) based on the Index Thomisticus (Busa, 1974), Perseus (Bamman and Crane, 2011) (53K tokens, Classical Latin) and Latin PROIEL (Haug and Jøhndal, 2008) (Classical Latin and the 4th century Vulgate New Testament translations). These are all partially available in Universal Dependencies format, including tokenization, lemmatization and dependency syntax (Nivre et al., 2016; Cecchini et al., 2018). Furthermore, there is the Late Latin Charter Treebank (Korkiakangas and Passarotti, 2011) (250k tokens, medieval Latin). There is some big data as well, specifically a 1.38 billion token corpus of Latin OCRed text (Bamman and Smith, 2012), a large but rather noisy resource due to mishaps in the OCR and automatic language detection processes.

Some Latin DS models exist: Latin data has been included in large multilingual semantic modeling (Grave et al., 2018) and parsing (Zeman et al., 2018) efforts, using automatic language detection to identify the material as Latin. Another large-scale approach was taken by Bjerva and Praet (2015), who trained embeddings on the aforementioned Bamman corpus (Bamman and Smith, 2012) using Word2vec (Mikolov et al., 2013). Parameters were taken from Baroni et al. (2014), who tuned on an English word similarity resource with models trained on a concatenation of large English-language corpora. The resulting models were not tuned or evaluated for Latin. Manjavacas et al. (2019) applied fastText to the same data to create embeddings for the task of semantic information retrieval, also without tuning, finding that more basic BOW methods outperform it and finding fastText to outperform Word2vec. The only study we are aware of that includes an evaluation of Latin word embeddings is by Sprugnoli et al. (2019), who create lemma embeddings from a manually annotated corpus of Classical Latin, the 1.7M token *Opera Latina* corpus, which includes manually created lemmatization. Sprugnoli et al. (2019) evaluate the lemma embeddings by extracting synonym sets from dictionaries and performing a synonym selection task on them. For a given target term, the cosine distance of its vector to a set of four other terms is computed, one of which is a synonym. To successfully complete the task, the synonym has to be nearer to the target term than the alternative terms. The alternative terms were manually checked to make sure they are not synonyms as well. They find that fastText-based models, which can represent subword units, perform better on this task than Word2vec-based model. They note that this may be due to Latin's heavily inflectional morphology, though when using lemmatized data, the effect of morphology should be limited.

In summary, there are no existing DS models relevant for addressing our research question, as Bjerva and Praet (2015)'s models were not evaluated on Latin and Sprugnoli et al. (2019)'s models were designed for Classical Latin. The relevance of the available corpora for creating Neo-Latin word embeddings is an open question that we will address.

2.2. Tiny data

The application of DS models to Latin involves working with smaller datasets than usual in DS. Some work has been done to evaluate the effect of data size and develop methods suited to learning from less data. Factorized count models have been found to work better on smaller datasets (Sahlgren and Lenci, 2016) compared to the Word2vec family of models (Mikolov et al., 2013). Herbelot and Baroni (2017)'s Nonce2Vec, however, shows that Word2vec can be adapted to learn even from a single sentence, if that sentence is highly informative. In an experiment on a small dataset of philosophical texts (Bloem et al., 2019), this method resulted in more consistent embeddings than a count-based model. The way in which Nonce2Vec can learn from such small amounts of data is by learning incrementally, starting from a semantic *background model* that is trained on a larger corpus, such as all Wikipedia text of a language. Given any term with one or a few sentences of context, that term can be placed into this background model, using nothing but those context sentences as training data. First, a simple additive model (Lazaridou et al., 2017) is used for initialization, taking the sum of the Word2vec background space vectors of all the context words of the target term. This additive model is also used as an evaluation baseline. Next, Nonce2Vec trains the background skipgram model on the context sentences for the target term vector, without modifying the network parameters of the background space[3], with an initial high learning rate, large window size and little subsampling. In this way, Nonce2Vec can learn a vector for a target term based on only one or a few sentences of context, even if that term does not occur in the larger background corpus. As we currently have only tiny amounts of in-domain data, and larger corpora are available that can be used as background (see section 2.1.), we use Nonce2Vec to take distributional information from a general-domain background corpus and further train it on our tiny in-domain dataset.

2.3. Evaluation

Distributional semantic models are typically evaluated by comparing similarities between its word embeddings to a gold standard of word similarity scores based on human ratings, such as the MEN dataset (Bruni et al., 2014) or the SimLex-999 dataset (Hill et al., 2015) for English. However, this is a rarely feasible method in specialised domains and low-resource situations. Not only do such datasets not exist for Latin, but even for English, the meaning of words reflected in these resources may differ from their meaning in the philosophical domain (Bloem et al., 2019).

Evaluation sets can also be created automatically using existing resources. Synonym sets, e.g. from lexical semantic databases, can be used as gold standard data by means of a synonym selection task, which measures how often the nearest neighbour of a vector is its synonym. This method was used for Latin by extracting information from dictionaries (Sprugnoli et al., 2019), but for our use case, this approach

---

[2] http://thelatinlibrary.com/, available as part of the Classical Language Toolkit: https://github.com/cltk/latin_text_latin_library

[3] Nonce2Vec can also modify the background model in newer versions (Kabbach et al., 2019), but this can lead to a snowball effect, where the context sentence vectors are significantly moved towards the position of the new context through backpropagation, which would worsen the quality particularly of small models.

may also have the issue of not reflecting domain-specific meanings. General dictionary synonyms may not reflect the way words are used in our target domain. Herbelot and Baroni (2017) evaluate Nonce2Vec by using vectors from a Word2vec model of Wikipedia text as gold vectors. The Word2vec model was in turn evaluated using word similarity scores from the MEN dataset. This evaluation can be conducted for any language in which Wikipedia is available, although for Latin, we do not have a word similarity test collection equivalent to the MEN dataset to evaluate a Word2vec model trained on Vicipaedia.

Some aspects of embedding quality can be measured without a gold standard. The metric of *reliability* quantifies the randomness inherent in some predictive distributional semantic models, and to what extent it can affect the results (Hellrich and Hahn, 2016). Bloem et al. (2019) propose *consistency* as a metric for evaluating low-resource DS models, defining a model as consistent "if its output does not vary when its input should not trigger variation (e.g. because it is sampled from the same text)". The consistency metric computes the ability of a model to learn similar embeddings from different parts of homogeneous data, and does not require 'gold' vectors to compute as it only compares learned vectors to each other. Multiple vectors for a single target term but with different context sentences are trained from identically parametrized models, and compared to each other in terms of nearest neighbour rank and cosine similarity. Higher similarity and nearest neighbour rank between these different vectors of the same target term indicates that the model is more consistent at the level of the domain of text that the context sentences are sampled from (a time period, author, genre, topic etc.). While this measure does not capture all aspects of model quality, it can be used to quantify what model configurations and which background corpora produce consistent embeddings.

To evaluate in-domain term meaning, domain-specific knowledge should be used in the evaluation. Comparative intrinsic evaluation (Schnabel et al., 2015) — i. e. letting users compare and rank terms from a list of nearest neighbours against a query term for semantic similarity — can be used to have experts assess the output of a model, and quantify the outcome. When evaluating models of philosophical concepts, this is not a trivial task. As even domain experts might be unaware of all possible expressions of a concept used by a particular author, constructing ground truths of in-domain key concepts paired off with known terms is necessary for evaluation, as shown by Meyer et al. (2019). This, in turn requires a large in-domain corpus. Although we are currently in the process of constructing a corpus with these exact characteristics, we do not have it yet in a form that is suitable for evaluation based on expert ground truths. If constructed properly in a machine-readable way, such a ground truth would enable automatic evaluation of model output in comparison to the ground truth.

3. Tasks

Considering the constraints on data size and evaluation for our domain, we perform two evaluations of Nonce2Vec on Latin data. The first evaluation aims to replicate Herbelot and Baroni (2017)'s English definitional dataset and evaluation for Latin, and shows us that Nonce2Vec can learn meaning representations from a single sentence that are similar to those learned from a larger corpus. In the second task, we evaluate vectors trained on a tiny dataset composed of sentences from texts relevant to our research question on Wolff's mathematical method. We perform the consistency evaluation of Bloem et al. (2019), while testing different background models for initialization. The second evaluation task shows us that Nonce2Vec can learn word embeddings from these sentences consistently even without access to a background corpus from the target domain.[4]

3.1. Vicipaedia definitional dataset evaluation

We built a dataset of terms and their definitional sentences, following Herbelot and Baroni (2017)'s definitional dataset for English using the same procedure as much as possible. We used Vicipaedia as a source, downloaded and extracted using Witokit[5]. This source was chosen because Herbelot and Baroni (2017) also used Wikipedia and because it is relatively close in time to 18th century Neo-Latin, is large, and is free of OCR errors. The dataset was constructed by taking Vicipaedia page titles containing one word only, taking that page title as a target term and taking the first sentence of the corresponding article as the definitional sentence. The sentences were tokenized using Polyglot[6] and we removed punctuation. We then filtered out target terms that occur fewer than 50 times in Vicipaedia to ensure that they are well-represented in the background model. Herbelot & Baroni used a frequency cutoff of 200 in the UkWaC corpus, but our corpus is smaller so we chose a lower cutoff. We also filtered out terms for which the definitional sentence is shorter than 10 words, to ensure there is some context to learn from. Terms for which the title word does not literally occur in the first Vicipaedia sentence were filtered as well. Occurrences of the target term were replaced by the string '___', ensuring that a new vector is learned for that term. We then randomly sampled 1000 of these terms and sentences, splitting them into 700 tuning and 300 test instances. All of this replicates Herbelot and Baroni (2017)'s extraction procedure for English.

To estimate the quality of the extracted material, we manually checked 99 of the randomly sampled definitional sentences and found that 70 contained proper definitions, 21 contained definitions with additional non-definitional information and 8 did not contain proper definitions. As Herbelot and Baroni (2017) extracted full sentences, definitions with additional information also occur in their sets, so we accept these cases. After updating our automatic extraction procedure, of the 8 non-definitional cases, 3 were excluded by excluding cases with parentheses in the title, 2 were resolved by including words between parentheses in the sentence extraction, 1 is a proper name without definition, and 2 now include a definition but also additional material.

Nonce2Vec can use these definitional sentences to perform one-shot learning of the target term. This newly learnt vector

---

[4]A branch of Nonce2Vec that includes these evaluations and datasets can be found at `https://github.com/bloemj/nonce2vec/tree/nonce2vec-latin`

[5]`https://github.com/akb89/witokit`

[6]`https://github.com/aboSamoor/polyglot`

can then be compared to the vector produced by a standard (skipgram) Word2vec model trained over the entire Vicipaedia. It is expected that a well-performing system will learn from the definitional sentence a vector that is close to the Vicipaedia vector: their Reciprocal Rank (RR) will be high. We calculate RR between the learned vector and the gold Vicipaedia vector from the background model, over all target terms, and take the resulting Mean Reciprocal Rank (MRR) as a measure of model quality. As a baseline, we use the additive model which just sums context vectors from the background space, following Herbelot and Baroni (2017).[7]

3.2. Neo-Latin dataset evaluation

We built a Neo-Latin dataset consisting of terms and their context sentences. This material is lifted from a small portion (about 20%) of a Neo-Latin corpus that is being used in our ongoing work (Van den Berg et al., ongoing). The full corpus includes 162 books in Latin and 146 books in German published in Germany between 1720 and 1790. We estimate the page count of the Neo-Latin corpus at roughly 40.000. The full corpus has several distinctive characteristics. It is (i) built by a team of experts towards a specific scholarly purpose, that of investigating the concept of *mathematical method* in 18th century Germany; (ii) it presents linguistic variation and vocabulary typical of Neo-Latin corpora (see section 2.1.); additionally, the texts contained in the corpus are more recent in comparison to Neo-Latin corpora from e.g. the 15th century. Another characteristic of our corpus is (iii) that it includes *only* academic philosophy, logic and science in general. In addition to focusing on specific topics and their corresponding technical language, the corpus thus also provides insight into the social context of the authors (Europeans with a deep command of Latin, (writing under) male (names), of a certain age and socio-economic background).

Manual annotations on the Neo-Latin corpus are currently ongoing. They aim at extracting lists of terms expressing certain philosophical concepts relevant to the study of the concept of mathematical method in 18th century Germany, as well as their (functional) synonyms, and the context in which they appear. A selection of contexts get manually typed in full. The Neo-Latin dataset we use in our task is a subset of the full annotation set, and is curated by the same annotator of the full Neo-Latin annotation set, a philosopher by training with knowledge of Latin (Maria Chiara Parisi). The dataset presents – *a fortiori* – the features of the full corpus indicated above and consists of a small, manually-typed and manually-checked set of 30 target terms and, for each term, three sentences (see Table 4) in which the term occurs. The target term (column 1) is replaced in the snippets (column 2, 3 and 4) with '___'. The Neo-Latin *corpusculum* we use is a tiny, but sufficient set of data to test the consistency of Neo-Latin word embeddings.

As we do not yet have the full corpus in a suitable machine-readable format, we cannot perform the same evaluation as for the definitional dataset, but we can measure vector *consistency* (Bloem et al. (2019), see 2.3.). We can use an out-of-domain background corpus, such as Vicipaedia, for initialization, in order to use Nonce2Vec to model these terms. Note that, doing this, we can no longer evaluate the resulting vectors by comparing the learned vectors to those from the background corpus. The background corpus is text of a different domain than 18th century mathematical text, and may not even contain the core terms from these works, or it may use them in a different way. Thus, unlike in Herbelot and Baroni (2017)'s Wiki definitions evaluation setup, vectors based on an out-of-domain background corpus cannot serve as a gold standard for vectors from our domain.

The consistency metric (Bloem et al., 2019) evaluates the stability of vector spaces generated by a particular model on a homogeneous dataset extracted from a particular domain of text, without a gold standard. In our case, the model is Nonce2Vec, and the homogeneous dataset is our tiny Neo-Latin mathematical method subset. Consistency is computed by measuring the similarity between vectors of the same word, trained over different samples of text (the sentences from the dataset). We can use this metric to compare different configurations of Nonce2Vec on the task and see which one results in more consistent embeddings. In particular, we are interested in trying different background models for initializing the Nonce2Vec vectors, trained on different background corpora. We hypothesize that a background model that leads to higher consistency scores on this task with our Neo-Latin dataset provides a better initialization for our in-domain term vectors. Such a model, we might conjecture, contains more of the relevant vocabulary, used in a more similar way to that of our texts.

4. Results

4.1. Definitional evaluation

In the first evaluation, we compare vectors trained on Vicipaedia definitional sentences to vectors from the Vicipaedia background model, for the same target term. We first train a standard Word2vec model on Vicipaedia, which Nonce2Vec does using the Gensim (Řehůřek and Sojka, 2010) implementation of Word2vec. While Herbelot and Baroni (2017) do not tune this model, as Vicipaedia is smaller than the English Wikipedia they use, we try to change the default parameters to accommodate this. We find that a higher learning rate ($\alpha = .01$), increased window size (15) and higher subsampling rate (1^{-4}) provides better results on our tuning set. Next, we tune and run Nonce2Vec on our Latin definitional dataset, using the background model for initialization and as the sum baseline. We performed a grid search of the same parameter space as Herbelot and Baroni (2017) do, containing different learning rates ($[0.5, 0.8, \mathbf{1}, 2, 5, 10, 20]$), the number of negative samples ($[\mathbf{3}, 5, 10]$), the subsampling rate ($[500, 1000, \mathbf{10000}]$), and window size ($[5, 10, \mathbf{15}, 20]$). The subsampling rate decay ($[1.0, 1.3, \mathbf{1.9}, 2.5]$) and window decay ($[1, 3, \mathbf{5}]$) are not relevant when training vectors on single sentences. Bold values are the best performing values in Herbelot and Baroni (2017).

Using the tuned Vicipaedia background model and applying it to the test set, the best performance is obtained for a window size of 5, a learning rate of 0.5, a subsampling rate of 500, and 3 negative samples. The lambda parameter was set

---

[7]We run the Nonce2Vec algorithm without the notion of informativeness incorporated by Kabbach et al. (2019), as that option requires the use of an additional language model.

Model	MRR	Median rank
N2V-best	0.01936	251
N2V-defaultbg	0.15832	1866
N2V-default	0.00410	5736
Sum	0.01263	322

Table 1: Results on definitional dataset

Model	cos-sim	rank	vocab
bamman-c50-d400	0.701	**47.5**	901K
bamman-c50-d100	**0.776**	202	901K
lattextlib-c50-d400	0.332	604	24.7K
lattextlib-c50-d100	0.450	1279	24.7K
lattextlib-c20-d400	0.505	**75**	50.4K
lattextlib-c20-d100	**0.621**	301	50.4K
vicipaedia-c50-d400	0.482	103	14.0K
vicipaedia-c50-d100	0.603	219	14.0K
vicipaedia-c20-d400	0.551	**47.7**	30.4K
vicipaedia-c20-d100	**0.674**	244	30.4K
treebanks-c50-d400	0.133	292	810
treebanks-c50-d100	0.165	286	810
treebanks-c5-d400	0.298	1103	7.3K
treebanks-c5-d100	**0.390**	703	7.3K

Table 2: Consistency metrics on our Neo-Latin dataset using Nonce2Vec, initialized with various background models.

to the default 70. Table 1 shows results using these tuned parameters (N2V-best) and the default Nonce2Vec parameters from the English experiment (N2V-default) as compared to the sum baseline (Sum). The N2V-defaultbg result uses our tuned N2V parameters, but with the default background model parameters, and the N2V-default result uses default parameters from Herbelot and Baroni (2017) both for the background model and for training on the definitional data. On the test instances, we find that N2V shows an improvement over the simple additive model baseline. As shown in Table 1, the median rank of the gold vectors for our test instances is 251, out of 14,049 neighbours (the vocabulary size). For English, Herbelot and Baroni (2017) report a median rank of 623. While this number appears worse than our score, this metric is sensitive to vocabulary size: their English model has a vocabulary of 259,376 types due to the larger corpus, and ranking high is more difficult when there are more other vectors to rank. The Mean Reciprocal Rank (MRR) measure is 0.019 on the Latin definitions but 0.049 on the English definitions, showing that the nearest neighbours of the gold Wiki vectors rank higher among the nearest neighbours of the learned definitional vector for English than for Latin.

4.2. Neo-Latin consistency evaluation

Recall that for the Neo-Latin data that pertains to our philosophical research question, we do not have gold vectors, as there is no background corpus for our domain yet. Instead, we compute consistency between vectors trained over different context sentences of the same target term (shown in Table 4). We experiment with initializing our vectors based on models trained from various background corpora with various model parameters, in order to find out what background model leads to more consistent results for our domain of Latin text. As background corpora, we use the Vicipaedia, Latin Text Library, Latin Treebanks and Bamman corpora described in section 2.1. The Latin Text Library corpus was tokenized using Polyglot in the same way as the Vicipaedia corpus. The Bamman corpus was tokenized and lowercased by Ucto (van Gompel et al., 2017). Punctuation was removed and, as these may be disruptive to distributional models, we let Ucto replace items that are less lexical, such as numbers of any type, dates, etc. by class labels. Of the treebanks, we use the Universal Dependencies versions of the Index Thomistius Treebank (165K tokens), the Perseus LDT (29K) and Proiel (200K).

For each background model, we compute consistency metrics over the vectors learned by Nonce2Vec of all 30 Neo-Latin target terms. We have three vectors per term, one from each context sentence, and compute the metrics between all pairs of the three vectors ($\vec{a_1}$-$\vec{a_2}$, $\vec{a_2}$-$\vec{a_3}$, $\vec{a_1}$-$\vec{a_3}$). This evaluation data is shown in Table 4. We consider two metrics for comparing a pair of vectors $\vec{a_1}$ and $\vec{a_2}$: by similarity, where a higher cosine similarity indicates more consistency, or by nearest neighbor rank, where a higher rank of $\vec{a_1}$ among the nearest neighbors of $\vec{a_2}$ indicates more consistency. Every vector in the background model, as well as $\vec{a_2}$, is ranked by cosine similarity to $\vec{a_1}$ to compute this rank value.

We use the same Nonce2Vec parameters across all experiments: the ones that performed best in our definitional evaluation (section 4.1.). We experiment with background models with different dimensionality: d400 (the Nonce2Vec default) and d100 (found to perform better by Sprugnoli et al. (2019) on lemmatized Latin data). We also vary the frequency cutoff, as when working with smaller data, we may wish to include more words even if they are infrequent. We try a cutoff of 50 (c50), the nonce2vec default, and c20 or c5 depending on the size of the corpus. The results of Nonce2Vec with the different background models are listed in Table 2. We observe that the most consistent vectors are obtained using the largest dataset as a background corpus, the Bamman corpus. Using the largest Bamman model (bamman-c50-d400), we find that different vectors for the same term trained on a different sentence are on average rank 47 in each other's nearest neighbours, out of a vocabulary of 901K types, computed over all 30 test instances. On average, the cosine similarity between these vectors is 0.7. Among the 90 total comparisons between the 3 vectors for the 30 target terms, there were 59 cases where both target term vectors were each other's nearest neighbour (65.6%), with a greater cosine similarity to each other than to any of the other 901K words in the vocabulary. This is an impressive score with a vocabulary of almost a million words. The best-performing Wiki model, with a lower frequency cutoff (vicipaedia-c20-d400) achieves a similar average rank among a vocabulary of 30.4K types, and 51% of comparisons have rank 1 consistency. The cosine similarities are lower, though (0.55). On their synonym detection task for Classical Latin, Sprugnoli et al. (2019) achieve an accuracy of 86.9%, but here, the model only needs to choose between four alternative words, instead of almost 1 million. Furthermore, we observe

Term		$\vec{a_1}$ NNs	$\vec{a_2}$ NNs
	1	essentialis	demonstrabilia
genus	2	metaphysica	quidditative
	3	substantialitas	universaha
	1	expucetur	possibiles
conceptus	2	demonstrabilia	universaliores
	3	universaha	aliquee

Table 3: Qualitative examination of some nearest neighbours of target term vectors computed over two different context sentences of those terms.

that for the bamman-c50-d400 model, the average rank of a target term vector from the background model among the nearest neighbours of the learned Neo-Latin vector for that same term is 50,737 with a cosine similarity of 0.41. This shows that the model does learn from the Neo-Latin data, deviating from the background vector, and does not achieve consistency simply by learning nothing consistently.

Generally, we see in Table 2 that a lower word frequency cutoff (keeping a larger vocabulary) leads to more consistent results. All of this indicates that more background data leads to more consistent vectors on our Neo-Latin data. The Vicipaedia-based models slightly outperform the Latin Text Library-based models, despite their smaller vocabulary. This shows that data size is not the only factor — similarity to our target domain may also be relevant here, as Vicipaedia data may be closer to Neo-Latin scientific text than the contents of the Latin Text Library. Lastly, the models based on the small Classical Latin treebanks perform worst, a corpus that is not only small but also highly varied.

These results show that the Bamman models lead to more consistent embeddings on our data, even though they are based on rather noisy data. We have a closer look at this result by cherry-picking some examples. Table 3 shows the three nearest neighbours for two vectors each for the target terms *genus* (kind) and *conceptus* (concept). $\vec{a_1}$ is trained over the first context sentence for this term from our dataset, and $\vec{a_2}$ over the second. For *genus*, most of these look reasonable — certainly, *essentialis* (essential), *quidditative* (relating to the essence of someone or something) and *substantialitas* (the quality of being substantial or having substance) are semantically related to *genus* in the context of the mathematical method. *Universaha*, while related, is an OCR error (*universalia* (universals)). In this case, the two vectors are also each other's nearest neighbours, so the results for this term are consistent. The nearest neighbours of *conceptus*, on the other hand, are not a very good result. To start, the additive model initialization from the background model for *conceptus* $\vec{a_1}$ has as its nearest neighbours the words *sdbygoogle*, *ibygoogic* and *digfeedbygoogle*, clearly Google Books artifacts. After training, the nearest neighbours are as listed in Table 3: they have improved compared to the initial additive vector's neighbours and are now vaguely on-topic, but still full of OCR errors. This shows that consistent results are not necessarily of high quality in other respects.

5. Discussion

Our definitional dataset evaluation has shown that Nonce2Vec can learn Latin word embeddings from a sin-

gle definitional sentence, though slightly less well than it can for English. This is likely because the task of training a DS model is harder on Latin text due to the highly inflectional nature of the language and the smaller size of the Latin Wikipedia. There is less statistical evidence for the usage patterns of more different word forms.

Our Neo-Latin evaluation has shown that Nonce2Vec can consistently learn Neo-Latin word embeddings for terms relevant to a certain concept (i.e. the mathematical method), without access to a background corpus from this domain and without tuning on the consistency metric or Neo-Latin data. The evaluation demonstrates that this method can be used even when nothing but a limited number of sentences is available for the target domain. This is likely due to transfer of word usage information from the general-domain background corpus to the domain-specific sentence context, caused by the way in which Nonce2Vec initializes vectors based on a background corpus. At least two factors may affect the outcome: the size of the background corpus, and how similar it is to Neo-Latin text. Since lack of high-quality corpora in the relevant domain and lack of expert ground truths are typical features of research in low-resource settings, the relevance of our result becomes clear. It is useful in such settings to know that Nonce2Vec learns even from very tiny Neo-Latin corpora – *corpuscula* –, as long as background corpora are available, and that the latter can even be (a) in a different variety of the same language (b) noisy, as long as they are large. Based on this finding, tools that allow information retrieval and visualization using DS models (e.g. BolVis, van Wierst et al. (2018)) can be developed for Latin and applied to digital versions of the relevant texts, in order to find passages relevant to particular research questions in the history of ideas (Ginammi et al., 2020).

Clearly, however, to the aim of addressing our research question on the mathematical method with appropriate scholarly precision, high-quality Neo-Latin word embeddings based on data that is relevant to our concept of interest will be necessary. We encountered several issues related to the morphology of Latin. Among the target terms automatically extracted from Wikipedia, there were many proper names, as they are less affected by morphology. They occur more frequently in their lemma form and are more likely to pass frequency cutoffs. Other Wikipedia lemmas are not frequently used in their lemma form in natural text. In our Neo-Latin dataset, multiple sentences containing the same word form are scarce for the same reason — important terms can be inflected in many ways and each form will get a distinct vector in a standard Word2vec model. Lemmatization has been shown to improve language model performance on highly inflected languages. (Cotterell et al., 2018).

For this reason, Sprugnoli et al. (2019) used lemma embeddings instead of word embeddings. They were able to do this by having a manually lemmatized corpus. For Nonce2Vec, to create lemma embeddings, any background corpus used would have to be lemmatized. Of the corpora we used, only the small treebank corpora that mostly contain Classical Latin contained lemmatization, and none of the better-performing larger corpora exist in lemmatized form. While lemmatizers exist (see Eger et al. (2015) for an overview and evaluation on medieval church Latin) evaluation is costly and results may vary across different varieties of Latin. Still, for our type of research questions lemmatization carries natural benefits, because, as philosophers focussing on meaning change and concept drift, we are interested in studying concepts independently of the morphological variants of the terms expressing them. In future work, the issue could be addressed with an extrinsic evaluation on our tasks and evaluation across Latin varieties in the context of the EvaLatin shared task (Sprugnoli and Passarotti, 2020).

Despite impressive consistency scores, we also saw that other aspects of the quality of these embeddings may be lacking. Using the top-scoring Bamman model for initialization, we observe many OCR errors among the nearest neighbours of our learned Neo-Latin vectors. This is cause for concern, as Word2vec models based on this same data have already been used in a study of concepts in the works of Cassiodorus (Bjerva and Praet, 2015). We must therefore consider in what ways our evaluation is incomplete. The consistency evaluation does not capture all aspects of embedding quality: after all, a model can be consistently bad as well as consistently good. The definitional evaluation we conducted is only grounded in a larger Word2vec model (the background model) which has not been evaluated for Latin. We also cannot just assume that this model works well on Latin just because it works well on English — as illustrated by the fact that in most of our experiments, the English parameter settings did not perform well on the Latin data. This uncertainty leads us to propose an additional evaluation that is directly grounded in domain expert knowledge, to test whether the learned Neo-Latin word embeddings are not only consistent, but also conceptually sound.

5.1. Grounding the evaluation

To identify whether the word embeddings are consistently good or consistently bad, we need to evaluate them by comparing the domain expert's knowledge of the philosophical data with the embeddings. In Meyer et al. (2019), we propose a first step towards this form of evaluation for a 20th century English corpus of the philosophical works of Quine. For this corpus, we semi-formally defined the relations of some key terms to other terms (e.g., in Quine's oeuvre, *denotation* signifies a relation between a *general term* in language and (*physical*) *objects* in the ontology). By defining these interrelations between terms in the corpus, the expert knowledge of the meaning of a term within the corpus is reflected by how the term relates to other terms. In the case of our Neo-Latin corpus, the domain expert identified that *definitio* (definition) and *axioma* (axiom) are functional synonyms of *principium* (principle). Similar to the task discussed above, to successfully complete this task, the cosine distance of the vector of a given target term has to be nearer to the vectors of their functional synonyms than alternative terms. In the case of *principium*, *definitio* and *axioma*, the cosine distance of the vectors of these terms are expected to be nearer to each other than to other terms. Such a conceptual evaluation grounded in expert knowledge provides a method to evaluate word embeddings intrinsically and, thereby, the quality of their consistency.

5.2. Conclusion

Our results show that consistent Neo-Latin word embeddings can be learned by using methods that are designed to handle tiny data. These methods have not been applied to Latin before. Nonce2Vec might be a good DS model to use in such low-resource settings, although further evaluation and refinement is necessary, in particular in the context of humanities research. In addition, we demonstrate and discuss evaluation methods appropriate for our task. Using both a grounded evaluation and a consistency evaluation can tell us to what extent the learned vectors represent the conceptual distinctions we are interested in, and to what extent they can be learned consistently from the same text source. We have great plans for the future. We are actively digitizing a comparable German and Neo-Latin corpus of philosophical works. We seek to cooperate with existing initiatives and intend to add value to available collections. For e.g. the Bamman corpus this will entail improving the overall text quality by applying fully automatic OCR post-correction as provided by Text-Induced Corpus Clean-up or TICCL (Reynaert, 2010). To equip TICCL for appropriately handling Latin, we will apply the TICCLAT method (Reynaert et al., 2019) for linking morphologically related word forms to each other, to their diachronic and their known typographical variants. This follows from our observation that there is much room for improvements in embedding quality by having lemmatized and cleaned datasets and background corpora. Tiny data methods can also be further explored, as recent work incorporating a notion of informativity and more incrementality into Nonce2Vec (Kabbach et al., 2019) and recent context-based approaches outperforming Nonce2Vec on the English definitional dataset (e.g. Schick and Schütze (2019)) was not explored here. Having high-quality embeddings learned from historical text, and downstream applications that make use of them, will help us in obtaining large-scale evidence for research questions in the history of ideas that is impossible to obtain otherwise.

6.   Acknowledgements

We thank the UvA e-Ideas group for their fruitful discussion of a draft of this paper. We also thank the anonymous reviewers for their time and valuable comments. This research was supported by Arianna Betti's VICI grant *e-Ideas* (277-20-007) financed by the Dutch Research Council (NWO) and by Human(e)AI UvA grant *Small data, big challenges*. Yvette Oortwijn has also been supported by *CatVis* (NWO research grant 314-99-117). M. Reynaert is also affiliated to the Tilburg School of Humanities and Digital Sciences, Tilburg University.

Appendix: Neo-Latin evaluation dataset

We here present the Neo-Latin evaluation dataset, non-preprocessed for legibility. Best scores are shown. Provenances of the snippets are documented in the metadata to the online distribution of the experimental data.[8] Shown are smaller excerpts of the longer snippets in the actual dataset.

---

[8]`https://github.com/bloemj/nonce2vec/`
`tree/nonce2vec-latin`

Target	PoS	Snippet 1	Snippet 2	Snippet 3	AR	AD
Mathematica	A	methodum meditationis, et inveniendi, et probandi, potest huc commode referri methodus __	Unde reliquis omnibus praeferenda methodus __	Ubi methodus __ adhibetur, ibi & principia sunt indubitata, & modus concludendi legitimus	1	0.848
Mathesin	N	Hoc insuper ipsum me circa __ particulatim reverä ?	Quamobrem ut __ huic instituto accommodationem efficierem, omnes disciplinas in eum ordinem digessi.	medium as scientiam perveniendi certissimum est accurata & indefessa matheseos tractatio & methodi ibidem observatae ad alia extra __ obvia applicatio	1	0.793
Wolfius	PN	__ certe totum opus replevit meris axiomatibus, & postulatis, & observationibus, de quibus nemo facile dubitaverit	Accuratius ergo Illustris __ in brevi comment. de meth. math. Elementis math. praemissa 30 afferit.	Quicunque itaque Philosophus hoc intelligit, __ suum sicuti minime concedet.	1.6	0.678
Methodo	N	Possunt etiam quaedam themata tractari __ mathematica, illa scilicet, quae clara & evidentia principia admittunt.	Methodus demonstrandi synthetica eadem quoque, cum __ ratiocinandi, est	__ mathematica itaque ad scientiam & subiective & obiective talem possumus pervenire.	1	0.738
Universalis	A	Methodus __ dirigit totam disciplinam, ejusque disponit.	ac propterea haud immerito elementa matheseos __ dici queant, suo loco prolixius docebitur.	Methodus __ dirigit totam disciplinam, ejusque disponit.	115	0.680
Disciplinae	N	quia ex eo certae __ conclusiones omnes sunt probandae.	qumm pleraeque __ aliae, quae illam quidem admittant, res solo intellectu comprehensibiles tradant.	Mathesi enim accurate loquendo non est una disciplina, sed ex variis __ derceptae particulae quantitatem subiecti in unaquaque tractantes	1	0.750
Axiomata	N	Inveniuntur __ duobus fontibus adhibitis, vel per inductionem, vel per definitiones	Quae enim immediate ex definitiones fluunt, propositiones, si theroreticae sunt, __, si practicae, POSTULATA, vocantur.	secundò has ipsas definitiones in se considerabo, & hinc deductas proprietas appellabo __	20	0.721
Postulata	N	__ ,seu principia generalia, non quidem evidentia ac per se nota, sed tamen aliunde certa aut probata.	Propositiones, quae ex definitione unica adeoque citra ratiocinorum ambagem, manifestae sunt, dicuntur axiomata, si theoreticae fuerint; __, si praticae.	tum ponantur axiomata & __, & tandem ipsae demonstrationes subiugantur.	1	0.779
Sequitur	V	cuicunque competit definitum, ei competat definitio, et quicquid ex definitione __, vel alias de definitio praedicatur.	Sponte sua hinc __, conclusiones ex hisce principiis derivari posse, quarum inde probetur veritas.	Propositio, quae ex unica definitione __, legitime tornata statim tanquam vera terminis intellectis patet, modo illa definitio adducatur	4.3	0.696
Definitio	N	Ad cognitionem tria requiruntur: __, DIVISIO, DEMONSTRATIO	Est autem __ nihil aliud, quam rei naturae, ex qua ipsa componitur, commoda explicatio.	Et __ quidem est propositio rem ita determinans	129	0.612
Definitum	A	Notas ad __ agnoscendum & ab aliis discernendum sufficientes praebent genus atque differentia specifica.	Id quod definitur, vocatur __	definitionem & __ esse terminos diversos non solum quoad voces significantes sed etiam quoad conceptus significatos & objectivos	8.6	0.639
Notio	N	__ completa est quae obiecto, omnes ideas in quas necessario resolvitur substituit.	__, quam habemus, aut solas rei notas continet	definitio dicitur, quae est __ distincta completa speciei vel generis.	6.7	0.652
Ideas	N	Unde simul patet, __ simplices, eo quod ex aliis non componantur, non quoque posse definiri.	__ mediatas simplices nominabo, quibus opponuntur ideae mediatae compositae	omnes __ claras quodammodo simplices, distinctas vero semper compositas simul, esse.	1	0.746
Conceptus	N	Definitio, generalissima accepta, est __ definiti naturam explicans	primò omnes possibiles primo __, ex quibus formantur reliqui, redigam in ordinem, atque imposterum Definitiones nominabo	quod denique continuum sic, unde __ completus hic est quod sit extensum ab uno loco ad alterum.	1.7	0.673
Rationem	N	quod vero __ sui in altero habet principiatum vocatur.	__ unius rei ex altera observantur	haec differentia inter __ sufficientem & determinantem est ratio	1	0.743
Cognitionem	N	Ad __ tria requiruntur: DEFINITIO, DIVISIO, DEMONSTRATIO	DE RERUM __ III. Ad cognitionem tria requiruntur: DEFINITIO, DIVISIO, DEMONSTRATIO.	intellectum ad veram rei __ ducere debet.	1000	0.652
Simplices	A	Deinde ideae vel __ sunt, in quibus nihil mente dividere possumus	Res __, quae nullas habent partes; definiri non possent.	Unde simul patet, ideas __, eo quod ex aliis non componantur, non quoque posse definiri.	1	0.736
Compositae	A	secundus gradus continet conditiones universales demonstrandi, quae sunt conditiones __ ex definitionibus principiorum.	Etenim si omnes ideae, quae essentiam ideae __ constituunt, evoluantur, definitio non potest non esse adequata definitio.	ideas mediatas simplices nominabo, quibus opponuntur ideae mediatae	1	0.757
Genus	N	Definitio Essentialis Metaphysica seu Logica est quae datur per __ & differentiam.	ideas mediatas compositae, propositio qua per __ & differentiam specificam declarantur	DEFINITIO, est Oratio explicans natura rei.1. PRIMARIA, quae affert __ & differentiam	2.3	0.729
Differentia	N	ideam, & quae ad essentiam rei primario pertinet, qua a reliquis omnibus distinguitur, comprehendere debeat, adeoque constare ex genere & __ specifica.	Partes autem rei Metaphysica sunt Genus, & __.	Sed attributum substantive expressum dicitur genus, adiective expressum __	90	0.608
Principia	N	certa & evidentia axiomata, quae non probantur, sed supponuntur a scientiis, ideoque vocantur prima __	Et hoc ipso etiam efficit, ut ex ea __ clara & evidentia derivari queant.	Quoniam itaque __ ista immota sunt definitiones, axiomata & experientiae clarae.	1.3	0.726
Terminos	N	definitionem & definitum esse __ diversos non solum quoad voces significantes sed etiam quoad conceptus significatos & objectivos	Scientia, cujus vult principia invenire, & aliqua notitia habita illius ponit aliquos __ principiorum	quod sit indemonstrabile, ut possit a quodlibet, __ modo intelligente, ob evidentiam cognosci.	1	0.729
Intellectus	N	definitio, divisio, argumentatio sunt recta __ operatio.	definitio, divisio, argumentatio sunt recta cognitio __	nexu necessario et evidenti, demonstrantur, ut de illarum veritatem __ nullo modo dubitare possit.	6.3	0.765
Veritas	N	per axiomata relatio inter certas ideas ostenditur, ut nova inde cognoscatur __	a quorum evidentia __ totius discursus continua serie deducitur	Quomodo vocatur illa __, a qua alia procedit vel dependet?	3	0.611
Propositiones	N	Et huinc Axiomata vocantur etiam Maximae, subintellige, __	quibus verae __ possint etiam perfecta fieri & accuratae, quibus nihil, quo fiant meliores, addii posset	Principia dirigentia, sunt axiomata, id est __ per se notae	1	0.699
Scientia	N	Logica est __ veritatis	__ est cognitio certa & evidens rei per causam &c.	Primo dicitur __, quia conclusiones certas ex principiis certis deducit.	2.6	0.659
Theoremata	N	Propositionem vero theoreticam ex pluribus definitionibus inter se collatis erutam, __ appellant.	Si plures definitiones inter se contenderis: facile reperies __ & PROBLEMATA.	cum videlicet principia sunt vocantur vel axiomata vel __	6	0.593
Demonstrationes	N	Principia __ sunt definitiones	tertius gradus continet __ universales ex principiis & conditiones universalibus productas	__ autem legitima consequentia ex iis tandem deducant propositiones per se non manifestas.	12.6	0.617
Derivari	V	universalissimum principium est constituendum, a quo cetera omnia facili negotio possunt __	Qua ratione autem axiomata ex definitione __ queant ostendit.	ac quaevis alia requirit methodus, plura possint hinc __, quam per aliam quamcumque methodum	1	0.725
Demonstrari	V	quod aliunde __ potest, ac debet, cuius id eo duplex est respectus, alius ad conclusionem, alius ad principium prius clarius	conclusiones ex hisce principiis __ posse, quarum inde probetur veritatis.	nulla est alia propositio per quam __ possit veritas hujus propositionis tandem est demonstrativa caeterarum.	1	0.756

Table 4: Neo-Latin consistency evaluation set. Legend: AR = Average Rank, AD = Average Distance, Part-of-speech tags: A = adjective, N = noun, PN = proper noun, V = Verb.

7. Bibliographical References

Bamman, D. and Crane, G. (2011). The ancient Greek and Latin dependency treebanks. In *Language technology for cultural heritage*, pages 79–98. Springer.

Bamman, D. and Smith, D. (2012). Extracting two thousand years of Latin from a million book library. *Journal on Computing and Cultural Heritage (JOCCH)*, 5(1):1–13.

Baroni, M., Dinu, G., and Kruszewski, G. (2014). Don't count, predict! A systematic comparison of context-counting vs. context-predicting semantic vectors. In *Proceedings of the 52nd Annual Meeting of the Association for Computational Linguistics (Volume 1: Long Papers)*, pages 238–247.

Bengio, Y., Ducharme, R., Vincent, P., and Jauvin, C. (2003). A neural probabilistic language model. *Journal of machine learning research*, 3(Feb):1137–1155.

Betti, A., van den Berg, H., Oortwijn, Y., and Treijtel, C. (2019). History of Philosophy in Ones and Zeros. In Mark Curtis et al., editors, *Methodological Advances in Experimental Philosophy*, Advances in Experimental Philosophy, pages 295–332. Bloomsbury.

Bjerva, J. and Praet, R. (2015). Word embeddings pointing the way for late antiquity. In *Proceedings of the 9th SIGHUM Workshop on Language Technology for Cultural Heritage, Social Sciences, and Humanities (LaTeCH)*, pages 53–57.

Bloem, J., Fokkens, A., and Herbelot, A. (2019). Evaluating the consistency of word embeddings from small data. In *Proceedings of the International Conference on Recent Advances in Natural Language Processing (RANLP 2019)*, pages 132–141, Varna, Bulgaria, September. INCOMA Ltd.

Bruni, E., Tran, N.-K., and Baroni, M. (2014). Multimodal distributional semantics. *Journal of Artificial Intelligence Research (JAIR)*, 49(1-47).

Busa, R. (1974). *Index Thomisticus Sancti Thomae Aquinatis Operum Omnium Indices Et Concordantiae in Quibus Verborum Omnium Et Singulorum Formae Et Lemmata Cum Suis Frequentiis Et Contextibus Variis Modis Referuntur*.

Cecchini, F. M., Passarotti, M., Marongiu, P., and Zeman, D. (2018). Challenges in converting the Index Thomisticus Treebank into Universal Dependencies. In *Proceedings of the Second Workshop on Universal Dependencies (UDW 2018)*, pages 27–36.

Clark, S. (2015). Vector space models of lexical meaning. *The Handbook of Contemporary semantic theory*, pages 493–522.

Cotterell, R., Mielke, S. J., Eisner, J., and Roark, B. (2018). Are all languages equally hard to language-model? In *Proceedings of the 2018 Conference of the North American Chapter of the Association for Computational Linguistics: Human Language Technologies, Volume 2 (Short Papers)*, pages 536–541, New Orleans, Louisiana, June. Association for Computational Linguistics.

Eger, S., vor der Brück, T., and Mehler, A. (2015). Lexicon-assisted tagging and lemmatization in Latin: A comparison of six taggers and two lemmatization methods. In *Proceedings of the 9th SIGHUM Workshop on Language Technology for Cultural Heritage, Social Sciences, and Humanities (LaTeCH)*, pages 105–113, Beijing, China, July. Association for Computational Linguistics.

Erk, K. (2012). Vector space models of word meaning and phrase meaning: A survey. *Language and Linguistics Compass*, 6(10):635–653.

Frängsmyr, T. (1975). Christian Wolff's Mathematical Method and its Impact on the Eighteenth Century. *Journal of the History of Ideas*, 36(4):653–668.

Ginammi, A., Bloem, J., Koopman, R., Wang, S., and Betti, A. (2020). Bolzano, Kant and the Traditional Theory of Concepts - A Computational Investigation [R&R 16 dec 2019 for volume under contract]. In Andreas de Block et al., editors, *The Dynamics of Science: Computational Frontiers in History and Philosophy of Science*. Pittsburgh University Press.

Grave, E., Bojanowski, P., Gupta, P., Joulin, A., and Mikolov, T. (2018). Learning word vectors for 157 languages. *arXiv preprint arXiv:1802.06893*.

Haug, D. T. and Jøhndal, M. (2008). Creating a parallel treebank of the old Indo-European Bible translations. In *Proceedings of the Second Workshop on Language Technology for Cultural Heritage Data (LaTeCH 2008)*, pages 27–34.

Hellrich, J. and Hahn, U. (2016). Bad company - neighborhoods in neural embedding spaces considered harmful. In *Proceedings of COLING 2016, the 26th International Conference on Computational Linguistics: Technical Papers*, pages 2785–2796.

Herbelot, A. and Baroni, M. (2017). High-risk learning: acquiring new word vectors from tiny data. In *Proceedings of the 2017 Conference on Empirical Methods in Natural Language Processing*, pages 304–309.

Hill, F., Reichart, R., and Korhonen, A. (2015). Simlex-999: Evaluating semantic models with (genuine) similarity estimation. *Computational Linguistics*, 41(4):665–695.

Hinrichs, E., Hinrichs, M., Kübler, S., and Trippel, T. (2019). Language technology for digital humanities: introduction to the special issue. *Language Resources and Evaluation*, 53(4):559–563, Dec.

Kabbach, A., Gulordava, K., and Herbelot, A. (2019). Towards incremental learning of word embeddings using context informativeness. In *Proceedings of the 57th Conference of the Association for Computational Linguistics: Student Research Workshop*, pages 162–168, Florence, Italy, July. Association for Computational Linguistics.

Korkiakangas, T. and Passarotti, M. (2011). Challenges in annotating medieval Latin charters. *Journal for Language Technology and Computational Linguistics*, 26(2):103–114.

Lazaridou, A., Marelli, M., and Baroni, M. (2017). Multimodal word meaning induction from minimal exposure to natural text. *Cognitive science*, 41:677–705.

Manjavacas, E., Long, B., and Kestemont, M. (2019). On the feasibility of automated detection of allusive text reuse. In *Proceedings of the 3rd Joint SIGHUM Workshop on Computational Linguistics for Cultural Heritage,*

Social Sciences, Humanities and Literature, pages 104–114.

McGillivray, B. and Kilgarriff, A. (2013). Tools for historical corpus research, and a corpus of Latin. *New Methods in Historical Corpus Linguistics*, (3):247–257.

Meyer, F., Oortwijn, Y., Sommerauer, P., Bloem, J., Betti, A., and Fokkens, A. (2019). The semantics of meaning: distributional approaches for studying philosophical text. Unpublished manuscript.

Mikolov, T., Chen, K., Corrado, G., and Dean, J. (2013). Efficient estimation of word representations in vector space. In *Proceedings of the ICLR Workshop*.

Nivre, J., De Marneffe, M.-C., Ginter, F., Goldberg, Y., Hajic, J., Manning, C. D., McDonald, R., Petrov, S., Pyysalo, S., Silveira, N., et al. (2016). Universal dependencies v1: A multilingual treebank collection. In *Proceedings of the Tenth International Conference on Language Resources and Evaluation (LREC'16)*, pages 1659–1666.

Passarotti, M. (2019). The project of the Index Thomisticus Treebank. In Monica Berti, editor, *Digital Classical Philology. Ancient Greek and Latin in the Digital Revolution*, volume 10 of *Age of Access? Grundfragen der Informationsgesellschaft*, pages 299–319. De Gruyter.

Řehůřek, R. and Sojka, P. (2010). Software Framework for Topic Modelling with Large Corpora. In *Proceedings of the LREC 2010 Workshop on New Challenges for NLP Frameworks*, pages 45–50, Valletta, Malta, May. ELRA. http://is.muni.cz/publication/884893/en.

Reynaert, M., Bos, P., and van der Zwaan, J. (2019). Granularity versus Dispersion in the Dutch Diachronical Database of Lexical Frequencies TICCLAT. In *Proceedings of CLARIN Annual Conference 2019 – Conference Proceedings*, pages 169–172, Leipzig, Germany. CLARIN ERIC.

Reynaert, M. (2010). Character confusion versus focus word-based correction of spelling and OCR variants in corpora. *International Journal on Document Analysis and Recognition*, pages 1–15. 10.1007/s10032-010-0133-5.

Sahlgren, M. and Lenci, A. (2016). The effects of data size and frequency range on distributional semantic models. In *Proceedings of the 2016 Conference on Empirical Methods in Natural Language Processing*, pages 975–980.

Schick, T. and Schütze, H. (2019). Rare words: A major problem for contextualized embeddings and how to fix it by attentive mimicking. *arXiv preprint arXiv:1904.06707*.

Schnabel, T., Labutov, I., Mimno, D., and Joachims, T. (2015). Evaluation methods for unsupervised word embeddings. In *Proceedings of the 2015 Conference on Empirical Methods in Natural Language Processing*, pages 298–307.

Sprugnoli, R. and Passarotti, M., (2020). *EvaLatin 2020 Shared Task Guidelines*. Version 1.0, December 10, 2019.

Sprugnoli, R., Passarotti, M., and Moretti, G. (2019). Vir is to Moderatus as Mulier is to Intemperans: Lemma embeddings for Latin. In *Sixth Italian Conference on Computational Linguistics*, pages 1–7.

Turney, P. D. and Pantel, P. (2010). From frequency to meaning: Vector space models of semantics. *Journal of artificial intelligence research*, 37:141–188.

Van den Berg, H., Betti, A., Oortwijn, Y., Parisi, M. C., Wang, S., and Koopman, R. (ongoing). The Spread of the Mathematical Method in Eighteenth-Century Germany: A Quantitative Investigation.

van Gompel, M., van der Sloot, K., Reynaert, M., and van den Bosch, A. (2017). FoLiA in practice: The infrastructure of a linguistic annotation format. In J. Odijk et al., editors, *CLARIN-NL in the Low Countries*, chapter 6, pages 71–81. Ubiquity (Open Access).

van Wierst, P., Hofstede, S., Oortwijn, Y., Castermans, T., Koopman, R., Wang, S., Westenberg, M. A., and Betti, A. (2018). Bolvis: visualization for text-based research in philosophy. In *3rd Workshop on Visualization for the Digital Humanities*.

Zeman, D., Hajic, J., Popel, M., Potthast, M., Straka, M., Ginter, F., Nivre, J., and Petrov, S. (2018). CoNLL 2018 shared task: Multilingual parsing from raw text to universal dependencies. In *Proceedings of the CoNLL 2018 Shared Task: Multilingual parsing from raw text to universal dependencies*, pages 1–21.

Proceedings of 1st Workshop on Language Technologies for Historical and Ancient Languages, pages 94–99
Language Resources and Evaluation Conference (LREC 2020), Marseille, 11–16 May 2020
© European Language Resources Association (ELRA), licensed under CC-BY-NC

Latin-Spanish Neural Machine Translation: from the Bible to Saint Augustine

Eva Martínez Garcia, Álvaro García Tejedor
CEIEC-Universidad Francisco de Vitoria
Edificio H, Campus de Pozuelo, Universidad Francisco de Vitoria.
Carretera Pozuelo-Majadahonda km. 1,800. 28223 Pozuelo de Alarcón (Madrid).
{eva.martinez, a.gtejedor}@ceiec.es

Abstract

Although there are several sources where to find historical texts, they usually are available in the original language that makes them generally inaccessible. This paper presents the development of state-of-the-art Neural Machine Systems for the low-resourced Latin-Spanish language pair. First, we build a Transformer-based Machine Translation system on the Bible parallel corpus. Then, we build a comparable corpus from Saint Augustine texts and their translations. We use this corpus to study the domain adaptation case from the Bible texts to Saint Augustine's works.

Results show the difficulties of handling a low-resourced language as Latin. First, we noticed the importance of having enough data, since the systems do not achieve high BLEU scores. Regarding domain adaptation, results show how using in-domain data helps systems to achieve a better quality translation. Also, we observed that it is needed a higher amount of data to perform an effective vocabulary extension that includes in-domain vocabulary.

Keywords: Machine Translation, domain adaptation, low resourced

1. Introduction

There exist several digital libraries that store large collection of digitalized historical documents. However, most of these documents are usually written in Latin, Greek or other ancient languages, resulting in them being inaccessible to general public. Natural Language Processing (NLP) offers different tools that can help to save this language barrier to bring the content of these historical documents to people. In particular, Machine Translation (MT) approaches can reproduce these historical documents in modern languages.

We present a set of experiments in machine translation for the Latin-Spanish language pair. We build a baseline Transformer-based (Vaswani et al., 2017) system trained on the Bible parallel corpus (Christodoulopoulos and Steedman, 2015) to study the associated difficulties of handling morphologically rich low-resourced languages like Latin. Latin is a low-resourced language, with few publicly available parallel data (González-Rubio et al., 2010a; Resnik et al., 1999). This is a challenge for data-driven approaches in general, and state-of-the-art Neural Machine Translation (NMT) approaches in particular since these systems usually require a high amount of data (Zoph et al., 2016). We create a comparable corpus from Saint Augustine's works and we study the impact of adapting the baseline Bible translation system towards the Saint Augustine writings.

The paper is organized as follows. In Section 2., we revisit the state-of-the-art MT approaches and their application to Latin. Then, in Section 3. we describe both the parallel and the comparable data that we use in our experiments, explaining how we compiled the comparable corpus. Section 4. gives details on the set of experiments that we carried out to evaluate a baseline NMT trained on the Bible and its adaptation towards the Saint Augustine work. Finally, Section 5. discusses the conclusions and future work.

2. Related Work

There is a growing interest in the computational linguistic analysis of historical texts (Bouma and Adesam, 2017; Tjong Kim Sang et al., 2017). However, there are only a few works related to MT for ancient or historical languages. In (Schneider et al., 2017), the authors treat the spelling normalization as a translation task and use a Statistical Machine Translation (SMT) system trained on sequences of characters instead of word sequences. There exist shared tasks like the CLIN27 (Tjong Kim Sang et al., 2017), a translation shared task for medieval Dutch.

In the particular case of Latin, there exist several NLP tools, for instance, the LEMLAT morphological analyzer for Latin (Passarotti et al., 2017). However, there are only a few works involving MT for Latin. In particular, (González-Rubio et al., 2010b) describe the development of a Latin-Catalan Statistical Machine Translation System and the collection of a Latin-Catalan parallel corpus. However, to the best of our knowledge, the present work describes the first experiments in neural machine translation for the Latin-Spanish language pair.

Neural Machine Translation systems represent the current state-of-the-art for machine translation technologies and even some evaluations claim that they have reached human performance (Hassan et al., 2018). The first successful NMT systems were attentional encoder-decoder approaches based on recurrent neural networks (Bahdanau et al., 2015), but the current NMT state-of-the-art architecture is the Transformer (Vaswani et al., 2017). This sequence-to-sequence neural model is based solely on attention mechanisms, without any recurrence nor convolution. Although RNN-based architectures can be more robust in low-resourced scenarios, Transformer-based models usually perform better according to automatic evaluation metrics (Rikters et al., 2018). All the NMT systems built for our experiments follow the Transformer architecture.

Latin and Spanish can be considered closely-related languages. There are several works that study the benefits of using NMT systems in contrast to using Phrase-Based Statistical MT (PBSMT) systems (Costa-jussà, 2017), observing how NMT systems are better for in-domain translations. (Alvarez et al., 2019) pursue a similar study from the post-editing point of view, showing how NMT systems solve typical problems of PBSMT systems achieving better results.

3. Corpora

In this section, we describe the parallel and comparable data we use to train our NMT models.

3.1. Parallel Data

Latin is a low-resourced language in general, and parallel data for Latin-Spanish are scarce in particular. In the

Corpus	Description	sent. align.
Tatoeba	A collection of translated sentences from Tatoeba[1]	3.9k
Bible	A multilingual parallel corpus created from translations of the Bible	30.3k
wikimedia	Wikipedia translations published by the wikimedia foundation and their article translation system.	0.1k
GNOME	A parallel corpus of GNOME localization files.	0.9k
QED	Open multilingual collection of subtitles for educational videos and lectures collaboratively transcribed and translated over the AMARA[2] web-based platform.	6.1k
Ubuntu	A parallel corpus of Ubuntu localization files.	0.6k
	Total:	41.8k

Table 1: Description of Latin-Spanish corpora available in the OPUS repository. The *sent. align.* column shows the number of aligned sentences available per corpus.

OPUS (Tiedemann, 2012) repository there are only 6 Latin-Spanish parallel corpora of different domains. Table 1 shows the statistics of these corpora, with a total of only 41.8k aligned sentences available. For our work, we choose the Bible corpus (Christodoulopoulos and Steedman, 2015) since it is the largest corpus and the only one containing historical texts which are closer to the Saint Augustine texts domain.

3.2. Comparable Data

NMT systems usually need a considerable amount of data to achieve good quality translations (Zoph et al., 2016). We built a comparable Latin-Spanish corpus by collecting several texts from Saint Augustine of Hippo, one of the most prolific Latin authors. The Federación Agustiniana Española (FAE) promoted the translation into Spanish of the Saint Augustine works and make them available online. We used most of the texts from the Biblioteca de Autores Cristianos (BAC), published under the auspices of the FAE, one of the most complete collections of the Augustinian works in Spanish[3][4].

After gathering the texts in Spanish and Latin, we processed the corpus. First, we split the text into sentences using the Moses (Koehn et al., 2007) sentence splitter and we tokenize the text using the Moses tokenizer. Then, we use Hunalign (Varga et al., 2007) to automatically align the data sentence by sentence. We filter out those sentence alignments that have assigned an alignment score below 0. Notice that since we are using automatically aligned data, the resulting corpus is comparable and not a parallel one.

Corpus	#sents	#tokens la	#tokens es
Train	91,044	2,197,422	2,834,749
Development	1,000	22,914	28,812
Test	1,500	31,682	40,587
Total:	93,544	2,252,018	2,904,148

Table 2: Figures for the comparable corpus on Saint Augustine works, showing the number of aligned sentences (*#sents*) and the number of tokens in Latin (*#tokens la*) and in Spanish (*#tokens es*). *Train*, *Development* and *Test* represent the slices used for building the MT systems. *Total* shows the total amount of data.

4. Experiments

We want to study, first, the aplicability of the state-of-the-art NMT systems to the Latin-Spanish language pair. Once we have created the comparable corpus on the Saint Augustine writings, we analyze the impact of applying several domain-adaptation techniques to adapt our models from the Bible domain to the Saint Augustine domain.

4.1. Settings

Our NMT systems follow the Transformer architecture (Vaswani et al., 2017) and they are built using the OpenNMT-tf toolkit (Klein et al., 2018; Klein et al., 2017). In particular, we use the Transformer *small* configuration described in (Vaswani et al., 2017), mostly using the available OpenNMT-tf default settings: 6 layers of 2,048 inner-units with 8 attention heads. Word embeddings are set to 512 dimensions both for source and target vocabularies. Adam (Kingma and Ba, 2015) optimizer was used for training, using Noam learning rate decay and 4,000 warmup steps. We followed an early-stopping strategy to stop the training process when the BLEU (Papineni et al., 2002) on the development set did not improve more than 0.01 in the last 10 evaluations, evaluating the model each 500 steps.

---

[3]Saint Augustine texts are available in https://www.augustinus.it

[4]We use all the texts except the *Tractates on the Gospel of John* and Sermons from *Sermon 100th* onward.

Training data was distributed on batches of 3,072 tokens and we used a 0.1 dropout probability. Finally, a maximum sentence length of 100 tokens is used for both source and target sides and the vocabulary size is 30,000 for both target and source languages. Vocabularies are set at the subword level to overcome the vocabulary limitation. We segmented the data using *Sentencepiece* (Kudo and Richardson, 2018) trained jointly on the source and target training data used for building each model, following the unigram language model (Kud, 2018). The *Sentencepiece* models were trained to produce a final vocabulary size of 30,000 subword units.

We evaluate the quality of the outputs by calculating BLEU, TER (Snover et al., 2006) and METEOR (Denkowski and Lavie, 2011) metrics. We used *multeval* (Clark et al., 2011) to compute these scores on the truecased and tokenized evaluation sets.

4.2. Results

First, we trained a baseline model on the Bible parallel corpus. Table 3 shows the results of the automatic evaluation of this system in its in-domain development and test sets. The *checkpoint-30000* is the model that achieved the best BLEU score on the development data. Following a usual technique to improve the translation quality, we averaged the 8 checkpoints with the best BLEU on the development set resulting in the *avg-8* model. In this particular case, the average model is able to improve +0.47 on the development set and +0.78 on the test set with respect to the *ckpt-30000* model. Also, the *avg-8* system improves the TER metric both on the development and the test set by 1.4 and 1.5 points respectively.

Bible	dev		test	
models	BLEU ↑	TER↓	BLEU↑	TER↓
ckpt-30000	11.6	76.8	9.7	82.3
avg-8	**12.2**	**75.4**	**10.5**	**80.8**

Table 3: Automatic evaluation of the Bible NMT models on the development (*dev*) and test sets extracted from the Bible corpus. *ckpt-30000* is the model resulting from the training step 30000, and the *avg-8* is the average of 8 checkpoints.

We selected the *avg-8* for adapting it to the Saint Augustine text via fine-tuning (Crego et al., 2016; Freitag and Al-Onaizan, 2016), that is, by further training the *avg-8* on the in-domain data (hereafter the *Bible* model). We created two systems adapted by fine-tuning, the first one uses the Bible vocabulary (*Bible-ft*), and the second one updates the Bible vocabulary by adding those missing elements from the Saint Augustine texts vocabulary (*Bible-ft-vocabExt.*). Furthermore, we also built a model trained only using the comparable corpus (*SAugustine*) and a model trained on the concatenation of the data from the Bible and the Saint Augustine comparable data (*Bible+SAugustine*) [5]. For all the systems, we selected those models that achieved the best BLEU scores on the development sets, considering also the models resulting from averaging 8 checkpoints with higher

---

[5]The concatenated corpus resulted in 119,330 sentence pairs.

BLEU scores on the development set like we did for the Bible model.

System	BLEU ↑	METEOR↑	TER↓
Bible	0.9	6.9	106.1
Bible-ft	9.4	25.3	79.2
Bible-ft-vocabExt.	7.1	21.9	84.4
SAugustine	9.1	25.2	79.7
Bible+SAugustine	**10.1**	**26.6**	**78.5**

Table 4: Automatic evaluation of the different MT systems on the in-domain manually validated Saint Augustine test set.

Table 4 shows the results of the automatic evaluation of the different systems on the *ValTest* from the Saint Augustine texts.

The best system is *Bible+SAugustine*, the one trained on the concatenated data, improving +0.7 points on BLEU regarding the best-adapted model *Bible-ft*. Also, it outperforms the model trained only on the in-domain data. These results show the importance of having enough data to train an NMT system as well as having an important percentage of data from the working domain.

The impact of using in-domain data to tune or train the translation models is remarkable. All the fine-tuned models outperform significantly the *Bible* model performance, gaining up to 8.5 points of BLEU. Notice that the fine-tuned model (*Bible-ft*) uses the same vocabulary as the *Bible* model. These numbers support the importance of having in-domain data for developing MT systems. Since many of the Saint Augustine writings discuss texts from the Bible, these results also evidence the sensitivity of MT systems to capture characteristics from different writing styles. These features can come from different authors or different time periods, which can be very important when studying historical texts, giving a wider sense to the domain definition.

Extending the vocabulary when fine-tuning the *Bible* model does not result in improvements regarding any of the automatic metrics. In fact, the *Bible-ft-vocabExt.* model is 2.3 BLEU poins below the *Bible-ft* model. Although the model with the extended vocabulary can have wider coverage, it does not have enough data to learn a good representation for the new elements in the vocabulary.

We observe also that the *SAugustine* model obtains better scores than the *Bible* model since its training data is larger and belongs to the test domain, although it was trained on comparable data. However, the results of the adapted model *Bible-ft* are slightly better than the *SAugustine*. This evidences the importance of having data of quality to model the translation from Latin to Spanish.

5. Conclusions and Future Work

We built NMT systems for translating from Latin to Spanish. We identified the typical issues for low-resourced languages for the particular case of Latin-Spanish. Since we only found few parallel corpora available for this particular language pair, we collected the work of Saint Augustine of Hippo in Spanish and Latin and built a comparable corpus of 93,544 aligned sentences. Furthermore, we created a manually validated test set to better evaluate the translation quality of our systems.

We built 5 NMT models trained on different data. First, we built a baseline system trained on the Bible parallel corpus. Then, we adapted the *Bible* model towards the Saint Augustine domain by fine-tuning it in two ways: maintaining the Bible vocabulary and extending this vocabulary by including new elements from the Saint Augustine data. Finally, we trained two models using directly the in-domain data. We built a model trained only on the comparable Saint Augustine corpus and, finally, we trained an NMT on the concatenation of the Bible and the Saint Augustine writings corpora. The automatic evaluation results show significant differences among the *Bible* model and the rest of the models that somehow include information from the in-domain data when translating the manually validated Saint Augustine test set, showing the importance of the in-domain data. The best system was the one trained on the concatenated data *Bible+SAugustine*, showing the importance of having enough data to train an NMT model.

As future work, we want to study the behavior of training NMT systems in the other direction: from Spanish to Latin. We find interesting to analyze if the issues observed when trying to translate into other morphologically rich languages like Basque (Etchegoyhen et al., 2018) or Turkish (Ataman et al., 2020) can be observed when dealing with Latin. In this line, we want to study the impact of using morphologically motivated subword tokenization like the ones proposed by (Alegria et al., 1996) for Basque and by (Ataman et al., 2020; Ataman et al., 2017) for Turkish. Also, we want to include a more in depht analysis of the linguistic related issues that can appear for these closesly-related languages (Popović et al., 2016).

In order to deal with the low resource feature of the Latin-Spanish language pair, we want to continue with our work by applying data augmentation techniques like back-translation (Sennrich et al., 2016) to artificially extend the training data. The Latin-Spanish scenario seems to apply the unsupervised NMT approaches (Artetxe et al., 2018; Artetxe et al., 2019; Lample et al., 2018), since there are available resources in both languages but only a few parallel data. Also, we want to explore how a Latin-Spanish MT system can benefit from other languages in a multilingual scenario (Johnson et al., 2017; Lakew et al., 2018), i.e. romance languages, to improve the final translation quality.

6. Acknowledgements

We would like to thank Beatriz Magán and Miguel Pajares for their assistance during the development of this research work. We would also like to thank the Federación Agustiniana Española (FAE) and the Biblioteca de Autores Cristianos (BAC) for making available online the Spanish translations of the Saint Augustine's works.

7. Bibliographical References

Alegria, I., Artola, X., Sarasola, K., and Urkia, M. (1996). Automatic morphological analysis of basque. *Literary and Linguistic Computing*, 11(4):193–203.

Alvarez, S., Oliver, A., and Badia, T. (2019). Does NMT make a difference when post-editing closely related languages? the case of Spanish-Catalan. In *Proceedings of Machine Translation Summit XVII Volume 2: Translator, Project and User Tracks*, pages 49–56, Dublin, Ireland, August. European Association for Machine Translation.

Artetxe, M., Labaka, G., Agirre, E., and Cho, K. (2018). Unsupervised neural machine translation. *Proceedings of the ICLR2018*.

Artetxe, M., Labaka, G., and Agirre, E. (2019). An effective approach to unsupervised machine translation. *Proceedings of the 57th Annual Meeting of the Association for Computational Linguistics*.

Ataman, D., Negri, M., Turchi, M., and Federico, M. (2017). Linguistically motivated vocabulary reduction for neural machine translation from turkish to english. *The Prague Bulletin of Mathematical Linguistics*, 108(1):331–342.

Ataman, D., Aziz, W., and Birch, A. (2020). A latent morphology model for open-vocabulary neural machine translation. *Proceedings of the ICLR2020*.

Bahdanau, D., Cho, K., and Bengio, Y. (2015). Neural machine translation by jointly learning to align and translate. In *Proceedings of the 3rd International Conference on Learning Representations (ICLR)*.

Gerlof Bouma et al., editors. (2017). *Proceedings of the NoDaLiDa 2017 Workshop on Processing Historical Language*, Gothenburg, May. Linköping University Electronic Press.

Christodoulopoulos, C. and Steedman, M. (2015). A massively parallel corpus: the bible in 100 languages. In *Language Resources and Evaluation*.

Clark, J. H., Dyer, C., Lavie, A., and Smith, N. A. (2011). Better hypothesis testing for statistical machine translation: Controlling for optimizer instability. In *Proceedings of the 49th Annual Meeting of the Association for Computational Linguistics: Human Language Technologies: short papers-Volume 2*, pages 176–181. Association for Computational Linguistics.

Costa-jussà, M. R. (2017). Why Catalan-Spanish neural machine translation? analysis, comparison and combination with standard rule and phrase-based technologies. In *Proceedings of the Fourth Workshop on NLP for Similar Languages, Varieties and Dialects (VarDial)*, pages 55–62, Valencia, Spain, April. Association for Computational Linguistics.

Crego, J., Kim, J., Klein, G., Rebollo, A., Yang, K., Senellart, J., Akhanov, E., Brunelle, P., Coquard, A., Deng, Y., et al. (2016). Systran's pure neural machine translation systems. *arXiv preprint arXiv:1610.05540*.

Denkowski, M. and Lavie, A. (2011). Meteor 1.3: Automatic metric for reliable optimization and evaluation of machine translation systems. In *Proceedings of the sixth workshop on statistical machine translation*, pages 85–91. Association for Computational Linguistics.

Etchegoyhen, T., Martínez Garcia, E., Azpeitia, A., Labaka, G., Alegria, I., Cortes Etxabe, I., Jauregi Carrera, A., Ellakuria Santos, I., Martin, M., and Calonge, E. (2018). Neural machine translation of basque.

Freitag, M. and Al-Onaizan, Y. (2016). Fast domain adaptation for neural machine translation. *arXiv preprint arXiv:1612.06897*.

González-Rubio, J., Civera, J., Juan, A., and Casacuberta, F. (2010a). Saturnalia: A latin-catalan parallel corpus for statistical mt. In *LREC*.

González-Rubio, J., Civera, J., Juan, A., and Casacuberta, F. (2010b). Saturnalia: A latin-catalan parallel corpus for statistical mt. In *LREC*.

Hassan, H., Aue, A., Chen, C., Chowdhary, V., Clark, J., Federmann, C., Huang, X., Junczys-Dowmunt, M., Lewis, W., Li, M., Liu, S., Liu, T., Luo, R., Menezes, A., Qin, T., Seide, F., Tan, X., Tian, F., Wu, L., Wu, S., Xia, Y., Zhang, D., Zhang, Z., and Zhou, M. (2018). Achieving human parity on automatic Chinese to English news translation. *CoRR*, abs/1803.05567.

Johnson, M., Schuster, M., Le, Q. V., Krikun, M., Wu, Y., Chen, Z., Thorat, N., Viégas, F., Wattenberg, M., Corrado, G., Hughes, M., and Dean, J. (2017). Google's multilingual neural machine translation system: Enabling zero-shot translation. *Transactions of the Association for Computational Linguistics*, 5:339–351.

Kingma, D. P. and Ba, J. (2015). Adam: A method for stochastic optimization. In *Proceedings of the ICLR2015*.

Klein, G., Kim, Y., Deng, Y., Senellart, J., and Rush, A. (2017). OpenNMT: Open-source toolkit for neural machine translation. In *Proceedings of ACL 2017, System Demonstrations*, pages 67–72, Vancouver, Canada, July. Association for Computational Linguistics.

Klein, G., Kim, Y., Deng, Y., Nguyen, V., Senellart, J., and Rush, A. (2018). OpenNMT: Neural machine translation toolkit. In *Proceedings of the 13th Conference of the Association for Machine Translation in the Americas (Volume 1: Research Papers)*, pages 177–184, Boston, MA, March. Association for Machine Translation in the Americas.

Koehn, P., Hoang, H., Birch, A., Callison-Burch, C., Federico, M., Bertoldi, N., Cowan, B., Shen, W., Moran, C., Zens, R., Dyer, C., Bojar, O., Constantin, A., and Herbst, E. (2007). Moses: Open source toolkit for statistical machine translation. In *Proceedings of the 45th Annual Meeting of the Association for Computational Linguistics on Interactive Poster and Demonstration Sessions (ACL)*, pages 177–180.

(2018). Subword regularization: Improving neural network translation models with multiple subword candidates. In *Kudo, Taku*.

Kudo, T. and Richardson, J. (2018). SentencePiece: A simple and language independent subword tokenizer and detokenizer for neural text processing. In *Proceedings of the 2018 Conference on Empirical Methods in Natural Language Processing (EMNLP)*, pages 66–71.

Lakew, S. M., Federico, M., Negri, M., and Turchi, M. (2018). Multilingual neural machine translation for zero-resource languages. *Italian Journal of Computational Linguistics. Volume 1, Number 1*.

Lample, G., Ott, M., Conneau, A., Denoyer, L., and Ranzato, M. (2018). Phrase-based & neural unsupervised machine translation. *Proceedings of the 2018 Conference on Empirical Methods in Natural Language Processing.*

Papineni, K., Roukos, S., Ward, T., and Zhu, W. (2002). BLEU: a method for automatic evaluation of machine translation. In *Proceedings of the 40th Annual Meeting on Association for Computational Linguistics (ACL)*, pages 311–318.

Passarotti, M., Budassi, M., Litta, E., and Ruffolo, P. (2017). The lemlat 3.0 package for morphological analysis of Latin. In *Proceedings of the NoDaLiDa 2017 Workshop on Processing Historical Language*, pages 24–31, Gothenburg, May. Linköping University Electronic Press.

Popović, M., Arčan, M., and Klubička, F. (2016). Language related issues for machine translation between closely related south Slavic languages. In *Proceedings of the Third Workshop on NLP for Similar Languages, Varieties and Dialects (VarDial3)*, pages 43–52, Osaka, Japan, December. The COLING 2016 Organizing Committee.

Resnik, P., Olsen, M. B., and Diab, M. (1999). The bible as a parallel corpus: Annotating the 'book of 2000 tongues'. *Computers and the Humanities*, 33(1-2):129–153.

Rikters, M., Pinnis, M., and Krišlauks, R. (2018). Training and adapting multilingual nmt for less-resourced and morphologically rich languages. In *Proceedings of the Eleventh International Conference on Language Resources and Evaluation (LREC 2018)*.

Schneider, G., Pettersson, E., and Percillier, M. (2017). Comparing rule-based and SMT-based spelling normalisation for English historical texts. In *Proceedings of the NoDaLiDa 2017 Workshop on Processing Historical Language*, pages 40–46, Gothenburg, May. Linköping University Electronic Press.

Sennrich, R., Haddow, B., and Birch, A. (2016). Improving neural machine translation models with monolingual data. In *Proceedings of the ACL2016 (Volume 1: Long Papers)*, pages 86–96.

Snover, M., Dorr, B., Schwartz, R., Micciulla, L., and Makhoul, J. (2006). A study of translation edit rate with targeted human annotation. In *Proceedings of the 7th Biennial Conference of the Association for Machine Translation in the Americas (AMTA)*, pages 223–231.

Tiedemann, J. (2012). Parallel data, tools and interfaces in opus. In Nicoletta Calzolari (Conference Chair), et al., editors, *Proceedings of the Eight International Conference on Language Resources and Evaluation (LREC'12)*, Istanbul, Turkey. European Language Resources Association (ELRA).

Tjong Kim Sang, E., Bollman, M., Boschker, R., Casacuberta, F., Dietz, F., Dipper, S., Domingo, M., van der Goot, R., van Koppen, J., Ljubešić, N., et al. (2017). The clin27 shared task: Translating historical text to contemporary language for improving automatic linguistic annotation. *Computational Linguistics in the Netherlands Journal*, 7:53–64.

Varga, D., Halácsy, P., Kornai, A., Nagy, V., Németh, L.,

and Trón, V. (2007). Parallel corpora for medium density languages. *Amsterdam Studies In The Theory And History Of Linguistic Science Series 4*, 292:247.

Vaswani, A., Shazeer, N., Parmar, N., Uszkoreit, J., Jones, L., Gomez, A. N., Kaiser, Ł., and Polosukhin, I. (2017). Attention is all you need. In *Proceedings of the 31st Annual Conference on Neural Information Processing Systems (NIPS)*, pages 6000–6010.

Zoph, B., Yuret, D., May, J., and Knight, K. (2016). Transfer learning for low-resource neural machine translation. In *Proceedings of the Conference on Empirical Methods in Natural Language Processing*, pages 1568 – 1575.

Proceedings of 1st Workshop on Language Technologies for Historical and Ancient Languages, pages 100–104
Language Resources and Evaluation Conference (LREC 2020), Marseille, 11–16 May 2020

Detecting Direct Speech in Multilingual Collection of 19th-century Novels

Joanna Byszuk[1], Michał Woźniak[1], Mike Kestemont[2], Albert Leśniak[1],
Wojciech Łukasik[1], Artjoms Šeļa[1,3], Maciej Eder[1]
[1]Institute of Polish Language, Polish Academy of Sciences; [2]University of Antwerp; [3]University of Tartu
Mickiewicza 31, 31120 Kraków, Poland; Prinsstraat 13, 2000 Antwerpen, Belgium; Ülikooli 18, 50090 Tartu, Estonia
{joanna.byszuk, michal.wozniak, albert.lesniak, wojciech.lukasik, artjoms.sela, maciej.eder}@ijp.pan.pl
mike.kestemont@uantwerp.be

Abstract

Fictional prose can be broadly divided into narrative and discursive forms with direct speech being central to any discourse representation (alongside indirect reported speech and free indirect discourse). This distinction is crucial in digital literary studies and enables interesting forms of narratological or stylistic analysis. The difficulty of automatically detecting direct speech, however, is currently under-estimated. Rule-based systems that work reasonably well for modern languages struggle with (the lack of) typographical conventions in 19th-century literature. While machine learning approaches to sequence modeling can be applied to solve the task, they typically face a severed skewness in the availability of training material, especially for lesser resourced languages. In this paper, we report the result of a multilingual approach to direct speech detection in a diverse corpus of 19th-century fiction in 9 European languages. The proposed method fine-tunes a transformer architecture with multilingual sentence embedder on a minimal amount of annotated training in each language, and improves performance across languages with ambiguous direct speech marking, in comparison to a carefully constructed regular expression baseline.

Keywords: direct speech recognition, multilingual, 19th century novels, deep learning, transformer, BERT, ELTeC

1. Introduction

Fictional prose can be broadly divided into narrative and discursive forms with direct speech being central to any discourse representation (alongside indirect reported speech and free indirect discourse). This distinction is crucial in digital literary studies and drives various forms of narratological or stylistic analysis: direct, or "mimetic" speech and thought (Gennette, 1980) was used to understand voice of literary characters (Burrows, 1987; Hoover, 2014) and study narrative representations of speech (Conroy, 2014; Katsma, 2014). Distinction between "mimetic" speech and "narration" helped to formalize free indirect discourse, defined as a linguistic mixture of these two types (Brooke, Hammond and Hirst, 2017; Muzny, Algee-Hewitt and Jurafsky, 2017). Sequences of direct exchanges between characters were studied to understand the evolution of dialogue as a literary device (Sobchuk, 2016) and dynamics of "dialogism" over the course of novel's history (Muzny, Algee-Hewitt and Jurafsky, 2017). Direct speech recognition is also closely related to the problem of identification and modeling fictional characters (He, Barbosa and Kondrak, 2013; Bamman, Underwood and Smith, 2014; Vala et al., 2015).

The majority of approaches to direct speech recognition (DSR) in prose remain language-specific and heavily rely on deep morphological and syntactic annotation of texts and depend on typographic conventions of marking direct speech within a given tradition. Rule-based solutions variably use punctuation, contextual heuristics, and morpho-syntactic patterns within clauses to identify direct and indirect speech (Krestel, Bergler and Witte, 2008; Alrahabi, Desclés and Suh, 2010; Brunner, 2013; Brooke, Hammond and Hirst, 2015; Muzny, Algee-Hewitt and Jurafsky, 2017), sometimes relying on external dictionaries of proper names and reporting verbs (Pouliquen, Steinberger and Best, 2007; Nikishina et al., 2019). When DSR does not use quotation marks, it utilizes pre-determined linguistic features – tense, personal pronouns, imperative mode or interjections – to guess speech type (Tu, Krug and Brunner, 2019). Similar assembling of mixed features that

might be relevant for direct speech is implemented in supervised machine learning approaches to DSR in two-class classification task (Brunner, 2013; Schöch et al., 2016). Jannidis et al. (2018) constructed a deep-learning pipeline for German that does not rely on manually defined features. It uses simple regular expressions for "weak" labeling of direct speech and then feeds marked text segments to the two-branch LSTM network (one for the "past" and one for the future context of a token) that assigns speech types on a word-to-word basis.

State-of-the-art DSR performance seems to be revolving around 0.9 F1-score with the highest (0.939) for French 19th-century fiction with Random Forests classification (Schöch et al., 2016), 0.87 (Brunner, 2013) or 0.9 (Jannidis et al., 2018) for German novels, 0.85 for Anglophone texts with noisy OCR (Muzny, Algee-Hewitt and Jurafsky, 2017). Despite relatively high performance, all implementations require either a general language-specific models (for tagging corpus and extracting features) or standardized typographic and orthographic conventions, which we cannot expect in historical texts across uneven literary and linguistic landscape. Few attempts to make multilingual DSR used highly conventional modern news texts and benefited from databases specific to the media; at their core these implementations remain a collection of rules adjusted to several selected languages (Pouliquen, Steinberger and Best, 2007; Alrahabi, Desclés and Suh, 2010).

In this paper we propose a multilingual solution for direct speech recognition in historic fictional prose that uses transformer architecture with multilingual sentence embedding and requires minimum amount of "golden standard" annotation.

2. Data

The project was born in relation to Distant Reading for European Literary History (COST Action CA16204) project, and one of its subtasks – direct speech markup. We have therefore focused on the problems as observed in the corpus created within the project: European Literary Text Collection (ELTeC), which is aimed to consist of "around 2,500 full-text novels in at least 10 different languages" (https://www.distant-reading.net/). Spanning from 1840 to 1920, ELTeC provides a cross-view of literary traditions and typography conventions.

The collection presents a number of challenges due to its historic variation, from typographic and orthographic differences, to old vocabulary, to the status of given languages at the time, with some, most notably Norwegian, undergoing at the time the process of being established as a standardized written language. Another challenge results from the varying origin of the texts in the subcollections – some were contributed from existing open-source collections, while others, e.g. Romanian, due to lack of digitized collections in respective languages were scanned, OCR-ed and annotated by the Action members specifically for ELTeC. Detailed information on the process and rules guiding the creation of the corpus can be found on the dedicated website https://distantreading.github.io/sampling_proposal.html.

We use ELTeC as in its first official release in Level 1 encoding (basic XML-TEI compliant annotation of the texts' division into chapters and paragraphs), covering the following languages: English, German, Italian, French, Romanian, Slovene, Norwegian, Portuguese, Serbian. We do not introduce changes in the original texts and select five samples per language of around 10,000 words each, with every sample drawn from a different novel. We use random sampling and preserve information about paragraphs and sentences.

The samples were manually annotated by JB, WŁ and AŠ, with two-fold purpose in mind: 1) they were used to train the model, 2) they were "the golden standard" to compare baseline performance to. At this early stage of the project we did not calculate inter-annotator agreement as in the case of some languages with which only one of us would be familiar the texts were annotated twice by the same person. In the next stage of the project we plan to involve the Action members in providing and verifying annotations, which will allow us to examine the quality of the annotations better.

Language	Paragraphs	Script	Direct speech ratio
English	989	Latin	0.684
French	1394	Latin	0.450
German	987	Latin	0.756
Italian	662	Latin	0.308
Norwegian	979	Latin	0.334
Portuguese	1573	Latin	0.583
Romanian	1522	Latin	0.597
Serbian	1278	Cyrillic	0.572
Slovene	1809	Latin	0.392

Table 1: Sample summaries and direct speech ratio (word level).

3. Method

3.1 Rule-based Approach and Baseline to Evaluate Model

Typographic conventions such as various quotation marks or dashes (see Table 2 below) are strong indicators of the direct speech. Based on them, we have constructed a baseline that relies on regular expressions to extract occurrences of unambiguously marked direct speech. In the languages that use dashes to mark dialogue, the challenge was to separate reporting clauses embedded in a sentence. The results obtained using this baseline were compared with those of manual annotation to assess its performance.

Language	Direct speech conventions
English	" … "
French	— … ; « … » ; « … ; » …
German	» … «
Italian	— … ; — …, —; « … » ; " … "
Norwegian	— … ; « … »
Portuguese	— … ; — …, —
Romanian	— … ; „ … "
Serbian	— … ; — … —
Slovene	" … " ; „ … "

Table 2: Conventions of marking direct speech across languages, as accounted for in the baseline (the above conventions apply to non-normalized ELTeC corpus, but not necessarily to the 19th-century typographic traditions in general).

For many European languages with a high degree of standardization of typographic conventions this approach is extremely effective. For example, in English where the words spoken are enclosed in double quotation marks, narrator's inclusions are easy to identify, therefore the example sentence: *"I see," said Rachel; "it is the same figure, but not the same shaped picture."* may be captured using simple regular expression: (".+?"). Other languages, like French, not only use different symbols for quotations («…»), but also tend to omit them in dialogues for the initial dashes. Despite this, the performance of the rules-based approach decreases only slightly.

Language	Precision	Recall	Accuracy	F1-score
English	0.98	0.99	0.99	0.98
Slovene	0.99	0.97	0.99	0.98
Portuguese	0.95	0.94	0.96	0.94
Romanian	0.90	0.94	0.94	0.92
German	0.99	0.86	0.94	0.92
French	0.92	0.92	0.95	0.92
Italian	0.87	0.88	0.94	0.88
Serbian	0.90	0.85	0.93	0.87
Norwegian	0.72	0.59	0.84	0.65

Table 3: Performance of regular expression baseline in direct speech detection on manually annotated samples.

However, frequently the formal structure of a compound sentence delimited by commas does not allow distinguishing the narration from the direct speech for the baseline. As, for instance, in the sentences —*Et la bonne Rosalie, la gouvernante de Frédéric, l'accompagne sans doute!* and —*Je ne demanderais pas mieux, dit Albert, en regardant madame Mansley*. With the lack of clear separation of the direct speech, which is often the case for the early 19th-century editions, baseline performance drops substantially: for the German sample without proper marks it achieves 0.68 accuracy and only 0.18 recall (F1 = 0.04).

Other common problems include no clear mark at the end of an utterance, no difference in marking direct speech and proper names, irony, or other pragmatic shifts that introduce subjective perspective, such as characters using metaphorical phrases, e.g. "*little man*" indicating not that the person addressed this way is short, but is treated with less respect by the speaker. These irregularities are the reason behind the decrease in baseline performance, with the worst results for Norwegian.

Deep learning solution that has distributed understanding of the direct speech features in multilingual environment may provide a way to get beyond typographic conventions or language-specific models.

3.2 Adopted Deep Learning Solution

While new developments in deep learning have had a significant impact on numerous natural language processing (NLP) tasks, one solution that has gained increased attention in recent months is BERT (Devlin et al., 2018), or Bidirectional Encoder Representations from Transformers. This new representation model holds a promise of greater efficiency of solving NLP problems where the availability of training data is scarce. Inspired by its developers' proposed examples of studies done on Named Entity Recognition (https://huggingface.co/transformers/examples.html), we adjusted discussed classifying method to work on the data annotated for direct speech utterances.

BERT is based on Transformer architecture, "an attention mechanism that learns contextual relations between words (or sub-words) in a text. In its vanilla form, Transformer includes two separate mechanisms – an encoder that reads the text input and a decoder that produces a prediction for the task." (Horev, 2018). As learning in BERT happens both in left-to-right and right-to-left contexts, it manages to detect semantic and syntactic relations with greater accuracy than previous approaches. The model is trained on the entire Wikipedia and Book Corpus (a total of ~3,300 million tokens), currently covering 70 languages. The last part was specifically important for our purposes, given that we aimed to provide a solution that could work well across all languages in ELTeC corpus.

Our solution consisted of several steps. First, we sampled five 10,000 word samples per language collection of ELTeC and manually annotated it for direct speech. We followed TEI guidelines annotating spoken and marked thought-out utterances into `<said>` `</said>` tags. Based on that, we converted our datasets into BERT-accepted column format of token and label (I for direct, O for indirect speech), with spaces marking the end of a paragraph (in alteration to NER solution that divided the text into sentences). Our sample paragraph `<said>»Ich bin derselben Meinung«</said>, rief Benno Tönnchen eifrig.</p>` would thus be turned into:

```
Ich I
bin I
derselben I
Meinung I
, O
rief O
Benno O
Tönnchen O
eifrig O
. O
```

In the next step, we collated our samples together and divided our dataset into train, test, and dev text files, following proportion of 0.8, 0.1, 0.1, ending with ~40,000 tokens per language, and 360,000 or 320,000 tokens total in training data, depending on the test conducted. The number depended on whether we included all languages or conducted a leave-one-out test. To ensure that the model learned a multilingual perspective, we introduced paragraph mixing, so a paragraph in a given language would occur every 8 or 9 paragraphs.

We trained our model with similar parameters as the NER solution we followed, that is with 3 or 2 epochs and batch size of 32. We found that decreasing the number of epochs to 2 improved model performance by 1–2%. We also increased the maximal length of a sequence, due to errors coming from longer sentences in some of the languages.

While we attempted increasing the number of epochs in the training, we realized the model performance was reaching its plateau at 3, pointing to the need to adopt other solutions to further boost its efficiency. We have also tried training on 1/2 and 3/4 of the training dataset, noting that performance drop would only occur when going to half of the training set, again indicating the possibility of having reached plateau, or a need for introducing more variance of conventions when increasing the amount of training data.

4. Results

General model performance is presented in Table 4. Aligning with our intuition, the overall behavior of the multi-language model performs slightly worse than the rule-based approach applied individually to each language.

Loss	Precision	Recall	F1-score
0.306	0.873	0.874	0.873

Table 4: General model performance.

To scrutinize the above intuition, we performed a series of leave-one-out tests, recording the performance of each model with one of the languages being excluded. The results are shown in Table 5. The scores obtained while excluding Norwegian and Italian suggest that in our composite model, some of the less-standardized languages might distort the final results. While this in itself might speak against choosing a multi-language approach, the fact that inclusion of the more-standardized languages in the model improves direct speech recognition for all languages indicates the usefulness of such model for automatic tagging of these parts of multilingual corpora for which regular expression based solutions are not good enough. The difference between the general model and the set of its leave-one-out variants turned out to be minor, leading to a conclusion that the general model exhibits some potential to extract direct speech despite local differences between the languages – suffice to say that the dispersion between the languages in the rule-based approach was much more noticeable.

Excluded language	Loss	Precision	Recall	F1-score
German	0.29	0.89	0.89	0.89
English	0.35	0.87	0.86	0.86
French	0.31	0.87	0.89	0.88
Italian	0.32	0.86	0.90	0.88
Norwegian	0.30	0.89	0.91	0.90
Portuguese	0.33	0.88	0.88	0.88
Romanian	0.30	0.89	0.89	0.89
Slovene	0.34	0.86	0.86	0.86
Serbian	0.40	0.87	0.88	0.89

Table 5: Leave-one-out performance.

Examination of the misclassifications of the model reveal three major sources of errors: narrative structures, size-related uncertainty and noise in pattern-learning. First person narration is often labeled as "direct speech" and linguistically these cases may appear inseparable. This applies not only to a general narrative mode of a novel, but also to the pseudo-documental entries (like letters, diaries) and other "intradiagetic" shifts, with characters becoming narrators. This points to the possible need of using separate DSR models for different narrative modes.

Size of the paragraph seems to influence model's judgement substantially: in longer paragraphs the model expects a mix of direct and indirect clauses (even if the text is homogenous), while one-sentence paragraphs tend to be marked as direct speech. This is in line with findings of Kovaleva et al. (2019) and Clark et al. (2019), showing that attention of BERT is strongly connected to delimiters between BERT input chunks and token alignment within them, as well as sentences across the training data that share similar syntax structure but not semantics. We also observed that many cases that would be easily detected by a rule-based approach are recognized wrongly by BERT-based model: this suggests a certain level of noise in model's decisions (e.g., quotation marks are used for different purposes within the corpus). Abundance of the `[reported clause] -> [reporting clause] -> [reported clause]` pattern also blurs the model and forces it to anticipate this structure.

It is unclear how important are linguistic features of direct and non-direct speech for the model, but errors suggest it pays some attention to imperative mode, personal pronouns, proper names, interjections and verb forms, while heavily relying on punctuation. The last one seems particularly important for misclassifications originating from the expectation that a sentence preceded by a colon or ending with a question or exclamation mark should be classified as direct speech. In a few cases we do not know if the model is wrong or right, because a context of one paragraph could be not enough for a human reader to make a correct judgement.

5. Conclusions

Our project gave us a number of findings in regard to the possibility of developing a uniform solution for direct speech annotation. First of all, we observe that inclusion of languages marking direct speech in more standardized conventions in the model boosts its general performance, improving classification also for literary traditions (or languages) with less regularities in spelling and typography. This is particularly important in the context of corpora such as ELTeC, which gather texts from several languages, including ones that are given relatively little attention in terms of the development of suitable NLP solutions, and present historical variants of the languages, often not well covered in contemporary language representations. It is also important for annotation of texts that feature extensive interjections from other languages, e.g. French dialogue in Polish and Russian novels, a phenomenon common in 19th-century literature involving gentry and bourgeoise characters.

The performance of the model also hints at possible latent imbalances in the corpus which may introduce additional noise and structural problems. In future tests it will be necessary to control the effects of texts coming from first editions (historical language and typographic conventions) and modern reprints (used in some of the ELTeC subcollections); and, while we have not observed significant correlated impact on the results, perhaps also account for language families (Germanic vs. Romance vs. Slavic) and scripts (Cyrillic vs. Latin). The impact of first-person narratives on the instability of the performance also seems to be a factor. Finally, imbalance of "quote"-based and "dash"-based conventions of marking direct speech in the corpus may have introduced additional punctuation-driven noise. Given the above, it is reasonable to attempt conducting experiments with removed direct speech marks altogether, examining the possibility of guiding a model away from the surface-level punctuation features.

Since the transformers-based solution performs better than the baseline in the situations of increased uncertainty and lack of orthographical marks, it is feasible to expect its stable performance also in texts with poor OCR or in historic texts in European languages unseen by the model. These conditions are easily testable in the future.

6. Acknowledgements

The project was launched as a part of a three-year collaborative research project "Deep Learning in Computational Stylistics" between the University of Antwerp and the Institute of Polish Language (Polish Academy of Sciences), supported by Research Foundation of Flanders (FWO) and the Polish Academy of Sciences. JB, ME, AL, AŠ and MW were funded by "Large-Scale Text Analysis and Methodological Foundations of Computational Stylistics" (NCN 2017/26/E/ HS2/01019) project supported by Polish National Science Centre.

7. Supplementary materials

Model and detailed results available at https://gitlab.ijp.pan.pl:11431/public-focs/detecting-direct-speech

8. Bibliographical References

Alrahabi, M., Desclés, J.-P. & Suh J. (2010). Direct Reported Speech in Multilingual Texts: Automatic Annotation and Semantic Categorization. In *Twenty-Third International FLAIRS Conference*. Menlo Park: AAAI Press, pp. 162–167.

Bamman, D., Underwood, T., & Smith N.A. (2014). A Bayesian Mixed Effects Model of Literary Character. In *Proceedings of the 52nd Annual Meeting of the Association for Computational Linguistics (Volume 1: Long Papers)*. Baltimore, Maryland: Association for Computational Linguistics, pp. 370–379.

Brooke, J., Hammond, A., & Hirst G. (2015). GutenTag: An NLP-Driven Tool for Digital Humanities Research in the Project Gutenberg Corpus. In *Proceedings of the Fourth Workshop on Computational Linguistics for Literature*. Denver: Association for Computational Linguistics, pp. 42–47.

Brooke, J., Hammond, A. & Hirst G. (2017). Using Models of Lexical Style to Quantify Free Indirect Discourse in Modernist Fiction. *Digital Scholarship in the Humanities*, 32(2), pp. 234–250.

Brunner, A. (2013). Automatic Recognition of Speech, Thought, and Writing Representation in German Narrative Texts. *Literary and Linguistic Computing*, 28(4), 563-575.

Burrows, J. (1987). *Computation into Criticism: A Study of Jane Austen's Novels*. Oxford: Clarendon Press.

Conroy, M. (2014). Before the 'Inward Turn': Tracing Represented Thought in the French Novel (1800–1929). *Poetics Today*, 35(1–2), pp. 117–171.

Devlin, J., Chang, M.-W., Lee K., and Toutanova K. (2019). BERT: Pre-Training of Deep Bidirectional Transformers for Language Understanding. ArXiv:1810.04805, (http://arxiv.org/abs/1810.04805).

Genette, G. (1980). *Narrative Discourse: An Essay in Method*. Ithaca, NY: Cornell University Press.

He, H., Barbosa, D., & Kondrak, G. (2013). Identification of Speakers in Novels. In *Proceedings of the 51st Annual Meeting of the Association for Computational Linguistics (Volume 1: Long Papers)*. Sofia, Bulgaria: Association for Computational Linguistics, pp. 1312–1320.

Hoover, D.L. (2014). The Moonstone and The Coquette : Narrative and Epistolary Style. In D.L. Hoover, J. Culpeper, K. O'Halloran. *Digital Literary Studies: Corpus Approaches to Poetry, Prose and Drama*. NY: Routledge, pp. 64–89.

Horev, R. (2018). BERT Explained: State of the art language model for NLP. *Medium*, 17.11.2018. https://towardsdatascience.com/bert-explained-state-of-the-art-language-model-for-nlp-f8b21a9b6270

Jannidis, F., Zehe, A., Konle, L., Hotho, A., & Krug M. (2018). Analysing Direct Speech in German Novels. In *DHd 2018: Digital Humanities. Konferenzabstracts*, pp. 114–118.

Katsma, Holst. (2014). Loudness in the Novel. *Stanford Literary Lab Pamphlets*, 7.

Krestel, R., Bergler, S., & Witte, R. (2008). Minding the Source: Automatic Tagging of Reported Speech in Newspaper Articles. In *Proceedings of the Sixth International Conference on Language Resources and Evaluation (LREC'08)*. Marrakech, Morocco: European Language Resources Association, pp. 2823–2828.

Muzny, G., Algee-Hewitt M., & Jurafsky D. (2017). Dialogism in the Novel: A Computational Model of the Dialogic Nature of Narration and Quotations. *Digital Scholarship in the Humanities*, 32(suppl. 2), pp. 1131–1152.

Nikishina, I.A., Sokolova I.S., Tikhomirov D.O., and Bonch-Osmolovskaya, A. (2019). Automatic Direct Speech Tagging in Russian prose markup and parser. In *Computational Linguistics and Intellectual Technologies*, 18.

Pouliquen, B., Steinberger R. & Best C. (2007). Automatic Detection of Quotations in Multilingual News. In *Proceedings of the International Conference Recent Advances in Natural Language Processing (RANLP'2007)*. Borovets, Bulgaria, pp. 487–492.

Schöch, C., Schlör D., Popp S., Brunner A., Henny U. & Calvo Tello J. (2016). Straight Talk! Automatic Recognition of Direct Speech in Nineteenth-Century French Novels. In *Digital Humanities 2016: Conference Abstracts*. Kraków: Jagiellonian University & Pedagogical University, pp. 346–353.

Sobchuk, O. (2016). The Evolution of Dialogues: A Quantitative Study of Russian Novels (1830–1900). *Poetics Today*, 37(1), pp. 137–154.

Tu, N.D.T., Krug, M. & Brunner, A. (2019). Automatic Recognition of Direct Speech without Quotation Marks. A Rule-Based Approach. In *DHd 2019 Digital Humanities: multimedial & multimodal. Konferenzabstracts*. Frankfurt am Main, Mainz, pp. 87–89.

Vala, H., Jurgens D., Piper A., & Ruths, D. (2015). Mr. Bennet, His Coachman, and the Archbishop Walk into a Bar but Only One of Them Gets Recognized: On the Difficulty of Detecting Characters in Literary Texts. In *Proceedings of the 2015 Conference on Empirical Methods in Natural Language Processing*. Lisbon, Portugal: Association for Computational Linguistics, pp. 769–774.

9. Language Resource References

ELTeC (2019). European Literary Text Collection. Distant Reading for European Literary History (COST Action CA16204), https://github.com/COST-ELTeC.

Overview of the EvaLatin 2020 Evaluation Campaign

Rachele Sprugnoli, Marco Passarotti, Flavio M. Cecchini, Matteo Pellegrini
CIRCSE Research Centre, Università Cattolica del Sacro Cuore
Largo Agostino Gemelli 1, 20123 Milano
{rachele.sprugnoli,marco.passarotti,flavio.cecchini}@unicatt.it
matteo.pellegrini@unibg.it

Abstract

This paper describes the first edition of EvaLatin, a campaign totally devoted to the evaluation of NLP tools for Latin. The two shared tasks proposed in EvaLatin 2020, i. e. Lemmatization and Part-of-Speech tagging, are aimed at fostering research in the field of language technologies for Classical languages. The shared dataset consists of texts taken from the Perseus Digital Library, processed with UDPipe models and then manually corrected by Latin experts. The training set includes only prose texts by Classical authors. The test set, alongside with prose texts by the same authors represented in the training set, also includes data relative to poetry and to the Medieval period. This also allows us to propose the *Cross-genre* and *Cross-time* subtasks for each task, in order to evaluate the portability of NLP tools for Latin across different genres and time periods. The results obtained by the participants for each task and subtask are presented and discussed.

Keywords: evaluation, lemmatization, PoS tagging

1. Introduction

EvaLatin 2020 is the first campaign being totally devoted to the evaluation of Natural Language Processing (NLP) tools for the Latin language.[1] The campaign is designed following a long tradition in NLP,[2] with the aim of answering two main questions:

- How can we promote the development of resources and language technologies for the Latin language?

- How can we foster collaboration among scholars working on Latin and attract researchers from different disciplines?

EvaLatin is proposed as part of the *Workshop on Language Technologies for Historical and Ancient Languages* (LT4HALA), co-located with LREC 2020.[3] EvaLatin is an initiative endorsed by the Italian association of Computational Linguistics[4] (AILC), and is organized by the CIRCSE research centre[5] at the Università Cattolica del Sacro Cuore in Milan, Italy, with the support of the *LiLa: Linking Latin* ERC project.[6]

Data, scorer and detailed guidelines are all available in a dedicated GitHub repository.[7]

2. Tasks and Subtasks

EvaLatin 2020 has two tasks:

1. **Lemmatization**, i. e. the process of transforming any word form into a corresponding, conventionally defined "base" form, i. e. its lemma, applied to each token;

2. **Part-of-Speech tagging**, in which systems are required to assign a lexical category, i. e. a Part-of-Speech (*PoS*) tag, to each token, according to the Universal Dependencies (UD) PoS tagset (Petrov et al., 2011).[8]

Each task has three subtasks:

1. **Classical**: the test data belong to the same genre and time period of the training data;

2. **Cross-genre**: the test data belong to a different genre, namely lyric poems, but to the same time period compared to the ones included in the training data;

3. **Cross-time**: the test data belong to a different time period, namely the Medieval era, compared to the ones included in the training data.

Through these subtasks, we aim to enhance the study of the portability of NLP tools for Latin across different genres and time periods by analyzing the impact of genre-specific and diachronic features.

Shared data and a scorer are provided to the participants, who can choose to take part in either a single task, or in all tasks and subtasks.

3. Dataset

The EvaLatin 2020 dataset consists of texts taken from the Perseus Digital Library (Smith et al., 2000).[9] These texts

---

[1] https://circse.github.io/LT4HALA/

[2] See for example other campaigns such as MUC (Message Understanding Conference), a competition dedicated to tools and methods for information extraction, SemEval (Semantic Evaluation), which is focused on the evaluation of systems for semantic analysis, CoNLL (Conference on Natural Language Learning), which since 1999 has been including a different NLP shared task in every edition, and EVALITA, a periodic evaluation campaign of NLP tools for the Italian language.

[3] https://lrec2020.lrec-conf.org/en/

[4] http://www.ai-lc.it/

[5] https://centridiricerca.unicatt.it/circse_index.html

[6] https://lila-erc.eu/

[7] https://github.com/CIRCSE/LT4HALA/tree/master/data_and_doc

[8] https://universaldependencies.org/u/pos/index.html

[9] http://www.perseus.tufts.edu/

are first processed by means of UDPipe models (Straka and
Straková, 2017) trained on texts by the same author, and
then manually corrected by Latin language experts.

Our author-specific models are trained on *Opera Latina*
(Denooz, 2004), a corpus which has been manually annotated at the *Laboratoire d'Analyse Statistique des Langues
Anciennes* (LASLA) of the University of Liège since 1961.[10]
Based on an agreement with LASLA, the *Opera Latina* corpus cannot be released to the public, but we are allowed to
use it to create models for NLP tasks. Thus, we convert the
original space-separated format of the *Opera Latina* into
the field-based CoNLL-U format,[11] on which we train annotation models using the UDPipe pipeline.[12] These models are then run on the raw texts extracted from the Perseus
files,[13] which are originally in XML format, after removing
punctuation. Finally, the outputs of our automatic annotation are manually checked and corrected by two annotators;
any doubts are resolved by a third Latin language expert.

Figure 1 and Figure 2 show examples of our CoNLL-U-
formatted training and test data respectively. Please note
that our training and test data lack any tagging of syntactic dependencies or morphological features, since EvaLatin
2020 does not focus on the corresponding tasks; besides,
tree-structured syntactic data are not available from the
Opera Latina corpus.

3.1. Training data

The texts provided as training data are by five Classical authors: Caesar, Cicero, Seneca, Pliny the Younger and Tacitus. For each author we release around 50,000 annotated
tokens, for a total of almost 260,000 tokens. Each author is
represented by prose texts: treatises in the case of Caesar,
Seneca and Tacitus, public speeches for Cicero, and letters
for Pliny the Younger. Table 1 presents details about the
training dataset of EvaLatin 2020.

AUTHORS	TEXTS	# TOKENS
Caesar	De Bello Gallico	44,818
Caesar	De Bello Civili (book II)	6,389
Cicero	Philippicae (books I-XIV)	52,563
Seneca	De Beneficiis	45,457
Seneca	De Clementia	8,172
Pliny the Younger	Epistulae (books I-VIII)	50,827
Tacitus	Historiae	51,420
TOTAL		259,646

Table 1: Texts distributed as training data.

3.2. Test data

Tokenization is a central issue in the evaluation of Lemmatization and PoS tagging: as each annotation system possibly applies different tokenization rules, these might lead
to outputs which are difficult to compare to each other. In

order to avoid such problem, we provide our test data in an
already tokenized format, one token per line, with a white
line separating each sentence.

Our test data consist only of tokenized words, but neither
lemmas nor PoS tags, as these have to be added by the participating systems submitted for the evaluation. The composition of the test dataset for the *Classical* subtask is given
in Table 2. Details for the data distributed in the *Cross-
genre* and *Cross-time* subtasks are reported in Tables 3 and
4 respectively.

AUTHORS	TEXTS	# TOKENS
Caesar	De Bello Civili (book I)	10,898
Cicero	In Catilinam	12,564
Seneca	De Vita Beata	7,270
Seneca	De Providentia	4,077
Pliny the Younger	Epistulae (book X)	9,868
Tacitus	Agricola	6,737
Tacitus	Germania	5,513
TOTAL		56,927

Table 2: Test data for the *Classical* subtask.

AUTHORS	TEXTS	# TOKENS
Horatius	Carmina	13,290

Table 3: Test data for the *Cross-genre* subtask.

AUTHORS	TEXTS	# TOKENS
Thomas Aquinas	Summa Contra Gentiles (part of Book IV)	11,556

Table 4: Test data for the *Cross-time* subtask.

4. Evaluation

The scorer employed for EvaLatin 2020 is a modified
version of that developed for the *CoNLL18 Shared Task
on Multilingual Parsing from Raw Text to Universal
Dependencies*.[14] The evaluation starts by aligning the
outputs of the participating systems to the gold standard:
given that our test data are already tokenized and split by
sentences, the alignment at the token and sentence levels is
always perfect (i. e. 100.00%). Then, PoS tags and lemmas
are evaluated and the final ranking is based on accuracy.

Each participant was permitted to submit runs for either one
or all tasks and subtasks.

It was mandatory to produce one run according to the so-
called "closed modality": the only annotated resources that
could be used to train and tune the system were those distributed by the organizers. Also external non-annotated resources, like word embeddings, were allowed.

The second run could be produced according to the "open
modality", for which the use of annotated external data, like
the Latin datasets present in the UD project, was allowed.

As for the baseline, we provided the participants with the
scores obtained on our test data by UDPipe, using the

---

[10]http://web.philo.ulg.ac.be/lasla/
textes-latins-traites/
[11]https://universaldependencies.org/
format.html
[12]http://ufal.mff.cuni.cz/udpipe
[13]https://github.com/PerseusDL/
canonical-latinLit

[14]https://universaldependencies.org/
conll18/evaluation.html

```
# sent_id = 306
# text = Debere se suspicari simulata Caesarem amicitia quod
exercitum in Gallia habeat sui opprimendi causa habere
1    Debere       debeo      VERB    _  _  _  _  _  _
2    se           sui        PRON    _  _  _  _  _  _
3    suspicari    suspicor   VERB    _  _  _  _  _  _
4    simulata     simulo     VERB    _  _  _  _  _  _
5    Caesarem     Caesar     PROPN   _  _  _  _  _  _
6    amicitia     amicitia   NOUN    _  _  _  _  _  _
7    quod         quod       SCONJ   _  _  _  _  _  _
8    exercitum    exercitus  NOUN    _  _  _  _  _  _
9    in           in         ADP     _  _  _  _  _  _
10   Gallia       Gallia     PROPN   _  _  _  _  _  _
11   habeat       habeo      VERB    _  _  _  _  _  _
12   sui          sui        PRON    _  _  _  _  _  _
13   opprimendi   opprimo    VERB    _  _  _  _  _  _
14   causa        causa      NOUN    _  _  _  _  _  _
15   habere       habeo      VERB    _  _  _  _  _  _
```

Figure 1: Format of training data.

```
# sent_id = 1
# text = Quaesisti a me Lucili quid ita si prouidentia mundus
regeretur multa bonis uiris mala acciderent
1    Quaesisti     _  _  _  _  _  _  _  _
2    a             _  _  _  _  _  _  _  _
3    me            _  _  _  _  _  _  _  _
4    Lucili        _  _  _  _  _  _  _  _
5    quid          _  _  _  _  _  _  _  _
6    ita           _  _  _  _  _  _  _  _
7    si            _  _  _  _  _  _  _  _
8    prouidentia   _  _  _  _  _  _  _  _
9    mundus        _  _  _  _  _  _  _  _
10   regeretur     _  _  _  _  _  _  _  _
11   multa         _  _  _  _  _  _  _  _
12   bonis         _  _  _  _  _  _  _  _
13   uiris         _  _  _  _  _  _  _  _
14   mala          _  _  _  _  _  _  _  _
15   acciderent    _  _  _  _  _  _  _  _
```

Figure 2: Format of test data.

Classical		Cross-genre		Cross-time	
UDPipe-open 1	96.19 (0.89)	UDPipe-open 1	87.13	UDPipe-open 1	91.01
UDPipe-closed 1	95.90 (0.83)	JHUCB-closed 2	85.49	UDPipe-closed 1	87.69
JHUCB-closed 2	94.76 (1.04)	UDPipe-closed 1	85.47	JHUCB-closed 2	85.75
Leipzig-closed 1	94.60 (1.11)	JHUCB-closed 1	82.69	Leipzig-closed 1	83.92
JHUCB-closed 1	94.22 (1.38)	Leipzig-closed 1	81.69	JHUCB-closed 1	83.76
Baseline	72.26 (2.88)	Baseline	62.19	Baseline	76.78

Table 5: Results of the Lemmatization task for the three subtasks in terms of accuracy. The number in brackets indicates standard deviation calculated among the seven documents of the test set for the *Classical* subtask.

model trained on the Perseus UD Latin Treebank[15] (Bamman and Crane, 2011), the same available in the tool's web interface.[16]

5. Participants and Results

A total of five teams are taking part in the PoS tagging task; three of them are also taking part in the Lemmatization task. All the teams have submitted runs for all three subtasks. Only one team (namely, UDPipe) has submitted a run following the open modality for each task and subtask, whereas the others have submitted runs in the closed modality, thus eschewing additional training data. In total, we have received five runs for the Lemmatization task and nine runs for the PoS tagging task. Details on the participating teams and their systems are given below:

- UDPipe, Charles University, Prague, Czech Republic. This team proposes a multi-task model jointly predicting both lemmas and PoS tags. The architecture is a bidirectional long short-term memory (BiLSTM) softmax classifier fed by end-to-end, character-level, pre-trained and contextualized word embeddings. In the run submitted for the open modality, they use all UD Latin treebanks as additional training data (Straka and Straková, 2020).

- Leipzig, Leipzig University, Germany. PoS tags are predicted with a gradient boosting framework fed with word embeddings pre-computed on a corpus of Latin texts of different genres and time periods. Lemmatization is instead based on a character-level translation performed by a long short-term memory (LSTM) sequence-to-sequence model (Celano, 2020).

- JHUBC, Johns Hopkins University and University of British Columbia, Canada. This team tests two systems for both Lemmatization and PoS tagging. The first one is an off-the-shelf neural machine translation toolkit, whereas the second puts together two different learning algorithms in an ensemble classifier: the aforementioned machine translation system and a BiLSTM sequence-to-sequence model (Wu and Nicolai, 2020).

- Berkeley, University of California, Berkeley, USA. The proposed model for the PoS tagging task consists in a grapheme-level LSTM network whose output is the input of a word-level BiLSTM network. This model is fed by a set of grapheme and word embeddings pre-trained on a corpus of over 23 million words (Bacon, 2020).

- TTLab, Goethe University, Frankfurt, Germany. This team tests three approaches to the PoS tagging task (Stoeckel et al., 2020): 1) an ensemble classifier based on a two-stage recurrent neural network combining the taggers MarMoT (Müller et al., 2013) and anaGo;[17] 2) a BiLSTM-CRF (conditional random fields) sequence tagger using pooled contextualized embeddings and a FLAIR character language model (Akbik et al., 2019); 3) another ensemble classifier combining the taggers MarMoT, anaGo, UDify (Kondratyuk and Straka, 2019) and UDPipe.

Tables 5 and 6 report the final rankings, showing the results in terms of accuracy, including our baseline. For each run, the team name, the modality and the run number are specified. Please note that for the *Classical* subtask the score corresponds to the macro-average accuracy obtained on the single text.

---

[15]https://github.com/
UniversalDependencies/UD_Latin-Perseus/

[16]http://lindat.mff.cuni.cz/services/
udpipe/

[17]https://github.com/vunb/anago-tagger

Classical	
UDPipe-open 1	96.74 (0.65)
UDPipe-closed 1	96.65 (0.63)
TTLab-closed 2	96.34 (0.60)
Leipzig-closed 1	95.52 (0.65)
TTLab-closed 3	95.35 (0.85)
JHUCB-closed 2	94.15 (0.64)
TTLab-closed 1	93.24 (0.92)
JHUCB-closed 1	92.98 (1.27)
Berkeley-closed 1	90.65 (1.98)
Baseline	70.25 (1.65)

Cross-genre	
UDPipe-open 1	91.11
TTLab-closed 2	90.64
UDPipe-closed 1	90.15
Leipzig-closed 1	88.54
JHUCB-closed 2	88.40
TTLab-closed 3	86.95
TTLab-closed 1	83.88
JHUCB-closed 1	82.93
Berkeley-closed 1	73.47
Baseline	62.96

Cross-time	
UDPipe-open 1	87.69
TTLab-closed 3	87.00
UDPipe-closed 1	84.93
Leipzig-closed 1	83.96
TTLab-closed 2	82.99
JHUCB-closed 1	82.62
TTLab-closed 1	81.38
JHUCB-closed 2	80.78
Berkeley-closed 1	76.62
Baseline	67.58

Table 6: Results of the PoS tagging task for the three subtasks in terms of accuracy. The number in brackets indicates standard deviation calculated among the seven documents of the test set for the *Classical* subtask.

6. Discussion

All the participating teams employ deep learning, and largely overcome the baseline. Systems mainly adopt LTSM networks, often in a bidirectional variant. Two teams also test the efficiency of ensemble classifiers, and one team a neural machine translation approach. Different types of embeddings are adopted: for example, grapheme embeddings, word embeddings, contextualized embeddings. In many cases, these embeddings are trained specifically for EvaLatin 2020 starting from large collections of Latin texts available online.

Not surprisingly, the addition of annotated data to the training set proves to be beneficial: in particular, an increase in accuracy is registered in the *Cross-genre* (+1.64 points of accuracy with respect to the best system in the closed modality) and *Cross-time* (+3.32 points of accuracy with respect to the best system in the closed modality) subtasks of the Lemmatization task.

The standard deviation among the texts of the test set in the *Classical* subtask fluctuates between 0.83 and 1.30 in the Lemmatization task, and between 0.60 and 1.98 in the PoS tagging task. With regard to the Lemmatization task, the easiest text to tackle for all the systems is *In Catilinam* by Cicero (accuracy ranging from 95.94 to 97.61), followed by the first book of the *De Bello Civili* by Caesar (accuracy ranging from 95.66 to 96.94). In the PoS tagging task, the situation is reversed: all the systems obtain better scores on the *De Bello Civili* (accuracy ranging from 93.08 to 97.91) than on *In Catilinam* (accuracy ranging from 93.02 to 97.44).

All the systems suffer from the shift to a different genre or to a different time period with a drop in the performances which, in some cases, exceeds 10 points. Taking a more in-depth look at the results, we can notice that, in general, the participating systems perform better on the Medieval text by Thomas Aquinas than on the Classical poems by Horace in the Lemmatization task, whereas the opposite is true for the PoS tagging task.

As for Lemmatization, Thomas Aquinas presents a less rich and varied vocabulary with respect to Horace: the lemma/token ratio is 0.09 and the percentage of out-of-vocabulary lemmas (i.e. lemmas not present in the training data) is 26%, while in the *Carmina* the lemma/token ratio is 0.26 and the percentage of out-of-vocabulary lemmas is 29%.

As for PoS tagging, Thomas Aquinas proves to be more challenging than Horace. This is probably due to the higher percentage and different distribution of tokens belonging to the categories of prepositions (ADP), conjunctions (CCONJ and SCONJ), auxiliaries (AUX) and numerals (NUM), as a consequence of a different textual and syntactic structure (with respect to the training set) that is more similar to that of modern Romance languages.

In particular, in Thomas Aquinas we observe a more frequent use of prepositional phrases: in Classical Latin, case inflection alone often suffices to convey the syntactic role of a noun phrase, whereas in the same context Medieval Latin might prefer that same phrase to be introduced by a preposition, extending a trend that is already present in Classical Latin (Palmer, 1988). We also find a greater number of subordinate clauses introduced by subordinating conjunctions (for example, the Classical construction of *Accusativus cum infinitivo* tends to be replaced by subordinate clauses introduced by subordinating conjunctions like *quia/quod/ut* 'that' (Bamman et al., 2008)), as well as of coordinated structures with coordinating conjunctions, the latter fact being possibly due to the very infrequent use of the enclitic particle *-que* 'and'. As for auxiliaries, their high number in the text of Thomas Aquinas is due to the fact that its annotation, carried out in the context of the *Index Thomisticus* Treebank (IT-TB) project (Passarotti, 2019), strictly follows the UD guidelines, so that the AUX tag is applied also to verbal copulas. This rule does not apply to the other texts employed in EvaLatin 2020, thus causing a discrepancy in the annotation criteria. Finally, the high occurrence of numerals is caused by the frequent use of biblical quotations (e.g. *Iob 26 14* 'Book of Job, chapter 26, verse 14', from *Summa contra Gentiles*, book 4, chapter 1, number 1).

7. Conclusion

This paper describes the first edition of EvaLatin, an evaluation campaign dedicated to NLP tools and methods for the Lemmatization and PoS tagging of the Latin language.

The call for EvaLatin 2020 has been spurred by the realization that times are mature enough for such an initiative. Indeed, despite the growing amount of linguistically annotated Latin texts which have become available over the last decades, today large collections of Latin texts are still lacking any layer of linguistic annotation, a state of affairs that prevents users from taking full advantage of digital corpora for Latin.

One aspect that heavily impacts on any NLP task for Latin is the high degree of variability of the texts written in this language, due to its wide diachronic and diatopic diversity, which spans across several literary genres all over Europe in the course of more than two millennia. Just because we need to understand how much this aspect of Latin affects NLP, two subtasks dedicated respectively to the cross-genre and cross-time evaluation of data have been included in EvaLatin 2020.

If it holds true that variation is a challenging issue that affects NLP applications for Latin, one advantage of dealing with Latin data is that Latin is a dead language, thus providing a substantially closed corpus of texts (contemporary additions are just a few, like for instance the documents of the Vatican City or song lyrics (Cecchini et al., forthcoming)). This warrants us to speak of a possible complete linguistic annotation of all known Latin documents in the future.

In the light of such considerations, we have decided to devote the first edition of EvaLatin to Lemmatization and PoS tagging, as we feel the need to understand the state of the art of these two fundamental annotation layers for what concerns Latin.

We hope that the results of our evaluation campaign will help the community move towards the enhancement of an ever-increasing number of Latin texts by means of Lemmatization and PoS tagging as a first step towards a full linguistic annotation that includes also morphological features and syntactic dependencies, and that it will also help foster interest for Latin among the NLP community, confronting the challenge of portability of NLP tools for Latin across time, place and genres.

8. Acknowledgments

This work is supported by the European Research Council (ERC) under the European Union's Horizon 2020 research and innovation programme via the *LiLa: Linking Latin* project - Grant Agreement No. 769994. The authors also wish to thank Giovanni Moretti for his technical assistance.

9. Bibliographical References

Akbik, A., Bergmann, T., Blythe, D., Rasul, K., Schweter, S., and Vollgraf, R. (2019). FLAIR: An easy-to-use framework for state-of-the-art NLP. In Waleed Ammar, et al., editors, *Proceedings of the 2019 Conference of the North American Chapter of the Association for Computational Linguistics (Demonstrations)*, pages 54–59, Minneapolis, MN, USA, June. Association for Computational Linguistics (ACL).

Bacon, G. (2020). Data-driven Choices in Neural Part-of-Speech Tagging for Latin. In Rachele Sprugnoli et al., editors, *Proceedings of the LT4HALA 2020 Workshop - 1st Workshop on Language Technologies for Historical and Ancient Languages, satellite event to the Twelfth International Conference on Language Resources and Evaluation (LREC 2020)*, Paris, France, May. European Language Resources Association (ELRA).

Bamman, D. and Crane, G. (2011). The Ancient Greek and Latin Dependency Treebanks. In Caroline Sporleder, et al., editors, *Language technology for cultural heritage*, Theory and Applications of Natural Language Processing, pages 79–98. Springer, Berlin - Heidelberg, Germany.

Bamman, D., Passarotti, M., and Crane, G. (2008). A Case Study in Treebank Collaboration and Comparison: Accusativus cum Infinitivo and Subordination in Latin. *The Prague Bulletin of Mathematical Linguistics*, 90(1):109–122, December.

Cecchini, F. M., Franzini, G. H., and Passarotti, M. C. (forthcoming). Verba Bestiae: How Latin Conquered Heavy Metal. In Riitta Valijärvi, et al., editors, *Multilingual Metal: Sociocultural, Linguistic and Literary Perspectives on Heavy Metal Lyrics*, Emerald Studies in Metal Music and Culture. Emerald group publishing, Bingley, UK.

Celano, G. (2020). A Gradient Boosting-Seq2Seq System for Latin PoS Tagging and Lemmatization. In Rachele Sprugnoli et al., editors, *Proceedings of the LT4HALA 2020 Workshop - 1st Workshop on Language Technologies for Historical and Ancient Languages, satellite event to the Twelfth International Conference on Language Resources and Evaluation (LREC 2020)*, Paris, France, May. European Language Resources Association (ELRA).

Denooz, J. (2004). Opera Latina: une base de données sur internet. *Euphrosyne*, 32:79–88.

Kondratyuk, D. and Straka, M. (2019). 75 Languages, 1 Model: Parsing Universal Dependencies Universally. In Kentaro Inui, et al., editors, *Proceedings of the 2019 Conference on Empirical Methods in Natural Language Processing and the 9th International Joint Conference on Natural Language Processing (EMNLP-IJCNLP)*, pages 2779–2795, Hong Kong, China, November. Association for Computational Linguistics (ACL).

Müller, T., Schmid, H., and Schütze, H. (2013). Efficient Higher-Order CRFs for Morphological Tagging. In David Yarowsky, et al., editors, *Proceedings of the 2013 Conference on Empirical Methods in Natural Language Processing*, pages 322–332, Seattle, WA, USA, October. Association for Computational Linguistics (ACL).

Palmer, L. R. (1988). *The Latin language*. Oklahoma University Press, Norman, OK, USA. Reprint.

Passarotti, M. (2019). The Project of the Index Thomisticus Treebank. In Monica Berti, editor, *Digital Classical Philology*, volume 10 of *Age of Access? Grundfragen der Informationsgesellschaft*, pages 299–320. De Gruyter Saur, Munich, Germany, August.

Petrov, S., Das, D., and McDonald, R. (2011). A Universal Part-of-Speech Tagset. *ArXiv e-prints*. arXiv:1104.2086 at https://arxiv.org/abs/1104.2086.

Smith, D. A., Rydberg-Cox, J. A., and Crane, G. R. (2000). The Perseus Project: A digital library for the humanities. *Literary and Linguistic Computing*, 15(1):15–25.

Stoeckel, M., Henlein, A., Hemati, W., and Mehler, A. (2020). Voting for PoS tagging of Latin texts: Using the flair of FLAIR to better Ensemble Classifiers by Example of Latin. In Rachele Sprugnoli et al., editors, *Proceedings of the* LT4HALA *2020 Workshop - 1st Workshop on Language Technologies for Historical and Ancient Languages, satellite event to the Twelfth International Conference on Language Resources and Evaluation (*LREC *2020)*, Paris, France, May. European Language Resources Association (ELRA).

Straka, M. and Straková, J. (2017). Tokenizing, PoS Tagging, Lemmatizing and Parsing UD 2.0 with UDPipe. In Jan Hajič et al., editors, *Proceedings of the CoNLL 2017 Shared Task: Multilingual Parsing from Raw Text to Universal Dependencies*, pages 88–99, Vancouver, Canada, August. Association for Computational Linguistics (ACL). Available at `http://www.aclweb.org/anthology/K/K17/K17-3009.pdf`.

Straka, M. and Straková, J. (2020). UDPipe at EvaLatin 2020: Contextualized Embeddings and Treebank Embeddings. In Rachele Sprugnoli et al., editors, *Proceedings of the* LT4HALA *2020 Workshop - 1st Workshop on Language Technologies for Historical and Ancient Languages, satellite event to the Twelfth International Conference on Language Resources and Evaluation (*LREC *2020)*, Paris, France, May. European Language Resources Association (ELRA).

Wu, W. and Nicolai, G. (2020). JHUBC's Submission to LT4HALA EvaLatin 2020. In Rachele Sprugnoli et al., editors, *Proceedings of the* LT4HALA *2020 Workshop - 1st Workshop on Language Technologies for Historical and Ancient Languages, satellite event to the Twelfth International Conference on Language Resources and Evaluation (*LREC *2020)*, Paris, France, May. European Language Resources Association (ELRA).

Proceedings of 1st Workshop on Language Technologies for Historical and Ancient Languages, pages 111–113
Language Resources and Evaluation Conference (LREC 2020), Marseille, 11–16 May 2020
© European Language Resources Association (ELRA), licensed under CC-BY-NC

Data-driven Choices in Neural Part-of-Speech Tagging for Latin

Geoff Bacon
Department of Linguistics
University of California, Berkeley
bacon@berkeley.edu

Abstract

Textual data in ancient and historical languages such as Latin is increasingly available in machine readable forms, yet computational tools to analyze and process this data are still lacking. We describe our system for part-of-speech tagging in Latin, an entry in the EvaLatin 2020 shared task. Based on a detailed analysis of the training data, we make targeted preprocessing decisions and design our model. We leverage existing large unlabelled resources to pre-train representations at both the grapheme and word level, which serve as the inputs to our LSTM-based models. We perform an extensive cross-validated hyperparameter search, achieving an accuracy score of up to 93 on in-domain texts. We publicly release all our code and trained models in the hope that our system will be of use to social scientists and digital humanists alike. The insights we draw from our inital analysis can also inform future NLP work modeling syntactic information in Latin.

Keywords: Part-of-speech tagging, Latin, LSTM, grapheme tokenization

1. Introduction

Textual data in historical and ancient languages (such as Latin and Ancient Greek) is increasingly available in digital form. As such, computational tools for analyzing and processing this data are highly useful among social scientists and digital humanists. In order to promote the development of resources and language technologies for Latin, the CIRCSE research centre[1] organized EvaLatin: a shared competition on part-of-speech tagging and lemmatization in Latin. This paper describes our system that participated in the part-of-speech tagging task of EvaLatin (Sprugnoli et al., 2020).

Our system was heavily informed by a detailed exploratory analysis of the training data. This analysis guided both our preprocessing decisions as well as the structure of the model. We assembled a large unlabelled corpus of Latin to train embeddings at both the grapheme and word level. Our system combines these pre-trained embeddings in LSTMs to predict part-of-speech tags. In this way we are able to leverage the wealth of unlabelled but machine-readable text in Latin available, as well as recent progress in neural network models of language. To fine-tune our system, we perform an extensive cross-validated hyperparameter search.

The remainder of the paper is structured as follows. In the next section, we outline the main findings of our exploratory data analysis that guided our approach. We then discuss the preprocessing decisions that were informed by this analysis in section 3. Section 4 describes our system, including our cross-validated hyperparameter optimization. In section 5 we present our results. Finally, section 6 highlights our plans for improving our method as well as the open and reproducible nature of this research.

2. Exploratory data analysis

Prior to making any modeling decisions, we performed a detailed exploratory analysis of the EvaLatin dataset. The goal was to find insights in the data that could be leveraged during the modeling stage. To do this, we analyzed the training data from three viewpoints, each focusing on a different level of the data: dataset-wide, orthographic forms and part-of-speech labels. In this section, we highlight the main findings from our analysis that guided the development of our system.

The training dataset contains 14,399 sentences with a total of 259,645 words. This is sizeable yet still significantly smaller than part-of-speech datasets in many other languages. The moderate size of labelled data available motivated us to investigate external unlabelled data (described in Section 4.1). Most (75%) sentences have under 24 tokens, with the average having 18. The vast majority (95%) of sentences have at most 40 tokens. A common concern in sequence-based neural networks is their recency bias which is a shortcoming when the data displays long-distance dependencies. However, with sentences of such moderate length, this concern is not pressing.

At the level of the orthographic form, we found numerous insights that guided our modeling. There are 43,767 unique forms in the training data, of which more than half (24,376) only appear once. The vast majority (90%) of forms appear at most 7 times in the training data. The large number of forms, and especially the large number of hapax legomena, suggest the need to include sub-word information, e.g. character-based models. There are 126 unique characters in the training data, a number which we could massively reduce by focusing on Latin characters (47 unique). Within the Latin characters, we noted that over 98% of instances are lower case. We further noted that capitalization is used in one of four ways: i) as the first character of a sentence, ii) as the first character of a proper noun (abbreviated or not), iii) in Roman numerals, or iv) in the token "HS". Although capital letters are an important signal for proper nouns, case folding would again halve the size of the character vocabulary. Full stops were also used in one of four ways: i) in abbreviations of proper nouns, ii) in lacunae, iii) for the noun "salus", almost always preceded by "suus", or iv) other abbreviations, whose full form is not found elsewhere in the sentence. As all Greek forms have the part-of-speech X, we can effectively represent any Greek word with a single

---

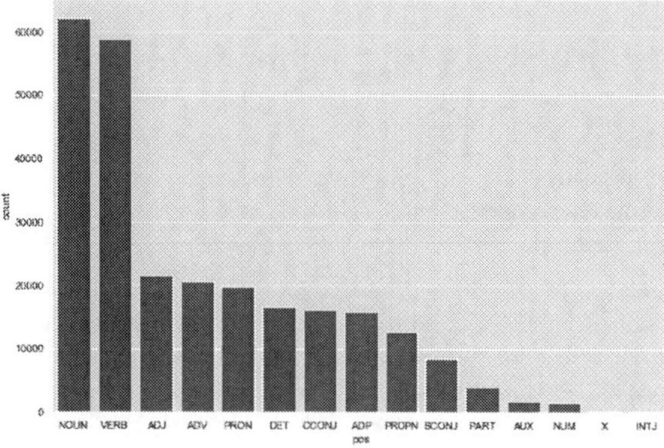

Figure 1: The frequency distribution over part-of-speech tags in the training data. Nouns and verbs are by far the most frequent tags, while AUX, NUM, X and INTJ are extremly rare.

form. Taken together, these insights suggest heavy preprocessing to reduce the character vocabulary, which we describe in Section 3.

Although there are a total of 15 part-of-speech tags in the dataset, the tags are clearly separated into three groups by frequency. The distribution over tags is illustrated in 1. Nouns and verbs are by far the most frequent tags (each accounting for around 23% of all tokens, totalling over 45% together). The next group consists of ADJ, ADV, PRON, DET, CCONJ, ADP, PROPN, SCONJ and PART tags, and each account for 1-8% of tags. The last group consists of AUX, NUM, X and INTJ tags, which each account for less than 1% of tokens. As a baseline, predicting NOUN for all words would have an accuracy of 23% in the training data. The NOUN, VERB, ADJ tags and PRON are identified by lexical root, morphology and syntactic context. Thus, it is important to explicitly include these information sources in the model, for example, with a contextual model. The ADV, DET, ADP and CCONJ tags are often tied to a particular orthographic form, which suggests that word-type representations would be effective in identifying them. Identifying tags which rely on inflectional morphology could be handled by character-based models and sub-word representations. As Latin's inflectional morphology is entirely suffixing, models would benefit from explicit end of word information.

3. Preprocessing

Based on our initial data analysis, our preprocessing was designed to remove as much noise from the data as possible that is not relevant to the task of part-of-speech tagging. To that end, we made significant preprocessing decisions. We replaced the following classes of word forms with placeholder characters as their specific forms do not matter for part-of-speech tagging: i) Greek words, ii) proper noun abbreviations and iii) lacunae. All remaining forms were lowercased. We also added start and end characters for word boundaries to assist modeling inflectional morphology. Furthermore, we tokenized orthographic forms

into graphemes rather than characters (Moran and Cysouw, 2018). Thus, character bigrams such as ⟨qu⟩ and ⟨ph⟩ are represented as a single grapheme in our models, rather than two.

4. System

Our system is broadly composed of three sections: i) pretrained domain-specific grapheme and word embeddings, ii) grapheme-level LSTMs, and iii) word-level bidirectional LSTMs. In this section, we first describe the unlabelled corpus of Latin text we curated to pre-train embeddings. We then describe the training procedure of the embeddings, followed by the structure of our model. Finally, we describe our extensive hyperparameter search to fine-tune our system.

4.1. Unlabelled corpus

Given the moderate size of the labelled training data discussed in Section 2, we opted to leverage unlabelled data to improve performance. Concretely, we curated an unlabelled corpus of Latin texts in order to learn non-contextual grapheme and word embeddings. We sourced this corpus from the Perseus Project, the Latin Library and the Tesserae Project through the CLTK library (Johnson, 2014 2020). The resulting corpus totalled over 23 million words.

4.2. Embeddings

We trained grapheme and word embeddings on this unlabelled corpus. In order to capture as much inflectional morphology as possible in the word embeddings, we used fastText (Bojanowski et al., 2017) which benefits from sub-word information. For grapheme embeddings, where subsymbolic information is not available we used the closely related word2vec (Mikolov et al., 2013). We trained grapheme embeddings of dimension $d_g \in \{5, 10, 20\}$ and word embeddings of dimension $d_w \in \{10, 25, 50, 100, 200, 300\}$ with n-gram lengths from 2 to 4. As part-of-speech tagging is a syntactic task, we fixed a low window size (3) for both sets of embeddings and trained for 10 epochs.

4.3. Model

Our part-of-speech tagging model is structured as follows. A unidirectional LSTM reads words as the preprocessed sequence of graphemes, representing them with their pre-trained embeddings. The final hidden state of that model is concatenated with the pre-trained word embedding. This concatenation (of size $d_g + d_w$) represents the input to a bidirectional LSTM at a single time step. At each time step, the output of the bidirectional LSTM is passed through a linear layer to produce probabilities over part-of-speech tags. All parameters within the model, including the pre-trained embeddings, are trainable.

4.4. Hyperparameter optimization

We ran extensive hyperparameter optimization to fine-tune our model. In particular, we performed a grid search over the following hyperparameters: grapheme embeddings ($d_g \in \{5, 10, 20\}$), word embeddings ($d_w \in \{10, 25, 50, 100, 200, 300\}$), hidden size of bidirectional

Subtask	Text	Accuracy
Classical	Bellum Civile	93.08
	In Catilinam	93.02
	De Providentia	90.63
	De Vita Beata	90.72
	Agricola	89.71
	Germania	87.38
	Epistulae	90.02
Cross-Genre	Carmina	73.47
Cross-Time	Summa Contra Gentiles	76.62

Table 1: The official evaluation results of our system on the EvaLatin shared task. Our system performed well on other Classical texts but saw significant performance drops on out-of-domain texts.

LSTM ($d_h \in \{50, 100, 200, 300\}$) and batch size ($b \in \{8, 16\}$). To evaluate each hyperparameter setting, we used 5-fold cross-validation of the training data. We trained for up to 10 epochs, with early stopping. In total, we trained 1,440 models on a single GPU.

5. Results

In this section, we analyze the results of our hyperparameter search and the errors our system makes, as well as report on the official evaluation.

Averaging over the five cross-validation folds, our best performing model achieved 95.3% accuracy on the training set. We observed a strong positive correlation between the dimensionality of the word embeddings and performance (Pearson's correlation $\rho = 0.725$) and a moderate positive correlation between the dimensionality of the hidden state of the bidirectional LSTM and performance ($\rho = 0.253$). The dimensionality of the grapheme embeddings and performance were weakly correlated ($\rho = 0.042$). All of the 1,440 models we trained achieved above 99% top 3 accuracy. The most common errors we observed were incorrectly tagging adjectives as nouns (12 % of errors) or nouns as adjectives (11%).

The official evaluation metric used in the EvaLatin evaluation was accuracy. The scores of our model on individual texts across the three subtasks are illustrated in Table 1. Our system performed well on in-domain texts (the Classical subtask) but saw significant drops in performance in out-of-domain texts spanning different genres and time periods of the language.

6. Discussion

Our approach was one heavily informed by an initial exploratory data analysis of the training dataset. We relied on significant preprocessing to remove noise from the data and leveraged a large unlabelled corpus of Latin texts. Our extensive hyperparameter search fine-tuned our system. Although our system performed well on in-domain texts, this high performance did not carry well across to other domains and time periods. Future work could investigate the use of external labelled resources to improve performance out of domain.

In order to facilitate engagement with our work, we make all our code and trained models publicly available at `https://github.com/geoffbacon/verrius`. In future work, we plan to make our models freely available through an API for research purposes. With the increased availability of digitized documents in ancient languages like Latin, computational tools for processing linguistic data grow in usage. We hope that our system will be of use to social scientists and digital humanists alike.

7. References

Bojanowski, P., Grave, E., Joulin, A., and Mikolov, T. (2017). Enriching word vectors with subword information. *Transactions of the Association for Computational Linguistics*, 5:135–146.

Johnson, K. (2014–2020). CLTK: The classical language toolkit. `https://github.com/cltk/cltk`.

Mikolov, T., Sutskever, I., Chen, K., Corrado, G. S., and Dean, J. (2013). Distributed representations of words and phrases and their compositionality. In *Advances in neural information processing systems*, pages 3111–3119.

Moran, S. and Cysouw, M. (2018). *The unicode cookbook for linguists: managing writing systems using orthography profiles*.

Sprugnoli, R., Passarotti, M., Cecchini, F. M., and Pellegrini, M. (2020). Overview of the evalatin 2020 evaluation campaign. In Rachele Sprugnoli et al., editors, *Proceedings of the LT4HALA 2020 Workshop - 1st Workshop on Language Technologies for Historical and Ancient Languages, satellite event to the Twelfth International Conference on Language Resources and Evaluation (LREC 2020)*, Paris, France, May. European Language Resources Association (ELRA).

Proceedings of 1st Workshop on Language Technologies for Historical and Ancient Languages, pages 114–118
Language Resources and Evaluation Conference (LREC 2020), Marseille, 11–16 May 2020
© European Language Resources Association (ELRA), licensed under CC-BY-NC

JHUBC's Submission to LT4HALA EvaLatin 2020

Winston Wu, Garrett Nicolai

Johns Hopkins University, University of British Columbia
Baltimore, USA, Vancouver, Canada
`wswu@jhu.edu, garrett.nicolai@ubc.ca`

Abstract

We describe the JHUBC submission to the EvaLatin Shared task on lemmatization and part-of-speech tagging for Latin. We view the task as a special case of morphological inflection, and adopt and modify a state-of-the-art system from this task. We modify a hard-attentional character-based encoder-decoder to produce lemmas and POS tags with separate decoders, and to incorporate contextual tagging cues. We observe that although the contextual cues both POS tagging and lemmatization with a single encoder, the dual decoder approach fails to leverage them efficiently. While our results show that the dual decoder approach fails to encode data as successfully as the single encoder, our simple context incorporation method does lead to modest improvements. Furthermore, the implementation of student-forcing, which approximates a test-time environment during training time, is also beneficial. Error analysis reveals that the majority of the mistakes made by our system are due to a confusion of affixes across parts-of-speech.

Keywords: evalatin, morphology, encoder-decoder, lemmatization, pos-tagging

1. Introduction

In this paper, we describe our system as participants in the EvaLatin Shared Task on lemmatization and part-of-speech (POS) tagging of Latin (Sprugnoli et al., 2020). Latin represents an interesting challenge for POS taggers — unlike English, its substantial inflectional morphology leads to significant data sparsity, resulting in large numbers of out-of-vocabulary (OOV) words for type-based taggers. Additionally, its word order is much more fluid than languages like English, handicapping n-gram taggers such as HMMs that rely on language modeling to produce tag sequences.

We consider lemmatization to be a special case of morphological reinflection (Cotterell et al., 2017), which takes as input one inflected form of a word and produces another, given the desired morpho-syntactic description (MSD) of the output form. Likewise, POS-tagging is a special case of morphological tagging but with a greatly reduced tagset.

Beginning with the state-of-the-art neural morphological generator of Makarov and Clematide (2018), we make several small modifications to both its input representation and its learning algorithm to transform it from a context-free generator into a contextual tagger. These modifications are described in Section 2. We also experiment with a neural machine translation system with no modifications.

Our results indicate that out-of-the-box tools already perform at a very high level for Latin, but that small boosts in performance can be observed through simple modifications and ensembling of different learning algorithms. We discuss our results in more detail in Section 5.

2. System Description

Since 2016, SIGMORPHON has hosted a series of Shared Tasks in morphological inflection (Cotterell et al., 2016; Cotterell et al., 2017; Cotterell et al., 2018; McCarthy et al., 2019). Increasingly, the tasks have become dominated by neural encoder-decoder architectures with heavy copy-biasing. Originally borrowed from the neural machine translation (NMT) community (Bahdanau et al., 2014), the systems have converged around hard-attentional transducers over edit actions (Aharoni and Goldberg, 2017).

Inflection Generation: Input   Output
                         lego 3;SG;IND;PRS   legit

This task: Input: Ut   legit scriptum ...
             ut   lego scriptum ...
             SCONJ VERB NOUN ...

Figure 1: The difference between inflection generation and contextual tagging.

2.1. System 1: Seq-to-seq morphological analysis

As our starting point, we take the system of Makarov and Clematide (2018), the highest performing system in the 2018 shared task. Note, however, that the inflection task is quite different from this one. In the 2018 task, participants were provided with an input lemma and MSD and were required to produce an inflected word out of context. Our task is in many ways the exact opposite: given a word *in context*, we must produce a lemma and a POS tag. Figure 1 illustrates this difference.

Our first task is to convert the initial system from a generator to a lemmatizer. This step is trivial: we simply specify the MSD for every input word as "LEMMA", producing a context-free lemmatizer. We expand to a context-free morphological analyzer by appending the POS to the end of the output — where the initial system would produce "lego" given `legit LEMMA`, our system now produces "lego+VERB". We refer to this system in future sections as the single-decoder without context (SDNC).

We introduce context into the system through a modification to the MSD, appending the two previous POS tags to the MSD. Given the example sequence in Figure 1, the input for "scriptum" would be `scriptum LEMMA;-2:SCONJ;-1:VERB`. We refer to this system as the single-decoder with context (SDC).

During training, it is common to feed the gold POS tags into the system as context, but at test time, the system must rely on its own predictions and may fall prey to overfitting, as it has trouble recovering from an incorrectly-predicted tag. To help mitigate this issue, we also introduce a sys-

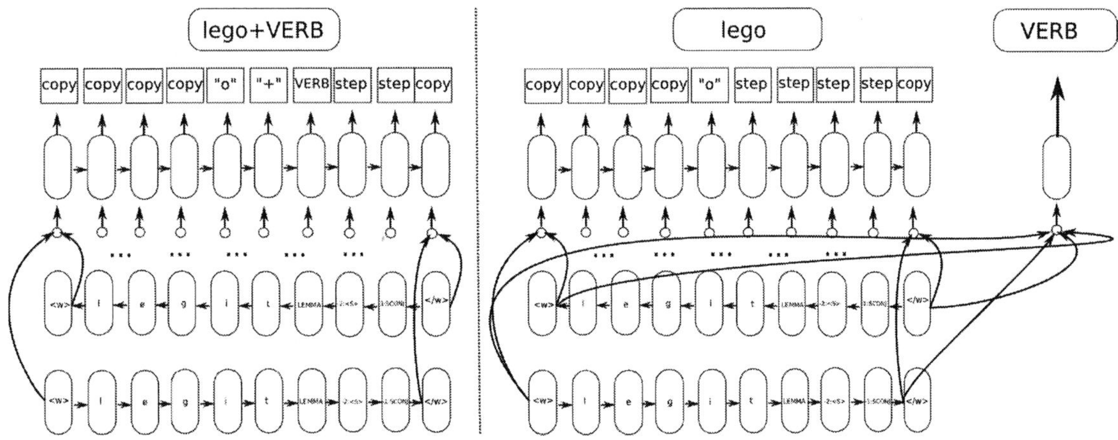

Figure 2: On the left - the single decoder architecture of Makarov et al.; On the right, the dual decoder architecture we introduce. Some connections have been removed to avoid clutter.

tem that learns via student-forcing, where the tags on the MSD are not the gold POS tags, but rather the predictions produced by the decoder. We refer to this system as the single-decoder with student forcing (SDSF).

Our most significant modification to the baseline system involves altering the architecture to produce lemmas and tags separately. By separating the decoders, we simplify the task of each decoder, allowing each decoder to specialize in its particular task. Each decoder has its own attention mechanism that allows it to focus on the parts of the input most significant to its task. The architecture is illustrated in Figure 2.

In both the single and dual decoder models, a bidirectional LSTM encoder reads in the input sequence (`legit LEMMA -2:<s> -1:<SCONJ>`) character-by-character[1]. In the single decoder, a hard attention mechanism feeds a decoder that generates edit actions (either "copy", "step", or "insert-x"), before producing the final output: `lego+VERB`. The dual decoder produces the lemma in the same way, but uses a second decoder with a global attention mechanism to produce a single POS tag.

2.2. System 2: Neural Machine Translation

Our second system submission is meant to serve as a strong baseline to compare with System 1. Treating the lemmatization and POS tagging tasks as a sequence prediction problem, we employ an off-the-shelf neural machine translation toolkit OpenNMT (Klein et al., 2017) with modifications to the data preprocessing. For both tasks, the input is the Latin word with its previous and next words in the sentence (including sentence boundary tokens). We train a SentencePiece (Kudo and Richardson, 2018) model with a vocabulary size of 8000 and apply it on both the input and output for lemmatization, and only the input for POS tagging. An example is shown in Table 1.

2.3. Ensembling

In addition to producing multiple individual systems, we ensemble each system, using a linear combination of each

Input:	_cum _dolore _in f i d e l it at is
Output (lemma):	dolor
Output (POS):	NOUN

Table 1: Data format for System 2 after processing with SentencePiece.

system's confidence scores from the decoder[2]. To aid the ensemble, we produce 10-best lists for each system, which requires a small modification to the beam search: each decoder produces a 10-best list of hypotheses, which are then combined with a linear combination of their confidence scores, with ties going to the prediction with the higher lemma score.

3. Experimental setup

We train our models on a 90% balanced subset of the provided training data, reserving 10% of the sentences in each document as a validation set. We train the single- and dual-decoder models identically. The encoders and decoders consists of a single layer with 200 hidden units, an embedding size of 100 for actions and characters, and 20 for POS tags. We train with a batch size of 32, using AdaDelta, a ReLU non-linearity function, and 50% dropout. All models are trained for a maximum of 60 epochs, with patience of 10 epochs.

For the NMT system, we use the default parameters of OpenNMT, which include a 2 layer encoder and decoder with 500 hidden units and an embedding size of 500. There is no difference in architectures for the lemmatization and POS tagging tasks. We train with a batch size of 64 using Adam, with 30% dropout, with a patience of 3 epochs.

4. Results

We now present the official test results of our systems in the three sub-tasks: classical, cross-genre, and cross-time. Our official submissions correspond to the Ensemble and

---

[1]MSDs are atomic.

[2]An incompatibility with OpenNMT's decoder prevents us from including the NMT system in the ensemble.

NMT baseline. The classical task presents test data by the same authors as were used in training, and consists of letters, speeches, and treatises. The cross-genre task tests on the Odes of Horace, also written in classical Latin but of a different genre (lyric poetry), while the cross-time task evaluates on a treatise by St. Thomas Aquinas written in the Ecclesiastical Latin of the 13th century.

System	Setting	Lemma	POS
Single	No Context	94.32	93.38
Dual	No Context	93.94	93.20
Single	Teacher	94.36	*93.87*
Dual	Teacher	93.61	92.73
Single	Student	*94.59*	93.8
Dual	Student	93.45	92.74
Ensemble	–	**94.76**	**94.15**
NMT	–	94.22	92.98

Table 2: Test Accuracy on Classical Task

System	Setting	Lemma	POS
Single	No Context	83.98	87.00
Dual	No Context	82.47	86.51
Single	Teacher	84.67	87.53
Dual	Teacher	82.42	86.39
Single	Student	*84.74*	*87.92*
Dual	Student	82.32	86.85
Ensemble	–	**85.49**	**88.40**
NMT	–	82.69	82.93

Table 3: Test Accuracy on Cross-Genre Task

System	Setting	Lemma	POS
Single	No Context	85.38	80.32
Dual	No Context	84.87	78.5
Single	Teacher	85.77	*82.49*
Dual	Teacher	85.36	80.06
Single	Student	***85.81***	81.58
Dual	Student	84.26	78.21
Ensemble	–	85.75	80.78
NMT	–	83.76	**82.62**

Table 4: Test Accuracy on Cross-Time Task

We observe that for all three sub-tasks, the single-encoder model outperforms our dual-decoder extension, for both lemmatization and POS-Tagging. It may be that lemmatization and POS-tagging provide complementary information that benefits a joint decoder, and splitting the decoders shifts much of the joint learning to the encoder, which is not able to learn a sufficient representation to accomodate the separate decoding mechanisms.

Encouragingly, the contextual information appears to have been captured by the encoder. POS-tagging and lemmatization both benefit from knowing the POS-tag of the previous POS tags in the sentence. We provide some discussion of this phenomenon in Section 5. We also observe that lemmatization benefits slightly from a student-forcing scenario.

	NN	VB	JJ	NNP	RB	AUX
NN	13333	182	356	63	50	0
VB	105	12037	114	9	12	69
JJ	204	140	4099	91	86	0
NNP	51	3	46	2437	6	0
RB	18	3	72	10	4188	0
AUX	0	273	0	0	0	480

Table 5: POS Confusion Matrix: open classes (y=gold)

Not surprisingly, ensembling multiple systems leads to small gains over any individual system. The sole exception occurs in the Cross-Time track, which sees the ensemble struggle to surpass the individual systems. We hypothesize that the low overall accuracy on this track harms the ensemble, as models produce hypotheses more consistent with classical Latin. A system that produces a correct medieval analysis is out-voted by the other systems.

5. Discussion

We now begin a detailed discussion of the types of errors made by our systems. As a test case, we consider the classical track; the types of errors encountered here are simply exacerbated in the other tracks.

We first consider the **open classes** of words: nouns, verbs, and adjectives. These classes demonstrate prolific inflectional morphology, and account for 82.3% of the lemmatization errors of our ensembled system. Of the remaining errors, 73% of false lemmatizations concern subordinating conjunctions or pronouns. Pronouns and conjunctions are regularly tagged as adverbs — they are incorrectly tagged as such nearly 10% of the time. All told, more than 90% of our system's errors can be attributed to either the open classes, or to closed words incorrectly tagged and lemmatized as such.

Table 5 shows the errors that our system makes on the open classes. Unsurprisingly, there is much confusion between auxiliary and main verbs. Given that these are often the finite form of a verb, the results suggest that our character-based model is heavily attending to the affixes of the word for POS-tagging. Likewise, we observe this phenomenon between common nouns, proper nouns, and adjectives, which must agree grammatically and often decline similarly. Perhaps the biggest surprise comes from the confusion between verbs and nouns/adjectives, which have very different inflectional systems, but account for nearly a quarter of all open-class errors.

Closer inspection reveals that nominal-verbal confusion comes about from incorrect affix-boundary identification. For example, the noun *evocatis* should be lemmatized as *evocati*, but is instead tagged as a verb, and lemmatized as *evoco*. The *-atis* ending is a common verbal suffix denoting the 2nd person plural, and indeed, the noun *evocati* "a veteran soldier called back to service" is derived from the verb *evoco* "to call out/summon" and in dictionaries is often listed as a subentry of *evoco*. In the other direction, *meritum* should be analyzed as a conjugation of the verb *mereor*, but is instead analysed as the noun *meritum*. *-tum* is a common

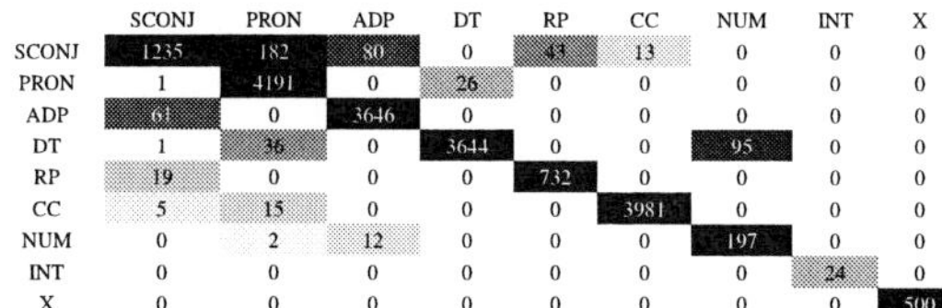

	SCONJ	PRON	ADP	DT	RP	CC	NUM	INT	X
SCONJ	1235	182	80	0	43	13	0	0	0
PRON	1	4191	0	26	0	0	0	0	0
ADP	61	0	3646	0	0	0	0	0	0
DT	1	36	0	3644	0	0	95	0	0
RP	19	0	0	0	732	0	0	0	0
CC	5	15	0	0	0	3981	0	0	0
NUM	0	2	12	0	0	0	197	0	0
INT	0	0	0	0	0	0	0	24	0
X	0	0	0	0	0	0	0	0	500

Table 6: POS Confusion Matrix: closed classes (y=gold)

nominal suffix, and *meritum* is the perfect passive participle of *mereor*, which itself belongs to a rare class of deponent verbs. We see that many of our verb misclassifications occur when the verb is inflected as a participle, which in Latin resemble and decline as ordinary adjectives.

Table 6 shows similar statistics for the **closed classes**. Outside of the aforementioned errors, we see some confusion between conjuctions and pronouns and adpositions, as well as between determiners and numbers. The latter is understandable, as the word *unus* and its inflections can be both determiner or number. For the former, many subordinating conjunctions share a suffix with relative pronouns (qui, quae, quod) and interrogative pronouns (quis, quod) and their inflections. One commonly misclassified word is *quod*, which can be translated as "because" (SCONJ) or "which" (PRON) depending on the context. Several subordinating conjunctions also function as adpositions depending on context, including *cum*, which is translated as "when" (SCONJ) or "with" (ADP). Accurately determining the function and translation of these words often requires first analyzing the verb, which may appear many words later in the sentence. A larger context window may allow our systems to more accurately analyze such words.

5.1. System variants

We next investigate the types of errors that are corrected by our system variants. As the single decoder dominates the dual decoder, we will focus our investigation on its variants in the classical task. When we add context to the model, we note a 7.5% relative error reduction on POS tagging. Many of the correct POS tags occur in the closed word classes.

As hinted above, several common Latin function words such as *ante* "before", *cum* "with/when", and the inflections of *unus* are ambiguous with respect to the part of speech. *Ante*, for example, can be an adverb, meaning "ago", such as in the sentence: *multis ante mensibus in senatu dixit …* – "He said many months *ago* in the senate …" However, it occasionally also operates as an adposition, as in English - *volui si possem etiam ante Kalendas Ianuarias prodesse rei publicae* – "I wished, if I could, to be useful to the state even *before* the first of January." Often, *ante* is used in its adverbial form when it follows an adjective or adverb, but as an adposition when it follows a verb. Knowing the prior contextual parts of speech can help disambiguate it, such as in the test sentence: *venisti paulo ante in senatum* – "You came a little while *ago* into the senate" – where the noncontextual model predicts an adposition, but the contextual system corrects it to an adverb.

The teacher-forcing model is heavily dependent on the quality of the contextual tags. At test time, the tags produced by the system will occasionally be incorrect, cascading to incorrect lemmatization and subsequent tagging. Contrary to the POS analysis, we see that it is the open word classes that benefit most from the student-forcing. POS accuracy stays stable, but the relative lemmatization error drops by 4%. The lemmatization model learns to rely less on the previous POS tags, which may now be incorrect, and to focus more on the shape of the word; nouns and verbs, in particular, seem to benefit the most from this model. Consider the form *speret*, which is the 3rd person singular present active subjunctive of the verb *spero* "to hope". Under the teacher forcing model, it is lemmatized as "*speo", likely following the deletion rule of other verbs like "nocere → noceo". In this particular POS context, "ere → eo" is much more common than "eret → ro" — the subjunctive is simply rarer than the indicative — so the model uses the contextually conditioned transition. Under the student forcing paradigm, the model makes less use of the POS context for lemmatization, and is able to correct the error.

Finally, we take a look at the dual decoder and why it fails with respect to the single decoder model. Comparing similar systems, we note that the dual decoder and single decoder are nearest in accuracy when no context is considered, and that adding context and noise degrades the dual decoder even as it improves the single encoder. We investigate some possible reasons why in this section.

The dual decoder fails to correctly apply contextual cues much more often than the single decoder model. For example, when *quod* is used as a pronoun, it should be lemmatized as *qui*. However, when used as a conjunction, it should remain as *quod*. The single decoder correctly identifies this difference, but the dual decoder invariably lemmatizes *quod* to the majority class *qui*. It would appear that although both decoders share an encoder and an embedding space, the lemmatizing decoder disregards contextual information for lemmas.

For part-of-speech tagging, somewhat surprisingly, the dual decoder also fails to leverage contextual information, even degrading as context is fed into the system. We are at a loss to describe such a phenomenon, and the errors describe no clear pattern. It is possible that the encoder is not strong enough to embed complementary information such that separate decoders can leverage it in different ways. In the future, we will investigate increasing the representational power of the encoder in the dual-decoder model.

6. Conclusion

We have described and analyzed the JHUBC submission to the 2020 EvaLatin Shared Task on Lemmatization and POS-Tagging. Viewing the task as an extension of morphological analysis, we adapted a strong morphological generator to the tasks, with a high level of success – contextual cues can be fed to the tagger via an extended tag vocabulary, and student-forcing can help the system recover from errors at test time. Our best systems perform well across a series of related tasks, and we feel that our system provides a strong, intuitive system for future comparison.

7. Bibliographical References

Aharoni, R. and Goldberg, Y. (2017). Morphological inflection generation with hard monotonic attention. In

Proceedings of the 55th Annual Meeting of the Association for Computational Linguistics (Volume 1: Long Papers), pages 2004–2015, Vancouver, Canada, July. Association for Computational Linguistics.

Bahdanau, D., Cho, K., and Bengio, Y. (2014). Neural machine translation by jointly learning to align and translate. *arXiv preprint arXiv:1409.0473*.

Cotterell, R., Kirov, C., Sylak-Glassman, J., Yarowsky, D., Eisner, J., and Hulden, M. (2016). The SIGMORPHON 2016 shared task—morphological reinflection. In *Proceedings of the 14th SIGMORPHON Workshop on Computational Research in Phonetics, Phonology, and Morphology*, pages 10–22. Association for Computational Linguistics.

Cotterell, R., Kirov, C., Sylak-Glassman, J., Walther, G., Vylomova, E., Xia, P., Faruqui, M., Kübler, S., Yarowsky, D., Eisner, J., et al. (2017). CoNLL-SIGMORPHON 2017 shared task: Universal morphological reinflection in 52 languages. *arXiv preprint arXiv:1706.09031*.

Cotterell, R., Kirov, C., Sylak-Glassman, J., Walther, G., Vylomova, E., McCarthy, A. D., Kann, K., Mielke, S., Nicolai, G., Silfverberg, M., et al. (2018). The CoNLL–SIGMORPHON 2018 shared task: Universal morphological reinflection. *arXiv preprint arXiv:1810.07125*.

Klein, G., Kim, Y., Deng, Y., Senellart, J., and Rush, A. (2017). OpenNMT: Open-source toolkit for neural machine translation. In *Proceedings of ACL 2017, System Demonstrations*, pages 67–72, Vancouver, Canada, July. Association for Computational Linguistics.

Kudo, T. and Richardson, J. (2018). Sentencepiece: A simple and language independent subword tokenizer and detokenizer for neural text processing. *arXiv preprint arXiv:1808.06226*.

Makarov, P. and Clematide, S. (2018). Neural transition-based string transduction for limited-resource setting in morphology. In *Proceedings of the 27th International Conference on Computational Linguistics*, pages 83–93, Santa Fe, New Mexico, USA, August. Association for Computational Linguistics.

McCarthy, A. D., Vylomova, E., Wu, S., Malaviya, C., Wolf-Sonkin, L., Nicolai, G., Kirov, C., Silfverberg, M., Mielke, S. J., Heinz, J., et al. (2019). The SIGMORPHON 2019 shared task: Morphological analysis in context and cross-lingual transfer for inflection. *arXiv preprint arXiv:1910.11493*.

Sprugnoli, R., Passarotti, M., Cecchini, F. M., and Pellegrini, M. (2020). Overview of the evalatin 2020 evaluation campaign. In Rachele Sprugnoli et al., editors, *Proceedings of the LT4HALA 2020 Workshop - 1st Workshop on Language Technologies for Historical and Ancient Languages, satellite event to the Twelfth International Conference on Language Resources and Evaluation (LREC 2020)*, Paris, France, May. European Language Resources Association (ELRA).

Proceedings of 1st Workshop on Language Technologies for Historical and Ancient Languages, pages 119–123
Language Resources and Evaluation Conference (LREC 2020), Marseille, 11–16 May 2020
© European Language Resources Association (ELRA), licensed under CC-BY-NC

A Gradient Boosting-Seq2Seq System for
Latin POS Tagging and Lemmatization

Giuseppe G. A. Celano
Leipzig University
Augustusplatz 10, 04109 Leipzig
celano@informatik.uni-leipzig.de

Abstract

The paper presents the system used in the EvaLatin shared task to POS tag and lemmatize Latin. It consists of two components. A gradient boosting machine (LightGBM) is used for POS tagging, mainly fed with pre-computed word embeddings of a window of seven contiguous tokens—the token at hand plus the three preceding and following ones—per target feature value. Word embeddings are trained on the texts of the Perseus Digital Library, Patrologia Latina, and Biblioteca Digitale di Testi Tardo Antichi, which together comprise a high number of texts of different genres from the Classical Age to Late Antiquity. Word forms plus the outputted POS labels are used to feed a Seq2Seq algorithm implemented in Keras to predict lemmas. The final shared-task accuracies measured for Classical Latin texts are in line with state-of-the-art POS taggers (∼96%) and lemmatizers (∼95%).

Keywords: Latin, gradient boosting, Seq2Seq, POS tagging, lemmatization, treebank

1. Introduction

The EvaLatin shared task (Sprugnoli et al., 2020) consists of two NLP tasks, (coarse-grained) POS tagging and lemmatization, each of which can be addressed in two modalities, closed and open.

Closed modality does not allow use of annotated external resources, such as treebanks or lexica, while non-annotated resources, such as word embeddings, can be used. In open modality, use of any external resource is allowed.

Participation to the shared task in closed modality only is possible, the open-modality approach being optional. The Latin texts provided for training are 7,[1] and belong to different works (see Table 1).

author	work	tokens
Caesar	Bellum Civile	6,389
	Bellum Gallicum	44,818
Cicero	Philippica	52,563
Plinius Secundus	Epistulae	50,827
Seneca	De Beneficiis	45,456
	De Clementia	8,172
Tacitus	Historiae	51,420

Table 1: Training data

The Latin data differ in age (slightly) and genre, because the goal of the shared task is to evaluate how models perform not only on similar, but also different, kinds of text. Caesar's and Tacitus' works are historical accounts, Cicero's Philippica are speeches, Plinius' work consists in letters, while Seneca's are philosophical essays. Caesar (100 BC–44 BC) and Cicero (106 BC–43 BC) belong to the Golden Age, while Plinius (61 AD–c. 113 AD), Seneca (c. 4 BC–65 AD), and Tacitus (c. 56 AD–c. 120 AD) belong to the Silver Age.

The released data are provided in the conllu format, with

sentence split and tokenization/word segmentation already performed. It is to note that the organizers decided to remove punctuation marks and to not tokenize enclitic *que* (i.e., "and"), although it usually is, in Latin treebanks, on syntactic grounds. As a consequence, tokenization/word segmentation could also be easily accomplished from raw text by splitting on whitespaces.[2]

Each token is aligned with only POS and lemma labels according to the Universal Dependencies (UD) scheme (Zeman et al., 2019).[3] As is known, the UD scheme provides general definitions for its morphosyntactic labels, in that they are supposed to be used for annotation of many typologically different languages.

There are currently three different UD Latin treebanks,[4] which use the same morphosyntactic labels slightly differently. For example, there is no consensus on whether a substantivized adjective should be morphologically annotated as an adjective or a noun (which will affect also lemma annotation), or how to treat, for example, "ubi" ("where") without an antecedent: is it a relative adverb or a subordinate conjunction? Unfortunately, there are many such problematic cases, still inadequately covered in guidelines. Notably, they cause not only divergencies between different treebanks, but also, often, inconsistencies within a treebank

---

[1]https://circse.github.io/LT4HALA/
EvaLatin.html.

[2]Identifying enclitic *que* is probably the main word segmentation problem for Latin, because of its high frequency and the fact that a high number of other words end in non-enclitic *que*, such as, for example, *quisque*, *quicumque*, or *aeque*. While almost all of these can be identified via rule-based algorithms, the series of tokens *quique*, *quaeque*, and *quodque* cannot: these word forms signify both pronouns ("everyone") and relative pronouns + enclitic *que*, and therefore can be disambiguated only by considering their syntactic contexts.

[3]See also, more specifically, https://
universaldependencies.org/guidelines.html.

[4]See https://universaldependencies.org/. The UD Latin treebanks derive from conversion of similarly annotated treebanks (Celano, 2019).

itself, annotators getting easily confused.[5]

For this reason, I decided to participate only to the closed modality of the shared task, by proposing a two-step system (see Figure 1) which employs (i) a gradient boosting machine for POS tagging and (ii) a Seq2Seq algorithm leveraging POS labels for lemmatization.[6] I present the former in Section 3 and the latter in Section 4. In Section 2, I discuss the pre-computed word embeddings which feed the gradient boosting machine, while Section 5 contains some concluding remarks.

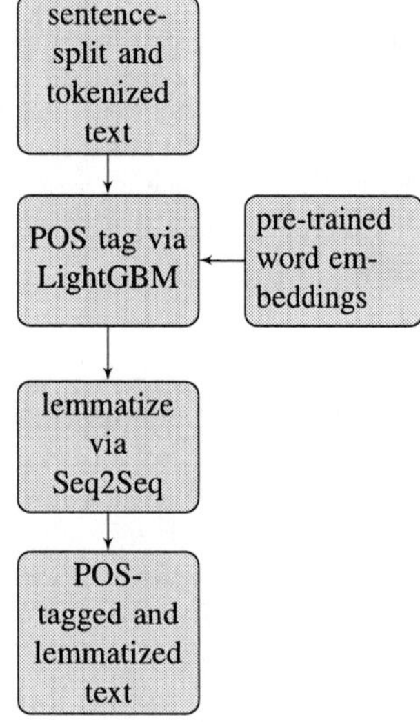

Figure 1: System pipeline

2. Data preparation and pre-computed word embeddings

Each text of the released data has been divided into three sets: training (80%), development (10%), and test (10%). By the union of all the training, development, and test sets, the final training, development, and test sets to use for machine learning have been created. This splitting strategy guarantees that each final set is, with respect to the data released, balanced and representative.

Token order within a sentence has been preserved because, as is shown in Section 3, preceding and following tokens of any given token has been used to predict the POS of such a given token. Order of sentences has also been kept because it is assumed to be irrelevant for the purposes of the machine learning task at hand.

Word embeddings are a common way to vectorize word forms. In recent years, FastText (Bojanowski et al., 2016)

has emerged as a successful library for word representation. Differently from other word embedding algorithms, such as Word2vec (Goldberg and Levy, 2014), FastText represents words as the sum of character n-grams, thus allowing any prefixes, infixes, or suffixes to be weighted.

Some models for Latin, such as the one based on texts from Common Crawl and Wikipedia, have already been computed and are freely available.[7] However, since the data released for the shared task are literary texts without punctuation, a new model trained exclusively on punctuation-free literary texts from sources derived from high quality digitization and post-scan processing is probably expected to perform better than less specific—even if already available—models.

I therefore trained a model using the texts from the Perseus Digital Library (PDL),[8] Patrologia Latina (PL),[9] and Biblioteca Digitale di Testi Tardo Antichi (BDTTA).[10] As the shared task also aims to evaluate a model on texts of different (i) age and (ii) genre, using the above mentioned collections, which together comprise most of the existing pre-medieval Latin texts, guarantees that both variables are adequately represented.

Another most crucial reason to create a new model is that the released data adopts the convention of only using the grapheme "u" to represent both the Latin vocalic (/u/) and semivocalic (/w/) phonemes. As is known, editors of Latin texts adopt different conventions in this respect, and therefore non-normalized texts are very likely to generate underperforming models for the shared task at hand.

FastText requires raw text as an input. Its extraction from the annotated XML files of especially the PDL is a nontrivial task, which would require a separate study. The texts of the PDL, as well as those of the PL and BDTTA, follow the Epidoc Schema, which is a subset of the TEI schema. An original text is interspersed with a lot of "markup text" introduced by XML elements such as "del"—to signal that a certain word should be deleted—or "note"—to add a comment on a specific point in the text.

The PDL texts also represent a particular challenge because some of them cannot be parsed by XML parsers:[11] indeed, a number of externally defined character references, such as "ē", raise exceptions, and therefore require preprocessing.

After extracting the text from the above mentioned collections and converting all "v" into "u",[12] I trained a model through FastText with the following hyperparameters: skipgram mode, minimum length of char n-gram 2, maximum length of char n-gram 5, dimensions 300, and learning rate

---

[5] A solution for this are more precise guidelines and word lists to account for specific phenomena, such as `https://git.informatik.uni-leipzig.de/celano/latinnlp/-/tree/master/guidelines` and `https://git.informatik.uni-leipzig.de/celano/latinnlp/blob/master/tokenize/to-tokenize.xml`.

[6] The models are made available at `https://github.com/gcelano/evalatin2020`.

[7] `https://fasttext.cc/docs/en/crawl-vectors.html`.

[8] `https://github.com/PerseusDL/canonical-latinLit/tree/master/data`.

[9] `https://github.com/OpenGreekAndLatin/patrologia_latina-dev/tree/master/corrected`.

[10] `http://digiliblt.lett.unipmn.it/g_bulk_opere.php`.

[11] I used the Java SAXParser, available in BaseX 9.3.1.

[12] I did not lowercase the texts, because I did not verify that this improves accuracy.

0.03.[13]

The model so created outperformed the Latin model provided by FastText in a number of preliminary tests. I also experimented with a lot of different hyperparameters and even texts: it is worth mentioning that models relying on the PHI Latin texts[14] turned out to perform worse than the one based on the above mentioned collections, probably because the PHI Latin texts comprise a considerable number of fragmentary works, whose texts mainly consist of broken words.

3. LightGBM: a powerful gradient boosting machine

LightGBM (Ke et al., 2017) is an efficient gradient boosting machine which combines high accuracies, fast training speed, and easy of use. It is developed by Microsoft, and has so far been successfully employed for a high number of different machine learning challenges.

Two kinds of features are employed to predict the POS labels:[15] (i) word embeddings and (ii) 2-character token endings. Word embeddings are calculated for any given token and its three preceding and three following tokens. Position is always calculated within a given sentence: if no token precedes or follows, a vector of 0 is used. Similarly, 2-character endings of any of the above mentioned tokens are extracted and made independent variables—if no token precedes or follows an underscore is used. Vectorization for the endings is automatically performed by LightGBM. After some experimenting, the following hyperparameter values turned out to be optimal: boosting_type = 'gbdt', num_leaves = 50, max_depth = -1, learning_rate = 0.03, n_estimators = 47946, subsample_for_bin = 100000, objective = 'multiclass', class_weight = None, min_split_gain = 0.0, min_child_weight = 0.001, min_child_samples = 1, subsample = 1.0, subsample_freq = 0, colsample_bytree = 1.0, reg_alpha = 0, reg_lambda = 0.001, random_state = 1, importance_type = 'split', max_bin = 500.

tagger	test accuracy	time
LightGBM	96.2	>3h
Marmot	95.18	31.9s
Lapos	95.22	18.78s

Table 2: Taggers compared

As Table 2 shows, the test accuracy of LightGBM[16] is higher than those of two popular taggers, Lapos (Tsuruoka et al., 2011) and Marmot (Mueller et al., 2013), which have been used with default hyperparameters. Striking is, however, training time, in that both Lapos and Marmot are extremely fast and do not require any pre-computed word embeddings. On the other hand, LightGBM required a very high number of estimators (47,946) in order to get about 1% more accuracy than the other taggers. This therefore

discouraged me, after finding the hyperparameters, from re-training the model with the train set + development set. With more training data (which could even include the test set), a winning accuracy for the shared task might have been achieved.

The LightGBM development accuracy calculated is 96.39%, while the test accuracy is 96.2%. These values are very similar to the final one calculated for Classical Latin on the shared task test set (95.52%). These accuracies are in line with state-of-the-art POS taggers for Classic Latin (Gleim et al., 2019).[17] As expected, the shared task cross-genre and cross-time accuracies calculated are lower (see Table 3).

classical	cross-genre	cross-time
95.52	88.54	83.96

Table 3: Final accuracy scores for POS tagging

4. A Seq2Seq algorithm for lemmatization

Lemmatization is the NLP task aiming to associate a group of morphologically associated word forms to one of these word forms which is conventionally taken as representative of the entire group.

Lemmas usually concide with dictionary entries. However, since dictionaries adopt slightly different conventions and sometimes are even inconsistent in themselves, there are a number of open issues, such as, for example, whether an adverb should be lemmatized with its related adjective.

To solve the lemmatization task, I adopt the Seq2Seq algorithm implemented in Keras.[18] It is a popular algorithm often employed for machine translation. It can be easily applied to the lemmatization task, in that lemmatization can be interpreted as a case of translation from a word form to another.

The algorithm allows translation on a character level. It consists of a LSTM layer functioning as an encoder, whose internal states are exploited by another LSTM layer, a decoder, to predict the target sequence.

In order to facilitate prediction, a target lemma is associated with a word form plus its POS label generated by LightGBM. POS labels are expected to disambiguate between morphologically ambiguous word forms.

The following hyperparameters were used: batch size 64, epochs 10, latent dimensions 2500. The development set accuracy calculated is 99.82%, while the test set accuracy is 97.63%. The accuracy calculated on the shared task test set is 94.6%. The drops in accuracy are arguably due to both some overfitting and the fact that the POS labels used for the test sets were not the gold ones, but those predicted by LightGBM, which therefore contained errors (see Table 4 for all final shared task accuracy scores).

One issue which was met when decoding some input tokens of the test data released for the shared task is that some Greek words in it contained a few Greek characters not

---

[13]Refer to the documentation for more details on hyperparameters: `https://fasttext.cc/docs/en/options.html`

[14]`https://latin.packhum.org/`.

[15]Morphological features are not required in EvaLatin.

[16]I checked that the POS tag assigned to a Greek word or "lacuna" is always "X", as required by the shared task guidelines.

[17]See also, for example, "la_proiel" at `https://universaldependencies.org/conll18/results-upos.html`.

[18]`https://keras.io/examples/lstm_seq2seq/`.

present in the training data. I had to substitute them with some Greek characters belonging to the set of those used in the training phase. This was not an issue at all, however, in that the lemma for any Greek word is always the placeholder "uox_graeca". Moreover, any "lacuna" in the text (i.e., any token including more than one period), which is always associated with "uox_lacunosa", has been automatically assigned the right lemma via a rule-based script. An unsolved problem is caused by Arabic numbers: they are not present in the training data provided, and therefore it is not clear what lemma labels should be predicted.

classical	cross-genre	cross-time
94.6	81.69	83.92

Table 4: Final accuracy scores for Lemmatization

5. Conclusion

The paper has shown a two-component system to POS tag and lemmatize Latin. The first consists in a LightGBM algorithm predicting POS labels from word embeddings and 2-character endings of a given token plus its three preceding and following tokens. The algorithm returns accuracies (∼96%) in line with those of state-of-the-art POS taggers for Classical Latin. The POS labels outputted plus word forms are then used to feed a Keras Seq2Seq algorithm, whose final result calculated on the shared task test set for Classical Latin (94.6%) can also be considered highly comparable to state-of-the-art lemmatizers (for example, the 1st ranked lemmatizer scored 95.9%, i.e., −1.3%).

6. Acknowledgements

This research has been funded by the Deutsche Forschungsgemeinschaft (DFG, German Research Foundation; project number 408121292).

7. Bibliographical References

Bojanowski, P., Grave, E., Joulin, A., and Mikolov, T. (2016). Enriching Word Vectors with Subword Information. *arXiv preprint arXiv:1607.04606*.

Celano, G. G. A. (2019). The Dependency Treebanks for Ancient Greek and Latin. *Digital Classical Philology*, pages 279–98.

Gleim, R., Eger, S., Mehler, A., Uslu, T., Hemati, W., Lücking, A., Henlein, A., Kahlsdorf, S., and Hoenen, A. (2019). Practitioner's View: A Comparison and a Survey of Lemmatization and Morphological Tagging in German and Latin. *Journal of Language Modelling*, 7(1):1–52.

Goldberg, Y. and Levy, O. (2014). Word2vec Explained: Deriving Mikolov et al.'s Negative-sampling Word-Embedding Method. *arXiv preprint arXiv:1402.3722*.

Ke, G., Meng, Q., Finley, T., Wang, T., Chen, W., Ma, W., Ye, Q., and Liu, T.-Y. (2017). LighGBM: A Highly Efficient Gradient Boosting Decision Tree. In *Advances in Neural Information Processing Systems*, pages 3146–3154.

Mueller, T., Schmid, H., and Schütze, H. (2013). Efficient Higher-Order CRFs for Morphological Tagging". In *Proceedings of the 2013 Conference on Empirical Methods in Natural Language Processing*, pages 322–332, Seattle, Washington, USA, October. Association for Computational Linguistics.

Sprugnoli, R., Passarotti, M., Cecchini, F. M., and Pellegrini, M. (2020). Overview of the EvaLatin 2020 Evaluation Campaign. In Rachele Sprugnoli et al., editors, *Proceedings of the LT4HALA 2020 Workshop - 1st Workshop on Language Technologies for Historical and Ancient Languages, satellite event to the Twelfth International Conference on Language Resources and Evaluation (LREC 2020)*, Paris, France, May. European Language Resources Association (ELRA).

Tsuruoka, Y., Miyao, Y., and Kazama, J. (2011). Learning with Lookahead: Can History-Based Models Rival Globally Optimized Models? In *Proceedings of the Fifteenth Conference on Computational Natural Language Learning*, pages 238–246. Association for Computational Linguistics.

8. Language Resource References

Zeman, D., Nivre, J., Abrams, M., Aepli, N., Agić, Ž., Ahrenberg, L., Aleksandravičiūtė, G., Antonsen, L., Aplonova, K., Aranzabe, M. J., Arutie, G., Asahara, M., Ateyah, L., Attia, M., Atutxa, A., Augustinus, L., Badmaeva, E., Ballesteros, M., Banerjee, E., Bank, S., Barbu Mititelu, V., Basmov, V., Batchelor, C., Bauer, J., Bellato, S., Bengoetxea, K., Berzak, Y., Bhat, I. A., Bhat, R. A., Biagetti, E., Bick, E., Bielinskienė, A., Blokland, R., Bobicev, V., Boizou, L., Borges Völker, E., Börstell, C., Bosco, C., Bouma, G., Bowman, S., Boyd, A., Brokaitė, K., Burchardt, A., Candito, M., Caron, B., Caron, G., Cavalcanti, T., Cebiroğlu Eryiğit, G., Cecchini, F. M., Celano, G. G. A., Čéplö, S., Cetin, S., Chalub, F., Choi, J., Cho, Y., Chun, J., Cignarella, A. T., Cinková, S., Collomb, A., Çöltekin, Ç., Connor, M., Courtin, M., Davidson, E., de Marneffe, M.-C., de Paiva, V., de Souza, E., Diaz de Ilarraza, A., Dickerson, C., Dione, B., Dirix, P., Dobrovoljc, K., Dozat, T., Droganova, K., Dwivedi, P., Eckhoff, H., Eli, M., Elkahky, A., Ephrem, B., Erina, O., Erjavec, T., Etienne, A., Evelyn, W., Farkas, R., Fernandez Alcalde, H., Foster, J., Freitas, C., Fujita, K., Gajdošová, K., Galbraith, D., Garcia, M., Gärdenfors, M., Garza, S., Gerdes, K., Ginter, F., Goenaga, I., Gojenola, K., Gökırmak, M., Goldberg, Y., Gómez Guinovart, X., González Saavedra, B., Griciūtė, B., Grioni, M., Grūzītis, N., Guillaume, B., Guillot-Barbance, C., Habash, N., Hajič, J., Hajič jr., J., Hämäläinen, M., Hà Mỹ, L., Han, N.-R., Harris, K., Haug, D., Heinecke, J., Hennig, F., Hladká, B., Hlaváčová, J., Hociung, F., Hohle, P., Hwang, J., Ikeda, T., Ion, R., Irimia, E., Ishola, Ọ., Jelínek, T., Johannsen, A., Jørgensen, F., Juutinen, M., Kaşıkara, H., Kaasen, A., Kabaeva, N., Kahane, S., Kanayama, H., Kanerva, J., Katz, B., Kayadelen, T., Kenney, J., Kettnerová, V., Kirchner, J., Klementieva, E., Köhn, A., Kopacewicz, K., Kotsyba, N., Kovalevskaitė, J., Krek, S., Kwak, S., Laippala, V., Lambertino, L., Lam, L., Lando, T.,

Larasati, S. D., Lavrentiev, A., Lee, J., Lê H`ông, P., Lenci, A., Lertpradit, S., Leung, H., Li, C. Y., Li, J., Li, K., Lim, K., Liovina, M., Li, Y., Ljubešić, N., Loginova, O., Lyashevskaya, O., Lynn, T., Macketanz, V., Makazhanov, A., Mandl, M., Manning, C., Manurung, R., Mărănduc, C., Mareček, D., Marheinecke, K., Martínez Alonso, H., Martins, A., Mašek, J., Matsumoto, Y., McDonald, R., McGuinness, S., Mendonça, G., Miekka, N., Misirpashayeva, M., Missilä, A., Mititelu, C., Mitrofan, M., Miyao, Y., Montemagni, S., More, A., Moreno Romero, L., Mori, K. S., Morioka, T., Mori, S., Moro, S., Mortensen, B., Moskalevskyi, B., Muischnek, K., Munro, R., Murawaki, Y., Müürisep, K., Nainwani, P., Navarro Horñiacek, J. I., Nedoluzhko, A., Nešpore-Bērzkalne, G., Nguy˜ên Thị, L., Nguy˜ên Thị Minh, H., Nikaido, Y., Nikolaev, V., Nitisaroj, R., Nurmi, H., Ojala, S., Ojha, A. K., Olúòkun, A., Omura, M., Osenova, P., Östling, R., Øvrelid, L., Partanen, N., Pascual, E., Passarotti, M., Patejuk, A., Paulino-Passos, G., Peljak-Łapińska, A., Peng, S., Perez, C.-A., Perrier, G., Petrova, D., Petrov, S., Phelan, J., Piitulainen, J., Pirinen, T. A., Pitler, E., Plank, B., Poibeau, T., Ponomareva, L., Popel, M., Pretkalniņa, L., Prévost, S., Prokopidis, P., Przepiórkowski, A., Puolakainen, T., Pyysalo, S., Qi, P., Rääbis, A., Rademaker, A., Ramasamy, L., Rama, T., Ramisch, C., Ravishankar, V., Real, L., Reddy, S., Rehm, G., Riabov, I., Rießler, M., Rimkutė, E., Rinaldi, L., Rituma, L., Rocha, L., Romanenko, M., Rosa, R., Rovati, D., Roșca, V., Rudina, O., Rueter, J., Sadde, S., Sagot, B., Saleh, S., Salomoni, A., Samardžić, T., Samson, S., Sanguinetti, M., Särg, D., Saulīte, B., Sawanakunanon, Y., Schneider, N., Schuster, S., Seddah, D., Seeker, W., Seraji, M., Shen, M., Shimada, A., Shirasu, H., Shohibussirri, M., Sichinava, D., Silveira, A., Silveira, N., Simi, M., Simionescu, R., Simkó, K., Šimková, M., Simov, K., Smith, A., Soares-Bastos, I., Spadine, C., Stella, A., Straka, M., Strnadová, J., Suhr, A., Sulubacak, U., Suzuki, S., Szántó, Z., Taji, D., Takahashi, Y., Tamburini, F., Tanaka, T., Tellier, I., Thomas, G., Torga, L., Trosterud, T., Trukhina, A., Tsarfaty, R., Tyers, F., Uematsu, S., Urešová, Z., Uria, L., Uszkoreit, H., Utka, A., Vajjala, S., van Niekerk, D., van Noord, G., Varga, V., Villemonte de la Clergerie, E., Vincze, V., Wallin, L., Walsh, A., Wang, J. X., Washington, J. N., Wendt, M., Williams, S., Wirén, M., Wittern, C., Woldemariam, T., Wong, T.-s., Wróblewska, A., Yako, M., Yamazaki, N., Yan, C., Yasuoka, K., Yavrumyan, M. M., Yu, Z., Žabokrtský, Z., Zeldes, A., Zhang, M., and Zhu, H. (2019). Universal Dependencies 2.5. LINDAT/CLARIAH-CZ Digital Library at the Institute of Formal and Applied Linguistics (ÚFAL), Faculty of Mathematics and Physics, Charles University.

Proceedings of 1st Workshop on Language Technologies for Historical and Ancient Languages, pages 124–129
Language Resources and Evaluation Conference (LREC 2020), Marseille, 11–16 May 2020
© European Language Resources Association (ELRA), licensed under CC-BY-NC

UDPipe at EvaLatin 2020: Contextualized Embeddings and Treebank Embeddings

Milan Straka, Jana Straková
Charles University
Faculty of Mathematics and Physics
Institute of Formal and Applied Linguistics
{straka,strakova}@ufal.mff.cuni.cz

Abstract

We present our contribution to the EvaLatin shared task, which is the first evaluation campaign devoted to the evaluation of NLP tools for Latin. We submitted a system based on UDPipe 2.0, one of the winners of the CoNLL 2018 Shared Task, The 2018 Shared Task on Extrinsic Parser Evaluation and SIGMORPHON 2019 Shared Task. Our system places first by a wide margin both in lemmatization and POS tagging in the open modality, where additional supervised data is allowed, in which case we utilize all Universal Dependency Latin treebanks. In the closed modality, where only the EvaLatin training data is allowed, our system achieves the best performance in lemmatization and in classical subtask of POS tagging, while reaching second place in cross-genre and cross-time settings. In the ablation experiments, we also evaluate the influence of BERT and XLM-RoBERTa contextualized embeddings, and the treebank encodings of the different flavors of Latin treebanks.

Keywords: EvaLatin, UDPipe, lemmatization, POS tagging, BERT, XLM-RoBERTa

1. Introduction

This paper describes our participant system to the EvaLatin 2020 shared task (Sprugnoli et al., 2020). Given a segmented and tokenized text in CoNLL-U format with surface forms as in

```
# sent_id = 1
1   Dum         _           _       _   . . .
2   haec        _           _       _   . . .
3   in          _           _       _   . . .
4   Hispania    _           _       _   . . .
5   geruntur    _           _       _   . . .
6   C.          _           _       _   . . .
7   Trebonius   _           _       _   . . .
```

the task is to infer lemmas and POS tags:

```
# sent-id = 1
1   Dum         dum         SCONJ   _   . . .
2   haec        hic         DET     _   . . .
3   in          in          ADP     _   . . .
4   Hispania    Hispania    PROPN   _   . . .
5   geruntur    gero        VERB    _   . . .
6   C.          Gaius       PROPN   _   . . .
7   Trebonius   Trebonius   PROPN   _   . . .
```

The EvaLatin 2020 training data consists of 260k words of annotated texts from five authors. In the closed modality, only the given training data may be used, while in open modality any additional resources can be utilized. We submitted a system based on UDPipe 2.0 (Straka et al., 2019a). In the open modality, our system also uses all three UD 2.5 (Zeman et al., 2019) Latin treebanks as additional training data and places first by a wide margin both in lemmatization and POS tagging.

In the closed modality, our system achieves the best performance in lemmatization and in classical subtask of POS tagging (consisting of texts of the same five authors as the

training data), while reaching second place in cross-genre and cross-time setting.

Additionally, we evaluated the effect of:

- BERT (Devlin et al., 2019) and XLM-RoBERTa (Conneau et al., 2019) contextualized embeddings;
- various granularity levels of treebank embeddings (Stymne et al., 2018).

2. Related Work

The EvaLatin 2020 shared task (Sprugnoli et al., 2020) is reminiscent of the SIGMORPHON2019 Shared Task (McCarthy et al., 2019), where the goal was also to perform lemmatization and POS tagging, but on 107 corpora in 66 languages. It is also related to CoNLL 2017 and 2018 Multilingual Parsing from Raw Texts to Universal Dependencies shared tasks (Zeman et al., 2017; Zeman et al., 2018), in which the goal was to process raw texts into tokenized sentences with POS tags, lemmas, morphological features and dependency trees of the Universal Dependencies project (Nivre et al., 2016), which seeks to develop cross-linguistically consistent treebank annotation of morphology and syntax for many languages.

UDPipe 2.0 (Straka et al., 2016; Straka, 2018) was one of the winning systems of the CoNLL 2018 shared task, performing the POS tagging, lemmatization and dependency parsing jointly. Its modification (Straka et al., 2019a) took part in the SIGMORPHON 2019 shared task, delivering best performance in lemmatization and comparable to best performance in POS tagging.

A new type of deep contextualized word representation was introduced by Peters et al. (2018). The proposed embeddings, called ELMo, were obtained from internal states of deep bidirectional language model, pretrained on a large text corpus. The idea of ELMos was extended to BERT by Devlin et al. (2019), who instead of a bidirectional recurrent language model employ a Transformer (Vaswani

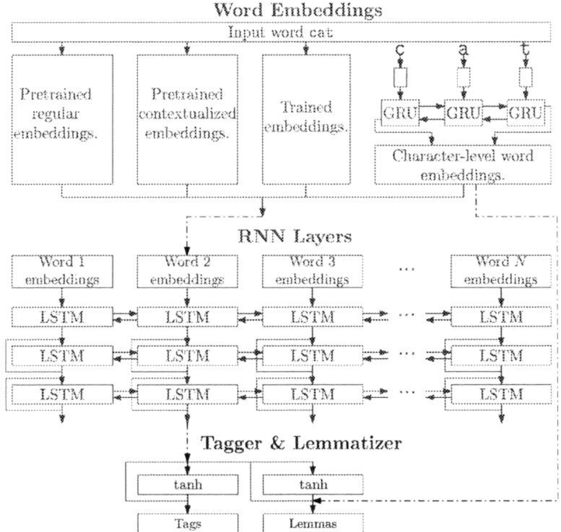

Figure 1: The UDPipe network architecture of the joint tagger and lemmatizer.

et al., 2017) architecture. A multilingual BERT model trained on 102 languages can significantly improve performance in many NLP tasks across many languages. Recently, XLM-RoBERTa, an improved multilingual model based on BERT, was proposed by Conneau et al. (2019), which appears to offer stronger performance in multilingual representation (Conneau et al., 2019; Lewis et al., 2019).

3. Methods

3.1. Architecture Overview

Our architecture is based on UDPipe entry to SIG-MORPHON 2019 Shared Task (Straka et al., 2019a), which is available at `https://github.com/ufal/sigmorphon2019`. The resulting model is presented in Figure 1.

In short, the architecture is a multi-task model predicting jointly lemmas and POS tags. After embedding input words, three shared bidirectional LSTM (Hochreiter and Schmidhuber, 1997) layers are performed. Then, softmax classifiers process the output and generate the lemmas and POS tags.

The lemmas are generated by classifying into a set of edit scripts which process input word form and produce lemmas by performing character-level edits on the word prefix and suffix. The lemma classifier additionally takes the character-level word embeddings as input. The lemmatization is further described in Section 3.2.

The input word embeddings are the same as in the previous versions of UDPipe 2.0:

- **end-to-end word embeddings**,
- **character-level word embeddings:** We employ bidirectional GRUs (Cho et al., 2014; Graves and Schmidhuber, 2005) of dimension 256 in line with (Ling et al., 2015): we represent every Unicode character with a vector of dimension 256, and concatenate GRU output for forward and reversed word characters. The character-level word embeddings are trained together with UDPipe network.
- **pretrained word embeddings:** We use FastText word embeddings (Bojanowski et al., 2017) of dimension 300, which we pretrain on plain texts provided by CoNLL 2017 UD Shared Task (Ginter et al., 2017), using segmentation and tokenization trained from the UD data.[1]
- **pretrained contextualized word embeddings:** We use the `Multilingual Base Uncased` BERT (Devlin et al., 2019) model to provide contextualized embeddings of dimensionality 768, averaging the last layer of subwords belonging to the same word.

We refer the readers for detailed description of the architecture and the training procedure to Straka et al. (2019a).

3.2. Lemmatization

The lemmatization is modeled as a multi-class classification, in which the classes are the complete rules which lead from input forms to the lemmas. We call each class encoding a transition from input form to lemma a *lemma rule*. We create a lemma rule by firstly encoding the correct casing as a *casing script* and secondly by creating a sequence of character edits, an *edit script*.

Firstly, we deal with the casing by creating a *casing script*. By default, word form and lemma characters are treated as lowercased. If the lemma however contains upper-cased characters, a rule is added to the casing script to uppercase the corresponding characters in the resulting lemma. For example, the most frequent casing script is "keep the lemma lowercased (don't do anything)" and the second most frequent casing script is "uppercase the first character and keep the rest lowercased".

As a second step, an *edit script* is created to convert input lowercased form to lowercased lemma. To ensure meaningful editing, the form is split to three parts, which are then processed separately: a prefix, a root (stem) and a suffix. The root is discovered by matching the longest substring shared between the form and the lemma; if no matching substring is found (e.g., form *eum* and lemma *is*), we consider the word irregular, do not process it with any edits and directly replace the word form with the lemma. Otherwise, we proceed with the edit scripts, which process the prefix and the suffix separately and keep the root unchanged. The allowed character-wise operations are character copy, addition and deletion.

The resulting *lemma rule* is a concatenation of a casing script and an edit script. The most common lemma rules present in EvaLatin training data are presented in Table 1.

Using the generated lemma rules, the task of lemmatization is then reduced to a multiclass classification task, in which the artificial neural network predicts the correct lemma rule.

3.3. Treebank Embedding

In the open modality, we additionally train on all three UD 2.5 Latin treebanks. In order to recognize and handle possible differences in the treebank annotations, we employ treebank embeddings following (Stymne et al., 2018).

---

[1] We use `-minCount 5 -epoch 10 -neg 10` options.

Lemma Rule	Casing Script	Edit Script	Most Frequent Examples
↓0;d¦	all lowercase	do nothing	et→et, in→in, non→non, ut→ut, ad→ad
↓0;d¦-+u+s	all lowercase	change last char to us	suo→suus, loco→locus, Romani→romanus, sua→suus
↓0;d¦---+o	all lowercase	change last 3 chars to o	dare→do, dicere→dico, fieri→fio, uidetur→uideo, data→do
↓0;d¦-+s	all lowercase	change last char to s	quid→quis, id→is, rei→res, omnia→omnis, rem→res
↓0;d¦----+o	all lowercase	change last 4 chars to o	hominum→homo, dedit→do, homines→homo
↓0;d¦--+o	all lowercase	change last 2 chars to o	habere→habeo, dicam→dico, ferre→fero, dat→do
↓0;d¦--+u+s	all lowercase	change last 2 chars to us	publicae→publicus, suis→suus, suam→suus, suos→suus
↓0;d¦-	all lowercase	remove last character	gratiam→gratia, causam→causa, uitam→uita, copias→copia
↓0;d¦-+u+m	all lowercase	change last char to um	belli→bellum, posse→possum, bello→bellum
↓0;d¦---+s	all lowercase	change last 3 chars to s	omnibus→omnis, rebus→res, nobis→nos, rerum→res
↑0¦↓1;d¦	1st upper, then lower	do nothing	Caesar→Caesar, Plinius→Plinius, Antonius→Antonius
↓0;d¦-----+o	all lowercase	change last 5 chars to o	uideretur→uideo, uidebatur→uideo, faciendum→facio
↓0;d¦--+i	all lowercase	change last 2 chars to i	quod→qui, quae→qui, quem→qui, quos→qui, quam→qui
↓0;d¦---	all lowercase	remove last 3 characters	quibus→qui, legiones→legio, legionum→legio, legionis→legio
↓0;d¦--+s	all lowercase	change last 2 chars to s	omnium→omnis, hostium→hostis, parte→pars, urbem→urbs
...	...	...	...
↓0;ais	all lowercase	ignore form, use is	eum→is, eo→is, ea→is, eorum→is, eam→is

Table 1: Fifteen most frequent lemma rules in EvaLatin training data ordered from the most frequent one, and the most frequent rule with an absolute edit script.

System	Lemmatization		
	classical	cross-genre	cross-time
UDPipe – open	96.19 (1)	87.13 (1)	91.01 (1)
UDPipe – closed	95.90 (2)	85.47 (3)	87.69 (2)
P2 – closed 1	94.76 (3)	85.49 (2)	85.75 (3)
P3 – closed 1	94.60 (4)	81.69 (5)	83.92 (4)
P2 – closed 2	94.22 (5)	82.69 (4)	83.76 (5)
Post ST – open	*96.35*	*87.48*	*91.07*
Post ST – closed	*95.93*	*85.94*	*87.88*

Table 2: Official ranking of EvaLatin lemmatization. Additionally, we include our best post-competition model in italic.

System	Tagging		
	classical	cross-genre	cross-time
UDPipe – open	96.74 (1)	91.11 (1)	87.69 (1)
UDPipe – closed	96.65 (2)	90.15 (3)	84.93 (3)
P4 – closed 2	96.34 (3)	90.64 (2)	87.00 (2)
P3 – closed 1	95.52 (4)	88.54 (4)	83.96 (4)
P4 – closed 3	95.35 (5)	86.95 (6)	81.38 (7)
P2 – closed 1	94.15 (6)	88.40 (5)	82.62 (6)
P4 – closed 1	93.24 (7)	83.88 (7)	82.99 (5)
P2 – closed 2	92.98 (8)	82.93 (8)	80.78 (8)
P5 – closed 1	90.65 (9)	73.47 (9)	76.62 (9)
Post ST – open	*96.82*	*91.46*	*87.91*
Post ST – closed	*96.76*	*90.50*	*84.70*

Table 3: Official ranking of EvaLatin lemmatization. Additionally, we include our best post-competition model in italic.

Furthermore, given that the author name is a known information both during training and prediction time, we train a second model with author-specific embeddings for the individual authors. We employ the model with author-specific embeddings whenever the predicted text comes from one of the training data authors (in-domain setting) and a generic model otherwise (out-of-domain setting).

4. Results

The official overall results are presented in Table 2 for lemmatization and in Table 3 for POS tagging. In the open modality, our system places first by a wide margin both in lemmatization and POS tagging. In the closed modality, our system achieves best performance in lemmatization and in classical subtask of POS tagging (where the texts from the training data authors are annotated), and second place in cross-genre and cross-time settings.

5. Ablation Experiments

The effect of various kinds contextualized embeddings is evaluated in Table 4. While BERT embeddings yield only a minor accuracy increase, which is consistent with (Straka et al., 2019b) for Latin, using XLM-RoBERTa leads to larger accuracy improvement. For comparison, we include the post-competition system with XLM-RoBERTa embeddings in Tables 2 and 3.

To quantify the boost of the additional training data in the open modality, we considered all models from the above mentioned Table 4, arriving at the average improvement presented in Table 5. While the performance on the in-domain test set (classical subtask) improves only slightly, the out-of-domain test sets (cross-genre and cross-time subtasks) show more substantial improvement with the additional training data.

The effect of different granularity of treebank embeddings in open modality is investigated in Table 6. When treebank embeddings are removed from our competition system, the performance deteriorates the most, even if only a little in absolute terms. This indicates that the UD and EvaLatin annotations are very consistent. Providing one embedding for EvaLatin data and another for all UD treebanks improves the performance, and more so if three UD treebank specific

Word embeddings	BERT embeddings	XLM-RoBERTa embeddings	Lemmatization			Tagging		
			classical	cross-genre	cross-time	classical	cross-genre	cross-time
Open modality								
✗	✗	✗	96.04	86.85	90.58	96.46	90.44	87.66
✓	✗	✗	96.27	87.28	90.80	96.64	91.16	87.78
✗	✓	✗	96.19	86.76	90.78	96.70	90.34	87.50
✗	✗	✓	96.33	86.48	90.95	96.80	90.67	87.79
✓	✓	✗	96.28	87.28	90.80	96.74	91.11	87.69
✓	✗	✓	96.35	87.48	91.07	96.82	91.46	87.91
Closed modality								
✗	✗	✗	95.62	84.62	87.63	96.14	88.90	83.59
✓	✗	✗	95.79	85.55	88.37	96.44	90.59	84.14
✗	✓	✗	95.65	84.76	87.58	96.44	89.08	84.84
✗	✗	✓	95.93	84.97	87.63	96.67	89.36	84.24
✓	✓	✗	95.96	85.52	88.04	96.65	90.15	84.93
✓	✗	✓	95.93	85.94	87.88	96.76	90.50	84.70

Table 4: The evaluation of various pretrained embeddings (FastText word embeddings, Multilingual BERT embeddings, XLM-RoBERTa embeddings) on the lemmatization and POS tagging.

	Lemmatization			Tagging		
	classical	cross-genre	cross-time	classical	cross-genre	cross-time
The improvement of open modality, i.e., using all three UD Latin treebanks	+0.430	+1.795	+2.975	+0.177	+1.100	+3.315

Table 5: The average percentage point improvement in the open modality settings compared to the closed modality. The results are averaged over all models in Table 4.

	Lemmatization			Tagging		
	classical	cross-genre	cross-time	classical	cross-genre	cross-time
Per-author embeddings, per-UD-treebank embeddings	96.28	87.28	90.80	96.74	91.11	87.69
Single EvaLatin embedding, per-UD-treebank embeddings	96.28	87.28	90.80	96.70	91.11	87.69
Single EvaLatin embedding, single UD-treebank embedding	96.23	87.22	90.78	96.68	91.14	87.63
EvaLatin and UD treebanks merged	96.18	87.23	90.77	96.52	91.01	86.12

Table 6: The effect of various kinds of treebank embeddings in open modality – whether the individual authors in EvaLatin get a different or the same treebank embedding, and whether the UD treebanks get a different treebank embedding, same treebank embedding but different from the EvaLatin data, or the same treebank embedding as EvaLatin data.

	Lemmatization	Tagging
	classical	classical
The improvement of using per-author treebank embeddings	0.027	0.043

Table 7: The average percentage point improvement of using per-author treebank embedding compared to not distinguishing among authors of EvaLatin data, averaged over all models in Table 4.

embeddings are used.

Lastly, we evaluate the effect of the per-author embeddings. While on the development set the improvement was larger, the results on the test sets are nearly identical. To get more accurate estimate, we computed the average improvement for all models in Table 4, arriving at marginal improvements in Table 7, which indicates that per-author embeddings have nearly no effect on the final system performance (compared to EvaLatin and UD specific embeddings).

6. Conclusion

We described our entry to the EvaLatin 2020 shared task, which placed first in the open modality and delivered strong performance in the closed modality.

For a future shared task, we think it might be interesting to include also segmentation and tokenization or extend the shared task with an extrinsic evaluation.

7. Acknowledgements

This work was supported by the grant no. GX20-16819X of the Grant Agency of the Czech Republic, and has been using language resources stored and distributed by the LINDAT/CLARIAH-CZ project of the Ministry of Education, Youth and Sports of the Czech Republic (project LM2018101).

8. Bibliographical References

Bojanowski, P., Grave, E., Joulin, A., and Mikolov, T. (2017). Enriching Word Vectors with Subword Information. *Transactions of the Association for Computational Linguistics*, 5:135–146.

Cho, K., van Merrienboer, B., Bahdanau, D., and Bengio, Y. (2014). On the Properties of Neural Machine Translation: Encoder-Decoder Approaches. *CoRR*.

Conneau, A., Khandelwal, K., Goyal, N., Chaudhary, V., Wenzek, G., Guzmán, F., Grave, E., Ott, M., Zettlemoyer, L., and Stoyanov, V. (2019). Unsupervised Cross-lingual Representation Learning at Scale. *CoRR*, abs/1911.02116.

Devlin, J., Chang, M.-W., Lee, K., and Toutanova, K. (2019). BERT: Pre-training of deep bidirectional transformers for language understanding. In *Proceedings of the 2019 Conference of the North American Chapter of the Association for Computational Linguistics: Human Language Technologies, Volume 1 (Long and Short Papers)*, pages 4171–4186, Minneapolis, Minnesota, June. Association for Computational Linguistics.

Graves, A. and Schmidhuber, J. (2005). Framewise phoneme classification with bidirectional lstm and other neural network architectures. *Neural Networks*, pages 5–6.

Hochreiter, S. and Schmidhuber, J. (1997). Long Short-Term Memory. *Neural Comput.*, 9(8):1735–1780, November.

Lewis, P., Oguz, B., Rinott, R., Riedel, S., and Schwenk, H. (2019). Mlqa: Evaluating cross-lingual extractive question answering. *ArXiv*, abs/1910.07475.

Ling, W., Luís, T., Marujo, L., Astudillo, R. F., Amir, S., Dyer, C., Black, A. W., and Trancoso, I. (2015). Finding Function in Form: Compositional Character Models for Open Vocabulary Word Representation. *CoRR*.

McCarthy, A. D., Vylomova, E., Wu, S., Malaviya, C., Wolf-Sonkin, L., Nicolai, G., Kirov, C., Silfverberg, M., Mielke, S. J., Heinz, J., Cotterell, R., and Hulden, M. (2019). The SIGMORPHON 2019 Shared Task: Morphological Analysis in Context and Cross-Lingual Transfer for Inflection. In *Proceedings of the 16th Workshop on Computational Research in Phonetics, Phonology, and Morphology*, pages 229–244, Florence, Italy, August. Association for Computational Linguistics.

Nivre, J., de Marneffe, M.-C., Ginter, F., Goldberg, Y., Hajič, J., Manning, C., McDonald, R., Petrov, S., Pyysalo, S., Silveira, N., Tsarfaty, R., and Zeman, D. (2016). Universal Dependencies v1: A multilingual treebank collection. In *Proceedings of the 10th International Conference on Language Resources and Evaluation (LREC 2016)*, pages 1659–1666, Portorož, Slovenia. European Language Resources Association.

Peters, M., Neumann, M., Iyyer, M., Gardner, M., Clark, C., Lee, K., and Zettlemoyer, L. (2018). Deep Contextualized Word Representations. In *Proceedings of the 2018 Conference of the North American Chapter of the Association for Computational Linguistics: Human Language Technologies, Volume 1 (Long Papers)*, pages 2227–2237. Association for Computational Linguistics.

Sprugnoli, R., Passarotti, M., Cecchini, F. M., and Pellegrini, M. (2020). Overview of the evalatin 2020 evaluation campaign. In Rachele Sprugnoli et al., editors, *Proceedings of the LT4HALA 2020 Workshop - 1st Workshop on Language Technologies for Historical and Ancient Languages, satellite event to the Twelfth International Conference on Language Resources and Evaluation (LREC 2020)*, Paris, France, May. European Language Resources Association (ELRA).

Straka, M., Hajič, J., and Straková, J. (2016). UDPipe: Trainable Pipeline for Processing CoNLL-U Files Performing Tokenization, Morphological Analysis, POS Tagging and Parsing. In *Proceedings of the 10th International Conference on Language Resources and Evaluation (LREC 2016)*, Portorož, Slovenia. European Language Resources Association.

Straka, M., Straková, J., and Hajic, J. (2019a). UDPipe at SIGMORPHON 2019: Contextualized Embeddings, Regularization with Morphological Categories, Corpora Merging. In *Proceedings of the 16th Workshop on Computational Research in Phonetics, Phonology, and Morphology*, pages 95–103, Florence, Italy, August. Association for Computational Linguistics.

Straka, M., Straková, J., and Hajič, J. (2019b). Evaluating Contextualized Embeddings on 54 Languages in POS Tagging, Lemmatization and Dependency Parsing. *arXiv e-prints*, page arXiv:1908.07448, August.

Straka, M. (2018). UDPipe 2.0 Prototype at CoNLL 2018 UD Shared Task. In *Proceedings of CoNLL 2018: The SIGNLL Conference on Computational Natural Language Learning*, pages 197–207, Stroudsburg, PA, USA. Association for Computational Linguistics.

Stymne, S., de Lhoneux, M., Smith, A., and Nivre, J. (2018). Parser training with heterogeneous treebanks. In *Proceedings of the 56th Annual Meeting of the Association for Computational Linguistics (Volume 2: Short Papers)*, pages 619–625, Melbourne, Australia, July. Association for Computational Linguistics.

Vaswani, A., Shazeer, N., Parmar, N., Uszkoreit, J., Jones, L., Gomez, A. N., Kaiser, L., and Polosukhin, I. (2017). Attention is all you need. *CoRR*, abs/1706.03762.

Zeman, D., Popel, M., Straka, M., Hajič, J., Nivre, J., Ginter, F., et al. (2017). CoNLL 2017 Shared Task: Multilingual Parsing from Raw Text to Universal Dependencies. In *Proceedings of the CoNLL 2017 Shared Task: Multilingual Parsing from Raw Text to Universal Dependencies*, pages 1–19, Vancouver, Canada. Association for Computational Linguistics.

Zeman, D., Hajič, J., Popel, M., Potthast, M., Straka, M., Ginter, F., Nivre, J., and Petrov, S. (2018). CoNLL 2018 Shared Task: Multilingual Parsing from Raw Text to Universal Dependencies. In *Proceedings of the CoNLL 2018 Shared Task: Multilingual Parsing from Raw Text to Universal Dependencies*, pages 1–20, Brussels, Belgium, October. Association for Computational Linguistics.

9. Language Resource References

Ginter, F., Hajič, J., Luotolahti, J., Straka, M., and Zeman, D. (2017). *CoNLL 2017 Shared Task - Automatically*

Annotated Raw Texts and Word Embeddings. Institute of Formal and Applied Linguistics, LINDAT/CLARIN, Charles University, Prague, Czech Republic, LINDAT/CLARIN PID: http://hdl.handle.net/11234/1-1989.

Zeman, D., Nivre, J., et al. (2019). *Universal Dependencies 2.5.* Institute of Formal and Applied Linguistics, LINDAT/CLARIN, Charles University, Prague, Czech Republic, LINDAT/CLARIN PID: http://hdl.handle.net/11234/1-3105.

Voting for POS Tagging of Latin Texts: Using the Flair of FLAIR to Better Ensemble Classifiers by Example of Latin

Manuel Stoeckel, Alexander Henlein, Wahed Hemati, Alexander Mehler

Text Technology Lab, Goehte-University Frankfurt

manuel.stoeckel@stud.uni-frankfurt.de, {henlein, hemati, mehler}@em.uni-frankfurt.de

https://www.texttechnologylab.org

Abstract

Despite the great importance of the Latin language in the past, there are relatively few resources available today to develop modern NLP tools for this language. Therefore, the EvaLatin Shared Task for Lemmatization and Part-of-Speech (POS) tagging was published in the LT4HALA workshop. In our work, we dealt with the second EvaLatin task, that is, POS tagging. Since most of the available Latin word embeddings were trained on either few or inaccurate data, we trained several embeddings on better data in the first step. Based on these embeddings, we trained several state-of-the-art taggers and used them as input for an ensemble classifier called LSTMVoter. We were able to achieve the best results for both the cross-genre and the cross-time task (90,64 % and 87,00 %) without using additional annotated data (closed modality). In the meantime, we further improved the system and achieved even better results (96,91 % on classical, 90,87 % on cross-genre and 87,35 % on cross-time).

Keywords: Part-of-Speech Tagging, Statistical and Machine Learning Methods, Corpus (Creation, Annotation, etc.)

1. Introduction

EvaLatin is the first evaluation campaign totally devoted to the evaluation of NLP tools for Latin (Sprugnoli et al., 2020). For this purpose, two tasks have been released (i.e. Lemmatization and Part of Speech (POS) tagging), each of which is divided into three subgroups: classical, cross-genre and cross-time. In this work we describe an approach to the task of EvaLatin regarding POS tagging, that is, the task of assigning each token in a text its part of speech. A part of speech is a category of words with similar grammatical properties. For many natural language processing (NLP) tasks, such as information retrieval, knowledge extraction or semantic analysis, POS tagging is a crucial pre-processing step. However, in morphologically rich languages such as Latin, this task is not trivial due to the variability of lexical forms. In order to perform POS tagging automatically, it has to be understood as a sequence labeling problem, where an output class is assigned to each input word so that the length of the input sequence corresponds to the length of the output sequence.

There already exist approaches for POS tagging for Latin (Gleim et al., 2019; vor der Brück and Mehler, 2016; Eger et al., 2016; Eger et al., 2015; Straka and Straková, 2017; Kestemont and De Gussem, 2016; Kondratyuk and Straka, 2019; Manjavacas et al., 2019). These approaches mostly utilize the increasingly popular neural network based methods for POS-tagging – by example of Latin. Part of this contribution is to extend this work and to train state-of-the-art neural network based sequence labeling tools (Straka and Straková, 2017; Lample et al., 2016; Akbik et al., 2019a; Kondratyuk and Straka, 2019) for Latin.

These neural network based sequence labeling tools usually require pre-trained word embeddings (e.g. Mikolov et al. (2013a) or Pennington et al. (2014)). These word embeddings are trained on large unlabeled corpora and are more useful for neural network sequence labeling tools if the corpora are not only large but also from the same do-

main as the documents to be processed. Therefore another part of this contribution is to create word embeddings for Latin for different genres and epochs. Since Latin is a morphologically rich language, sub-word-embeddings (Grave et al., 2018; Heinzerling and Strube, 2018) must be created to reflect its morphological peculiarities.

The various sequence labeling tools provide different results, making it advisable to combine them in order to bundle their strengths. For this reason LSTMVoter (Hemati and Mehler, 2019) was used to create a conglomerate of the various tools and models (re-)trained here.

To simplify the above mentioned process of training embeddings and sequence labeling tools on the one hand and creating an ensemble thereof, we developed a generic pipeline architecture which takes a labeled corpus in ConLLU format as input, trains the different taggers and finally creates an LSTMVoter ensemble. The idea is to make this architecture available for the solution of related tasks in order to systematically simplify the corresponding training pipeline.

The article is organized as follows: Section 2 describes the data sets we used to train our word embeddings. Section 3 describes the training process of the taggers and how they were integrated into our system. In Section 4, we present and discuss our results, while Section 5 provides a summary of this study and prospects for future work.

2. Datasets

This section gives a brief overview about the datasets supplied for EvaLatin as well as other corpora we used for the *closed modality* run of the POS task.

Current state-of-the-art sequence labeling systems for POS tagging make use of word embeddings or language models (Akbik et al., 2018; Bohnet et al., 2018; Gleim et al., 2019, *LMs*). These tools are usually trained and evaluated on high-resource languages; making use of the availability of large unlabeled corpora to build feature-rich word embeddings. This leads to an ever-increasing ubiquitousness of embeddings for all kinds of languages.

Unfortunately, the number of available, high-quality corpora for Latin is stretched thin; historically the Latin Wikipedia has often been used as a corpus for training word embeddings (Grave et al., 2018; Heinzerling and Strube, 2018). But the Latin Wikipedia is composed of modern texts written by scholars of different backgrounds, which cannot properly reflect the use of Latin language throughout history. Thus we compiled a corpus of historical, Medieval Latin texts covering different epochs which is presented in the following section.

2.1. Historical Corpora

An overview of the corpora used is shown in table 1. It lists each corpus together with its numbers of sentences, tokens and characters and provides a summary of the overall corpus with the total number and unique counts. In addition to the corpus published for EvaLatin, we added other publicly accessible corpora: the Universal Dependencies Latin (Nivre et al., 2016a, UD_Latin) corpora UD_Latin-PROIEL (Haug and Jøhndal, 2008), UD_Latin-ITTB (Cecchini et al., 2018) and UD_Latin-Perseus (Bamman and Crane, 2011a), the Capitularies (Mehler et al., 2015) and the Cassiodorus Variae (Variae, 2020). But the main bulk of text comes from the Latin text repository of the eHumanties Desktop (Gleim et al., 2009; Gleim et al., 2012) and the CompHistSem (Cimino et al., 2015) project comprising a large number of Medieval Latin texts.[1] For all corpora we extracted the plain text without annotations and compiled a single corpus called *Historical Latin Corpus* (HLC).

Corpus	Sentences	Tokens	Chars
UD-Perseus	2 260	29 078	1 444 884
Cassiodor. Variae	3 129	135 352	748 477
EvaLatin	14 009	258 861	1 528 538
Capitularies	15 170	477 247	2 432 482
UD-PROIEL	18 526	215 175	1 157 372
UD-ITTB	19 462	349 235	1 771 905
CompHistSem	2 608 730	79 136 129	384 199 772
Total	2 665 840	80 129 332	389 576 106
Unique		971 839	434

Table 1: Plain text corpora statistics.

3. System Description

3.1. Embeddings

While there are some word embeddings and language models trained on Latin texts, these are either trained on small, but higher-quality datasets (eg. Nivre et al. (2016b), trained on the Latin part of the UD corpus; Sprugnoli et al. (2019), trained on the 1 700 000 token *Opera Latin* corpus), or larger datasets which suffer from poor OCR quality (eg. Bamman and Crane (2011b) trained on noisy data) or are of modern origin (eg. Grave et al. (2018) and Heinzerling and Strube (2018) trained on Wikipedia). Therefore we trained

our own embeddings[2] on the HLC of Section 2.1 to obtain high quality word embeddings for our sequence labeling models. In the following sections we describe the type of embeddings we used and their hyperparameters adjusted during training.

3.1.1. Word Embeddings

wang2vec (Ling et al., 2015) is a variant of *word2vec* embeddings (Mikolov et al., 2013a; Mikolov et al., 2013b) which is aware of the relative positioning of context words by making a separate prediction for each context word position during training.

GloVe embeddings (Pennington et al., 2014) are trained on *global* word-word co-occurrence statistics across an entire corpus rather than considering *local* samples of co-occurrences.

3.1.2. Sub-word Embeddings

fastText embeddings (Grave et al., 2018) are trained on *character n-grams* of words rather than words themselves. They are able to capture character-based information which may be related to morphological information in addition to distributional information.

Byte-Pair Embeddings (Heinzerling and Strube, 2018, BPEmb) are composed of sub-word token embeddings. They utilize a vocabulary of character sequences which are induced from a large text corpus using a variant of byte-pair encoding for textual data (Sennrich et al., 2016). We used the *SentencePiece's*[3] implementation of the byte-pair algorithm to encode the HLC (see Section 4).

3.1.3. FLAIR Language Model

Current methods for sequence labeling use *language models* (LMs) trained on large unlabeled corpora to obtain *contextualized embeddings*, achieving state-of-the-art performance in POS tagging and named entity recognition for English, German and Dutch (Peters et al., 2018; Akbik et al., 2018). Some recent sequence labeling models with strong performance leverage *FLAIR character language models* (Akbik et al., 2018; Akbik et al., 2019b). These models are available through the *FLAIR framework* (Akbik et al., 2019a) which, since its first release, has been expanded with character language models for various languages by the NLP community, but none for Latin. Thus, we trained our own Latin character language model on the HLC of Section 2.1.

3.2. Taggers

In the following sections we briefly describe the taggers we have selected for our evaluation.

3.2.1. MarMoT

MarMoT is a generic CRF framework (Mueller et al., 2013). It implements a higher order CRF with approximations such that it can deal with large output spaces. It can also be trained to fire on predictions of lexical resources and on word embeddings.

---

[1] The texts are available via `www.comphistsem.org` or the eHumanities Desktop (`hudesktop.hucompute.org`).

[2] `http://embeddings.texttechnologylab.org`
[3] `https://github.com/google/sentencepiece`

3.2.2. anaGo

anaGo is a neural network-based sequence labeling system. It is based on the Glample Tagger (Lample et al., 2016), which combines a bidirectional *Long Short-term Memory* (LSTM) with *Conditional Random Fields* (CRF).

3.2.3. UDPipe

UDPipe provides a trainable pipeline for tokenization, tagging, lemmatization and dependency parsing. It offers 94 pre-trained models of 61 languages, each of which has been trained on UD Treebank (Nivre et al., 2016a) datasets. The POS model itself is based on MorphoDiTa (Straková et al., 2014) and can be easily trained on new data; no additional embeddings or features are required.

3.2.4. UDify

UDify is a single BERT-based (Devlin et al., 2018) model which was trained on 124 treebanks of 75 different languages for tagging, lemmatization and dependency parsing as well. Besides a pre-trained BERT model, the pipeline does not require any other features to be trained on new data.

3.2.5. FLAIR

Utilizing the FLAIR language model introduced above, we trained a BiLSTM-CRF sequence tagger using pooled contextualized embeddings (Akbik et al., 2019b, PCEs). PCEs are *aggregated* during the tagging process to capture the meaning of underrepresented words, which have already been seen by the tagger previously in contexts that are more specified.

3.2.6. Meta-BiLSTM

The **Meta-BiLSTM** tagger (Bohnet et al., 2018) combines two separate classifiers using a meta-model and achieves very good results on POS tagging. Each intermediate model is trained on the sequence labeling task using a different view of sentence-level representations, namely word and character embeddings. Then, a meta-model is trained on the same task while using the hidden states of the two other models as its input.

3.2.7. LSTMVoter

LSTMVoter (Hemati and Mehler, 2019) is a two-stage recurrent neural network system that integrates the optimized sequence labelers from our study into a single ensemble classifier: in the first stage, we trained and optimized all POS taggers mentioned so far. In the second stage, we combined the latter sequence labelers with two bidirectional LSTMs using an attention mechanism and a CRF to build an ensemble classifier. The idea of LSTMVoter is to learn, so to speak, which output of which embedded sequence labeler to use in which context to generate its final output.

4. Experiments

In this section we discuss our experiments and outline the parameters used to train each of the models. After the end of the task's evaluation window we were able to fine-tune our models using the gold-standard evaluation dataset. All of our experiments were conducted according to the *closed modality* of the second EvaLatin task, i.e. no additional labeled training data was used.

Tool	Classical	Cross-Genre	Cross-Time
LSTMVoterV1[e]	93,24 %	83,88 %	81,38 %
FLAIR[e†]	**96,34 %**	**90,64 %**	83,00 %
LSTMVoterV2[e]	95,35 %	86,95 %	**87,00 %**
UDPipe	93,68 %	84,65 %	86,03 %
UDify	95,13 %	86,02 %	87,34 %
Meta-BiLSTM[†]	96,01 %	87,95 %	82,32 %
FLAIR[†]	96,67 %	**90,87 %**	83,36 %
LSTMVoterV3[†]	**96,91 %**	90,77 %	**87,35 %**

Table 2: F1-scores (macro-average) for the different test datasets. All tools were trained according to the *closed modality*. [†] denotes models that were trained using our embeddings, while [e] denotes models which were submitted during the tasks evaluation window.

4.1. Training

4.1.1. Embeddings

For each of the methods mentioned in Section 3.1.1 we created 300 dimensional word embeddings by

- setting the window size to 10 for wang2vec and training for 50 epochs,
- using default parameters in the case of fastText and by training it for 100 epochs,
- choosing a window size of 15 with default parameters for GloVe and training for 100 epochs.

We encoded the HLC by means of the byte-pair algorithm, experimented with different vocabulary sizes $c \in \{5\,000, 10\,000, 100\,000, 200\,000\}$ and trained 300 dimensional GloVe embeddings on them using the same hyperparameters for GloVe as with the plain text corpus.

For our FLAIR language model we choose our parameters according to the recommendations of Akbik et al. (2018) and set the hidden size of both forward and backward language models to 1024, the maximum character sequence length to 250 and the mini-batch size to 100. We trained the model until after 50 epochs the learning rate annealing stopped with a remaining perplexity of 2,68 and 2,71 for the forward and backward model, respectively.

4.1.2. Taggers

We trained a BiLSTM-CRF sequence tagger using FLAIR with pooled contextualized embeddings together with our language model. We added all our word and subword embeddings as features for up to 150 epochs and used learning rate annealing with early stopping. In our experiments the byte-pair embeddings with the smallest vocabulary size of 5 000 performed best. We choose one hidden LSTM layer with 256 nodes and default parameters otherwise.

The Meta-BiLSTM tagger was trained with our GloVe embeddings using default parameters. UDPipe was trained with the default settings on the data set. POS was trained independently of the lemmatizer, as this achieved better results. The UDify BERT model was also only trained on POS, while all other modules were removed. This concerned a variant of BERT-Base-Multilingual[4] which also processed Latin data.

[4] https://github.com/google-research/bert/ blob/master/multilingual.md

	ADJ	ADP	ADV	AUX	CCONJ	DET	INTJ	NOUN	NUM	PART	PRON	PROPN	SCONJ	VERB	X
Classical															
Meta	90 %	99 %	93 %	85 %	99 %	97 %	**98** %	97 %	76 %	99 %	97 %	97 %	89 %	97 %	75 %
UDPipe	85 %	98 %	91 %	64 %	99 %	96 %	88 %	95 %	69 %	98 %	95 %	95 %	85 %	95 %	89 %
UDify	87 %	99 %	92 %	88 %	99 %	96 %	00 %	96 %	74 %	99 %	96 %	97 %	91 %	97 %	00 %
FLAIR	91 %	**99** %	**95** %	86 %	**99** %	**97** %	91 %	**97** %	78 %	**100** %	97 %	97 %	**93** %	98 %	82 %
VoterV1	83 %	98 %	90 %	67 %	99 %	96 %	70 %	94 %	69 %	99 %	95 %	95 %	86 %	95 %	00 %
VoterV2	88 %	99 %	93 %	84 %	**99** %	97 %	96 %	96 %	74 %	99 %	96 %	97 %	90 %	97 %	**95** %
VoterV3	**91** %	99 %	**95** %	**88** %	**99** %	97 %	96 %	97 %	**78** %	99 %	**98** %	**98** %	92 %	**98** %	90 %
Cross-Genre															
Meta	79 %	96 %	85 %	57 %	97 %	94 %	77 %	90 %	67 %	97 %	96 %	80 %	75 %	91 %	—
UDPipe	69 %	93 %	80 %	13 %	**98** %	92 %	79 %	86 %	55 %	98 %	96 %	86 %	75 %	87 %	—
UDify	73 %	97 %	80 %	50 %	98 %	89 %	00 %	88 %	55 %	**98** %	95 %	87 %	79 %	88 %	—
FLAIR	**82** %	97 %	**87** %	**80** %	98 %	**94** %	**91** %	**93** %	64 %	97 %	96 %	87 %	78 %	**94** %	—
VoterV1	66 %	95 %	81 %	29 %	98 %	92 %	70 %	86 %	**71** %	98 %	95 %	85 %	73 %	86 %	—
VoterV2	73 %	97 %	84 %	50 %	98 %	93 %	77 %	88 %	74 %	**98** %	96 %	86 %	78 %	89 %	—
VoterV3	79 %	**97** %	86 %	**80** %	98 %	93 %	80 %	92 %	71 %	**98** %	**97** %	**87** %	**80** %	93 %	—
Cross-Time															
Meta	74 %	97 %	**72** %	42 %	**90** %	89 %	60 %	89 %	29 %	**100** %	84 %	65 %	70 %	86 %	—
UDPipe	70 %	97 %	68 %	36 %	90 %	89 %	50 %	93 %	97 %	**100** %	82 %	**98** %	72 %	86 %	—
UDify	74 %	98 %	68 %	**46** %	90 %	87 %	00 %	**95** %	97 %	**100** %	85 %	93 %	**76** %	88 %	—
FLAIR	74 %	**98** %	71 %	44 %	90 %	86 %	75 %	90 %	50 %	**100** %	85 %	52 %	72 %	89 %	—
VoterV1	69 %	97 %	68 %	38 %	90 %	89 %	55 %	88 %	29 %	**100** %	81 %	55 %	70 %	86 %	—
VoterV2	73 %	98 %	69 %	43 %	90 %	89 %	**100** %	94 %	**97** %	**100** %	84 %	95 %	74 %	88 %	—
VoterV3	**75** %	98 %	**73** %	43 %	90 %	**89** %	46 %	94 %	96 %	**100** %	**86** %	81 %	74 %	**89** %	—

Table 3: F-Scores (micro-average) for each tool per tag and dataset. Model names are abbreviated: VoterV*i* denotes LSTMVoter V*i* and Meta denotes the Meta-BiLSTM model. Bold entries mark the best values prior to rounding.

For LSTMVoter we used a 40-10-40-10 split of the training data in line with Hemati and Mehler (2019). Using the first 40-10 split, all taggers from Section 3.2 were trained and their hyperparameters were optimized. The second split was then used to train LSTMVoter and to optimize its hyperparameters. We created the following ensembles:

V1: MarMoT and anaGo.

V2: MarMoT, anaGo and UDify, UDPipe.

V3: MarMoT, anaGo, UDify, UDPipe and FLAIR.

4.2. Results

An overview of the results of our taggers is provided by Table 2, while a more detailed report listing the performance of each tool for each POS and data type is given by Table 3. The first three rows of Table 2 show our submissions during the EvaLatin evaluation window. The best model for the classical and cross-genre sub-task is the FLAIR BiLSTM-CRF tagger with 96,34 % and 90,64 % while the LSTMVoter V2 model performs best on the cross-time sub-task with 87,00 %. With these results we placed first among other closed modality EvaLatin participants for both out-of-domain tasks and second for the Classical sub-task.

With fine-tuning after the release of the gold-standard annotations (while still following closed modality rules) we were able to increase all our results significantly by means of the third variant (V3) of our LSTMVoter ensemble model, while the performance of the fine-tuned FLAIR tagger only increased marginally.

5. Conclusion

We presented our experiments and results for the EvaLatin task on POS tagging. We trained and optimized various state-of-the-art sequence labeling systems for the POS tagging of Latin texts. Current sequence labeling systems require pre-trained word embeddings. In our experiments we trained a number of such models. In the end a combination of tools, which were integrated into an ensemble classifier by means of LSTMVoter, led to the best results. The reason for this might be that the LSTMVoter combines the strengths of the individual taggers as much as possible, while at the same time not letting their weaknesses get too many chances. The best model submitted during the evaluation window for the classical and cross-genre sub-task was the FLAIR BiLSTM-CRF tagger with 96,34 % and 90,64 % while the LSTMVoter V2 model performed at this time best on the cross-time sub-task with 87,00 %. With these results we placed first among other closed modality EvaLatin participants for both out-of-domain tasks and second for the classical sub-task. With fine-tuning after the release of the gold-standard annotations we were able to increase all our results significantly with the help of LSTMVoter V3. However, it is rather likely that we reached the upper bound of POS tagging for classic texts, because the inter-annotator agreement for POS tagging seems to be limited by a number in the range of 97 %–98 % (Brants, 2000; Plank et al., 2014). Our results for cross-genre and cross-time are top performers in EvaLatin, but they still offer potential for improvements. Future work should develop models that are specialized for each genre and time period. This also regards the inclusion of additional information such as lemma-related and morphological features to a greater extent, since Latin is a morphologically rich language.

The data and the code used and implemented in this study are available at https://github.com/texttechnologylab/SequenceLabeling; the embeddings are available at http://embeddings.texttechnologylab.org. All presented tools are accessible through the TextImager (Hemati et al., 2016) interface via the GUI [5] and as REST services[6].

---

[5] textimager.hucompute.org

[6] textimager.hucompute.org/rest/doku/

6. Bibliographical References

Akbik, A., Blythe, D., and Vollgraf, R. (2018). Contextual string embeddings for sequence labeling. In *COLING 2018, 27th International Conference on Computational Linguistics*, pages 1638–1649.

Akbik, A., Bergmann, T., Blythe, D., Rasul, K., Schweter, S., and Vollgraf, R. (2019a). FLAIR: An easy-to-use framework for state-of-the-art NLP. In *Proceedings of the 2019 Conference of the North American Chapter of the Association for Computational Linguistics (Demonstrations)*, pages 54–59, Minneapolis, Minnesota, June. Association for Computational Linguistics.

Akbik, A., Bergmann, T., and Vollgraf, R. (2019b). Pooled contextualized embeddings for named entity recognition. In *Proceedings of the 2019 Conference of the North American Chapter of the Association for Computational Linguistics: Human Language Technologies, Volume 1 (Long and Short Papers)*, pages 724–728, Minneapolis, Minnesota, June. Association for Computational Linguistics.

Bamman, D. and Crane, G. (2011a). The ancient greek and latin dependency treebanks. In *Language technology for cultural heritage*, pages 79–98. Springer.

Bamman, D. and Crane, G. R. (2011b). Measuring historical word sense variation. In Glen Newton, et al., editors, *Proceedings of the 2011 Joint International Conference on Digital Libraries, JCDL 2011, Ottawa, ON, Canada, June 13-17, 2011*, pages 1–10. ACM.

Bohnet, B., McDonald, R., Simões, G., Andor, D., Pitler, E., and Maynez, J. (2018). Morphosyntactic tagging with a meta-BiLSTM model over context sensitive token encodings. In *Proceedings of the 56th Annual Meeting of the Association for Computational Linguistics (Volume 1: Long Papers)*, pages 2642–2652, Melbourne, Australia, July. Association for Computational Linguistics.

Brants, T. (2000). Inter-annotator agreement for a German newspaper corpus. In *Proceedings of the Second International Conference on Language Resources and Evaluation (LREC'00)*, Athens, Greece, May. European Language Resources Association (ELRA).

Cecchini, F. M., Passarotti, M., Marongiu, P., and Zeman, D. (2018). Challenges in converting the *Index Thomisticus* treebank into universal dependencies. *Proceedings of the Universal Dependencies Workshop 2018 (UDW 2018)*.

Cimino, R., Geelhaar, T., and Schwandt, S. (2015). Digital approaches to historical semantics: new research directions at frankfurt university. *Storicamente*, 11.

Devlin, J., Chang, M.-W., Lee, K., and Toutanova, K. (2018). Bert: Pre-training of deep bidirectional transformers for language understanding. *arXiv preprint arXiv:1810.04805*.

Eger, S., vor der Brück, T., and Mehler, A. (2015). Lexicon-assisted tagging and lemmatization in Latin: A comparison of six taggers and two lemmatization methods. In *Proceedings of the 9th Workshop on Language Technology for Cultural Heritage, Social Sciences, and Humanities (LaTeCH 2015)*, Beijing, China.

Eger, S., Gleim, R., and Mehler, A. (2016). Lemmatization and morphological tagging in German and Latin: A comparison and a survey of the state-of-the-art. In *Proceedings of the 10th International Conference on Language Resources and Evaluation*, LREC 2016.

Gleim, R., Waltinger, U., Ernst, A., Mehler, A., Esch, D., and Feith, T. (2009). The eHumanities Desktop – an online system for corpus management and analysis in support of computing in the humanities. In *Proceedings of the Demonstrations Session of the 12th Conference of the European Chapter of the Association for Computational Linguistics EACL 2009, 30 March – 3 April, Athens*.

Gleim, R., Mehler, A., and Ernst, A. (2012). SOA implementation of the eHumanities Desktop. In *Proceedings of the Workshop on Service-oriented Architectures (SOAs) for the Humanities:Solutions and Impacts, Digital Humanities, Hamburg*.

Gleim, R., Eger, S., Mehler, A., Uslu, T., Hemati, W., Lücking, A., Henlein, A., Kahlsdorf, S., and Hoenen, A. (2019). A practitioner's view: a survey and comparison of lemmatization and morphological tagging in german and latin. *Journal of Language Modeling*.

Grave, E., Bojanowski, P., Gupta, P., Joulin, A., and Mikolov, T. (2018). Learning word vectors for 157 languages. In *Proceedings of the International Conference on Language Resources and Evaluation (LREC 2018)*.

Haug, D. T. and Jøhndal, M. (2008). Creating a parallel treebank of the old indo-european bible translations. In *Proceedings of the Second Workshop on Language Technology for Cultural Heritage Data (LaTeCH 2008)*, pages 27–34.

Heinzerling, B. and Strube, M. (2018). BPEmb: Tokenization-free Pre-trained Subword Embeddings in 275 Languages. In Nicoletta Calzolari (Conference chair), et al., editors, *Proceedings of the Eleventh International Conference on Language Resources and Evaluation (LREC 2018)*, Miyazaki, Japan, May 7-12, 2018. European Language Resources Association (ELRA).

Hemati, W. and Mehler, A. (2019). LSTMVoter: chemical named entity recognition using a conglomerate of sequence labeling tools. *Journal of Cheminformatics*, 11(1):7, Jan.

Hemati, W., Uslu, T., and Mehler, A. (2016). Textimager: a distributed uima-based system for nlp. In *Proceedings of the COLING 2016 System Demonstrations*. Federated Conference on Computer Science and Information Systems.

Kestemont, M. and De Gussem, J. (2016). Integrated sequence tagging for medieval latin using deep representation learning. *Journal of Data Mining and Digital Humanities*.

Kondratyuk, D. and Straka, M. (2019). 75 languages, 1 model: Parsing universal dependencies universally. In *Proceedings of the 2019 Conference on Empirical Methods in Natural Language Processing and the 9th International Joint Conference on Natural Language Processing (EMNLP-IJCNLP)*, pages 2779–2795, Hong Kong, China. Association for Computational Linguistics.

Lample, G., Ballesteros, M., Subramanian, S., Kawakami, K., and Dyer, C. (2016). Neural architectures for named entity recognition. *CoRR*, abs/1603.01360.

Ling, W., Dyer, C., Black, A. W., and Trancoso, I. (2015). Two/too simple adaptations of word2vec for syntax problems. In Rada Mihalcea, et al., editors, *NAACL HLT 2015, The 2015 Conference of the North American Chapter of the Association for Computational Linguistics: Human Language Technologies, Denver, Colorado, USA, May 31 - June 5, 2015*, pages 1299–1304. The Association for Computational Linguistics.

Manjavacas, E., Kádár, Á., and Kestemont, M. (2019). Improving lemmatization of non-standard languages with joint learning. *CoRR*, abs/1903.06939.

Mehler, A., vor der Brück, T., Gleim, R., and Geelhaar, T. (2015). Towards a network model of the coreness of texts: An experiment in classifying latin texts using the ttlab latin tagger. In Chris Biemann et al., editors, *Text Mining: From Ontology Learning to Automated text Processing Applications*, Theory and Applications of Natural Language Processing, pages 87–112. Springer, Berlin/New York.

Mikolov, T., Chen, K., Corrado, G., and Dean, J. (2013a). Efficient estimation of word representations in vector space. In Yoshua Bengio et al., editors, *1st International Conference on Learning Representations, ICLR 2013, Scottsdale, Arizona, USA, May 2-4, 2013, Workshop Track Proceedings*.

Mikolov, T., Sutskever, I., Chen, K., Corrado, G. S., and Dean, J. (2013b). Distributed representations of words and phrases and their compositionality. In Christopher J. C. Burges, et al., editors, *Advances in Neural Information Processing Systems 26: 27th Annual Conference on Neural Information Processing Systems 2013. Proceedings of a meeting held December 5-8, 2013, Lake Tahoe, Nevada, United States*, pages 3111–3119.

Mueller, T., Schmid, H., and Schütze, H. (2013). Efficient higher-order CRFs for morphological tagging. In *Proceedings of the 2013 Conference on Empirical Methods in Natural Language Processing*, pages 322–332, Seattle, Washington, USA, October. Association for Computational Linguistics.

Nivre, J., De Marneffe, M.-C., Ginter, F., Goldberg, Y., Hajic, J., Manning, C. D., McDonald, R., Petrov, S., Pyysalo, S., Silveira, N., et al. (2016a). Universal dependencies v1: A multilingual treebank collection. In *Proceedings of the Tenth International Conference on Language Resources and Evaluation (LREC'16)*, pages 1659–1666.

Nivre, J., de Marneffe, M., Ginter, F., Goldberg, Y., Hajic, J., Manning, C. D., McDonald, R. T., Petrov, S., Pyysalo, S., Silveira, N., Tsarfaty, R., and Zeman, D. (2016b). Universal dependencies v1: A multilingual treebank collection. In Nicoletta Calzolari, et al., editors, *Proceedings of the Tenth International Conference on Language Resources and Evaluation LREC 2016, Portorož, Slovenia, May 23-28, 2016*. European Language Resources Association (ELRA).

Pennington, J., Socher, R., and Manning, C. D. (2014). Glove: Global vectors for word representation. In *Empirical Methods in Natural Language Processing (EMNLP)*, pages 1532–1543.

Peters, M., Neumann, M., Iyyer, M., Gardner, M., Clark, C., Lee, K., and Zettlemoyer, L. (2018). Deep contextualized word representations. In *Proceedings of the 2018 Conference of the North American Chapter of the Association for Computational Linguistics: Human Language Technologies, Volume 1 (Long Papers)*, pages 2227–2237, New Orleans, Louisiana, June. Association for Computational Linguistics.

Plank, B., Hovy, D., and Søgaard, A. (2014). Learning part-of-speech taggers with inter-annotator agreement loss. In *Proceedings of the 14th Conference of the European Chapter of the Association for Computational Linguistics*, pages 742–751, Gothenburg, Sweden, April. Association for Computational Linguistics.

Sennrich, R., Haddow, B., and Birch, A. (2016). Neural machine translation of rare words with subword units. In *Proceedings of the 54th Annual Meeting of the Association for Computational Linguistics (Volume 1: Long Papers)*, pages 1715–1725, Berlin, Germany, August. Association for Computational Linguistics.

Sprugnoli, R., Passarotti, M., and Moretti, G. (2019). Vir is to moderatus as mulier is to intemperans lemma embeddings for latin. In *Sixth Italian Conference on Computational Linguistics*, pages 1–7. CEUR-WS. org.

Sprugnoli, R., Passarotti, M., Cecchini, F. M., and Pellegrini, M. (2020). Overview of the evalatin 2020 evaluation campaign. In Rachele Sprugnoli et al., editors, *Proceedings of the LT4HALA 2020 Workshop - 1st Workshop on Language Technologies for Historical and Ancient Languages, satellite event to the Twelfth International Conference on Language Resources and Evaluation (LREC 2020)*, Paris, France, May. European Language Resources Association (ELRA).

Straka, M. and Straková, J. (2017). Tokenizing, pos tagging, lemmatizing and parsing ud 2.0 with udpipe. In *Proceedings of the CoNLL 2017 Shared Task: Multilingual Parsing from Raw Text to Universal Dependencies*, pages 88–99, Vancouver, Canada, August. Association for Computational Linguistics.

Straková, J., Straka, M., and Hajic, J. (2014). Open-source tools for morphology, lemmatization, pos tagging and named entity recognition. In *Proceedings of 52nd Annual Meeting of the Association for Computational Linguistics: System Demonstrations*, pages 13–18.

Variae. (2020). Latin Text Archive (LTA) Version of the CompHistSem Working Group of the Corpus "Variae" by Flavius Magnus Aurelius Cassiodorus based on Cassiodori Senatoris Variae, rec. Theodorus Mommsen, Berlin: Weidmann, 1894 (MGH Auct. Ant. 12). Retrieved from the critical edition and prepared by the BMBF project "Humanist Computer Interaction under Scrutiny" (https://humanist.hs-mainz.de/en/). Available at https://www.comphistsem.org/texts.html.

vor der Brück, T. and Mehler, A. (2016). TLT-CRF: A lexicon-supported morphological tagger for Latin based on conditional random fields. In *Proceedings of the 10th International Conference on Language Resources and Evaluation*, LREC 2016.